SAP MM

for Beginners

SAP MM

for Beginners

THE X TEAM

Sandip Rakshit
Abhinav Kumar Sinha

Published in the USA by:

Arizona Business Alliance

SHROFF PUBLISHERS & DISTRIBUTORS PVT. LTD.
Mumbai *Bangalore* *Kolkata* *New Delhi*

SAP MM for Beginners

Sandip Rakshit, Abhinav Kumar Sinha

ISBN 13: 978-93-5023-649-9
Originally printed in India.

Published by Shroff Publishers & Distributors Pvt. Ltd., C-103, T.T.C. Industrial Area, M.I.D.C., Pawane, Navi Mumbai - 400 705, India. Tel: (91-22) 4158 4158
Fax: (91-22) 4158 4141, E-mail: spdorders@shroffpublishers.com.

Printing History:

First Edition: June 2012

Reprinted in the USA by Arizona Business Alliance.
Under license from Shroff Publishers & Distributors Pvt. Ltd., India.

First USA Reprint: July 2012
ISBN 13: 978-1-61903-046-6

Published by **Arizona Business Alliance LLC** 7169 W. Ashby Drive, Peoria AZ 85383
Tel: 623 297 4448, Fax: 623 687 9524 e-mail: aba.us@hotmail.com

Table of Contents

PART - 1 INTRODUCTION

PART - 2 MASTER DATA

PART - 4 RELATED PROCESSINGS

PART-1

INTRODUCTION

Chapter 1

INTRODUCTION TO MATERIALS MANAGEMENT

✪✪✪✪✪✪✪

An Introduction to Materials Management

(An End Users Guide Book)

✪✪✪✪✪✪✪

Overview

In this book we will study about the importance of the Materials Management module as a very important component of SAP software. MM contains many aspects like purchasing, goods movement important material storage, consumption-based planning and inventory and many other business functionalities. It is deeply integrated with many other modules such as

Finance (FI), Controlling (CO), Production Planning (PP), Sales and Distribution (SD), Quality Management (QM), Plant Maintenance (PM), Project System (PS) and Warehouse Management (WM).

SAP HISTORY

- SAP was founded in 1972 and is now a market and technology leader in client/server enterprise application software. SAP is constantly developing new products that allow stheir customers to respond to dynamic market conditions and help them maintain competitive advantage.
- In 1979, SAP released its mainframe product called R/2 & in 1992, SAP developed the client/server application we all know as R/3.
- SAP has been releasing new versions of SAP as Release 4.6, Release 4.7, Release 5, Release 6, Release 6.2 & further more new releases to come. Now question arises as what are these versions? Versions are nothing but the same software added with new patches which have advanced features and broader combinations of business process and requirements.

Components

There are several components of SAP software, Finance (FI), Controlling(CO), Human Resources(HR), Product Lifecycle Management, Plant & Production(PP), Quality Management(QM), and Supply Chain Management, Warehouses Management(WM), Plant & Production(PP), Materials Management(MM).

Now you can ask "what is ERP?" One may describe ERP as Enterprise Resource Planning, means this is a software through which the enterpriser can manage and plan his valuable resources be it manpower, raw materials or technologies and machineries to produce the best possible optimum utilization.

Materials Management is basically a part of Logistics Functionalities. The Logistics function in SAP includes the following:

- Materials Management (MM)
- Sales and Distribution (SD)
- Quality management (QM)
- Plant and Maintenance (PM)
- Production Planning (PP)
- Project System (PS)
- Finance (FI)
- Warehouse Management (WM)

- Logistics Information System (LIS)

Apart from these some other functions are also there like:-

- Batch Management
- Unit Management
- Variant Configuration
- Engineering Change Management
- Environment, Health and Safety (EHS)

These are important as per individual process requirements.

Chapter

2

ORGANIZATIONAL STRUCTURE

Organization of an Enterprise in the SAP System

In this section we will take a look on the organization of an enterprise in the SAP system in the domain of Materials Management. We will see how they are involved in purchasing.

Organizational Levels

In SAP R/3 System the enterprise structure may have the following organizational levels:

Client

It is a grouping or combination of legal, organizational, business and/or administrative units with a common purpose. You can mean it as group of companies.

Example: A corporate group in technical terms a client is a self-contained unit in an SAP system with saperate set of master records & tables

Company code:-

This is a level that represents an independent accounting unit within a client. Each company code has its own balance sheet and its own profit and loss statement.

Example: a single company within a group o companies.

Plant

This is an operational unit in a company code. The definition of a plant may vary depending upon the functionality of a particular plant. That means a production place or factory may be counted as a plant in SAP system and on the other hand a branch office also may be taken as a plant. Again just a stock point may work as same depending upon the functionality of plant.

Purchasing organization

This is an organizational unit which is responsible for procuring (purchasing) materials or services for one or more plants. It is also responsible for negotiating general conditions of purchase with vendors. It holds a legal responsibility for all external purchase transactions.

Purchasing group

For day-to-day activities the purchasing organization is subdivided into purchasing groups, which are responsible for day-to-day buying activities. The purchasing group may be a person or a group of responsible people for purchasing.

Storage Locations

In different domain this term has different meanings. But in Logistics it means as an organizational unit where various stocks of a material is kept in a plant. This is also a middle step between plant and the warehouse number.

Plant - purchasing organization/company code

To make the enterprise structure complete in the SAP system,

- A plant must be assigned to one or more purchasing organizations
- A plant must always be assigned to a company code.
- A purchasing organization must also be assigned to one company code if the purchasing organization is not assigned with one company code then the unassigned purchasing organization may work for multiple company codes.

Organized ways of Purchasing

There are two ways of organizing purchasing functions.

- Centralized
- Distributed Purchasing
- Plant Specific

You can organize your purchasing function in the following ways:

- Centralized purchasing process will have just one purchasing organization for a company code and all the plants are assigned to this only purchasing organization.
- Distributed purchasing process will have more than one purchasing organization and each purchasing organization will be responsible for procurement for different plants.

In case of Centralized purchasing only one purchasing organization is responsible for multiple company code's purchasing activities.

- Purchasing Organization 1000
- Company Code 1000
    - Plant 0001
    - Plant 0002
    - Plant 0003
- Company Code 2000
    - Plant 0004
    - Plant 0005
    - Plant 0006

Thus one purchasing organization will work for multiple company codes.

But in case of Decentralized purchasing or company specific purchasing

- Purchasing Organization 1000
- Company Code 1000
    - Plant 0001
    - Plant 0002
    - Plant 0003
- Purchasing Organization 2000
- Company Code 2000
    - Plant 0004
    - Plant 0005
    - Plant 0006

One more purchasing process is plant specific is purchasing. In this process one purchasing organization is responsible only for one plant

- Company Code 1000

- Purchasing Organization 1000
    - Plant 0001

Thus purchasing organizations will be different for each company codes

Reference Purchasing Organization:-

A Reference Purchasing Organization is a purchasing organization whose conditions or contracts may be used by other purchasing organizations, which are linked to it.

PART-2

MASTER DATA

Chapter 3

MATERIAL MASTER

Introduction

In SAP the term 'Procurement' symbolizes a complete process of purchasing something, be it material or service, for any reason be consumption or further utilization or just for stock holding. It starts from the requirement detection to taking possession of the material and invoice entry in the system.

Master Data

A number of data files are created in SAP system which are called 'Master data'. When implementing SAP, companies transfer their data base about customers and vendors, materials, different conditions and its records and so many others from one legacy system (format such as Excel or other data bases) into the SAP system. These data files contains information and records about the respective reason. These data and information will be used and utilized for future reference and calculations.

Material:-

Normally in non SAP, the term Material may means anything that we can feel, see and touch.

But in SAP, material means something of physical existence that may be consumed or further used in due course of production. The goods that are the subject of business activity. The material can be traded, used in manufacture, consumed, or produced.

Material Master:-

Material Master is a database that contains information about each material that a company deals in or consumes. When the information entered is used throughout the SAP system in due course of business. These data are created either manually or automatically.

Tables and fields:-

The Material Master is created by the users to enter all the relevant information of a particular item of material. As we know tables are frames that contain several fields to capture the combinations of information from the allowed information input range. These information are when entered and saved, updates some respective fields of correct tables. The information is further used for processing purpose and reporting purpose.

Create Material:-

Transaction Code – MM01 :-

When we make first entry of the material we have to enter transaction code MM01. Once we enter this t-code(short form of transaction code) first of all enter the material number.

Material Numbering:-

The material number that is name of the material item may be internal or external. Priority is given to the external material number that is entered by the person who is making entries, if material number is not entered manually then system will create a new number for that material automatically and that will fall within a particular number range which is defined and assigned with the related material type by the consultants while implementation.

Material Types:-

A material type is a group of materials with similar attributes. Each material item has to have from a predefined material type. This is defined and assigned by the consultants while implementation.

Now we will see an example how a material is created along with the information. In SAP easy access screen, enter MM01 in the transaction bar or follow the menu path given below and enter.

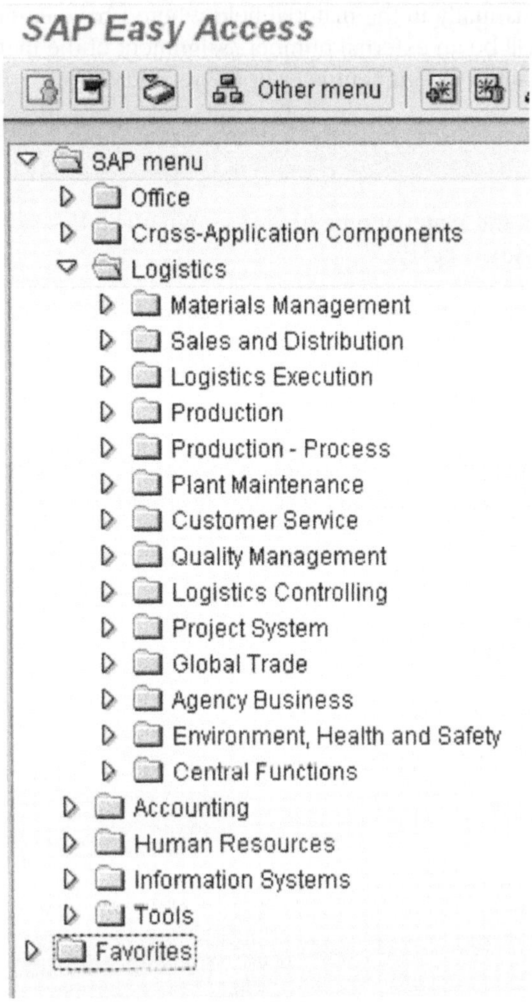

Program will be executed and initial screen of create material will come. Now if you want to do the process with me then you can follow what is explained below with screen shots.

Enter MM01 in the transaction bar.

Or follow the menu path as shown in the screen shots.

SAP Easy Access > Logistics > Materials Management > Material Master > Material > Create General.

Enter material number manually in the material field where I have entered AA, note that if you enter manually then it will be an external number assignment of the material. We will study this internal and external number assignment later in the related chapter.

Select from the drop down list (F4) from the industry sector. Take it as Mechanical Engineering (for example).

Select Material type from the material type field (F4). What is industry sector and what is what material type is are explained below.

If user does not enter or input any thing in the material field then system will generate a numerical number from predefined internal No. range.

Industry sector:-

Industry sector is a key that specifies the branch of industry to which the material is assigned. It determines the sequence o screens and industry specific fields on each of the selected screens.

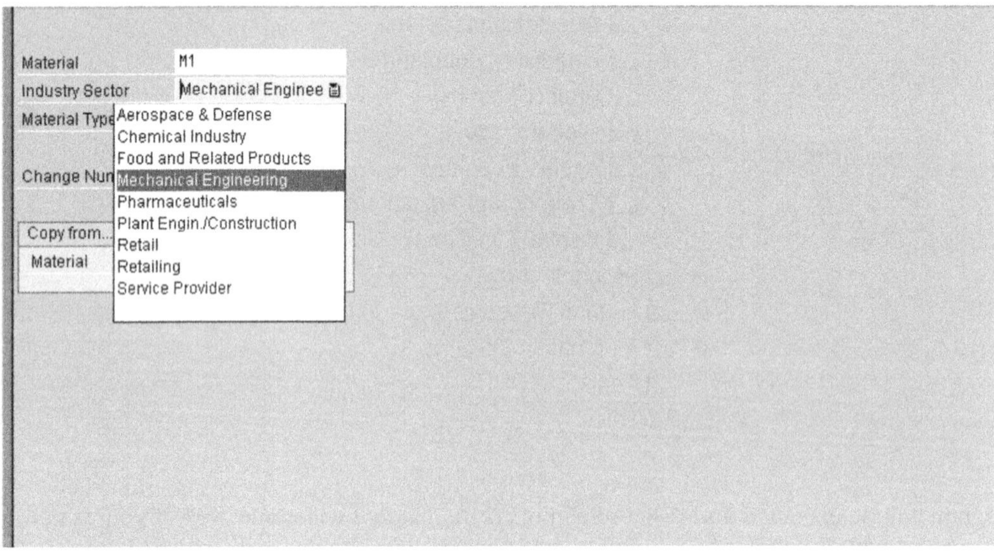

Material type:-

It is a key that assigns the material to a group of materials such as raw materials, operating supplies or trading goods, finished material or pipeline material.

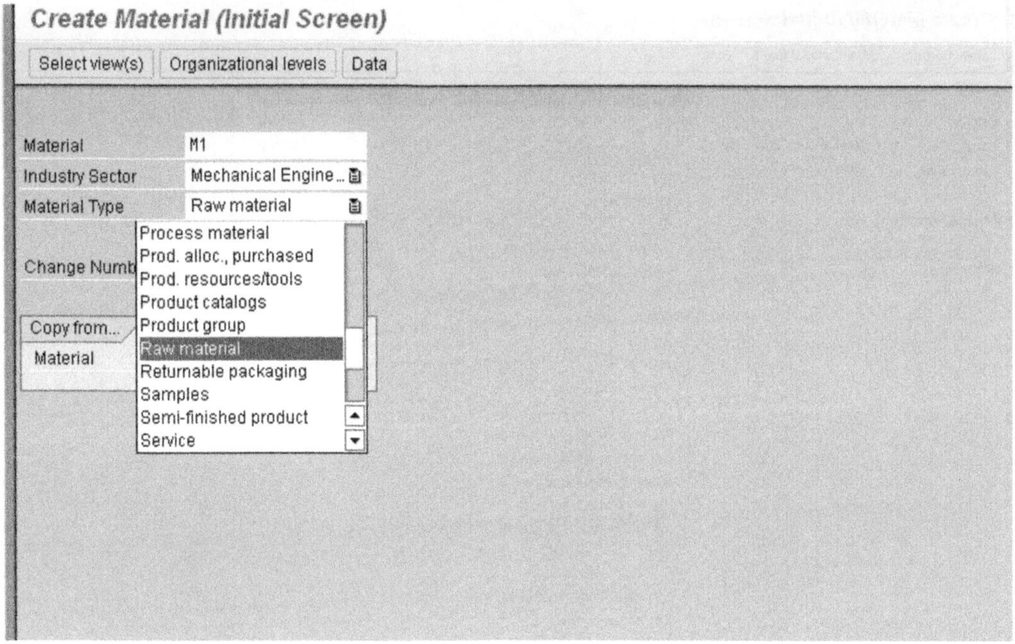

Use

The material type selection determines-

- Material number is assigned internally or externally
- The internal number range
- Screens for data entry
- Screen sequence
- Department-specific data fields.

After this press enter or select 'select view(s)' or F5. The following screen will come. This will have a list of the department specific screens to be selected.

Here select Basic Data 1, Purchasing, MRP 1, MRP 2 and Accounting 1 view. Now one may ask why only these a few view out of so many views. So answer is these are the views which are a must for any transaction to be done within the materials management domain. So these are the minimum views which must have relevant required data to proceed with the process. Apart from these views you can select other views also if required.

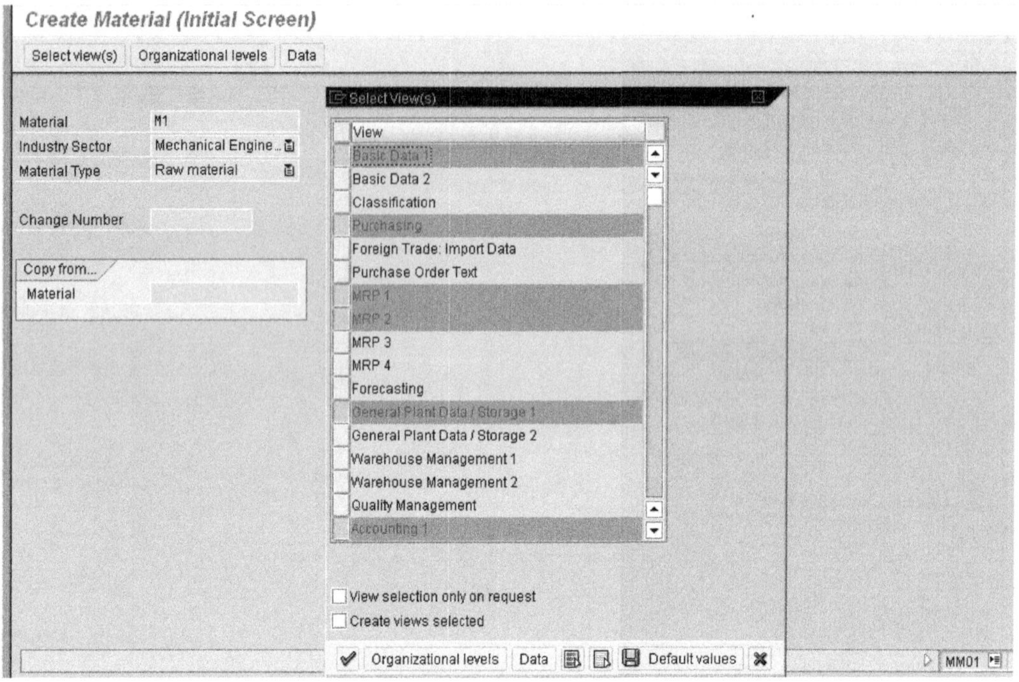

And then enter or go to Organization levels (F6).

Here two blank fields will come one is for Plant and another for Storage location.

Put the cursor in the plant field

It will fetch the drop down list of all the plants enlisted in the organization.

From here choose plant 1000.

And in the same way put the cursor in the storage location field.

And there also select storage location 0001 for example. See the screen shots below for both plant entry and storage location entry.

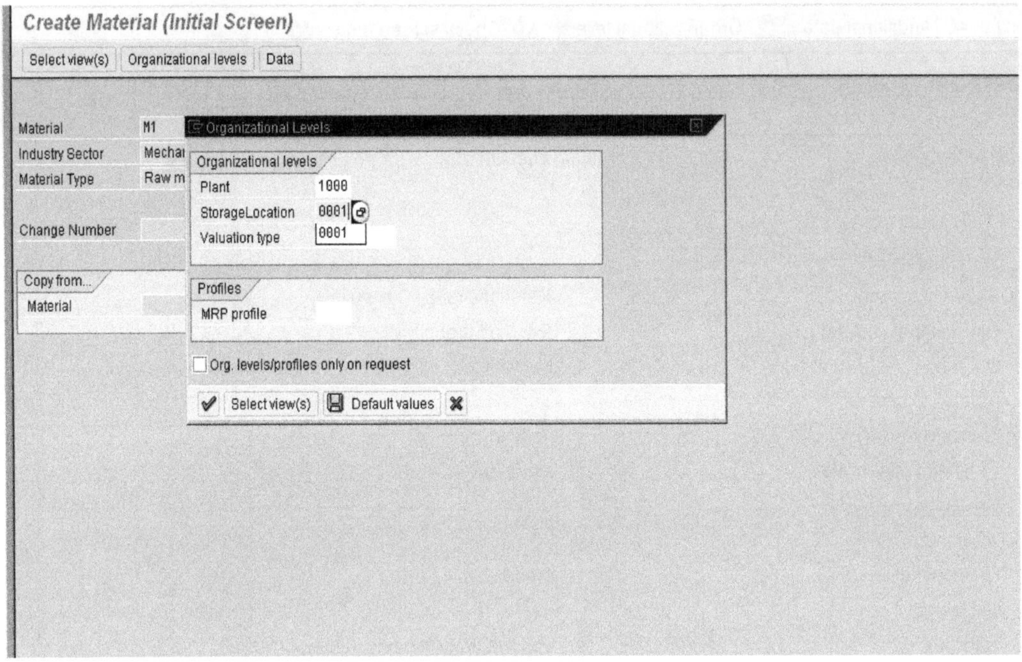

See blank fields.

Select 1000 and choose (F2)

Select 0001 for storage location field. Then below shown screen will come.

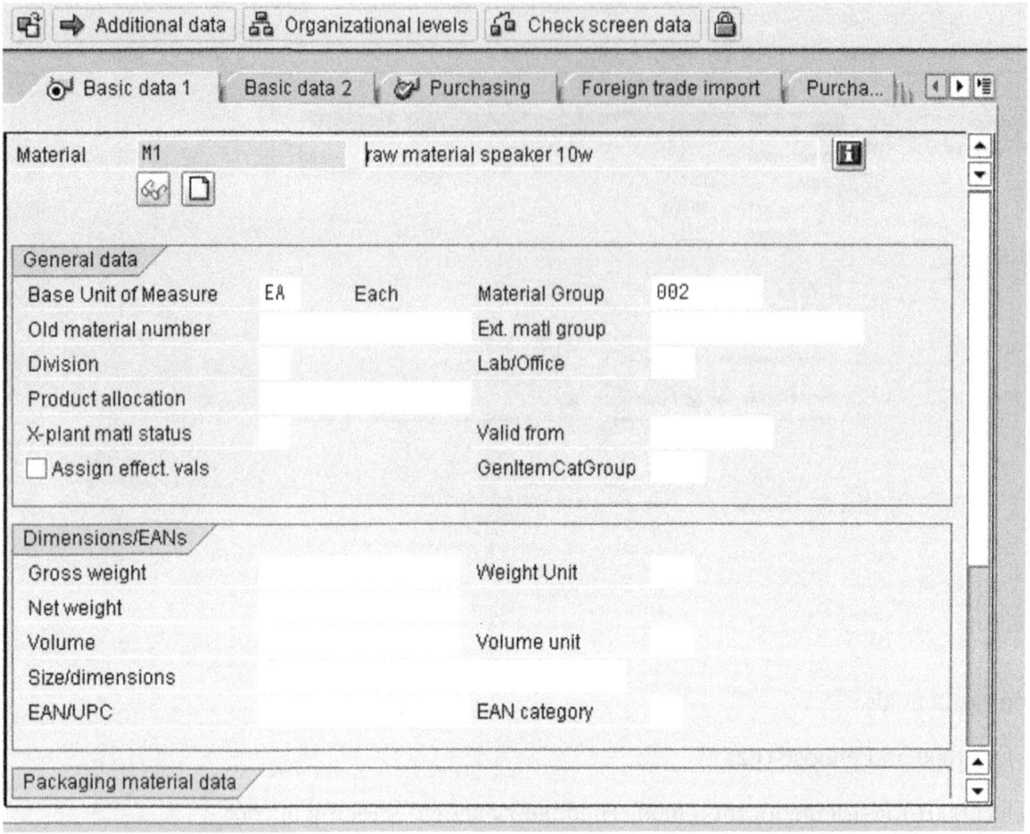

Description of material:-

- The first field to be entered is Material description is a Text that describes the material in more detail in the language. It may be of 40 character length.

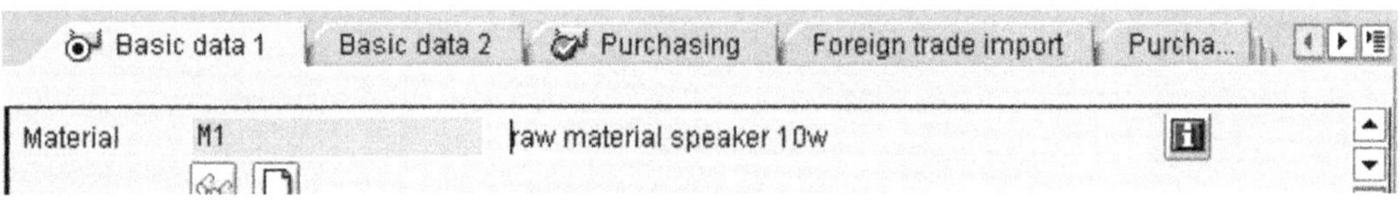

Base Unit of Measure:-

After this enter in the field of base unit of measure. This is the unit of measure in which material is calculated or weighted or counted. This is selected as per the basic characteristics of the respective material.

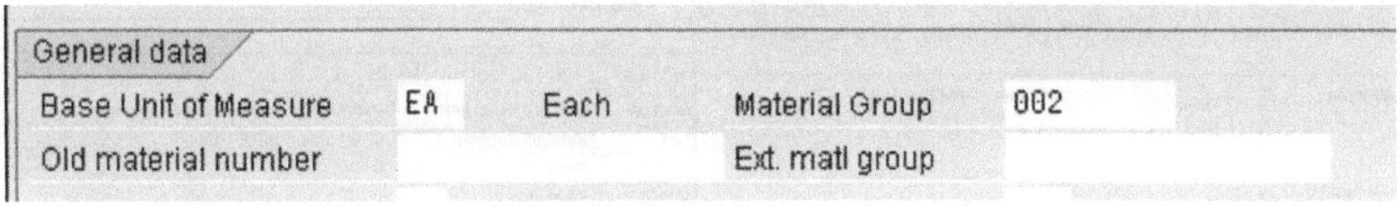

From the drop down select unit of measure as EA.

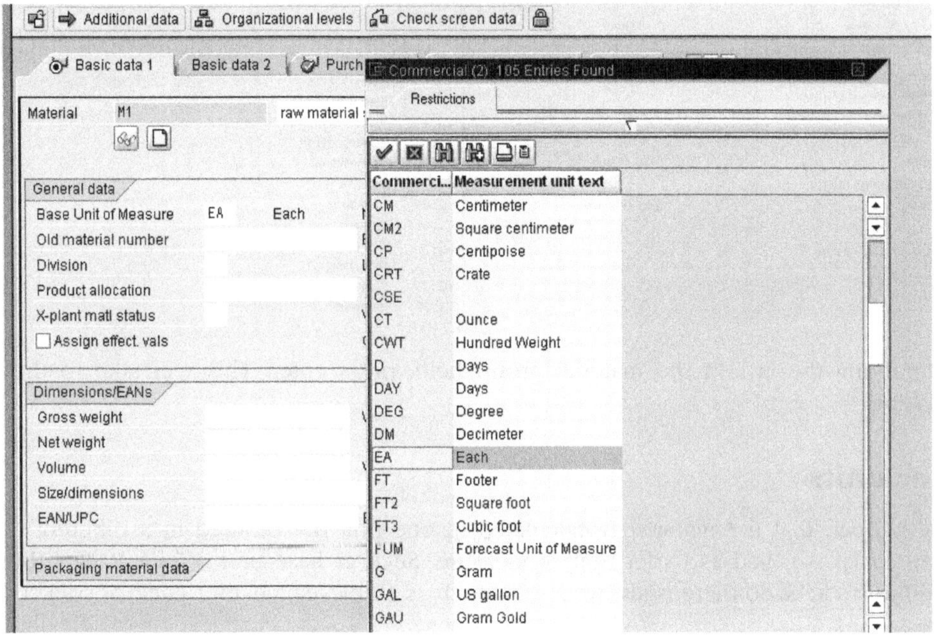

That means that this material item M1 white pen model is counted in each as 1,2,3... and so on.

Material group:-

This is a Key that is used to group together several material or service with the same attributes, and it is assigned them to a particular material group.

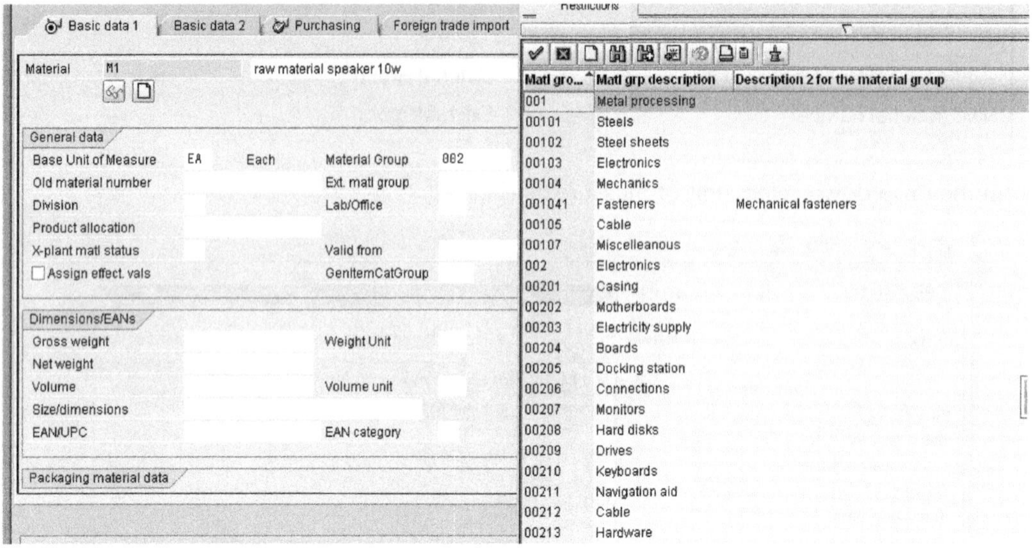

After entering the 001 in the material group field, press enter. This will take to the view purchasing.

Order unit:-

It may happen that the material is calculated in one unit but ordered in a different unit of measure. That is called as Order unit of measure. Such as base unit of pen is each but it is ordered in packets. So there is always a ratio such as 10 pieces means 1 pack or packet.

Purchase group:–

Purchase group is a person or group of people who is/are responsible for certain purchasing activities.

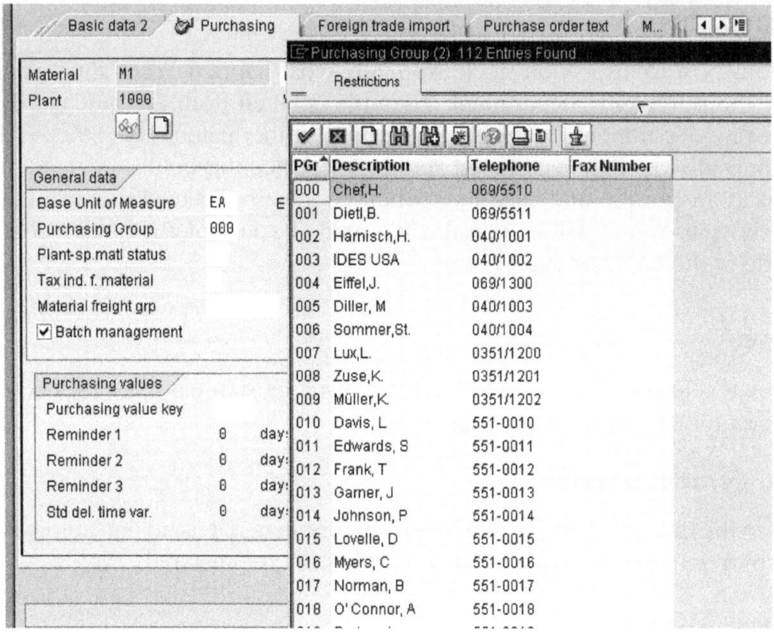

GR Processing time:-

Down there in the purchasing screen you can see GR processing time. This data is entered in days which mean the time taken (Number of workdays) by the data entry operator for counting the goods that have reached to their storage locations, verifying and entering those counted numbers into the SAP system. This time is further used in automatic procurement process and procurement time determination.

You can enter here day as 1.

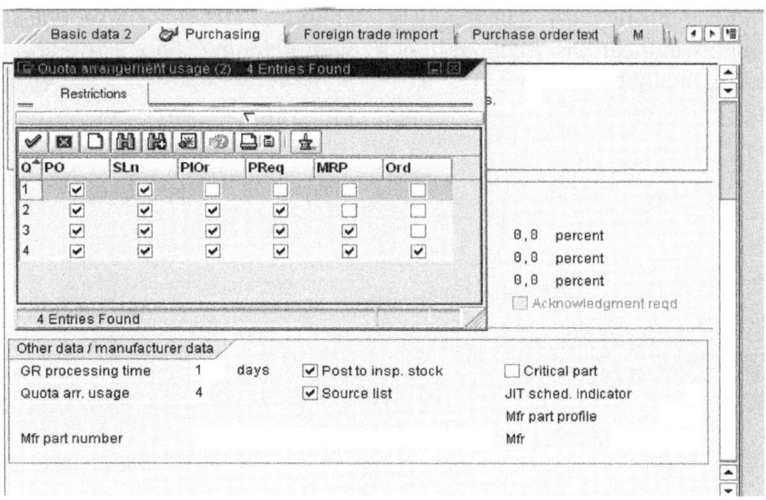

Post to Insp. Stock:-

This field means post to inspection stock. Normally what happens, each time when material is purchased by the purchasing department, a sample is taken from the purchased stock and is sent to the quality department for quality verification of the material lot. Stock of that material can be used only after quality department verification. Once this field is selected the material is subject to quality inspection and each time when goods are received that will be put into the quality inspection stock and will be consumable until checked by the quality department with the entry made in the SAP system.

Source list:-

This check box is selected if you wish to fix source list a must. It has to be created in the system before any procurement processing of the material.

Quota arrangement usage: -

This field is to be filled if vendor selection for this material is to be automated in quota arrangement process while multiple vendors may supply the material.

Next screen is MRP 1.

MRP means Material Requirement Planning. That is material requirement will be recorded automatically by the system on a particular time interval when material requirement planning program is run to know the requirement quantity and date.

MRP type:-

MRP type is a key which determines how Material will be planned for procurement.

In this field you have to select MRP type as per your business process requirement the requirement. Will it be automatically created by the system on a particular date, or will the requirement requisitions be created manually on requirement basis. Here we will select the MRP type as ND which will mean that Material Requirement Planning is not active and requirements will be created manually by the user.

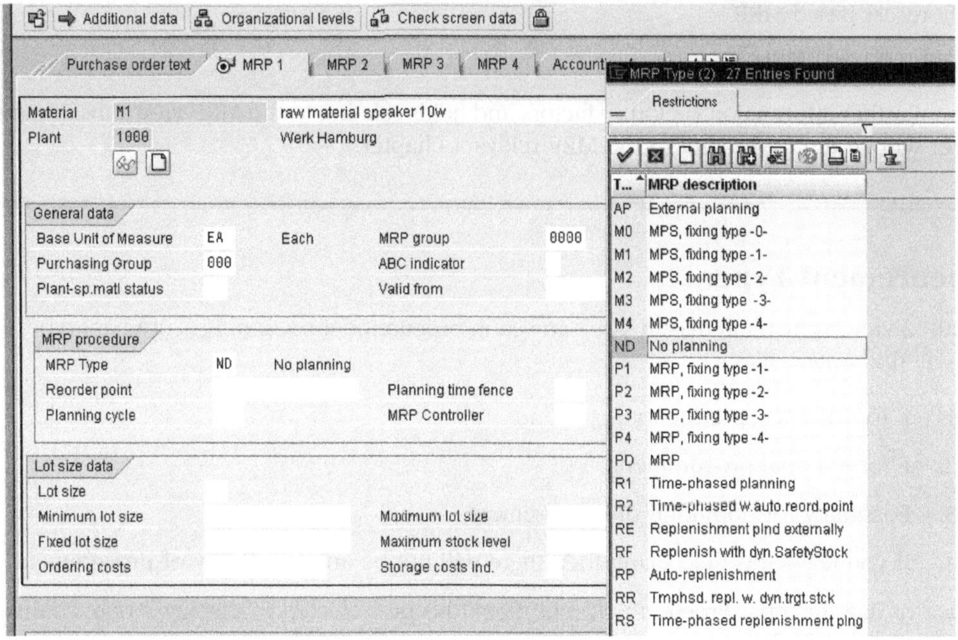

***** Note:--

1. MRP Type

   NORMAL MRP (2way configuration).

   Make to stock (MD61) - This is basically to have a back up stock of material for future requirement.

   Make to order (MD81) - This is basically to cater one or more sales order or production order.

   CONSUMPTION BASED MRP.

   Reorder point planning.

   Manual reorder point planning. (In manual reorder point planning, you define both the reorder level and the safety stock level manually in the appropriate material master.)

   Automatic reorder point planning. (In automatic reorder point planning, both the reorder level and the safety stock level are determined by the integrated forecasting program. The system uses past consumption data (historical data) to forecast future requirements. Past consumption data>future requirement>reorder level>safety stock level>taking the service level(by MRP controller>material's replenishment lead time)

Forecast Based MRP.

Time phased MRP.]

Note:- Further information on Other factors and fields relating to the MRP view tabs in material master will be discussed later in the MRP relevant chapter.

Procurement Type:-

In MRP 2 view in material master you can see in procurement section, Procurement type. Here you will find option like -

1. E for In-house production,
2. F for External procurement,
3. Possibility for both kind of procurement,
4. If you leave this field blank then there will not be any possibility of procurement.

In case of Raw material Procurement type F will be pre-selected in display mode, as this has been configured in the material type already.

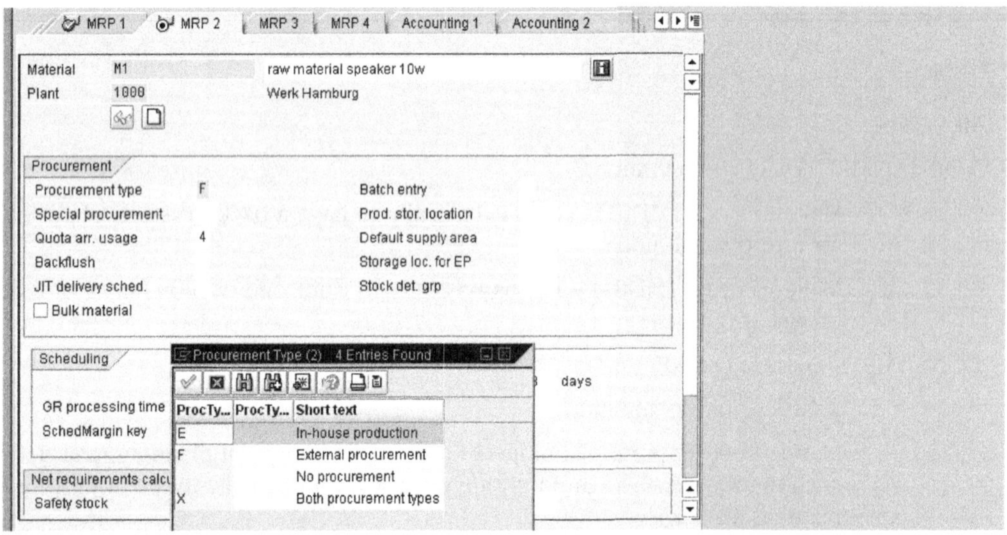

Special procurement:-

In the same view there is an another field is Special procurement. These are different procurement processes through which the same material can be procured. We will discuss broadly on these special procurement type in the relevant chapters

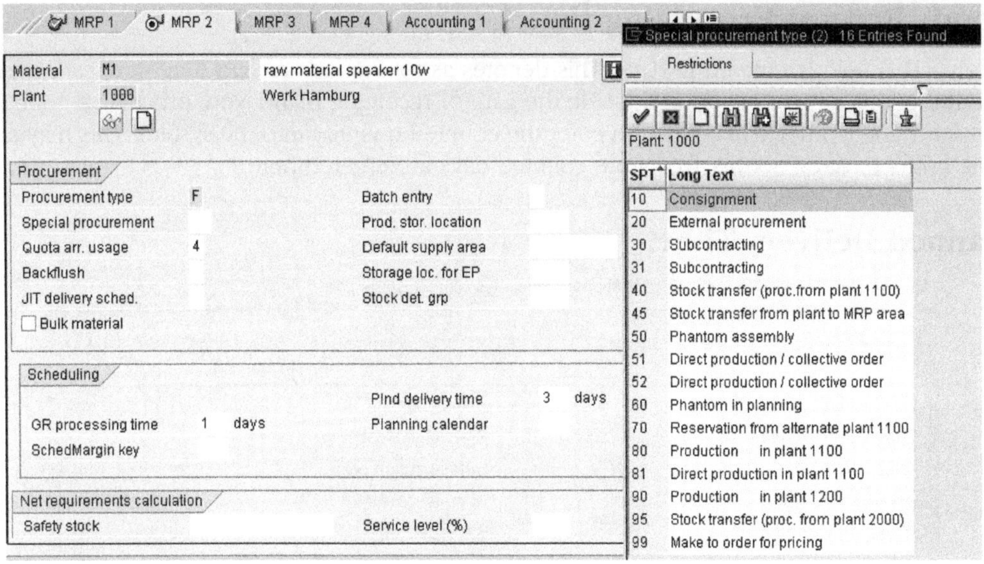

Quota Arrangement usage:-

This field is useful when the material is procured through quotation and bidding. You can see below several usage types, like 1, 2, 3, 4. These denote the area in which this quotation processing is used and utilized. We will further discuss this in the relevant chapter.

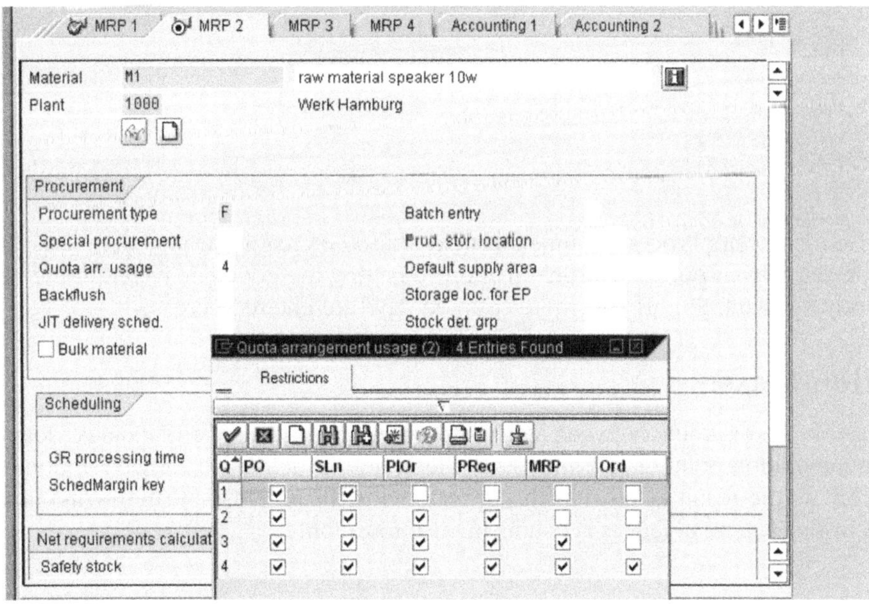

Goods Receipt Processing time:-

This field is entered in days. This denotes as total goods receipt time in days. Assume that, the goods delivery is done out side the gate of receiving plant. Now process of counting is to start. The worker will count and enter the counted quantity into the system. This may take some hours or days. So this 1 or more counted days are entered here.

Planned Delivery Time:-

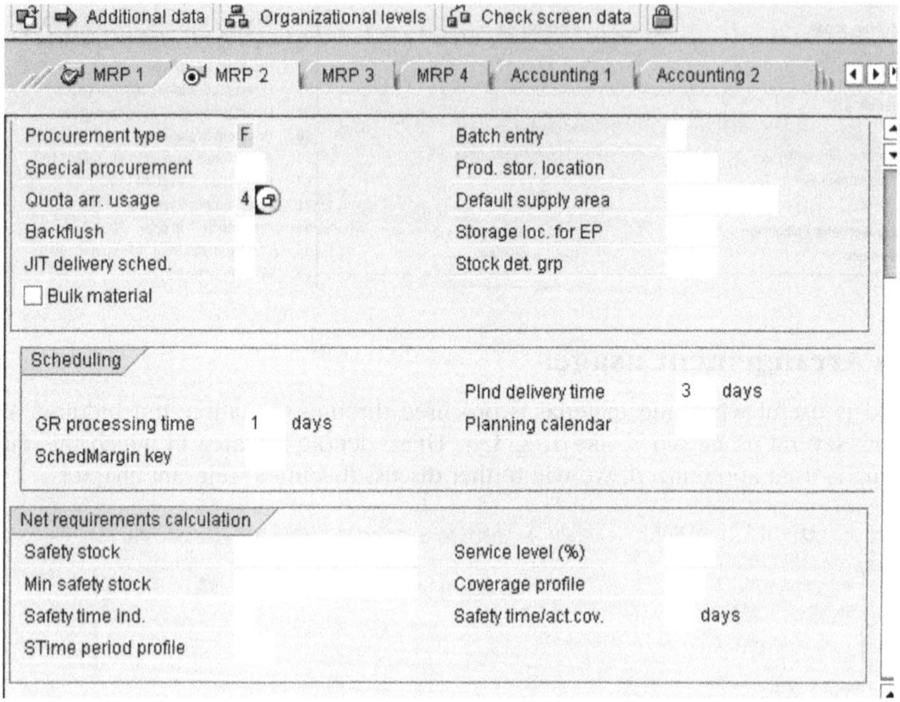

Just like Goods Receipt Processing time this field is also entered in the system in days. This time calculation starts from purchase order creation to getting the goods delivered at the door step of the receiving plant. So this 1 or more counted days are entered here.

Valuation Class:-

This valuation class is a link between Materials Management domain and Finance domain. This is also an integration point of MM and FI. By filling up this field from allowed options, general ledger entry as the result of movements of material is made. This valuation class is assigned with one or more general ledger accounts in customization.

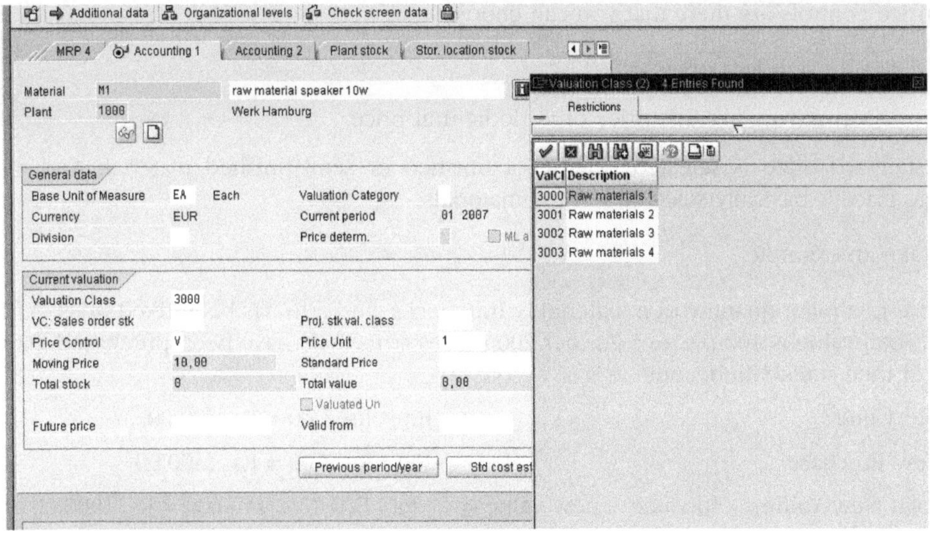

Price control:-

This price is the valuation price @ each unit of measure at the stock point. Or you can say total valuated stock in a particular plant will change with each goods receipt and average valuation stock will change accordingly.

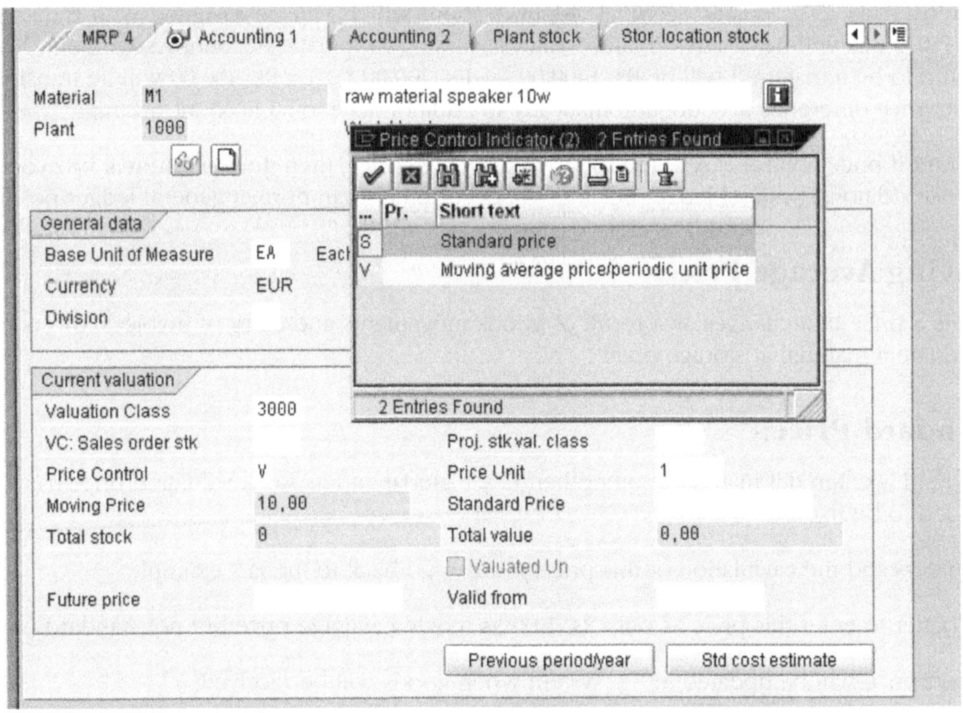

Two price controls are there that you can choose.

1. S – for standard price
2. V for moving average price or periodic unit price.

Now standard price is selected in case of finished or semi finished material. And moving average price is basically selected for raw materials.

Now take an example:

Suppose in a plant quantity of a material is 100 pieces, and rate has been fixed @ Rs. 5.00 per piece. Total value is 100 pieces * Further 200 pieces @ Rs. 7.00 have been purchased. Now the value of total stock will become as :-

Old value 100 * Rs. 5.00 = Rs. 500.00.

New Purchase 200 * Rs. 7.00 = Rs. 1400.00

Total New Value = old value + new value = (Rs.) 500.00 + 1400.00 = Rs. 1900.00

and average price will be = (Rs. 1900.00)/(100 + 200) = Rs. 6.33 per piece.

Since this total stock and new prices keeps on changing based on the material procured and its purchase order price or production cost, this value is called as moving average price.

S = Now resolution is that if standard price is selected as price control then the valuation price will not change but will remain same as earlier of Rs. 5.00 per piece. And increased value will be transferred to a separate general ledger account which will be assigned with transaction Key PRD(this will be discussed later while discussing Automatic Account Assignment. Means amount to be transferred will be Rs. 1400.00 – (Rs. 200.00 * 2) = Rs. 400.00 will be transferred to the price difference account automatically in addition to normal account postings.

V = And if price control is selected as Moving average price, then the amount will be averaged and no additional general ledger posting will occur other than normal general ledger postings.

Moving Average Price:-

This is a price that changes as a result of goods movements and entry of invoices, this is used to valuate a material at storage point.

Standard Price:-

This field is entered if material is other than raw material and its stock valuation price has been decided to be fixed.

To understand the calculation of this price you can go back to the last example.

It is better to enter this price as only Rs. 1.00 as moving average price but not standard price.

Correct price will be updated in the system when goods will be received.

Standard price: - This price is entered as estimated correct price of the material as a particular stock point or plant and later on this price does not change as effect of further goods movements.

After entering this value if you further enter then the material master will be created and will be saved.

So with this final step of saving you have completed the process of creation of material item.

Change Material:-

You can change the material master if you need to change any information of the material master which is already in the system. For this purpose you can use transaction code MM02 in the command line. You can also use menu path.

Display Material:-

You can display material to view any information as per your requirement in the transaction code MM03 in the command line.

Chapter 4

VENDOR MASTER

Introduction:-

As we have already studied about what is master data. These are data files which are created in SAP system which are called 'Master data'. When implementing SAP, companies transfer their data base about customers and vendors, materials, different conditions, records and other information from one legacy system (format such as Excel or other data bases) into the SAP system. These data files contain information and records about the respective reason. These data and information will be used and utilized for future reference and calculations.

And just like Material Master Vendor Master contains basic information of all the vendors like, vendors address, contact information, apart from that conditions applicable to the respective vendor.

In this section we will see the different factors of Vendor Master.

Create Vendor:-

You can follow the menu path just screened below.

Or alternatively you can enter XK01 in the transaction bar to reach to vendor creation screen as screened below.

Change Vendor:-

In the picture you can see a menu path to reach to the option of change vendor. Changing a vendor means updating the master data which already exists in the SAP system. Some times it is required when vendor wants to change the address or there may be some other changes relating to the vendor so in such cases information database has to be updated. The transaction code for this process is XK02.

Display Vendor:-

In this process you can view the database of the vendor which already exists. If you need to know some information relating to the vendor you can view that in display vendor transaction or XK03 transaction code. Alternatively you can also follow the menu path as it is shown in the picture above.

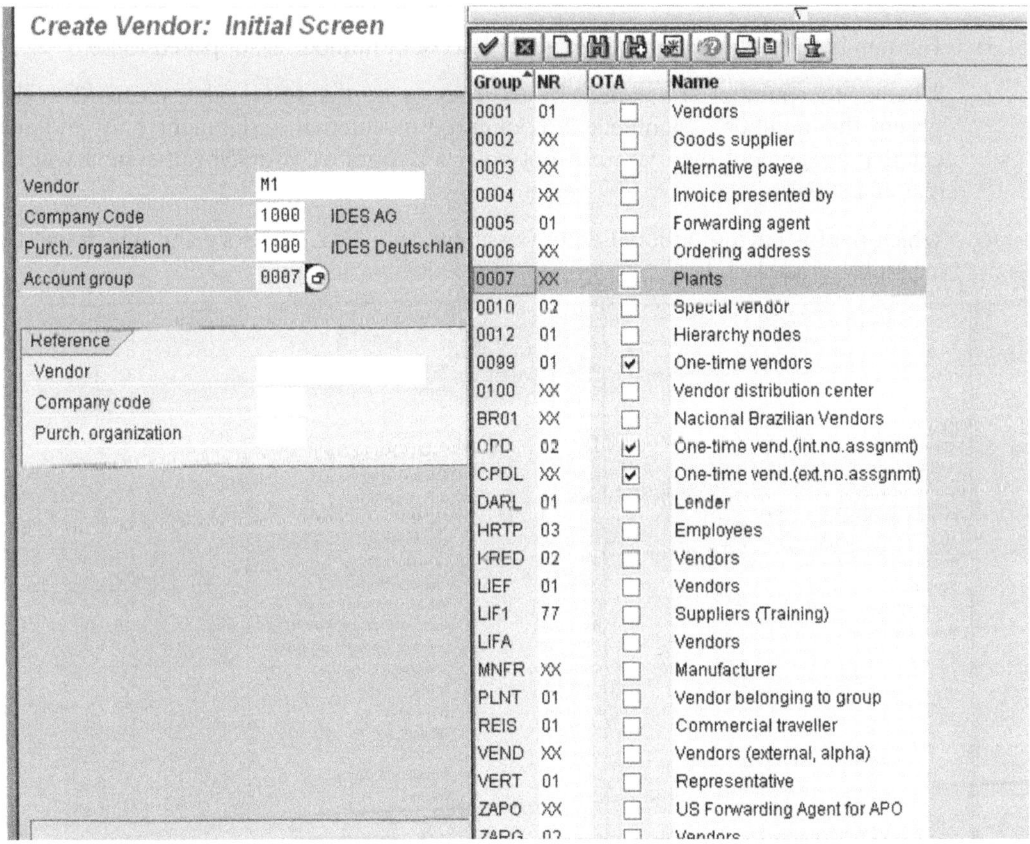

Here you can see the initial screen. You need to enter following information here.

• vendor code (vendor number):-

You have freedom to enter vendor number externally. But there is a limitation that you can enter vendor number only within the allowed number range which is already defined in the configuration settings. This number range is defined and assigned with the Vendor account group that you are to enter in the Account group field on the initial screen.

• Account Group:-

2nd entry to be made is Account Group from the allowed range which is configured in the system while implementation and later on. Now question is what account group is and why it is important. The account group classifies the vendor master record as whether vendor will be a regular vendor or an one time vendor.

The account group determines:

- o The number interval within which vendor account number is supposed to be,
- o Whether the number is assigned by the user or by the system that means if in the system the number assignment is configured as internal assignment only and not external assignment then you can not enter any number yourself but system will fix that in a serial.
- o Which field is having optional entry possibility, which compulsory and which will be in display mode only!

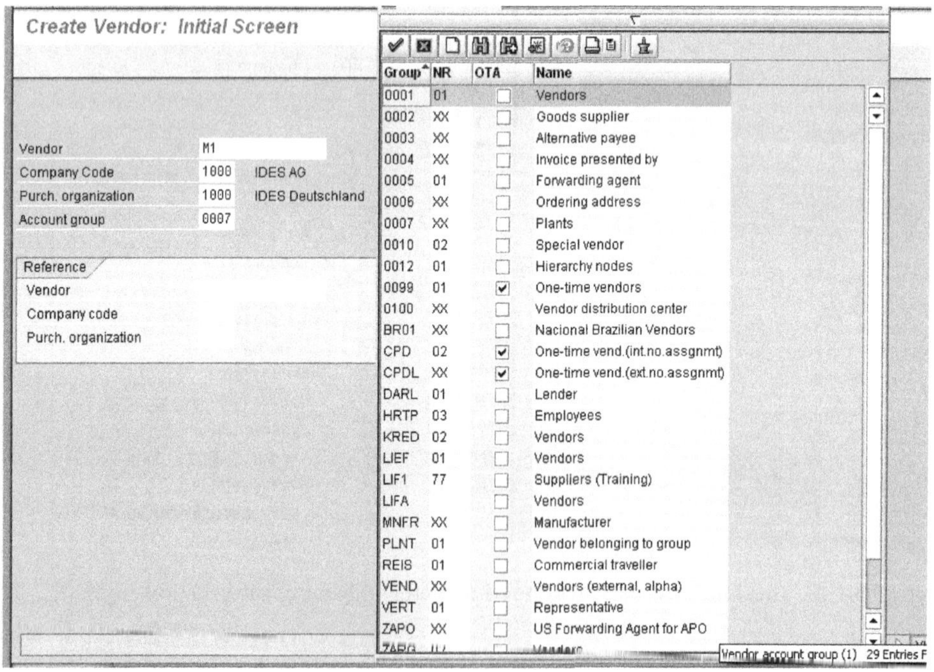

Now if only these two fields are entered and the creation is started without entering company code name and purchase organization code entry, then the kind of information that will be asked and be entered will be only of client level information and these information will be same in all the company code and all the purchasing organization level.

Company Code:-

Why to enter company code here? Yes because there may be more than one company code in one concern and there may be thousands of vendors some supplying some material to one company code and some to the other company code or even same vendor supplying same material to different company codes of same client. But depending on different factors purchasing conditions may vary, payment structure may vary or even simply currency may vary, and that may be a much deciding factor in profit making and billing or payment transaction.

Here you can enter company code 1000 because as we have already mentioned that in IDES system which is for educational and training purpose, company code 1000, purchase organization 1000, plant 1000, storage location 0001 and other storage locations are the best configured for the sequence and processing related to Materials management topics.

Purchasing Organization:-

Enter Purchasing Organization as 1000.

Press Enter.

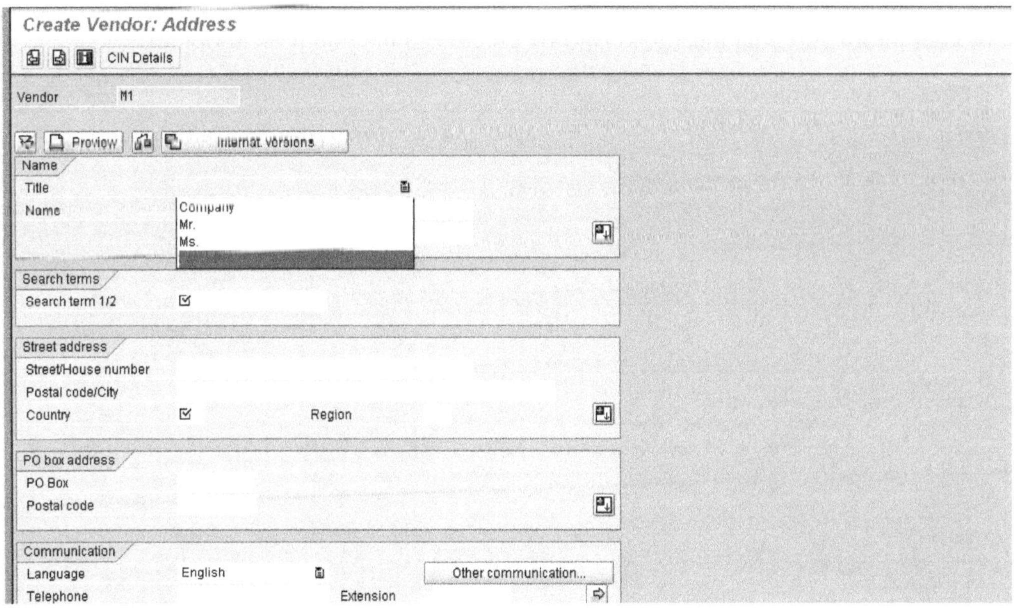

After Pressing Enter in the key board you can see a screen asking basic information about the name and address of the vendor.

Enter different information views.

Address:-

This view will contain address related information of the vendor.

Title:-

Enter any from the allowed options of Company / Mr. / Ms.

Name:-

Enter the name of the Vendor.

Search Term:-

This is used by he system to find a particular vendor's information when required. You can enter it same as name of the vendor or a unique short name which are better to trace the vendor.

Country:-

With other information the must field is to be entered as in country field option.

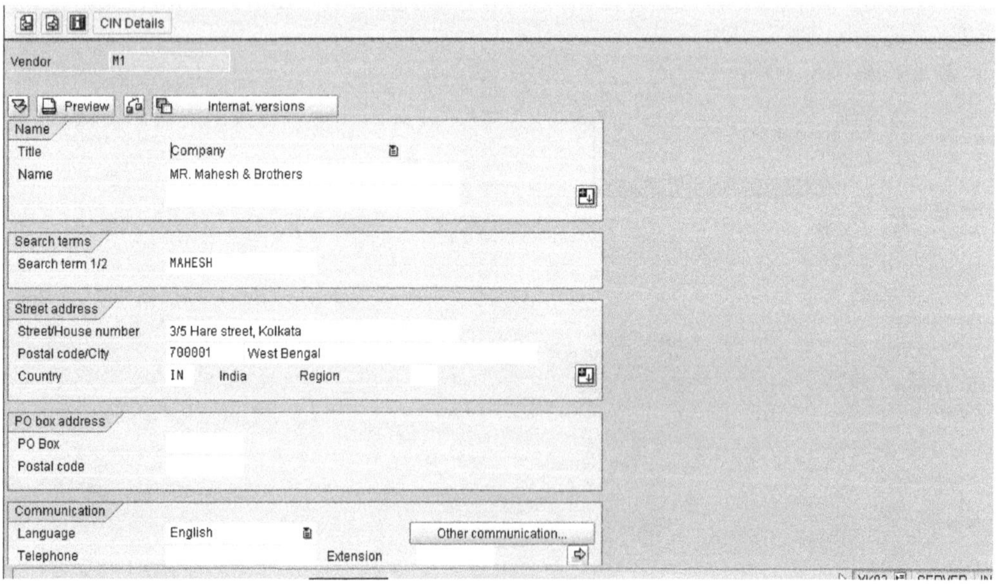

Other communication:-

You can also enter communication related other information updated in the pop-up.

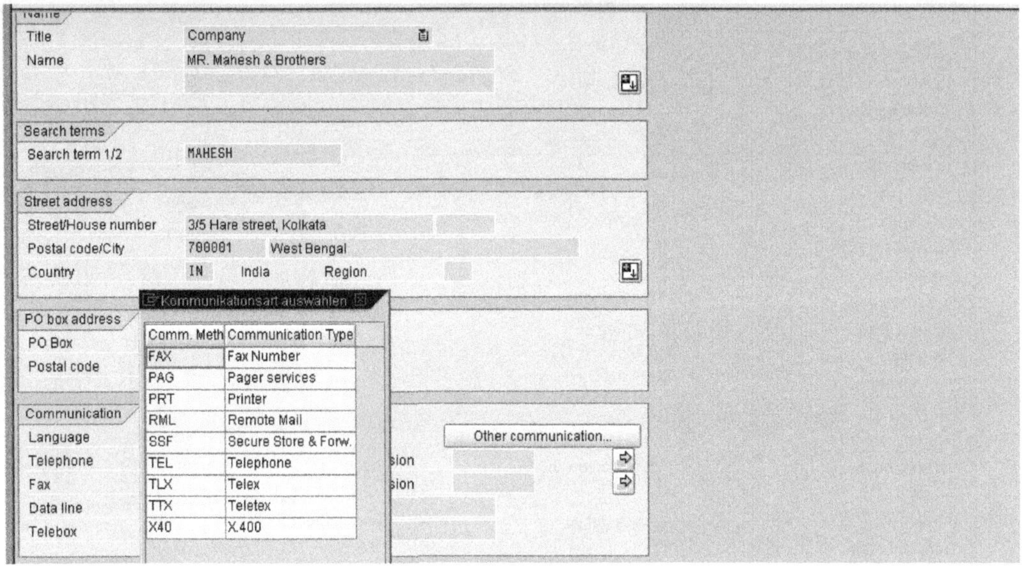

Apart from other information you can also see a link to CIN details. This is basically to enter information which is required to capture Tax information of the vendor as per India's law. This field will pop-up only if Indian tax structure is configured in the system for Indian company code.

Control:-

Then control view and payment transaction view are captured in the system. This view is to be maintained if the vendor's due is to be adjusted against customer in some cases.

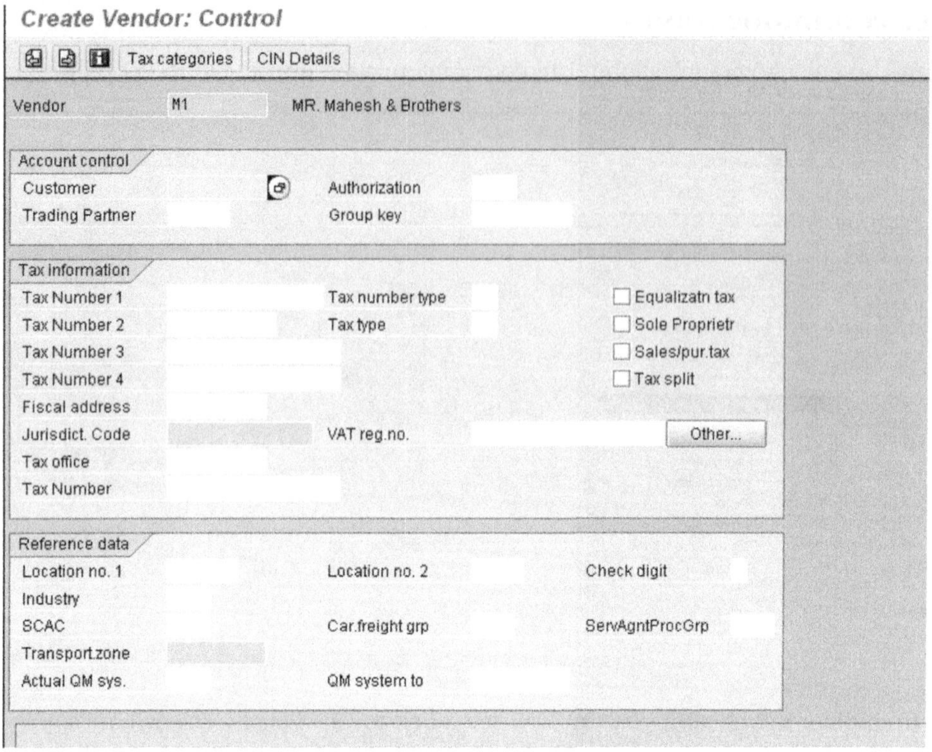

This information is related only to client level.

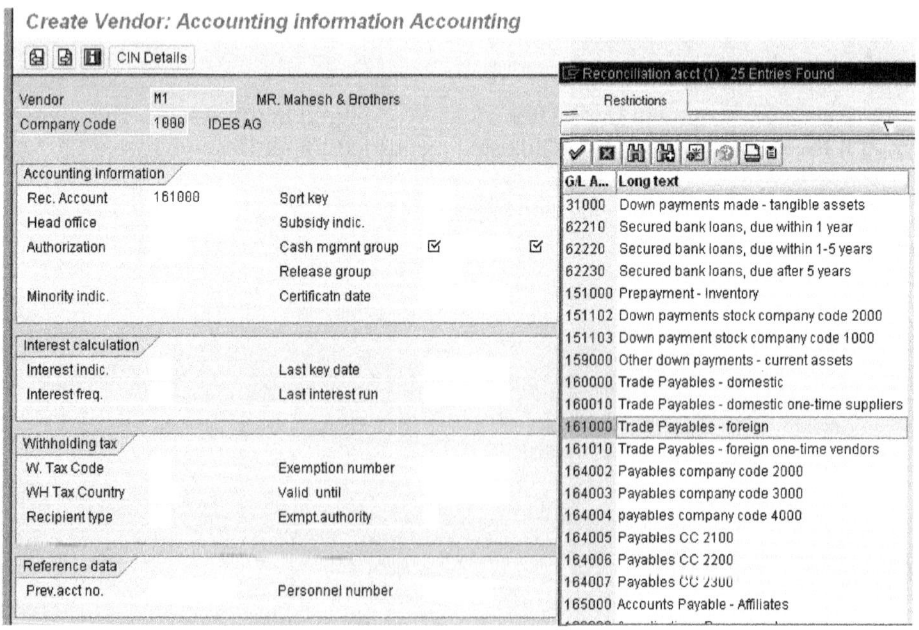

Now the next level of information will be Accounting Information Accounting at company code level.

That means these information will be available only within the specified company code.

Reconciliation Account:-

This information is required to link this vendor to Finance. This field will be entered with General Ledger. Press F4 or search option to find the relevant G/L account. This Ledger is updated with every transaction that happens with vendor. Here enter G/L account number 160000 in 1000 company code.

Cash Management Group:-

The vendors are linked to the planning group via cash management group. The planning group is used as a selection criterion with which you can restrict the selection of products to be planned in the production planning run: A procurement planning heuristic or an MRP heuristic may only plan a product in the production planning run if the product belongs to one of the planning groups specified in the product selection.

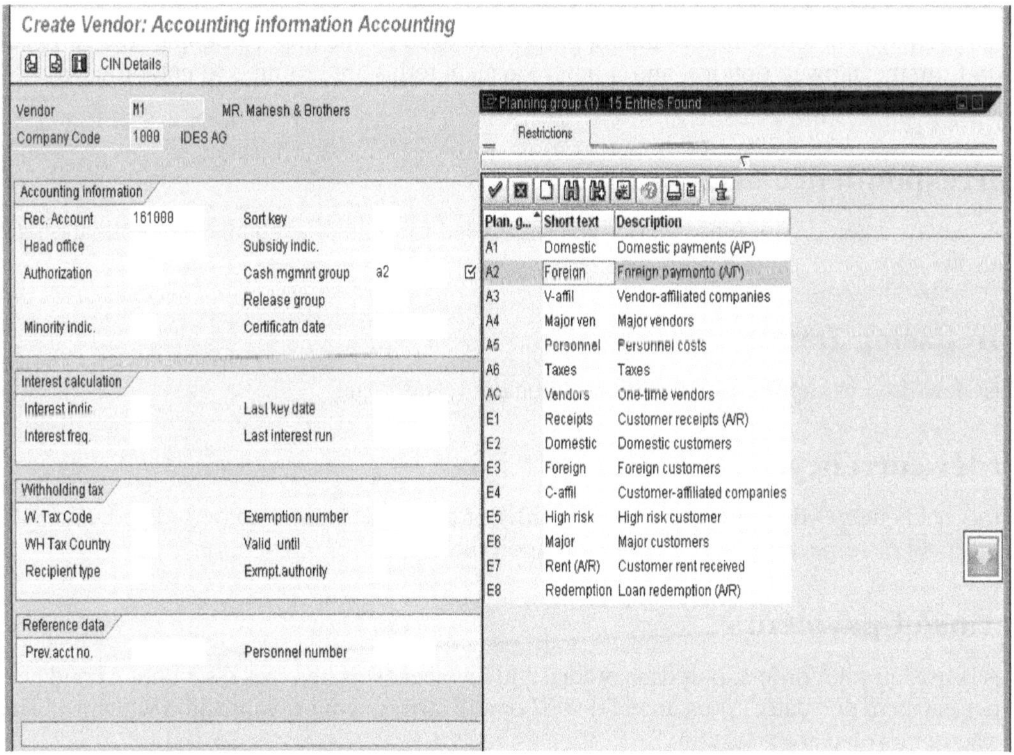

Payment Transactions Accounting:-

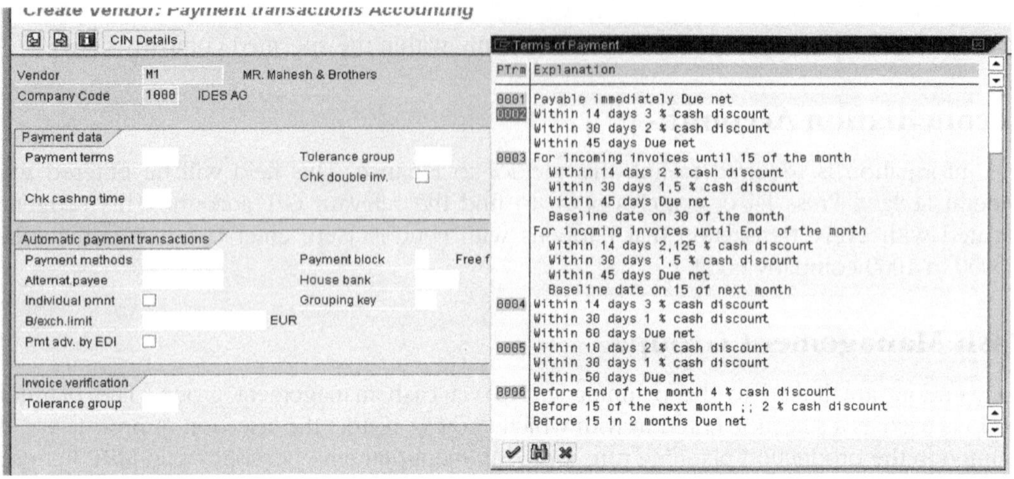

Payment Terms:-

These are payment terms for accounting purpose to filled by the finance people. You can make entry from the allowed options, and if other Payment terms are required to enter then you can customize that in customization in finance module.

Correspondence accounting:-

This view is entered with information which are used for regular exchange of information and controls.

Purchasing Data:-

This view used to capture purchasing requirement related data.

Order currency:-

In this field enter Order currency in which order or purchase order is to be ordered. Enter INR in this field or respect currency depending upon the country of the vendor.

Terms of payment:-

This is used in sales orders, purchase orders, and invoices. This involves discounting conditions as per payment due dates. You can enter 0002 or any other payment transaction which will later be used in invoice entry section.

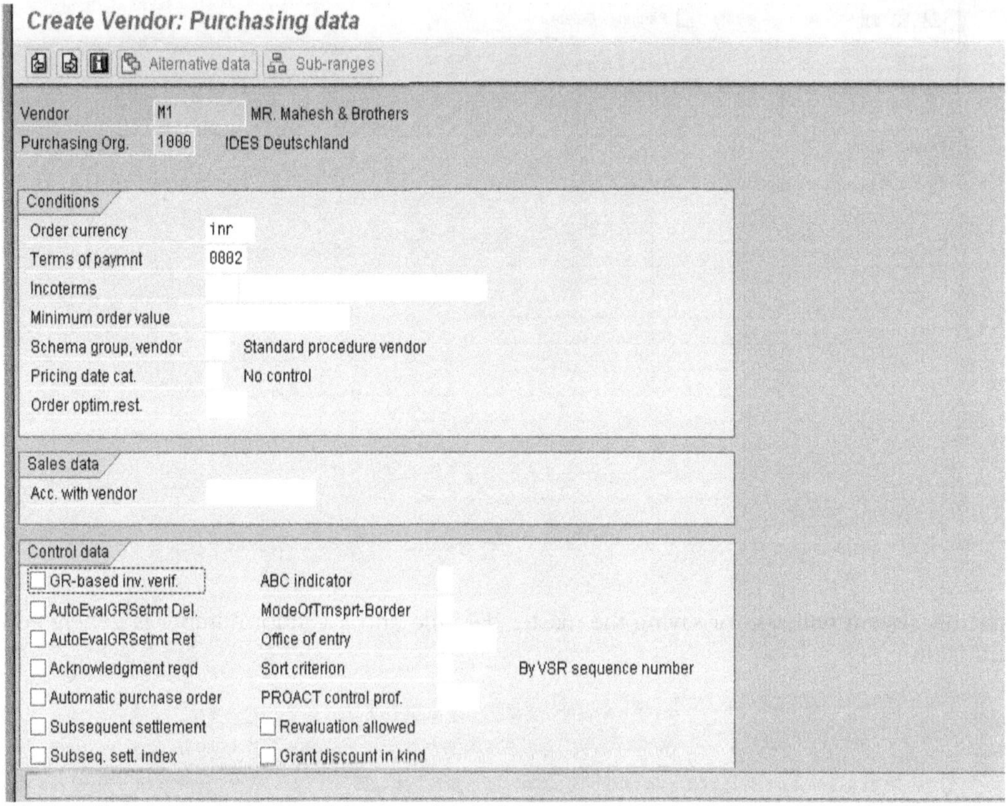

There is much information to be entered in the above fields to know right now about these fields you can press F1 and get the information. But we will study these information only when these are required.

Partner function:-

In the next view you can see Partner function related data and information. These data are asked only depending on some specific vendor account group. Now question arises what is a partner. In the business we have several business partners who perform their respective responsibilities based on respective roles to complete a transaction. They may be transporting agents, Invoice presented by, Forwarding agent, Goods Supplier and so on. Do not make any entry here.

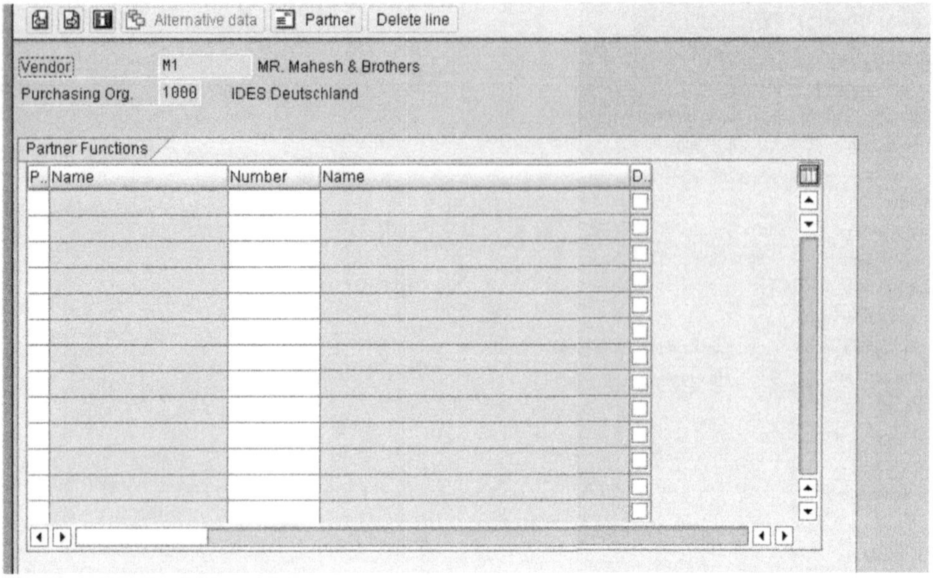

After this system will ask for saving the master data file and a vendor number is generated in the system.

Apart from that you can also Change the Vendor Master Data in XK02 and XK03 for displaying master data. So you can see only a few information are primarily required to input to do the normal business processing. But there are so many other check boxes in different view pages which are used for some or a few specific transactions and these will be discussed later on with proper context.

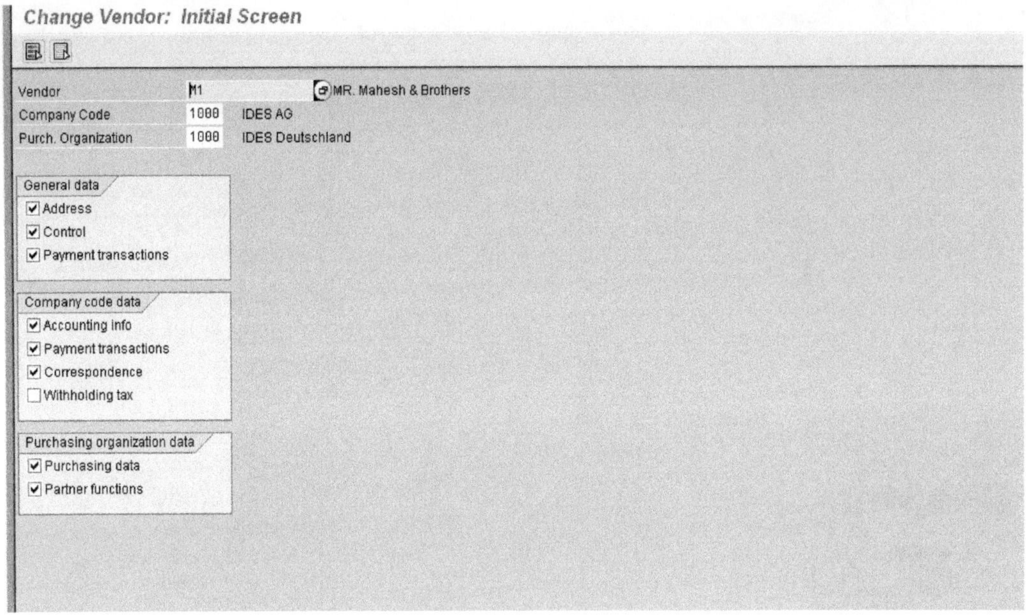

Yet if you are willing to know information about one or more field then you can put cursor in that field and press F1 function key to display help document.

Chapter

5

PURCHASING INFORMATION RECORD

Introduction:-

As the name suggests that this is a record which will contain purchasing related important information. This is basically a Master Data which is a semi compulsory prerequisite for the procurement process or purchasing process of any material. Now question may arise that, why semi compulsory?

First of all this is a master data which is to be created in the system manually before procurement process starts and this will contain purchase related information like price of a particular material in combination of a particular vendor. Combination will be as many materials and as many vendors will be created.

Why it is required?

Why it is required! Reason is that this info record contains information about discounting conditions and offers that may be available from a specified vendor or further expenses like freight charges delivery charges to be included in the price or not, and such kind of information this also contains applicable tax related information beforehand, as in some cases it is not possible to add tax codes or information in the invoice document manually. This information is used in the purchase order while initiating procurement process. This information works as a master data of condition and pricing information on a particular material procurement process.

Further you will come to know about the scenarios like consignment procurement and pipeline material's procurement. In these procurement processes tax codes are entered in the purchasing info record manually as a prerequisite because in these documents invoices are settled by the system automatically. So in this case info record is a compulsory.

Optional or Compulsory

No, except some scenarios this master record is not a compulsory one but optional. Results will be different depending on whether you have created this info record or you have not.

1. Suppose you have not created this record then while creating purchasing document system will not be able to search and fetch conditions and prices. In this case you will have to enter this information manually to determine applicable price. And once this purchasing document is saved, the info record will be generated out of this purchasing document (purchase order) automatically in the system.
2. Now suppose if it is already created then system will not ask for price information but price will be set automatically in the purchasing document (purchase order). And there will be no price related error if info record is created correctly.

Create Info Record:-

Info Record can be created by following menu path as shown in the picture below or alternatively you can enter ME11 in the transaction bar to fetch the initial screen.

Change Info Record:-

You can not re create any info record document but you can change this purchasing info record which is already created with one info category and same information. You can change this document in the transaction code ME12.

Display Info Record:-

You can view already created info record by the transaction code ME13.

Initial Screen:-

On the initial screen you can see a few fields to input.

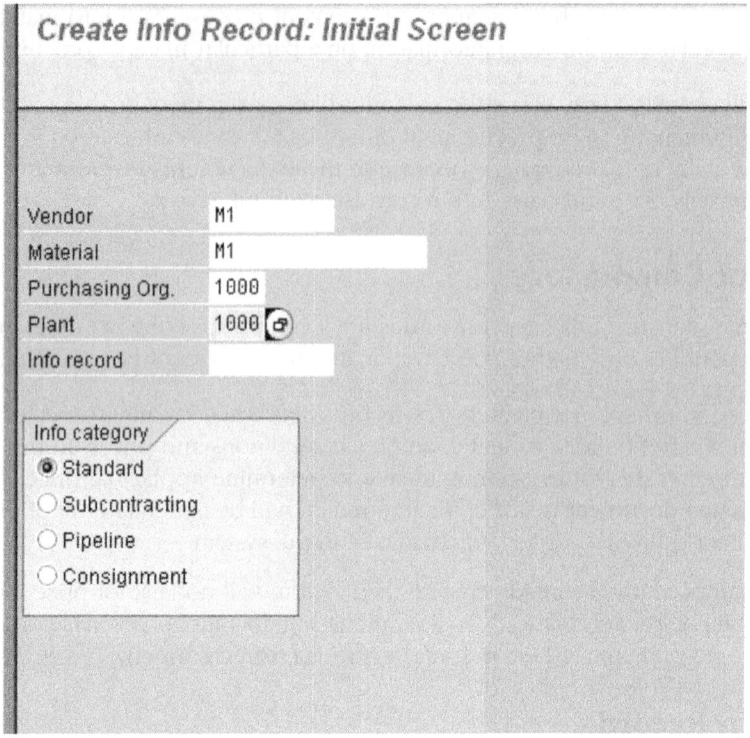

Input fields

1. Vendor

   First is for the vendor code number, from which you are going to procure the material.

2. Material

   2nd is for the material number which you are going to procure from the above mentioned vendor.

3. Purchase Org.

   3rd field is for the purchasing organization under which procurement process will take place.

4. Plant

   4th is for the plant at which level this purchasing info record will be created and for which this procurement will happen. So here you see that the info record should always be plant specific. Conditions and prices may or may not be different for each plant.

Organization level:-

Info record can be created at the following organizational levels:

1. At the Purchasing organization level, and
2. At the Plant level.

Info category:-

Next selection is for info category field. This is the next level, at which each info record will be different based on Info Category which is required for different types of procurement process, like Standard, Subcontracting, Pipeline, and Consignment procurement. Here you have to select the radio button as per your procurement flow as to select subcontracting radio button for subcontracting procurement and so on others.

Press Enter.

General Data Page

1st view will be of General data page. In this page you need not enter any information. Though there are several field which can provide vital information about the vendor.

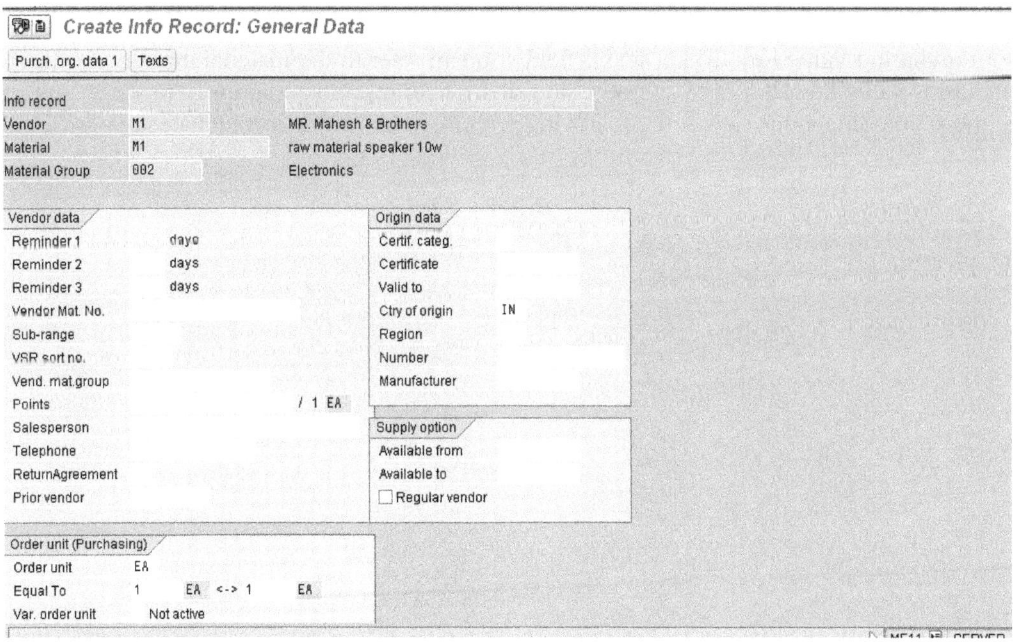

General Data:-

This is General Data page. This page is for general data input. Maximum of the information on this page will be fetched either from vendor master or material related information from material master. But yet there are a few information that will asked by the system.

Reminder:-

This is the number of days for first reminder, 2nd reminder or 3rd reminder letter to be issued to the vendor.

Use:-

This is basically to remind the vendor about the remaining days to some task or delivery date or deadline date for submission of quotation. And this goes on reducing. This is taken as negative reminder.

Similarly positive number of days can also be counted as number of days after some event or due date.

Procedure:-

The process of these time interval is first of all taken from purchasing info record and if it does not exist then it is taken from the material master record. The field in the material master record is of Purchasing Value Key. To know this field you can refer to the material master record. The purchasing value key also has some other important features and additions to process. You can see the purchasing value key in the following screen shot which is in purchasing data view.

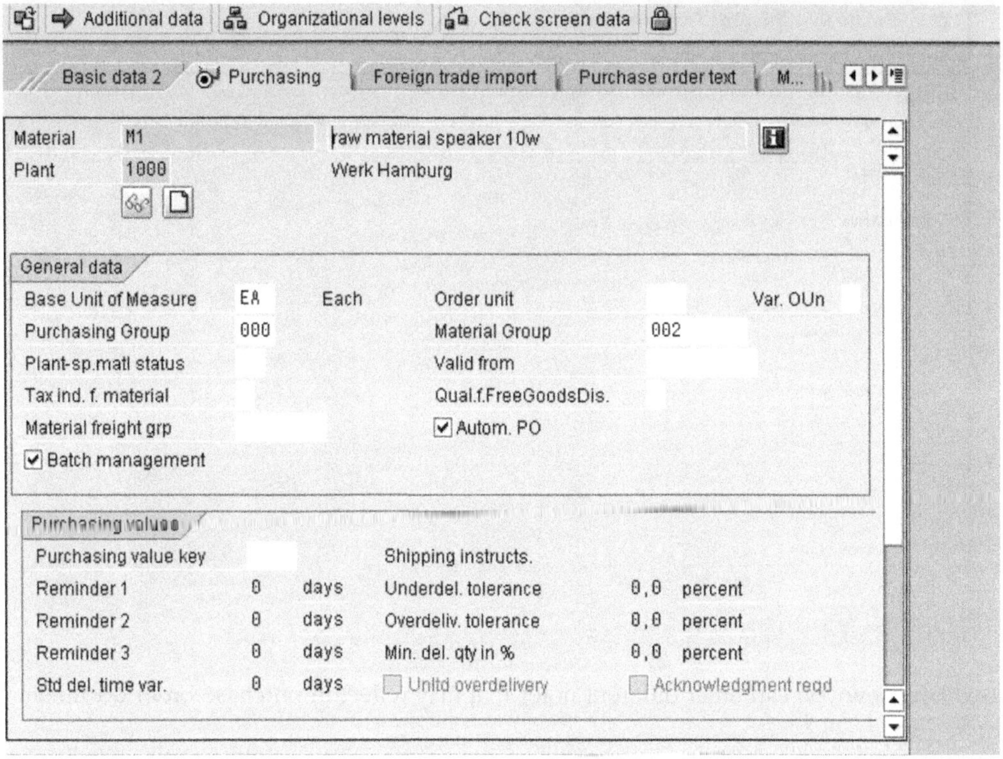

Dependencies:-

On this reminder, follow ups depend a lot, such as delivery date and some deadline dates.

Example:-

In case of delivery delay, you can send messages to the vendor to deliver the ordered materials. If delivery date is not matched then production of the company may hamper. So after the failure of delivery date management must remind the vendor as 1st reminder, 2nd reminder and 3rd reminder after some time interval.

Now click on Text.

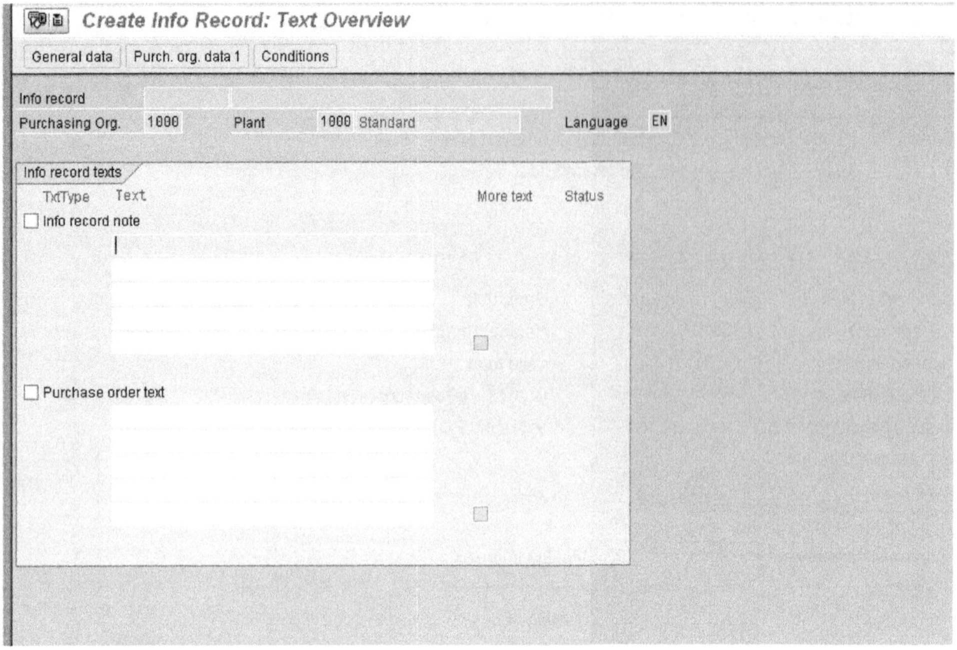

In text overview you can enter different notes that may reflect in purchase order document.

Texts in Purchasing Info Record:-

The info record also contains some texts which when specified, reflects in Purchase Order item. Some text is printed out and some texts are not printed

Info record memo:-

It is an internal note or comment. The info record memo is not printed out.

PO text:-

This purchase order text describes the order item in purchase order and same as the PO text in the material master record. It reflects in the PO item and is included in the printout of purchase order.

Short text

This short text (short description) is copied directly from the material master record of a particular and specified material and it reflects in the PO or the outline purchase agreement.

Click on condition.

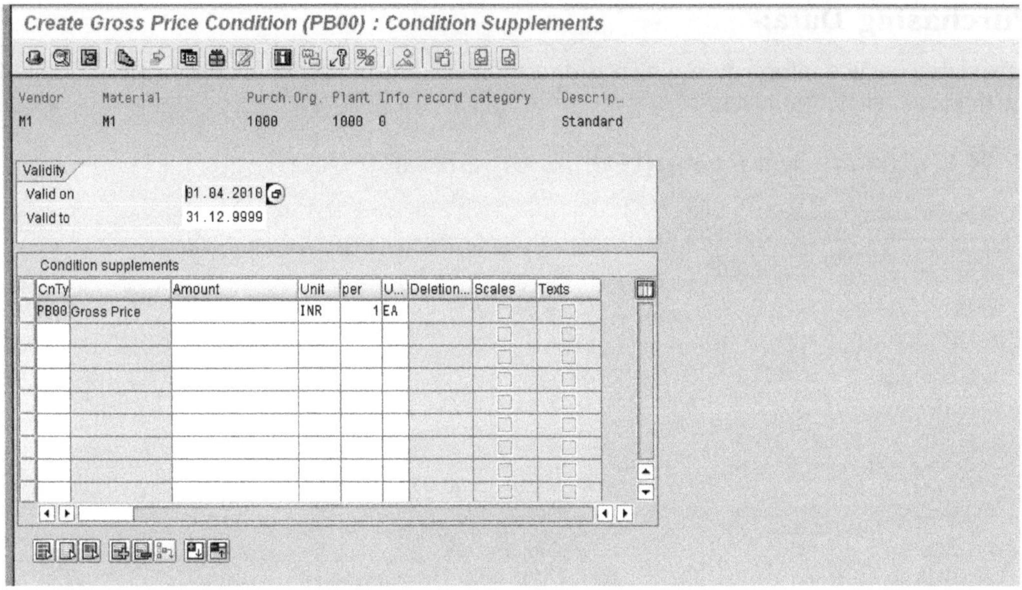

Here in this page you can enter price or gross price per unit of measure. You can also change the validity date and increase the date range so that purchase order creation date falls within this specified date range. Only then price in purchase order will be picked up from this field.

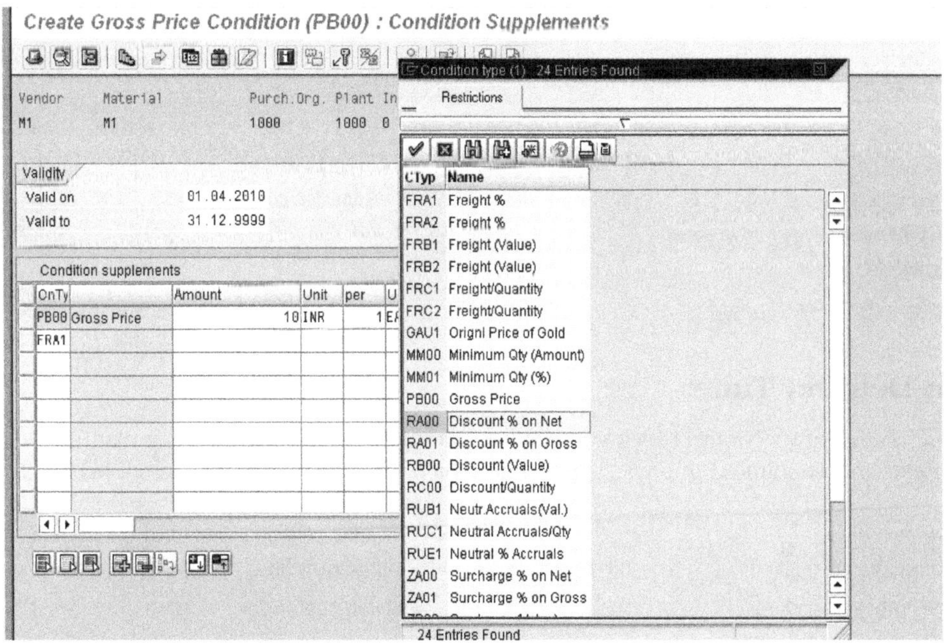

Info record also contains purchase order price history log which is charged for a material by a vendor.

Purchasing Data:-

This view contains information which is directly related to the procurement process. Some of the fields are circled in black.

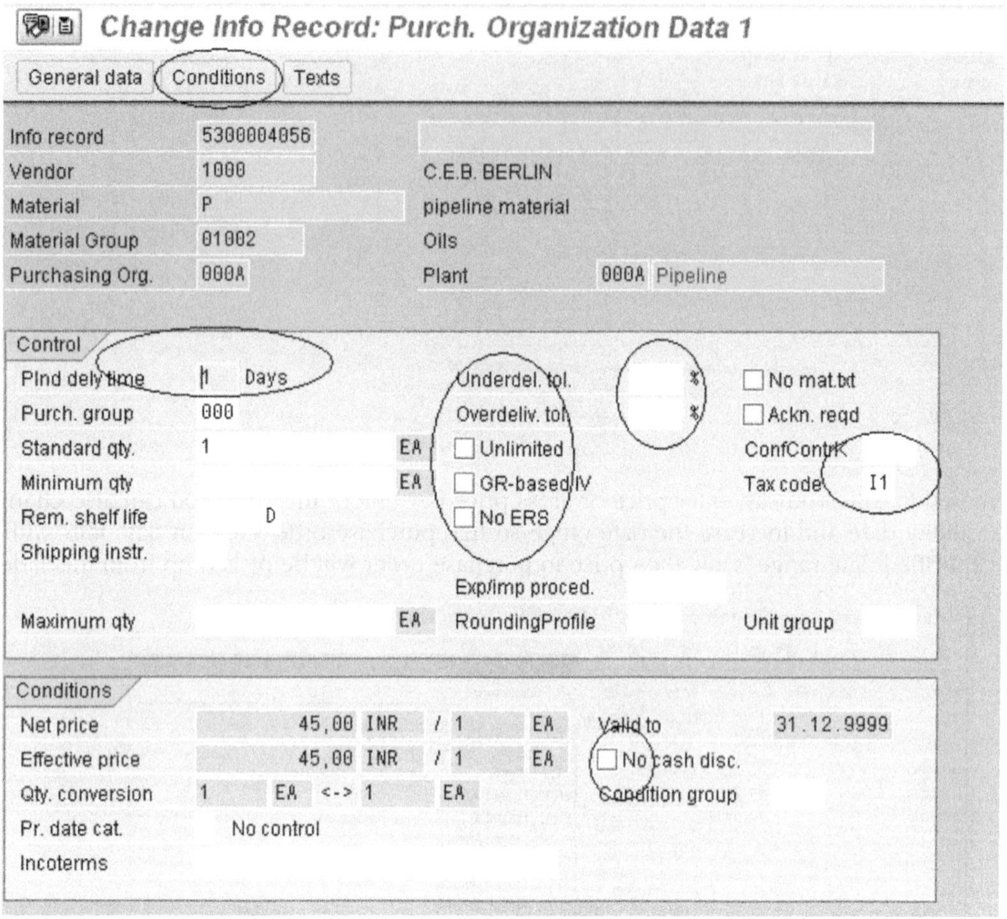

Plan Delivery Time:-

In purchasing view's control block you can see plan delivery time, which is a planned delivery time field. This is counted in days. This a time which is same as it is in material master.

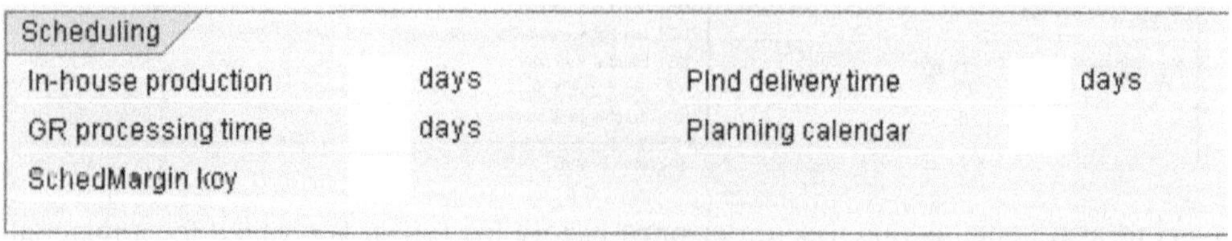

Just like Goods Receipt Processing time this field is also entered in the system in days. This time calculation starts from purchase order creation to getting the goods delivered at the door step of the receiving plant. So this 1 or more counted days are entered here. This is Vendor's planned delivery time which is used for scheduling of delivery of the material.

In the material master you can see the following view in MRP 2 view. Only difference is that in info record this planned delivery time is not material specific but rather vendor specific. The number of days a specified vendor takes to process the purchase order.

Purchase Group:-

In the purchasing view next comes Purchase group which is same as in material master's field. As we know purchase group is a person or a group of people who are responsible to negotiate with the vendor for purchasing a specified material. Apart from that purchase group is not a part of any specific organization level but it is at the client level. Here you press F4 and select the purchase group as per your requirement to whom you have assigned the job of procurement negotiation.

Standard Quantity:-

Standard Purchase order quantity is quantity of the material that is ordered form this vendor. This is used for price determination in depending upon the price scales that has been set in the purchasing info record's condition.

Use:-

The standard purchase order quantity is used to calculate and compute

- the effective prices in vendor evaluation
- The standard quantity may not be less than the minimum order quantity.
- To in determine to the effective price for which Material has scale (you can see the scales which is set below.).

Example: standard quantity 100 pieces.

Scale prices: 1-100 pieces. @ 10.00 and 101-200 pieces. @ 8.00

Price determined on basis of standard quantity: $10.00

Here you can see that how scaling process is done. I will explain the process how to set the scaling.

Step1- In the purchasing view's header you can see the tab condition.

Step2- Press that tab.

Step3- This will take you to the screen condition as you can see below in the screen shot.

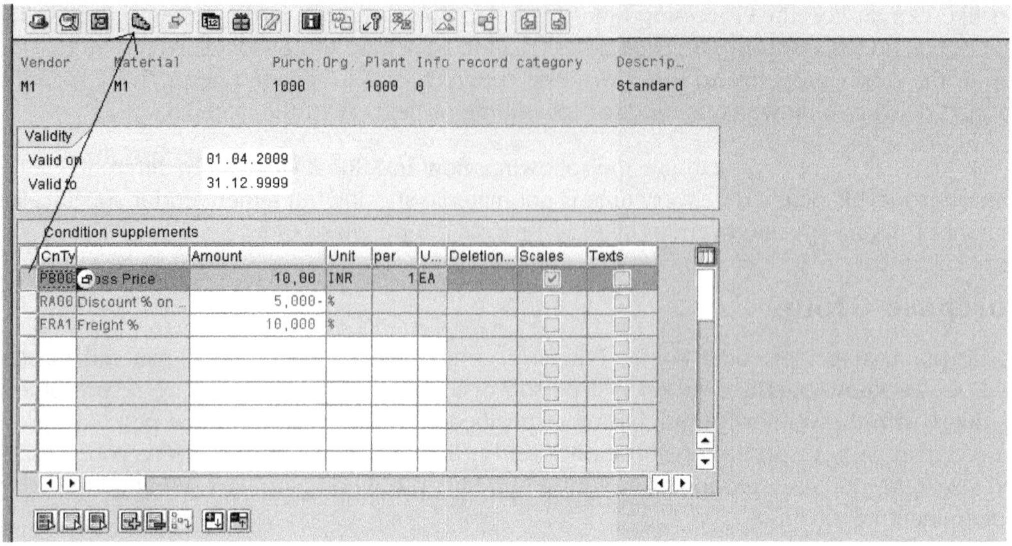

Here you enter price of the material in the amount field for the particular condition type for base price PB00.

Step4- Then press enter.

Step5- Then select the entire line of condition type.

Step6- And go to Scale and click as shown above in the screen shot.

Step7- Here you can see the view as below in the screen shot.

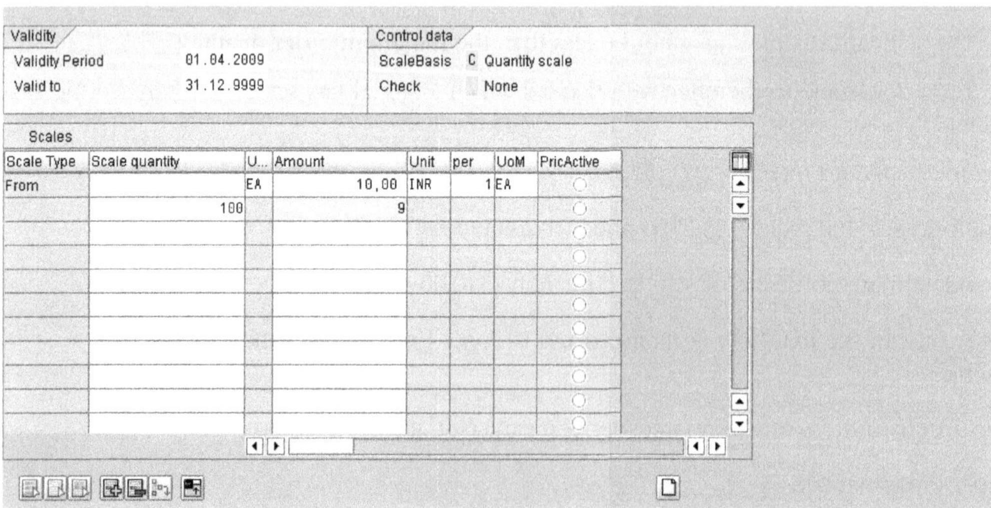

Here you do not enter any quantity in Scale Quantity field means keep it blank. And put 100 in the next line and the amount which you think should be or negotiated to be applicable for that quantity of material. So this means quantity

From 1-99 pieces will be priced @ Rs. 10.00 per piece.

From 100 and onwards will be priced @ Rs. 9.00 per piece till upper level is set.

You will be it's use and effect in the purchase order when you change the purchase order quantity in the quantity field. You will be able to see the changes there.

• Net price:-

In info record this is the price that is arrived at after taking all discounts and surcharges into account. You can go back to the last topic for how to set the condition type, which may be base price or other conditions like freight charges or discount.

• Condition type:-

This is a key that uniquely identifies the condition.

• Use

For example, whether, during pricing, the system suggests or calculates a price, a discount, a surcharge, or other pricing elements, such as freight costs and sales taxes. For each of these pricing elements, there is a condition type defined in the system

You can see condition types by pressing F4.

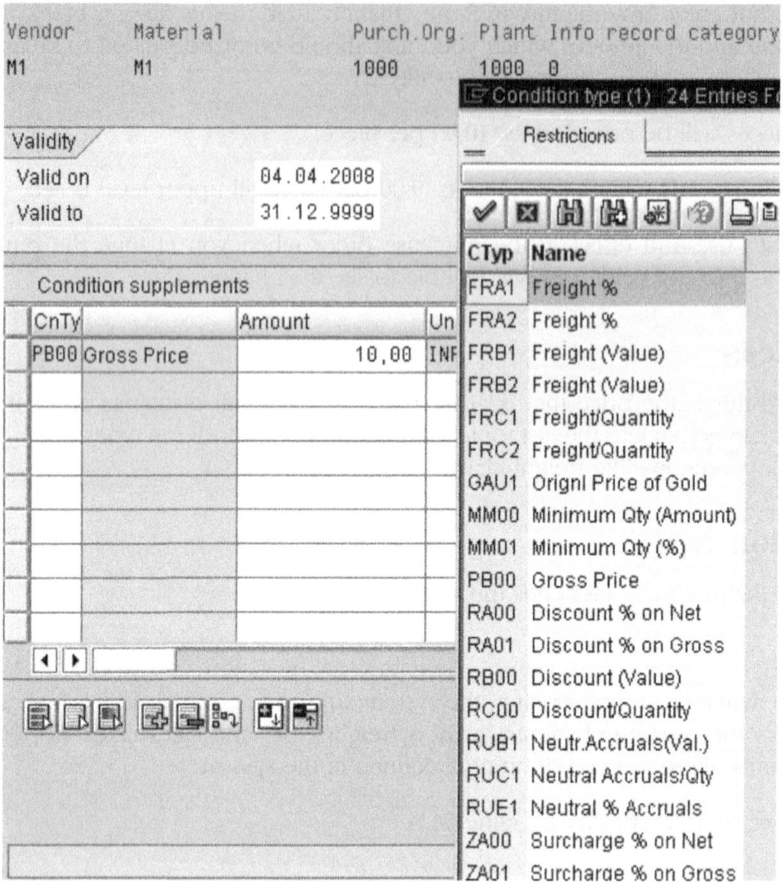

Use:-

This price is determined automatically by the system. In info record you will have to input it manually and if no other data record or price condition record found in the system as a prerequisite then system will take this price into account and will be displayed in the purchase order item.

Procedure:-

You can enter the following:

- The net price (this is the price which includes the vendor's discounts or surcharges).
- The gross price (this is the price which excluding discounts or surcharges).
- Further you also maintain the conditions (condition types) in the columns as it is shown in the screen shot for the item. Then applicable net price will be calculated by the system.
- Dependencies

During creation, you can only maintain the net price if you have not yet maintained the info record conditions. You must then maintain the price on the conditions screen. If the vendor's net price for the material has not been maintained in the info record, the net price of the last purchase order issued to the vendor is proposed when a new purchase order is created.

Tolerance data:-

Under delivery tolerance:-

You can see in Tol. Underdel and Tol. Overdel fields in the info record. You can set the limit in %. This value is taken into consideration for purchase order item or online agreement item. Based on this If goods delivery differs from purchase order or online agreement by more than this limit then system prompts for action.

Over Delivery tolerance:-

As mentioned above in case of under delivery tolerance applies, same is in case of over delivery tolerance also.

Indicator: Unlimited over delivery allowed:-

This is the Indicator that confirms that over delivery will not have any limit at the time of Goods receipt.

Dependencies

This selection is taken into consideration for purchase order item or online agreement item. Based on this If goods delivery differs from purchase order or online agreement by more than this limit then system prompts for action and if this indicator is set then there is no limit of over delivery.

• Indicator: GR-based invoice verification

This selection is taken into consideration for purchase order item, invoice will be accepted only to the extent goods are delivered and as many times goods are delivered. You have option to select invoice of some of the delivery and not of some of the delivered items. If this field is selected then GR based invoice verification filed is pre selected in purchase order item details.

• Indicator: No evaluated receipt settlement (ERS)

This is a selection field which confirms that payment will not be settled automatic without receipt of invoice of goods receipt from the vendor. Evaluated receipt settlement is a procedure which creates automatic settlement of goods receipts. In this procedure vendor does not send any invoice for purchase order item and goods receipt but the invoice document is automatically posted in the buyer's system as per goods receipt of purchase order item.

• Minimum remaining shelf life

It is a minimum time span for which the material may be kept in the system as usable before consumption date. This field may be entered in days, weeks, months, years as you select in the period indicator field.

Tax Code:-

This field is for tax code entry as in some cases or procurement processes the invoice is not entered manually but it is selected automatically by the system. So in this case you need to enter applicable tax code in the info record before hand. Consignment purchase or pipeline purchase may be a few examples. Tax codes are country specific and rates also vary.

• Order acknowledgment requirement:-

This field determines vendor confirms and sends the acknowledgement each time the vendor performs the part of the process for the purchase order. Vendor will send the letter of acknowledgement when shipment of the goods is done, and so on.

Use:-

To ensure that your purchase order or scheduling agreement delivery schedule has been received by the vendor, you can arrange for the latter to send you an acknowledgment.

• Dependencies

Once this indicator is set, this will be auto selected in the purchase order item or outline agreement when the documents are created.

Price valid until:-

This field will be filled up automatically by the system. If you need to change the validity date of purchasing info record, then you have to follow process in the screen shot.

To do the process first go to purchasing data view, there you can see condition field and select that. After that the above mentioned screen will where you can see valid from field and valid to field. Change the date as per your requirement. This validity period is very important because if the created purchase order does not fall within the info record's validity period the purchase order will not be able to fetch the price from the info record.

No cash discount:-

If this indicator is set then no discount will be prompted at the time of payment for the item.

• Inco terms

These are Commonly-used trading terms that comply with the standards established by the International Chamber of Commerce (ICC).

It is a code as per international rules for the interpretation of the commonly used terms in the international business.

Use

Inco terms specify certain internationally recognized procedures that the shipper and the receiving party must follow for the shipping transaction to be successfully completed.

After entering this information, press enter, system will prompt to save. Again press enter. System will save the purchasing info record and a info record number will be generated which will be unique. Now if you need to change this info record then use ME12, and for display info record use ME13.

Chapter 6

SOURCE LIST

Introduction:-

What is source list?

Source list is a master record which provides information that who are the people or vendors who can supply the specified material within a specified validity date.

The Menu Path:-

Fixed Vendor:-

You can define a source of supply as "fixed" for a certain period of time. After fixing this the fixed vendor will automatically be selected by the system in purchase requisition.

Blocked vendor:-

You can also define a source of supply as blocked for certain time interval. That means system will not propose the blocked vendor for procurement process.

Maintaining Source List:-

When you enter transaction code ME01 in the transaction bar, you can see following initial screen. Here you will have to enter a material and a plant for which material is going to be procured.

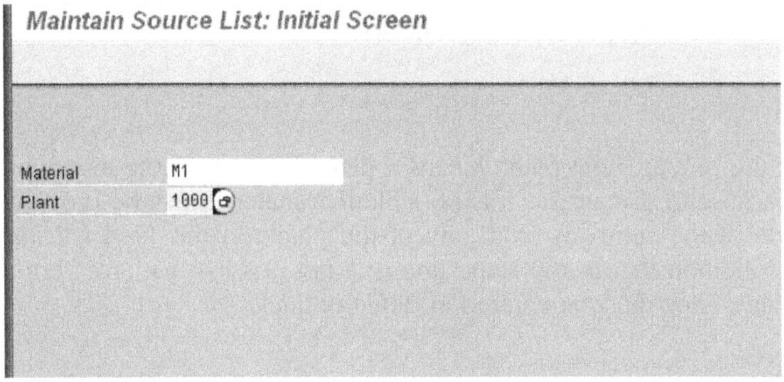

After entering this information press enter. System will take you into this screen as seen below.

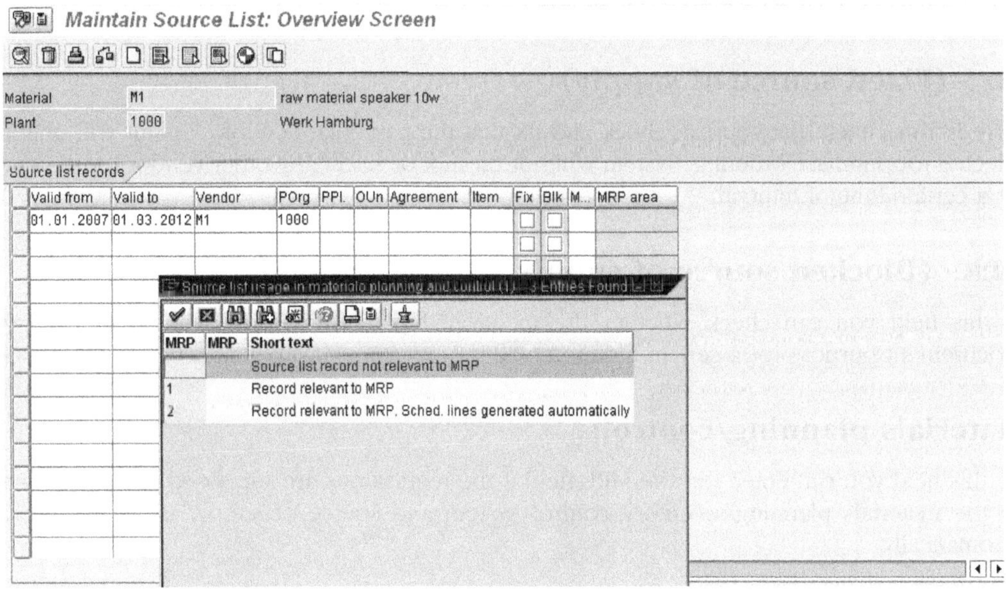

Valid from:-

In this column you will enter the start date from which this source list is applicable.

Valid to:-

In this column you will enter the end date till which this source list is applicable.

Vendor:-

This column will have list of all the vendors who will supply the already mentioned material.

Purchase Organization:-

This is the list of controlling purchase organization.

PPL:-

This field is for the procurement plant. Means a plant from which the mentioned material can be procured. Because in some cases it is possible that material may be procured from outside vendor or inside of the company from any of the plant. So this field will have plant code. But there is a condition that in the same line it is not possible to have vendor number and procurement plant. They must be entered in different lines.

Agreement:-

In this field you can enter the agreement document number if any has been created between the purchasing organization and the vendor.

Fix:- (Fixed source of supply)

Here in this check box you can check and fix that the particular vendor or plant will only be selected for purchase ordering. System will not prompt or select any other vendor for the same for a certain time of interval.

BLk:- (Blocked source of supply)

In this field you can check whether the mentioned plant or vendor will be blocked for procurement purpose for a certain time interval.

Materials planning/control:-

In this field you can enter 1 in the MRP field if the requisitions are supposed to be generated by the materials planning/inventory control system and source of supply is to be selected automatically.

Enter 2 if you have entered a scheduling agreement in the source list and the requisitions generated by the materials planning and control system should be automatically converted into delivery schedule lines.

After entering these information you can check by pressing an icon at the header. This will check the correctness of the entries that you have made. After this press save button and save it.

*****

Multiple ways of Maintaining source list:-

You can maintain source list records in different ways as per individual specific requirements. We have already seen how to create it manually. And automatically you can create a source list for a material by the system when you create info record for the material with the vendor or for each outline agreement item in which the material is specified.

Manual maintenance:

You can maintain source list manually by the process as mentioned above if you have to keep on making changes from time to time in the source list.

Automatic Maintenance from within an outline agreement:-

Apart from manual maintenance you can maintain it automatically also by maintaining outline agreement. The data will flow automatically when you create or make any changes in the outline agreement as you will be entering that number in the source list.

Automatic Maintenance from within an info record:-

With this procedure, you can enter a vendor in the source list when creating or making any changes in the purchasing info record.

Prerequisites

Before creating source list following must be maintained in the system.

Material:-

Material must be created in the system for which you are going to maintain source list.

Plant:-

Plant is the level for which material has been created and now source list will be maintained.

Validity period:-

You should have knowledge for which validity period this source list is required. According this is to be entered.

Source list requirement for plant:-

This is a very vital and important reason to maintain source list. Normally what happens that if you do not maintain source list and even after that you proceed to procure the material then system will not create any problem while creating purchasing document. Only problem will occur is that system will not find applicable source of supply automatically but you will have to enter manually.

But if you have maintained source list as a compulsory pre requisite for procurement in the material master purchasing data, then system will not allow you to procure the material unless and until you maintain the source list for the material under the plant.

Source list requirement in Customization:-

In Customization you maintain the source list requirement as compulsory.

- In easy access menu * Tools * Business Engineer * Customizing * Implementation Projects * Display SAP Reference IMG * Logistics * Material Management * Purchasing * Source list.

Or alternatively you can go to:-

- SPRO * Logistics * Material Management * Purchasing * Source list * Source List requirement at plant level. Here is the list of plants for which a source list requirement exists.

Maintaining a Source List while creating an Info Record

If you need to create source list while creating a Purchasing info record, choose Extras > Source list when creating an info record. Here Source list overview screen will appear. Here you can maintain the start and end dates of the period during which material will be procured from the specified vendor as specified in the info record.

Apart from that you can also maintain source list for a number of plants at a time by choosing Go to * Plant menu.

Save the Purchasing Info Record.

PART-3

PROCESS MANAGEMENT

Chapter 7

PROCUREMENT IN MATERIALS MANAGEMENT

Introduction

In general procurement word means a complete process of purchasing some material or service from some vendor or getting it from some plant in case of internal procurement as per the requirement.

The procurement cycle consist of the following steps. The procedure is same for material and service procurement.

Determination of Requirements:-

Material requirements are identified in the production department or in the respective cost center or consumption point where a particular material is required for some reason. Now the requirement may be generated via material requirement planning automatically which is controlled by inventory management, or manually (some person who is responsible for keeping consumption track recognizes the need of the material or service. This involves regular checking of stock levels of materials which is defined in the master records. In documented form this is not a legal document but only an internal document.

Source Determination:-

This is a purchasing component that helps you to determine who should be the most probable vendor for procurement purpose for the material or service. This may also involve past track record of the vendor along with other current factors like pricing, conditions, any agreement previously made etc.

Purchase requisition:-

Once the requirement is known, then the process of procurement starts. First of all requirement is recorded in documented form in Purchase Requisition. Here following information is recorded, like quantity required, delivery time of material, plant where the material is to be delivered, source of supply if already known etc. These are the basic information that are tracked and recorded in the Purchase requisition.

Request for quotation:-

Once purchase requisition is created then this is released for further processing. In this step with reference to the purchase requisition, Request for Quotation documents are created and this will be sent to different vendors for feedback and to get their offers on the material. After creation of documents separate documents numbers are created.

Quotation from the vendors:-

We know after creation of request for quotation separate document numbers are created for request for quotation for each vendor. These request for quotations are sent to the vendors. Vendors get the request for quotations and after that they study on this offer. After that they send their response in the form of quotation to the purchasing company. These quotations are again recorded in the purchasing company's system in the form of maintain Quotations.

In this step quotations are created with reference to the same request for quotation document number, Price and conditions are added in this document. Document numbers do not change.

Price comparisons:-

In this step the authority compares the quotation documents and decides minimum price that is beneficial for the organization. Based on this system proposes best possible vendor who should be given the order. In this comparison system takes into account all the conditions, price and discounts that are offered by the vendor.

Vendor Selection:-

After source of supply is proposed by the vendor then the management or purchasing officer confirms the vendor for purchasing and purchasing document is created.

Purchase Order Processing:-

Purchase order is created with reference to purchase requisition, request for quotation document numbers, and is sent to the vendor for procurement. Based on the item contents of the material or service in this purchase order the vendor send the material. Based on this the vendor will supply the material.

Purchase Order Follow-Up:-

After creating and sending purchase order to the vendor the system recalls the reminder periods as was set in the material master and the purchasing information record. If the vendor makes any delay in delivery of the material then system will trigger a reminder to the vendor.

Goods Receiving and Inventory Management:-

When goods sent by the vendor reaches to the doorstep of the storage location of a particular plant then the responsible goods receiving personnel counts the material quantity and then enters the counted number in the system as Goods received quantity. After making this entry one material document is created having all the information of the goods receipt and also the financial document for the material's valuation change at a particular plant level. At this point system will also check the over delivery and under delivery of the material if required.

Invoice Verification:-

After goods are received multiple copies of invoice documents are also received which are sent by vendor as per bills for payment. These invoice documents may come before goods receipt, with goods receipt or after goods receipt as per mode of dispatch. Then the accounts payable clerk checks the invoice, enters into the system and verifies that for any quantity or price variance in comparison to purchase order and goods receipt. And when everything is ok the officer posts the invoice for payment.

Payment:-

Based on entered invoice document the finance people pay the due amount to the vendor.

So these were basic procurement process in case of external procurement.

Chapter

8

PURCHASING DOCUMENTS

Introduction:-

A purchasing document is an instrument in documented form which is used by purchasing department to procure materials or services.

You can enlist various external purchasing documents which are available in the standard SAP System.

Purchase Requisition:-

Requirements of materials or services is recorded and reported to Purchasing by means of purchase requisitions. This is a purchasing document but an internal one. Internal is called because this remains within the organization for internal circulation. This document is used as a reference material for purchasing documents. This may be created at production point or consumption point.

Request for quotation (RFQ):-

This is a document which contains information about requirement on a particular date with required quantity of a material or service. This document is sent to the vendor to know their wiliness to supply the material.

Quotation:-

This document is created with reference to the request for quotation and it contains a vendor's prices and conditions along with the basic information on requirement and based on this document potential vendor is selected.

Purchase order (PO):-

This is a buying party's request to a selected vendor for external procurement to supply certain material or perform some service on a condition on a particular date or within a pre defined time interval.

Contract:-

In the SAP System this is a long term buying arrangement or agreement. This is a binding commitment to procure a certain or a range of material or service from a vendor over a certain time period.

Scheduling agreement:-

Same as Contract, this is also an agreement or long term buying arrangement. This provides delivery schedules of purchase quantity, delivery dates and precise time over a predefined period along with the normal contract.

Structure of a purchasing document

Each purchasing document is into two main parts: 1. header and 2. individual items. There may be several items within one header in a document.

Header:-

The header contains information which is relevant to the whole purchasing document.

Items:-

Items are detailed information which is material or service specific in a document which may be more than one to be procured.

For example, information about the vendor and the document number is contained in the document header, and the material description and the order quantity are specified in each item.

Additional Data:-

Additional data provides additional required information regarding purchasing document and item as per procurement process. It includes, for example, account assignments (such as cost center and G/L account) and the PO history for an item, and invoice receipts settings relating to the item.

Document Types:-

Different documents are differentiated by document types. Document types carry different number ranges to assign separate number for one document type. Along with number range this also determines the fields that are offered for data input as a default. This also determines that one particular field will be required or display or optional field for data input.

Document Number Range:-

Each document is assigned a unique number which is assigned serially within a predefined number range. The defined number may be alphanumeric code. These number can be assigned internally or externally, depending on the procedures followed by the organization. Internal number assignment means that system will automatically assign a unique number picking from predefined number range. External number assignment means the user will have authority to assign a particular number for the document or database.

Chapter

9

PURCHASE REQUISITION

Introduction

Suppose you have understood that some material or external service is required at some point due to some reason. Now you need to track that and forward this the relevant department and authority for fulfillment. This document is created to serve this purpose. These Purchase Requisitions can be created either directly or indirectly or say manually or automatically.

"A purchase requisition is a request or instruction to Purchasing to procure a certain quantity of a material or a service so that it is available at a certain point in time". SAP definition.

Manual Creation of Purchase Requisition:-

"Directly" or manual creation of purchase requisition means when this purchasing document is created by someone from the requesting department manually. The responsible person determines what and how much to order, and the delivery date.

Automatic Creation of Purchase Requisition:-

"Indirectly" or Automatic Creation of Purchase Requisition means that the purchase requisition is created automatically via another Process as per the requirement. It may be material requirement planning, a sales order or for any project.

After purchase requisition is created, it is possible that this purchase requisition might be required to be released based on specific requirements and processes. That is determined in Release procedure.

Requisitions can be created automatically:-

- **Via materials planning and control**

For this:-

- Make settings in Consumption-Based Planning.
- Maintain past consumption stock track.
- Maintain existing stock level.
- System automatically calculates all the prerequisites and the order quantity and the delivery date are determined automatically.

- **Via networks**

This is created in the domain of project system, if

- A material or an external service has been assigned to an operation which is a part of any project.
- The indicator allowing automatic generation of requisitions immediately when a network is saved has been set in the network.
- If the indicator has not been set, in the network then the system passes the data on to materials planning and control when the network is released.
- The latter component then creates the requisition.

- **Via maintenance orders**

This is created in the domain of Plant Maintenance and Service Management. If

- A material has been assigned to an operation, or
- An operation with the control key for external services has been created.
- Via production orders. In the domain of PP Production Planning and Control. If
    - The production order contains any external operation like subcontracting work.

      Texts are automatically adopted in the purchase requisitions.

Procurement Item Categories:-

Some times procurements may involve multiple procurement processes. So as per the requirement Purchase requisition will be assigned with procurement types in the procurement type field. Purchase requisition is defined for following procurement types:-

- Standard
- Subcontracting
- Consignment
- Stock transfer
- External service

Standard:-

This procurement type is used as a normal procurement process. In this procurement process item category field remains blank. Process is followed as normal one.

Subcontracting:-

In this procurement process is used when some material is manufactured or made up of some components. Components may be 1 or more. In this process 1st of all components are procured and then these components are provided to the potential subcontracting vendor. After this purchase requisition is created and sent to the purchasing department. With reference to this purchase requisition purchase order is created for the subcontracting material. And finally material is procured from the subcontracting vendor. Vendor is paid for the service that this vendor has rendered.

Consignment:-

In consignment procurement procedure stocks are procured from a consigner and stock is kept at the buyer's stock point in special stock. And vendor is paid only when stock is consumed and to the extent stock is consumed.

Stock transfer:-

This requisition type is used to transfer stock from one plant to another plant where value of stock may or may not change.

External Service:-

This requisition type is used to procure services that may be of any kind.

Create Purchase Requisition:-

Manually Purchase Requisition may be created multiple ways.

- Create Purchase requisition with master record.
- Create Purchase requisition without master record.
- Create Purchase requisition with reference technique (with reference to old purchase requisition).

Prerequisites:-

Before you proceed to create purchase requisition you will have to maintain some prerequisites depending upon the purchase requisition creation ways. You can use following organizational structure for your smooth practice. Why this organizational structure? This is just because in standard SAP training system this organizational structure is already configured.

- **For purchase requisition with master record:-**

  Use Organization Structure as

  - Company Code 1000
  - Purchase Organization 1000
  - Plant 1000
  - Storage location 0001 or any Storage location

- **Create Material Master Record**

  Use Organization Structure as

  - Plant 1000
  - Storage location 0001 or any Storage location

    (Which should be assigned with Company Code 1000, Purchase Organization 1000)

- **Create Vendor Master Record**
  - Company Code 1000
  - Purchase Organization 1000
  - Vendor account group as 0007 or any other

- **Create Purchasing Information Record, for info category standard use following information.**
  - Vendor with same organization levels
  - Material that you have created with same organization levels
  - Purchase Organization 1000
  - Plant 1000

- **Create Source list**
  - Material that you have created with same organization levels
  - Plant 1000

Menu Path:-

You can follow menu path as it is shown in the picture below. Alternatively you can also use transaction code ME51N in the command line. Proceed to create Purchase Requisition menu path as shown below in the picture.

You use the transaction code ME51N to create purchase requisition.

Choose Requisition ® Create.

The initial screen appears. This will look some what like,

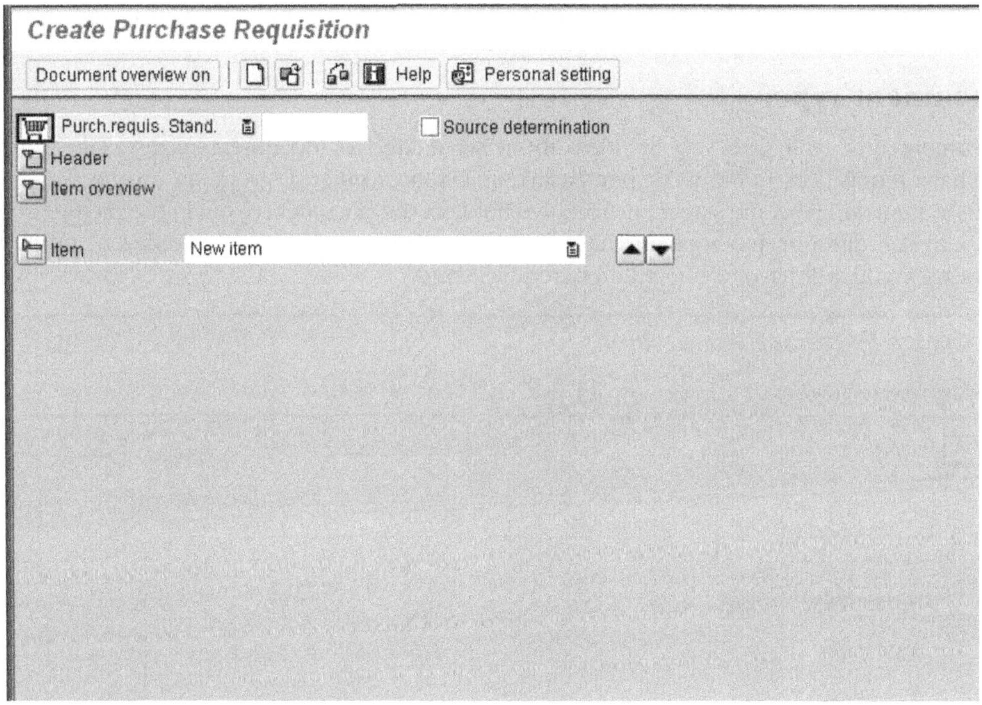

Header data:-

As you can see in the above picture icons for Header (Header Data), Item overview (Item data), Item Detail (Item Details Data). The header contains information which is relevant to the whole purchasing document.

Item overview:-

On the initial screen you can see Item overview icon. If you click this then it will take you to the item overview screen of the document. This will contain multiple items in a single purchasing document. These items lines may or may not be similar to any other line item in the same document. Here you will enter material number in the material field which you are going to procure and other fields as listed below.

Item details data:-

This view page will give you information which will be specific to a particular line item. The information about item will be in details with all relative required information.

Source Determination:-

On the right side you can see a check box for Source determination. If you put a check in this box to select this option then source will be determined automatically by the system based on the source of supply. Pre requisite for this optional benefit will be achieved only when you have source list master data in your system available or already created. If this check box is not checked then you will have to enter the source of supply (vendor number) manually.

Document type:-

Document type will give you an idea about what kind of document is this. Like normal purchase requisition, frame work purchase requisition or other. Depending on the document types system will reset the screen and relative fields of the document. Now in the picture below you can see different types of purchase requisition that will be used for different purposes. Right now you will have to select Purch. requis. Stand.

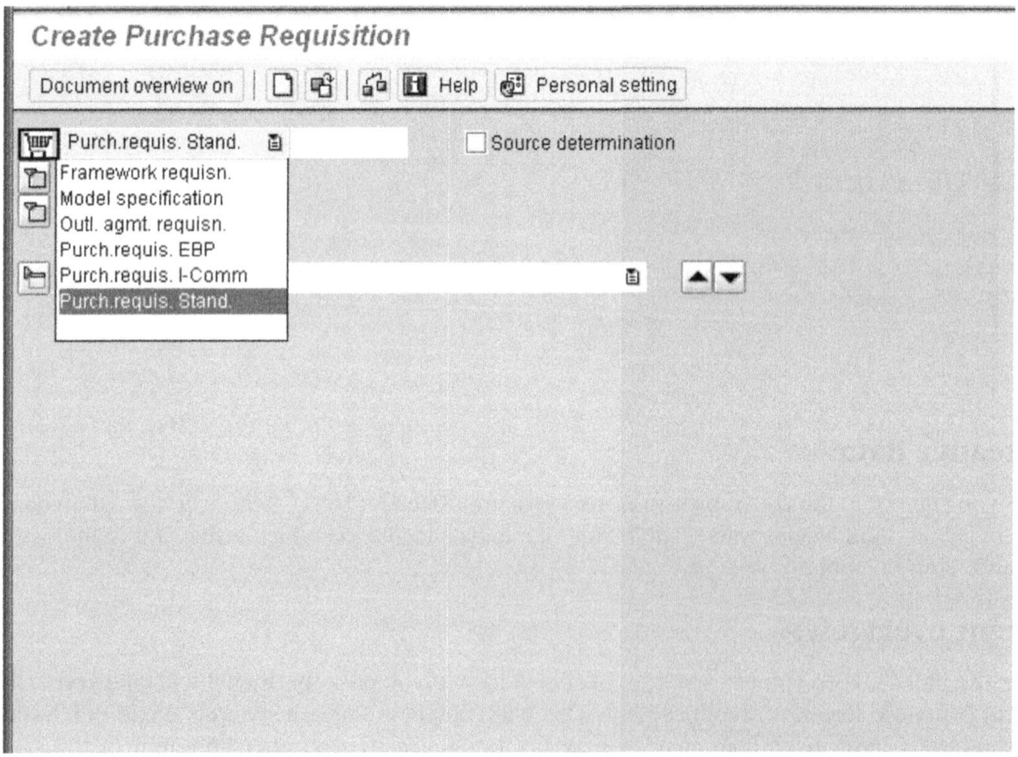

Document overview:-

On the left side you can see the document overview screen. This toggles as document overview on and document overview off status.

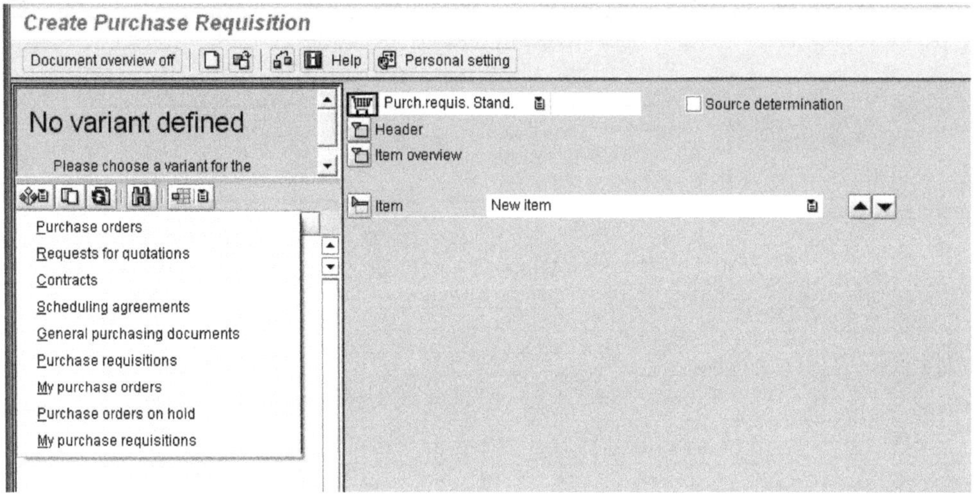

Here click on Variants. A drop down list will be opened. From this list select your required presiding reference document.

You can find your required purchasing document from here also.

As a default the initial screen will look something like the picture below.

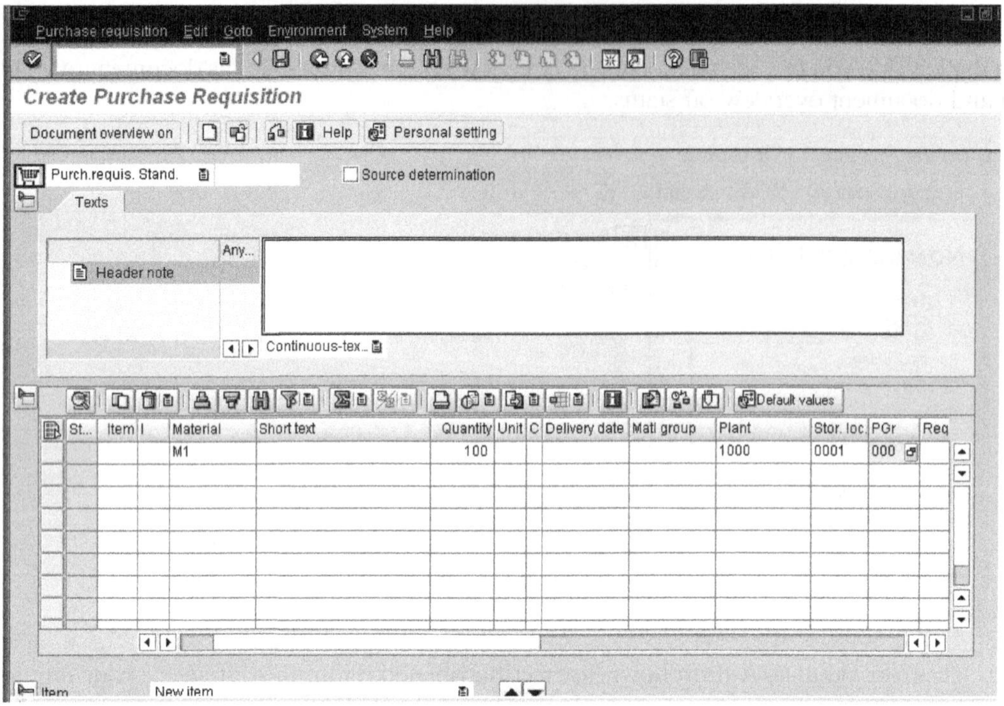

- o Enter the material (that you need to procure).
- o Press ENTER
- o The item overview appears.
- o For each item, enter the following data:
  - Purchasing group (buyer group) responsible for ordering the material (column PGr)
  - Requested quantity
  - Delivery date (If Purchasing is to set up an outline agreement, you will not be able to specify a delivery date.)
  - Plant for which you are going to procure. (Plant column) and
  - Storage location (if known).

You keep on entering data system will display only the descriptions of plant material storage location etc. So do not get confused. After entering data the screen will look something like

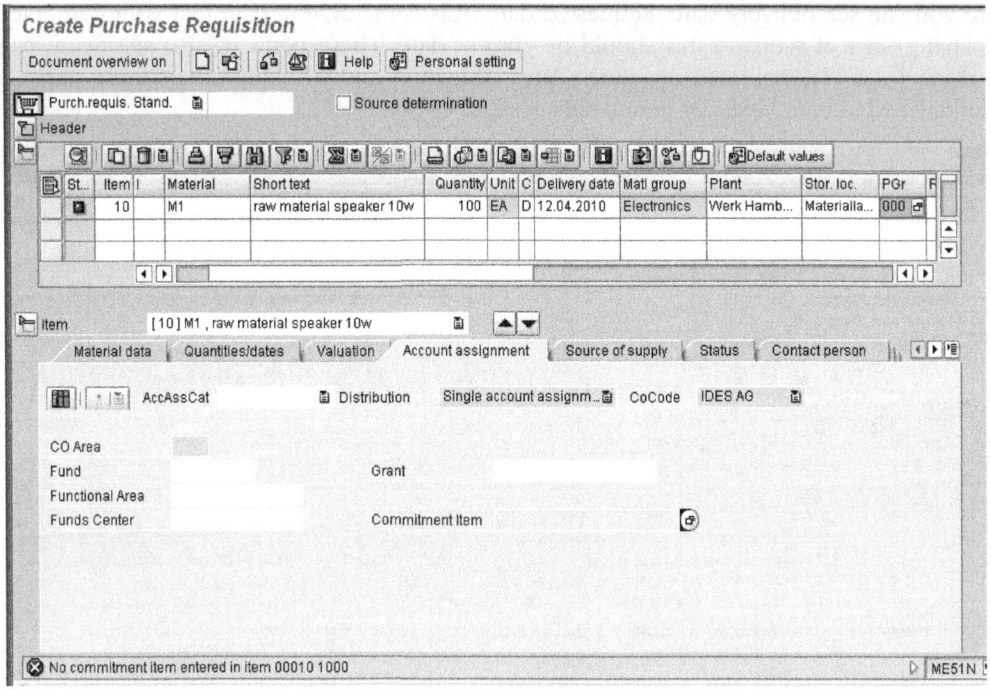

Here in commitment item field of account assignment tab page if you find any error then enter there 9993 and press enter. Commitment item defines the functional structure of the organization in funds management.

Select quantities/date tab page.

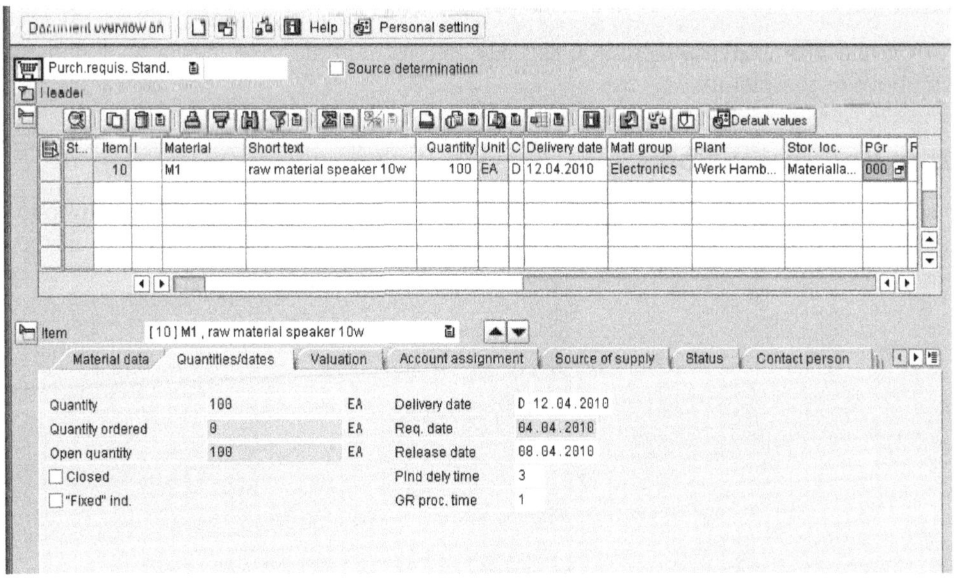

Here you can see delivery date, Requested date (this is the system date that your computer is displaying) in real scenario this should be current date. There you can also see many pages below there as Material data, quantities/dates, Valuation and so many others these pages are called tabs which are basically item details screen.

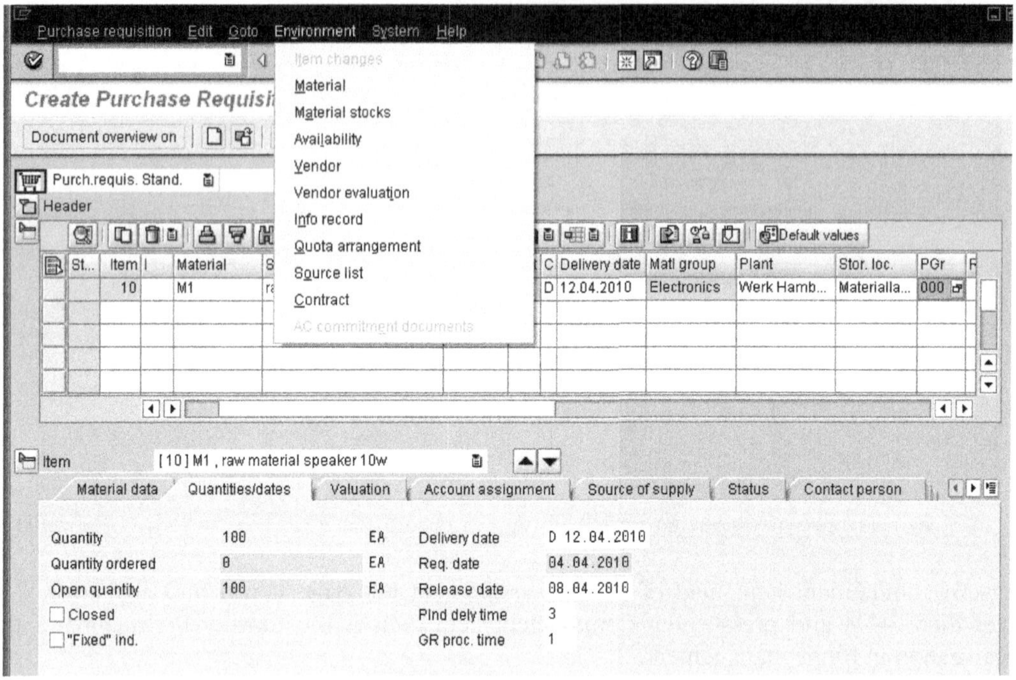

Navigation to different documents:-

Apart from that from Environment you can navigate to multiple master data or documents, as shown above in the picture.

Source determination:-

Now see since I have not checked the check box for Source determination in my purchase requisition system is not able to select the vendor automatically. You can see that in the next picture.

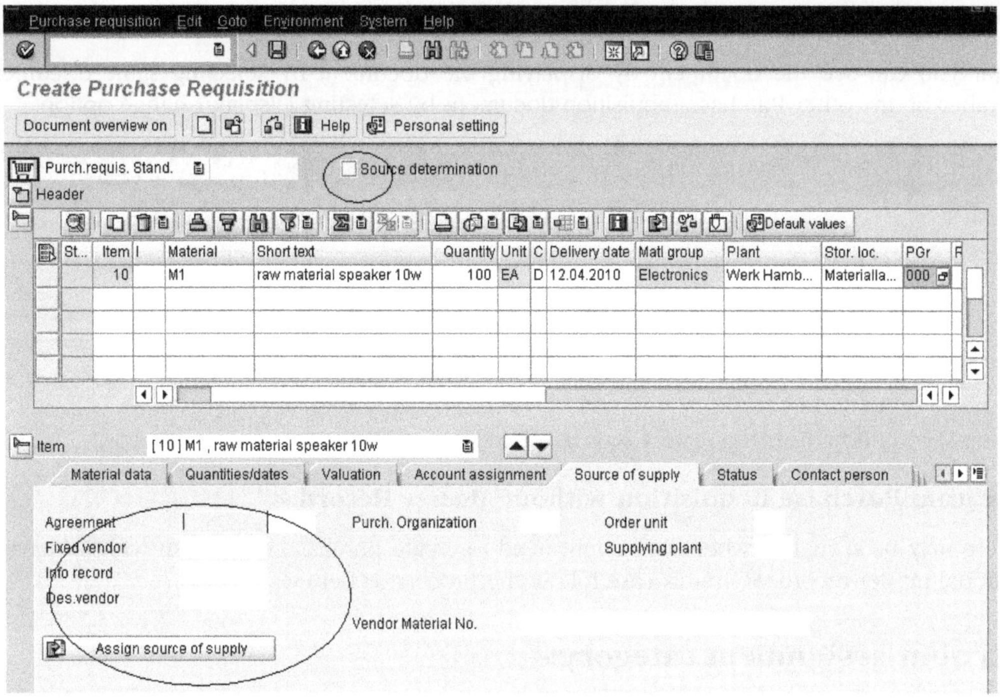

So you will have to put a check in the source determination check box for automatic vendor selection.

Assign source of supply:-

Other wise you can also press "Assign source of supply" in the Source of supply tab page as seen in the above picture. This will also act as the same check box for finding probable vendor automatically.

Fixed vendor:-

If you have selected source of supply check box on the top of the screen then this field will automatically populated. If you do not put a check in the box mentioned above then this field will not be populated automatically but you have option to select later in the document before saving it by pressing on the icon assign source of supply. And if you do not select any of these options then this field will remain blank. You have to enter the vendor number manually if required.

If none of these processes is followed then you have option of leaving vendor selection in this step. Later that will be selected while creating purchase order.

- Below in the status bar you can see the unique purchase requisition number.

Display/Change:-

Later you can see the document by displaying the document by selecting same document number or any other Purchase requisition document by selecting Display/Change option.

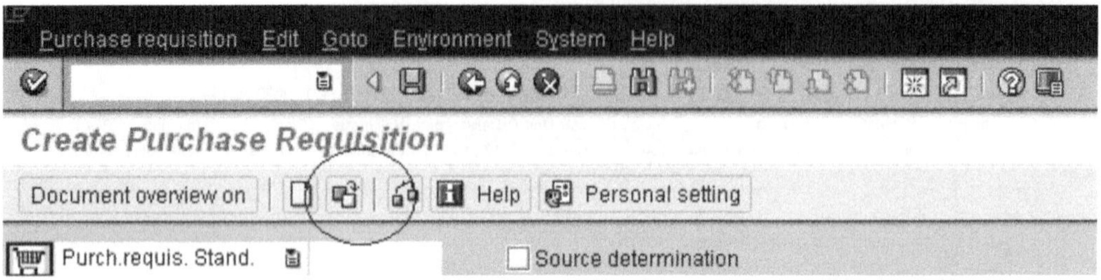

So now you know how to create a standard Purchase requisition with master record.

Creating Purchase Requisition without Master Record:-

There may be scenarios where you might need to create purchase requisition without having material master record. So in this case follow the process as below.

Account assignment category:-

This is to determine manual general ledger number assignment and cost occurring department. Account assignment category is used if it is known to the person who is creating purchase requisition at the time of creation whether the procurement is for consumption purpose or any other specific reason. At the of purchase requisition you can fix this document for the purpose.

Prerequisites

- If No material master record but material has to be procured.
- If Procurement is for direct usage or consumption,
    - o Assign the account for which the consumption will take place. This process is called as account assignment. The account may be any of the 17 account assignment categories. To select this you will have to press F4 in the Column "A" for Account assignment category.

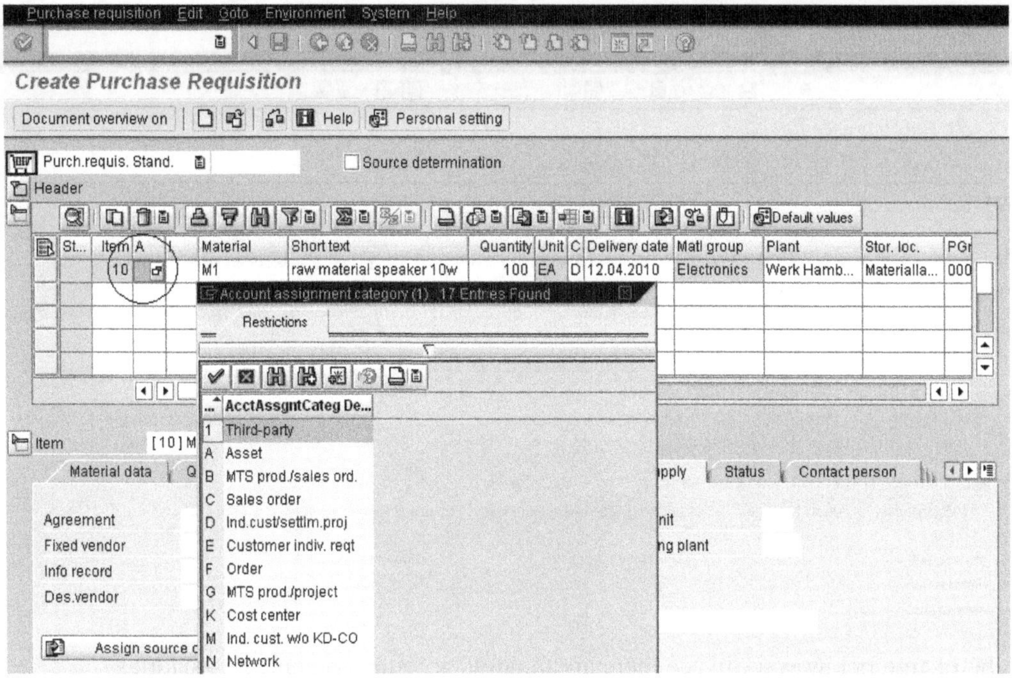

Procedure is as follows.

- Selcct account assignment category - U
- Plant - 1000
- Quantity - 100
- Purchase group - 000
- Unit of measure EA
- Short text(material short text) – office material
- Material group - any
- Valuation price -
- Delivery date normally this field is taken automatically but if not taken then you will have to enter manually.
- After this you just do a check from purchase requisition to check. If every thing is ok then press save button and the document will be saved.

Screen will look something like as below.

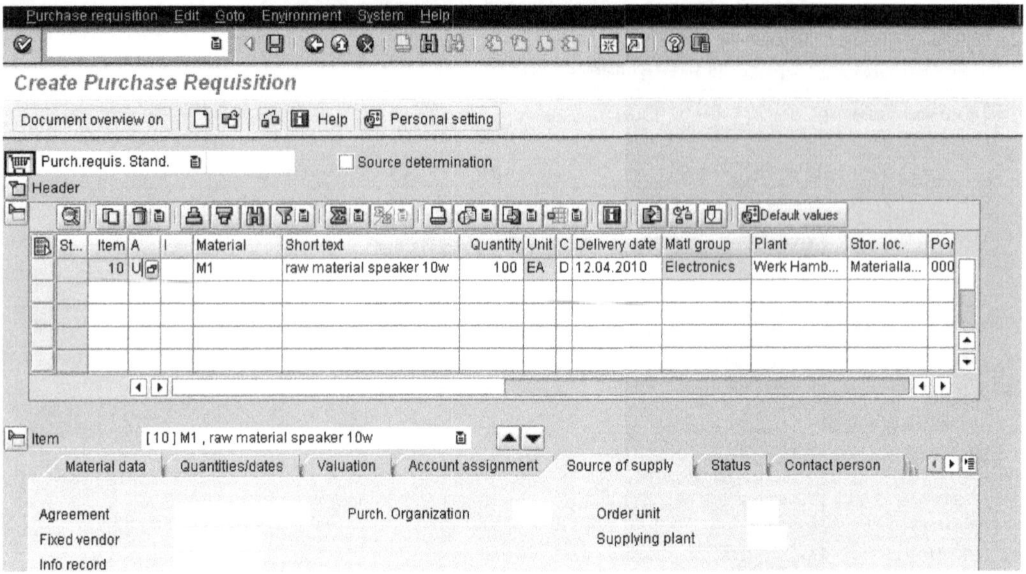

In the picture below you can see there are multiple account assignment categories.

Here in this field you can enter account assignment category as U (Unknown). If you select other account assignment category such as K for cost center, then you will have to enter cost center as the department or reason for which this procurement will take place. Also you will have to enter general ledger account and business area if required as defined in the system with this account assignment category.

After create all the information as you have done in the last step. At the end check the document and save it.

Later on you can take this document as reference and create purchase order for further process of procurement.

Archiving Purchasing Requisition:-

Once you created the purchase requisitions and these requisitions are utilized. The supposed material as purchase requisition is already procured. Now after a certain period these documents are not required for reporting purposes. So at that point of time you archive these documents.

To archive purchase requisitions, you can choose the path as:-

Requisition ® Follow-on functions ® Archive.

To generate a list of archived purchase requisitions, choose:-

Requisition ® List displays ® Archived requisitions

Chapter 10

PURCHASE ORDER

Purchase Order

A purchase order is a formal request or instruction from a purchasing organization to a vendor or a plant to supply or provide a certain quantity of goods or services at or by a certain point in time (SAP Definition).

A purchase order is a document in which you find some information which is applicable to the whole document (the terms of payment and the delivery terms are defined in the header) and some information which is applicable only a few and certain line items of material. There will be one header and multiple line items. Apart from that there will also be line item details which will give you detailed information of each line item individually.

Item Category:-

Some times procurements may involve multiple procurement processes. So as per the requirement Purchase requisition will be assigned with procurement types in the procurement type field. If purchase order is created with reference to purchase requisition then system will automatically take the default procurement process as it is in the purchase requisition. But if purchase order is not created with reference to the purchase requisition then you can create the purchase order by assigning item categories as per requirement.

The item category determines:-

- Whether material number is required and must be entered in purchase order.
- Whether an account assignment must be entered in purchase order.
- Whether the procured stock is to be managed as a stock item
- Whether the procurement Requires a goods receipt (GR) and/or an invoice receipt (IR)

The item categories in the purchase order are as follows.

- Standard
- Subcontracting
- Consignment
- Stock transfer
- External service

Standard:-

This procurement type is used as a normal procurement process. In this procurement process item category field remains blank. Purchase order is created in a normal way. The item category field remains blank.

Subcontracting:-

In this procurement process is used when some material is manufactured or made up of some components. Components may be 1 or more. In this process 1st of all components are procured and then these components are provided to the potential subcontracting vendor. After this purchase requisition is created and sent to the purchasing department. With reference to this purchase requisition purchase order is created for the subcontracting material. And finally material is procured from the subcontracting vendor against purchase order. In this item procurement process item category L is assigned with the purchase order for the material which will be procured from the subcontracting vendor. Vendor is paid for the service that this vendor has rendered.

Consignment:-

In consignment procurement procedure stocks are procured from a consigner and stock is kept at the buyer's stock point in special stock (Consignment Stock). And vendor is paid only when stock is consumed and to the extent stock is consumed. Liability does not gets transferred to the buyer unless and until stock is consumed.

Stock transfer:-

This procurement type is used to transfer stock from one plant to another plant where value of stock may or may not change. This is basically done for internal reason and process.

External Service:-

This procurement type is used to procure services that may be of any kind.

Third-Party

If in purchase order item category s is selected then this purchase order will be used in third-party processing. In this process you place a purchase order with a vendor to deliver goods or perform a service for a different company or vendor. Your company does not deliver the material to your customer but material is provided from the vendor to the customer's premises. Vendor sends invoice to you or your company and you pay for that. Apart from that you also send invoice to your customer and he pays you that.

Limit

This item category is selected with items which involves blanket purchase like there will be one purchase order without any material but a predefined time limit and also amount limit of purchase amount.

Document type of blanket purchase order is the document type FO. There is you can specify a validity period for the order, Instead of a specific delivery date.

In this process Goods receipts is not required. You can enter invoice for the amount of material receipt with making goods receipt entry.

Delivery schedule:-

You can break up delivery of the total quantity (or performance of the total volume of services) that is mentioned in the purchase order as an item and put it in a delivery schedule to be delivered or performed on different dates. In delivery schedule you can mention the delivery quantity or extent of service.

If you create Purchase order of a subcontracting material or material which will be procured from a subcontractor, you can find the explode component icon where you can see the components from which this material is created. In such kind of purchase order you can also input the components for this material and the ratio and combination required.

Conditions

Conditions can apply at various levels:

- Conditions for the entire purchase order (Header level)
- Condition for each item, as many different materials (Item level).
- Condition at service line level for individual services (tasks or activities)

Account Assignment

It is possible that procurement is done with an objective of stocking or for consumption purpose. So as per requirement the account assignment category is assigned with the purchase order so that cost can be assigned to various Controlling objects via the account assignment.

For an example, here in this field you can enter account assignment category as K (Cost center) or any other account assignment category. Then amount will be transferred to respective already assigned general ledger account. This amount transfer is confirmed only at the time of purchase order creation.

If you are creating a purchase order with reference to the purchase requisition then you can assign account assignment category in the purchase requisition itself and it will be take in the purchase order as a default then if required in the purchase order you can change the account assignment type. Such as select account assignment category U in the purchase requisition and then in the purchase order change that and assign any other account assignment category in the purchase order.

Vendor Confirmations

Vendor confirmation is a confirmation which is part of the procurement process, be it documented form or not. In this process information is sent to the buyer on receipt of purchase order or start of shipment or any other purchase order related activity. Vendor informs the buyer for each milestone covered in delivery process completion.

PO History

Once Purchase order is created then it is processed or sent to the vendor. He delivers the material which is again entered in the system as Goods Receipt. After this Incoming invoice is recorded. Now after performing all these steps or at any point of the in between process you can go back to that purchase order and you can see the history that has relevance and process that has been performed based on this purchase order. In Purchase order history tab page you can see the documents that are created and in the purchase order document header you can see the status of the material that has been ordered.

Partner Roles

In the business a vendor performs multiple roles. It may be to whom material is ordered, and vendor who will supply the material, vendor who will send the invoice as invoicing party, and who will be paid, and so on. But in some cases it may be possible that more than one vendor performs each role. So in this all these performer vendor as a business partner and in different processes different vendor's name appears for processing specification. This whole process is configured in the Partner determination process configuration.

Texts

In purchase order you can see different fields where you can enter texts. This text may be for different purposes.

- Header text: that applies to the entire document
- Item text: that applies only to the relevant item

Purchase Order creation:-

Now we create purchase order. In the picture you can see the menu path for purchase order creation and apart from that you can also enter ME21N in the command bar.

Manually Purchase Order may be created multiple ways.

- Create Purchase Order with master record.
- Create Purchase Order without master record.
- Create Purchase Order with reference technique (with reference to any purchase requisition, or any other document).

Prerequisites:-

Before you proceed to create purchase Order you will have to maintain some prerequisites depending upon the purchase Order creation ways.

- For purchase Order with master record:-

  Use Organization Structure as

  - Company Code 1000
  - Purchase Organization 1000
  - Plant 1000
  - Storage location 0001 or any Storage location
- Create Material Master Record

  Use Organization Structure as

  - Plant 1000
  - Storage location 0001 or any Storage location

(Which should be assigned with Company Code 1000, Purchase Organization 1000)

- Create Vendor Master Record
  - Company Code 1000
  - Purchase Organization 1000
  - Vendor account group as 0007 or any other
- Create Purchasing Information Record, info category standard.
  - Vendor with same organization levels
  - Material that you have created with same organization levels
  - Purchase Organization 1000
  - Plant 1000

- Create Source list
    - o Material that you have created with same organization levels
    - o Plant 1000

After entering the transaction code or getting into the transaction you will be able to see the initial screen for this process as below in the picture.

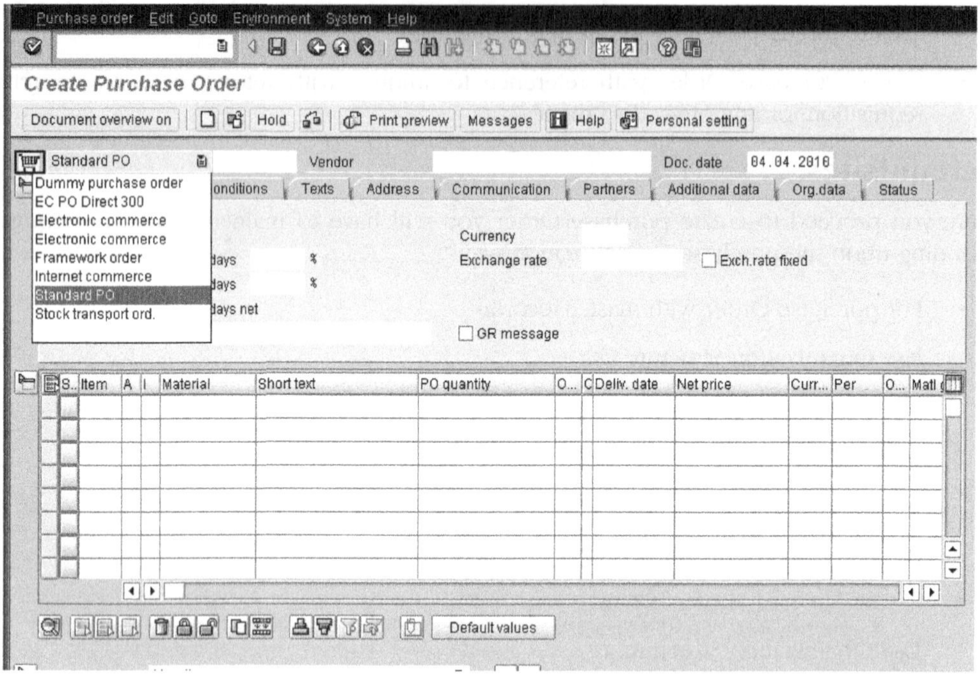

Document overview:-

Up there can see the document over view on and off which toggles if you click on that. This will display a list of all the purchase orders and all other purchasing documents which have been created till now.

Now in the picture above you can see header, item overview and item. We have already discussed on these topics.

Up there in the cart you can see Standard PO icon field. This is a drop down list from where you can select different document types for purchase order. As per your selection process will be decided.

On the right side you can see the field for vendor. This is for the vendor's name from whom you will procure the material.

Again right of this you can see the document date. This is always the current date.

Then you have to click on the header. Here you will be able to see multiple header items like Delivery/invoice, texts and others like Partners Org. Data. Status.

Org. Data:-

In organization data you will see purchase organization, purchase group and company code. This is the organization you are going to procure the material. So you will have to enter in these fields. Enter following details in these fields.

Purchasing organization – 1000

Company code – 1000

Enter

Then system will ask for purchase group input.

Enter Purchase group – 000

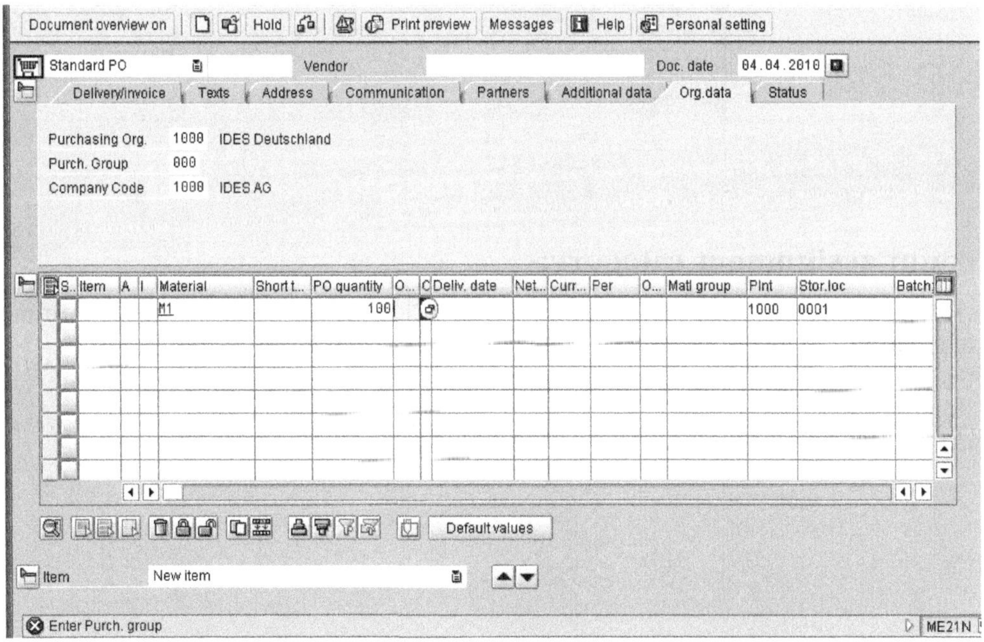

Item overview:-

After this select Item overview. Here you will enter material number in the material field which you are going to procure and other fields as listed below.

Item category:-

First you have to select item category as to determine which procurement process this purchase order involve. Leave this field blank as for standard purchase order. See below in the picture.

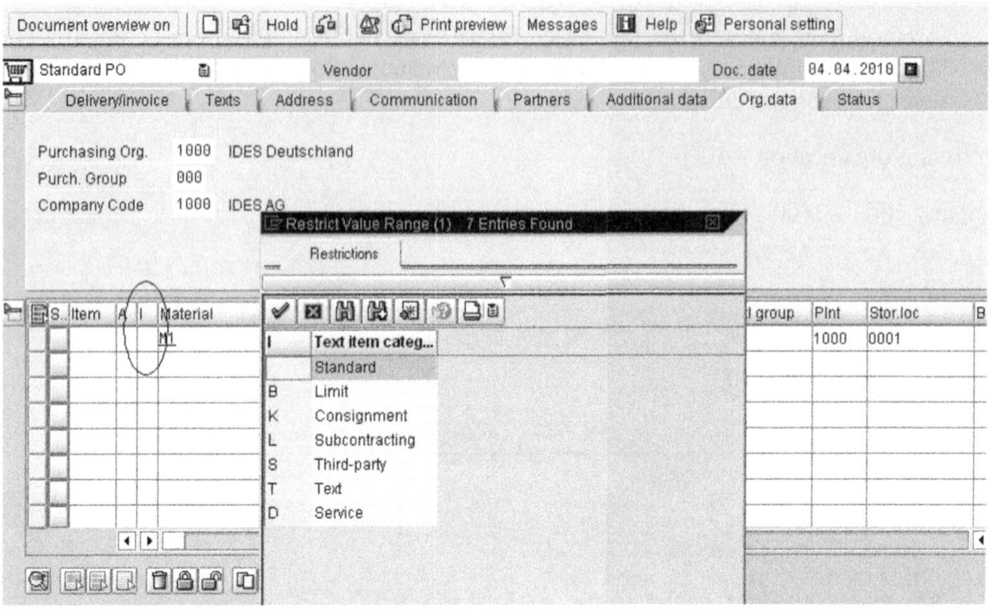

Account assignment category:-

This is to determine manual general ledger number assignment and cost occurring department. Leave it blank as in the picture below.

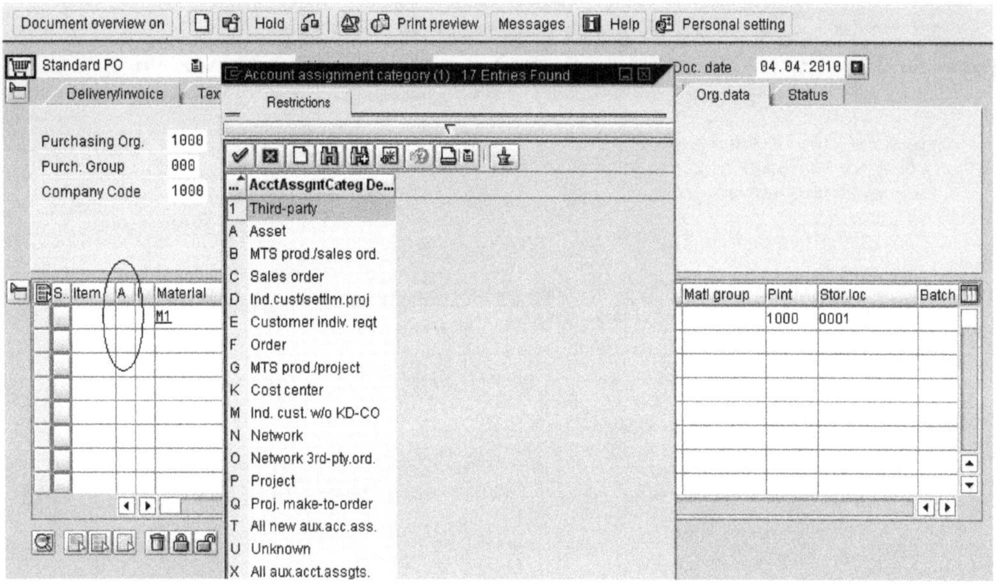

Vendor – Up there you can see the vendor field blank. Enter your desired vendor name there.

Material – that you have created with organization structure same.

Plant - 1000

Quantity – 100 or any

Enter.

You will see that price field is automatically filled up. You should remember that this field is determined automatically just because you already have created the info record for the same material and same vendor.

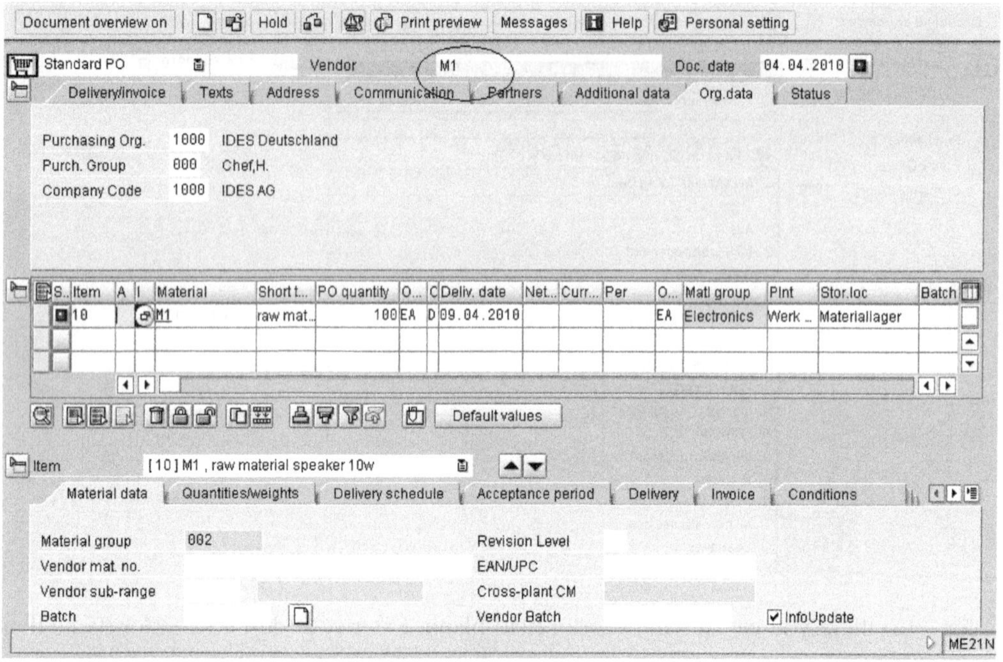

After entering these fields check all the tab pages one by one so that you will be able to know about the fields which are relevant to the specific tab page.

SC vendor:-

In delivery tab page you can see SC Vend field to be checked and Vendor number field blank. This is for subcontracting procurement process such as you are procuring some material from a vendor and you want this material to be dispatched to your subcontracting vendor's stock place. So in this requirement you will have to enter the subcontracting vendor number there and SC vend field checked.

Condition:-

In the condition tab page there you will be able to find the pricing and condition details. Select any condition type like Gross Price line and double click on condition record display then it will take you to the record or master data from where it has taken the price. Apart from this if you double click on Analysis then it will give you complete details of pricing procedure and condition technique's details. This procedure is shown in the pictures one by one.

Select the condition tab page.

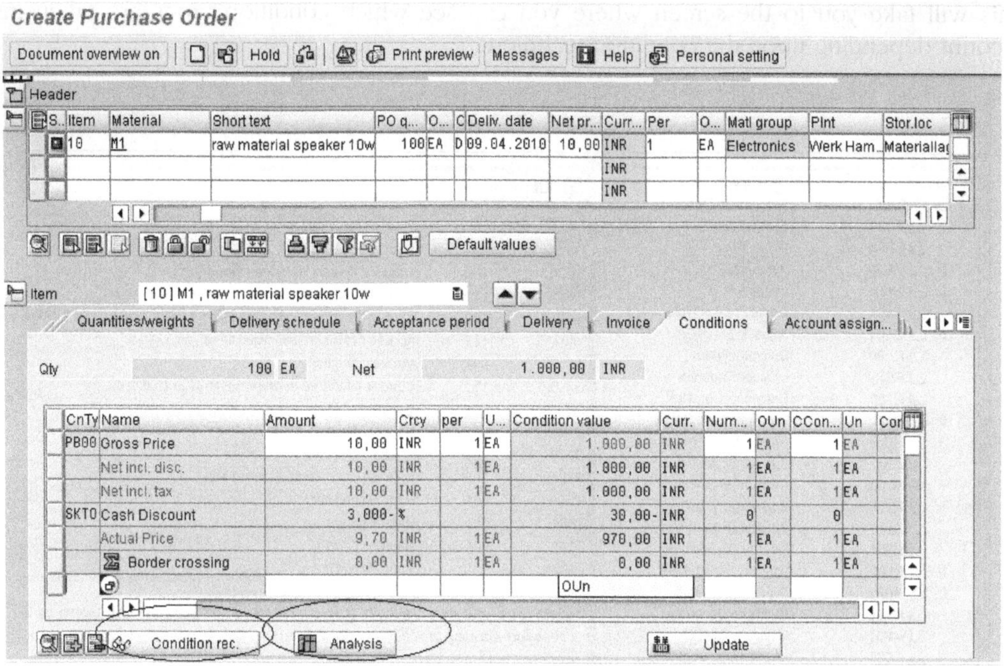

Select Condition record:-

This will take you to the condition record from where price is taken.

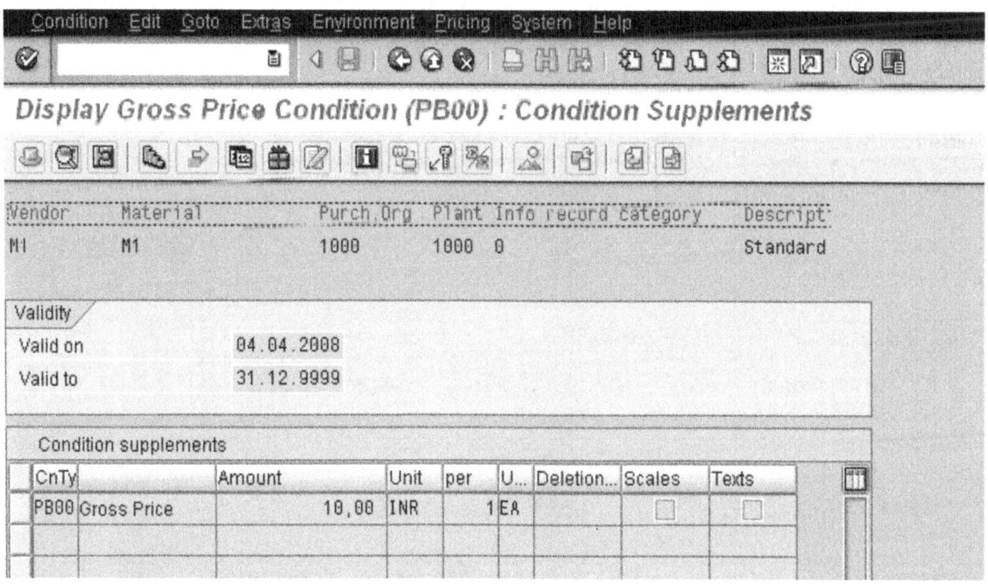

Click on back icon and select the condition line in the condition tab page. Select the analysis.

This will take you to the screen where you can see which condition types are taken into account depending upon the condition technique.

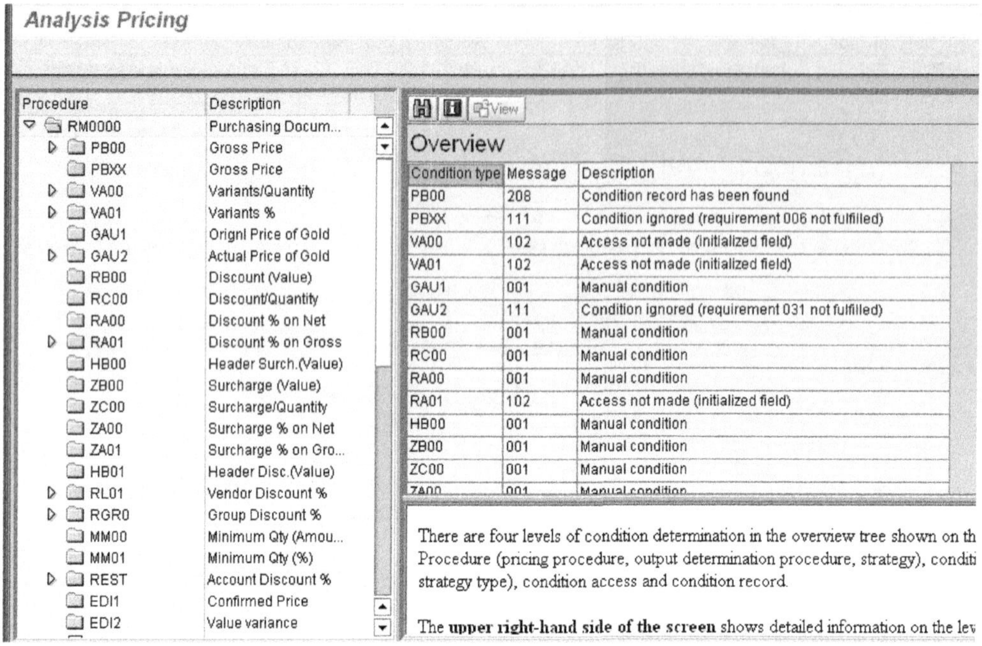

Apart from this on the header item also you can see a condition tab page. This condition is applicable for the whole purchase order document. You can see this in the picture below.

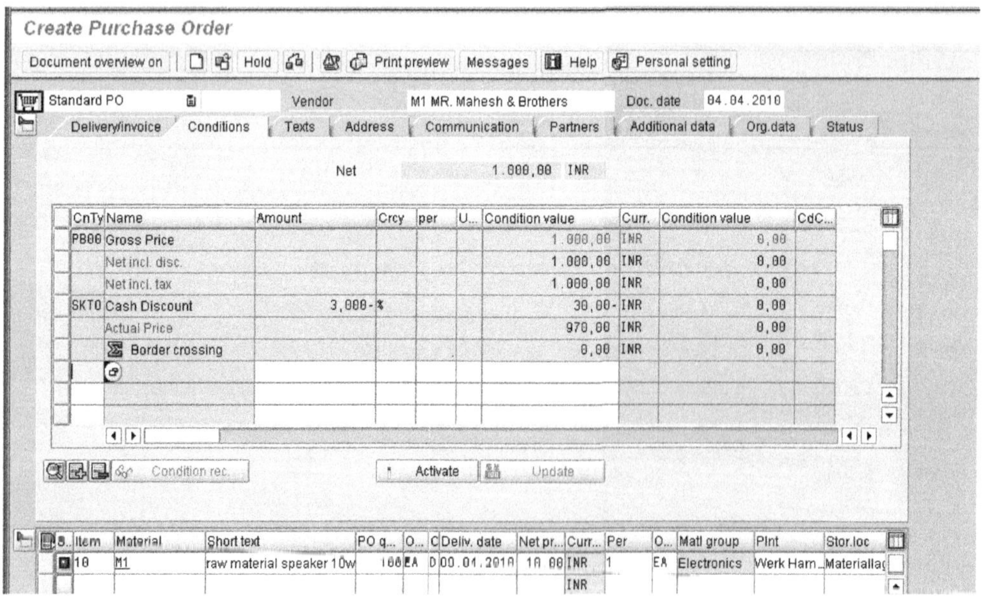

In the partner tab page you can see the details of partners which are tied up with your vendor and are enlisted in you company to perform different roles, as in the picture below.

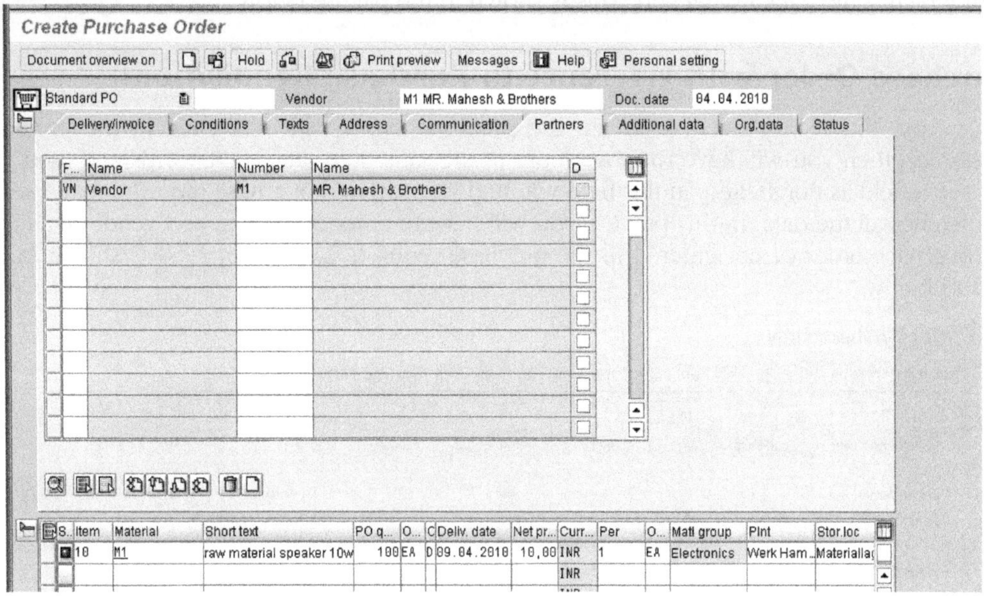

In the picture you can see the Status tab page. This will show you the processing status condition of the purchase order that you are creating or you have already created.

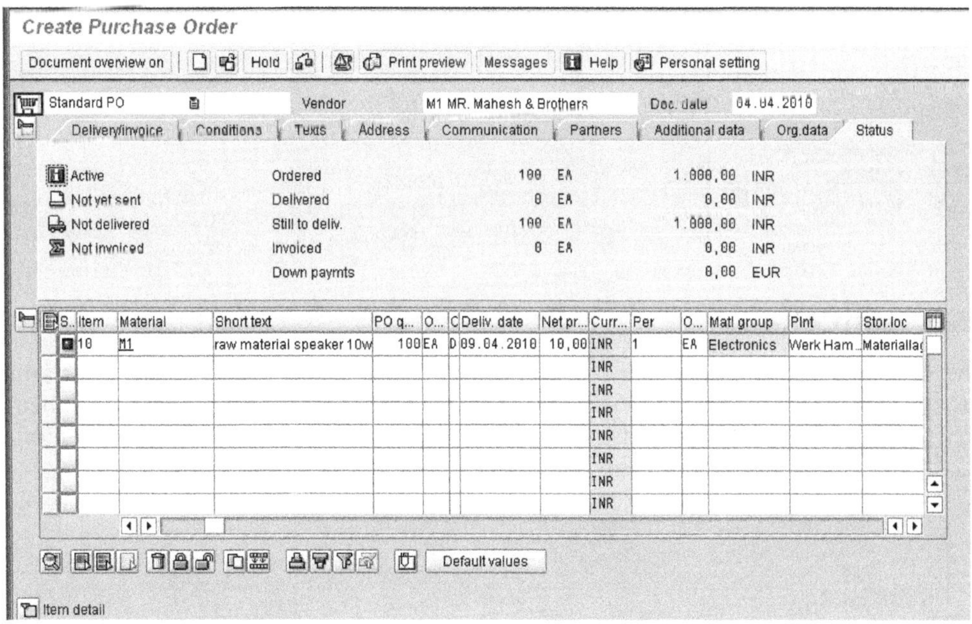

Now if you move right word on the line item of the material entered in the purchase order then in the Info Rec. field you can see the info record number which is relevant for this material and from which some data are fetched. This is shown in the picture below.

Purchase Order with reference to Purchase Requisition:-

Apart from this if you need to create the purchase order with reference to the purchase requisition then you will have to move more in the same item line right words and then you can see a field as Purch. Req. in this field you find your desired purchase requisition and select that fetches all the data. In this process you will have to enter only price and vendor details in the purchase order (if not entered in the purchase requisition). This process is shown in the picture below.

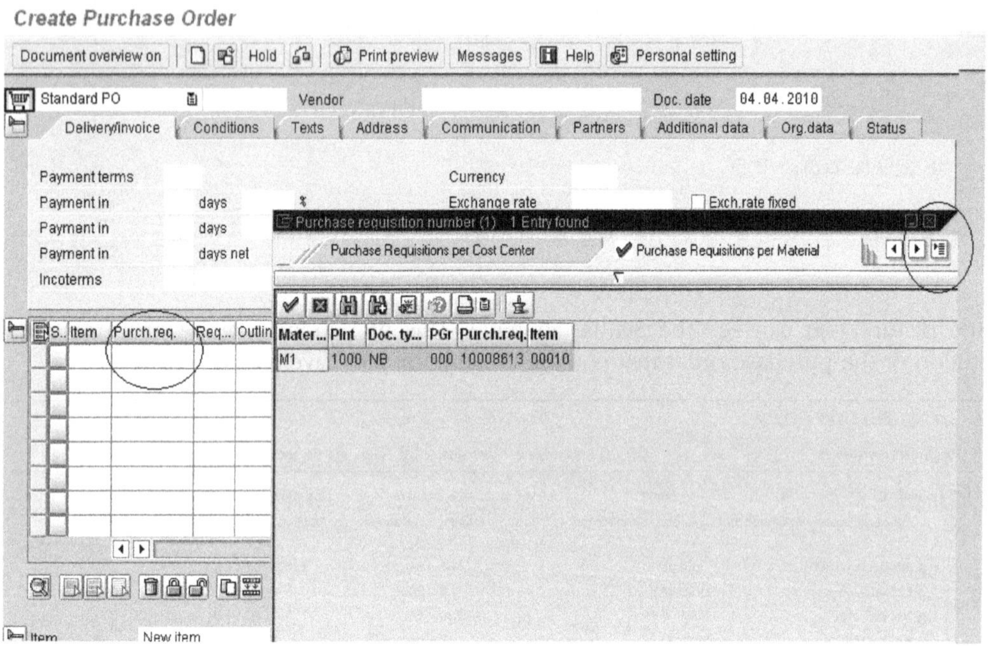

Free (Sample):-

In the same line you can make the procurement of the item free of cost as if it is for sample. For that you cam see on the item line a check box field as Free. If you select that field then this purchase order will serve as purchase order for sampling process against this goods receipt will be done against specific movement type and goods will be taken into the stores.

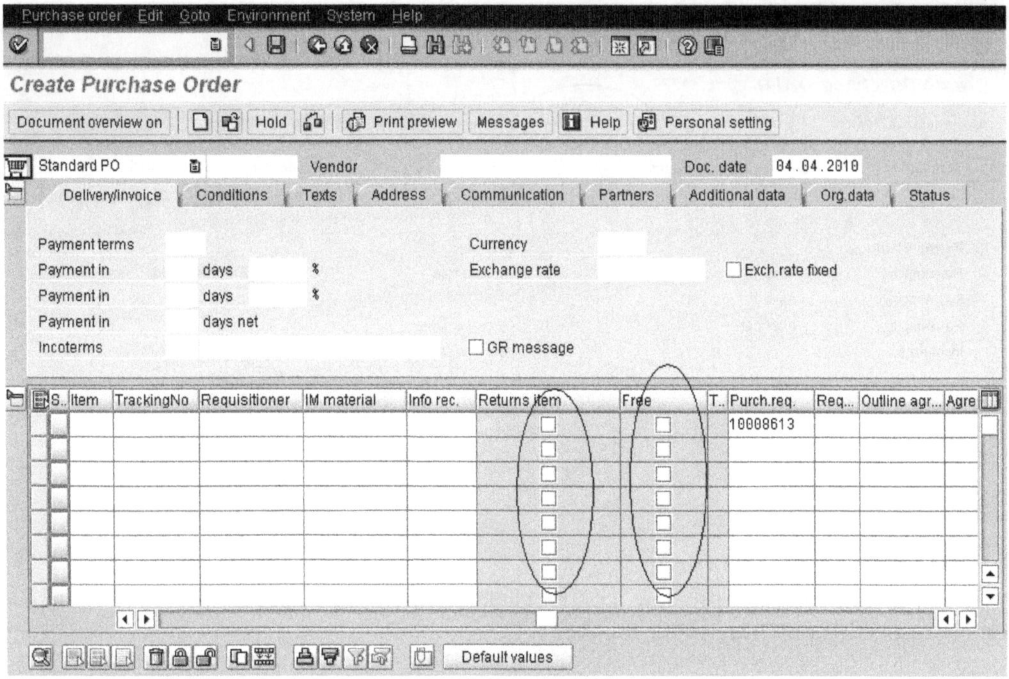

Returns item:-

On the item line you move right words then you can see the field Returns item check box this will be denoted for specific process. This specifies whether this item is returns item or not.

This field can be selected except following item category.

- Service items (item type D)
- Limit items (item type B)
- Items with invoicing plan

Outline agreement:-

Now suppose this may happen that the procured material is to be procured according to some outline agreement. So in this case the Outline agreement field is to be input with agreement number.

Request for Quotation (RFQ):-

If this purchase order is decided as per some quotation or request for quotation then RFQ field has to be input with the relevant RFQ number.

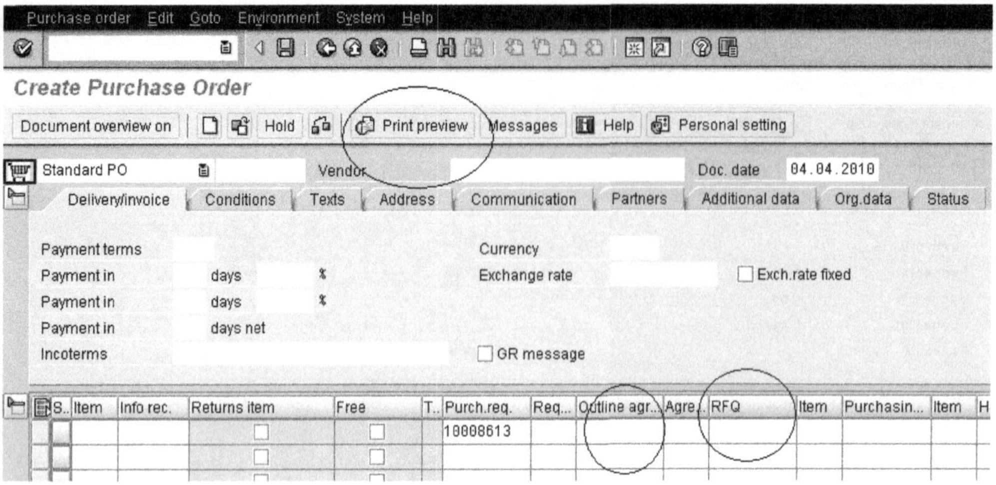

Print preview:-

Up there you can see Print preview icon by clicking where you can see the printed purchase order of respective purchase order number.

Delivery Schedule:-

You can break the purchase item quantity in different delivery dates and into respective schedule line quantities. You can do so in the Delivery schedule tab page in item details screen. This is shown as below.

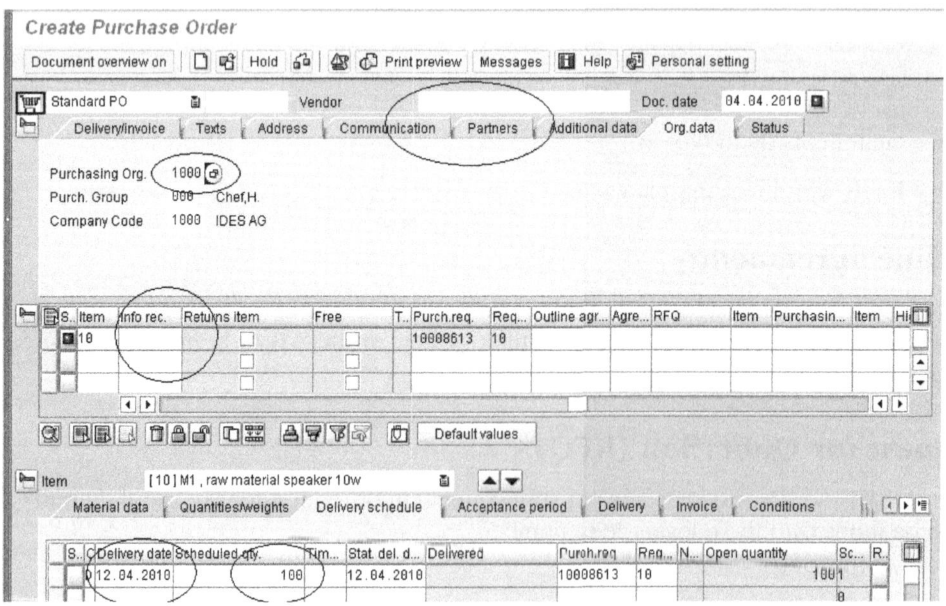

In the picture above you can see the marked fields. If there is any error prompt like purchasing organization then you can enter the responsible purchasing organization like 1000. You can view the info record number which you had created earlier about the mentioned vendor and material.

Delivery Completed indicator:-

On delivery tab page on item details page you can see the delivery completed indicatory field to be checked. If you check this field then material will be procured only once. Suppose you have created purchase order for 100 quantity of a material. Then you can receive goods only once for any quantity be it 1 piece or be it 50 piece or 100 piece. And you try to enter the 2nd goods receipt for the same purchase order then you can not make any goods receipt. This important control is provided in this field.

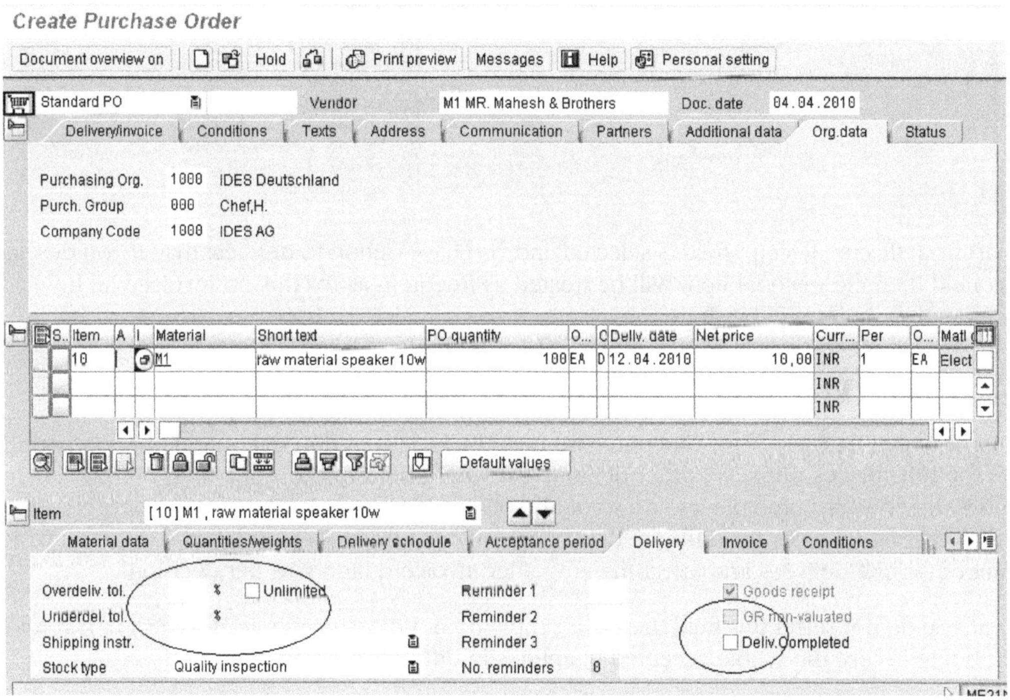

On the same page above in the delivery tab page you can set over delivery and under delivery limit in percentage (%) so that vendor can not deviate from the purchase order.

On the same delivery tab page you can also see the under delivery and under tolerance limits. That you can set in % so that deviation while delivery of the material should not vary more than mentioned limits.

In the invoice tab page you can see Tax code field. In the purchase order itself you can set the tax code that will be applicable and will be paid to the tax authority on due time.

This is shown as below in the picture.

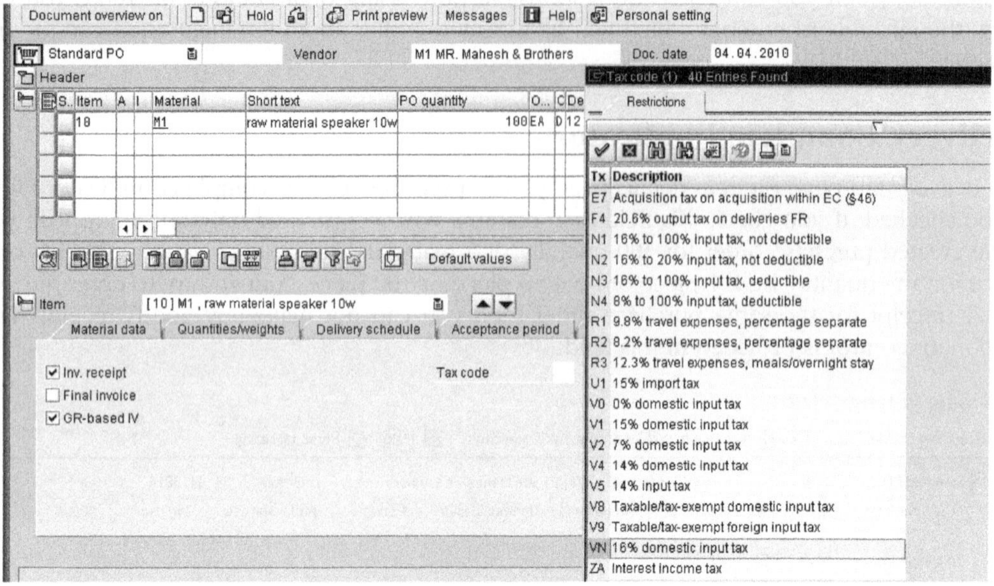

Apart from this inv Receipt field is selected and you have option to deselect that. If you deselect that field then the material item will be treated as free item as for this no invoice will be made and so no payment will be done.

GR based IV:-

It may happen that goods for one purchase quantity is delivered in different delivery schedules like for 1000 pieces purchase order quantity goods are delivered on one time 200 pieces, 2nd time 500 pieces, 3rd time pieces and so on. If you receive goods in such broken deliveries then while entering invoices for different deliveries you have freedom to select the desired invoice number for one delivery and reject the any other invoice quantity as per decision.

But if you do not select this field then you simply do not have any choice to select or not select that but to accept the whole accepted quantities in different dispatches.

Account Assignment Tab page:

If you select this field in the Account assignment category field in the line item depending upon the item category then you have to confirm the relevant entries in the account assignments in the account assignment tab page in item details tab page. This is shown as below. Such as you can procure material for any consumption then you can enter it for cost center and assign relevant information as prompted.

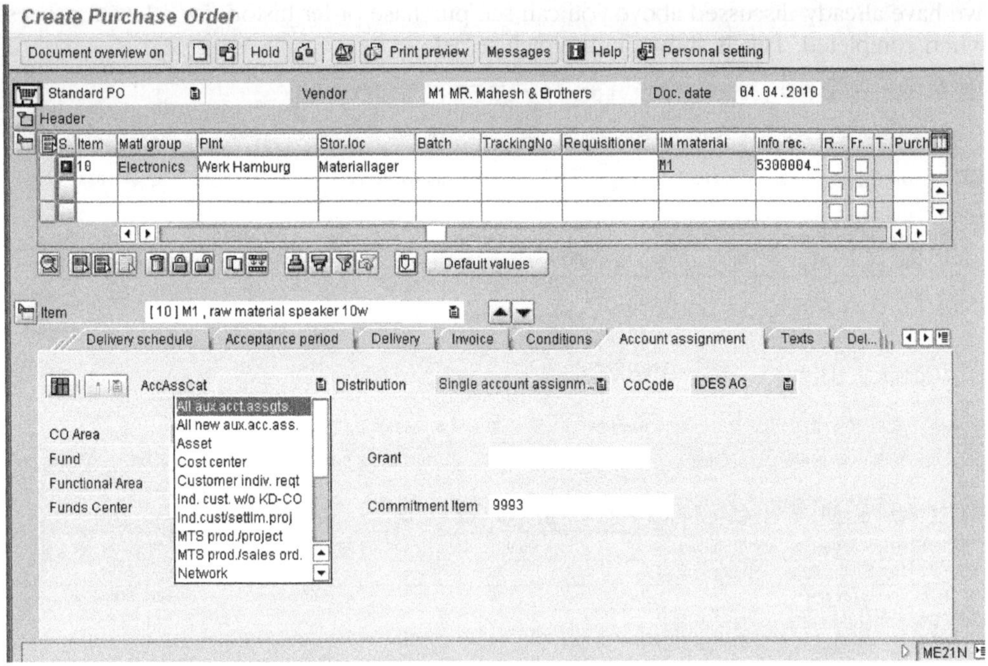

Multiple Account Assignment:-

As in the above after assigning account assignment category it may happen that same material might be being procured for different reasons. So in this case up there you can see the single account assignment field. This field will be activated when account assignment category field is selected and then you can change this field to multiple account assignment. There you can fill up multiple account assignment related data and break the order quantity of the material.

(If you need to process with multiple account assignment then select cost center as account assignment category and then click on cost center field, enter here 1000 as preconfigured cost center, GL account will be picked up automatically if it does not provide GL account automatically then you can enter GL account 400000 which was created in 1000 company code. After this click on multiple account assignment and assign further cost centers and quantities.)

As we have already discussed above you can see purchase order history for relevant processes as when completed. This is shown in the picture below.

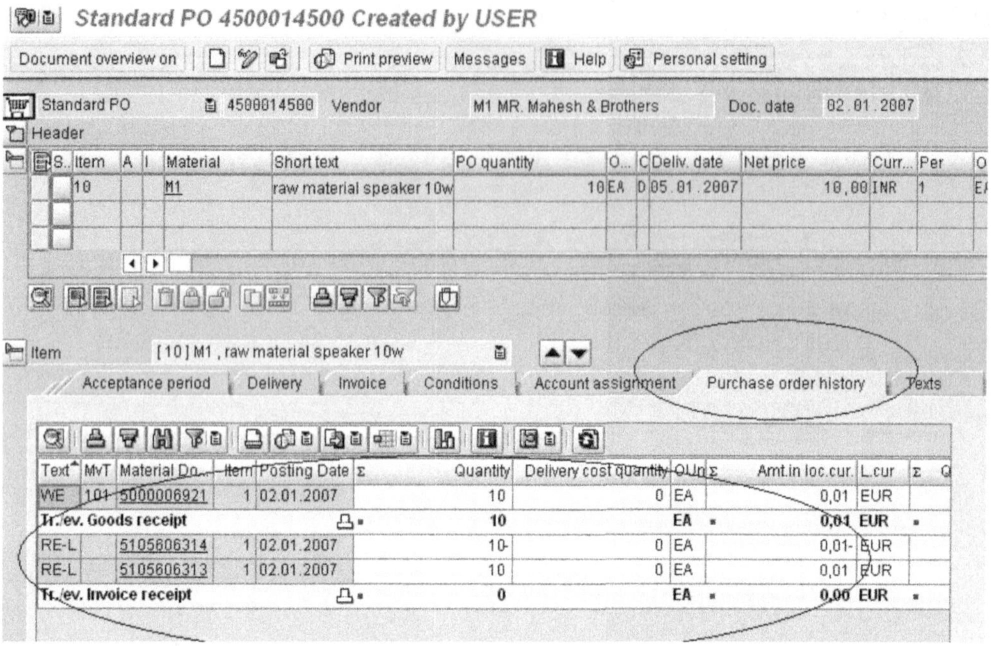

To summarize the process you can follow following details.

Material – Any that you have created with relevant organization levels.

Vendor - Any that you have created with relevant organization levels.

Purchase organization – 1000

Purchase group – Any

Plant – 1000

Quantity – 1000 or any quantity

Pricing procedure in PO is determined by the combination of vendor schema group in the vendor master and purchasing organization in the P. O.

Price – do not enter it will be taken from condition record or from purchasing info record. If the price is not taken from any master data then you can enter any amount in respective currency.

Delivery date – If required

Check the document and save.

If item category is entered then fill up the respective requested information in the relevant fields.

If account assignment category is selected then fill up the respective requested information in the relevant field.

I believe now you will be able to create the standard purchase order.

Change the Purchase Order:-

You can also change the purchase order document by the transaction code ME22N. You can also follow the menu path as it is shown in the picture below.

Display Purchase Order:-

As you can see in the picture above that ME23N is for display of the material.

Chapter

11

GOODS MOVEMENTS

Goods movement is a transaction which results in a change of stock.

This goods movement may be of any of this kind.

- **Goods receipt:-**

A goods receipt (GR) is a goods movement in which goods are received from a vendor in external procurement and from any production plant in internal procurement. Goods receipt increases stock status in inventory.

- **Goods issue:-**

A goods issue (GI) is a goods movement in which material is taken out of inventory stock for material consumption, or sent to a customer. A goods issue leads to a reduction in warehouse stock. Goods issue reduces the stock status in inventory.

- **Stock transfer:-**

A stock transfer is a goods movement in which the stocks are removed from one storage location and stock kept to another storage location. Stock transfers can occur either within the same plant or between two plants.

- **Transfer posting:-**

A transfer posting is a movement in which the stock type is changed, for an example as from blocked stock to quality stock or from quality stock to unrestricted use stock.

- Transfer postings from material to material:-
- Release from quality inspection stock into unrestricted use stock:-
- From unrestricted use stock to quality stock:-
- From unrestricted use stock to blocked stock:-
- Form blocked stock to unrestricted use stock:-
- From quality stock to blocked stock:-
- Transfer of consignment material into company's own stock:-

The Document Concept

According to the document concept in business, a document must be generated and stored in the system that changes stock quantity or value or status.

While posting any goods movement in SAP System, following documents are created:

- **Material document:-**

This is a proof of the movement and all related information like what, where, from whom, when, for what purpose with all the results and remarks if any.

- **Accounting document**

If the movement leads to an update of the G/L accounts, an accounting document is created parallel to the material document. G/L accounts are updated automatically taking information from automatic account assignment.

If the document is dependent on multiple currencies then you can switch between both currencies by choosing *Settings ® Currency display.*

Changes to a Document

Once material document or financial documents are created then you can not change the document but you can input some additional information if required. In place of changing the material or financial document you can reverse or cancel the document with proper reason.

Document Numbers

Any document is identified by a specific document number assigned to it and year of generation.

These number ranges are pre configured in the system. Material document number range and financial document number ranges are different.

Transaction/Event Types and Document Types

The material documents are divided into transaction/event types and accounting documents are divided into document types (see following table).

Transaction/Event Types and Document Types for Goods Movements (Examples)

Goods movement	Tr./Ev. type	Doc. type
Goods receipts for purchase orders	WE	WE or WN
Goods receipts for orders	WF	WE
Goods issues, transfer postings, other goods	WA	WA
Goods issues for deliveries	WL	WL

For each transaction/event type, a number range is defined. System created material document out of these number ranges. Same is in case of financial document.

Movement Type:-

A movement type is a three-digit identification key that determines screen display and other input requisites for a goods movement.

Some movement types are

Goods Movements and Movement Types

Goods receipt for a purchase order	101
Goods issue for a cost center	201
Release from quality inspection stock	321

A movement type effects:-

- Quantity and updates that,
- Stock and consumption accounts,
- In determining which fields will be displayed during entry of a document in the system

For display and reporting purpose there are several options where from you can check different documents and stock status. *You can choose Environment ® List Displays ® Material Documents*

Stock types:-

In SAP system you can maintain a stock in different ways. Such as if the stock is procured and is fit for immediate consumption then you can put it in an unrestricted use stock. If you need a quality check for the stock received then you can put it in quality stock. If you have received the stock but there is some dispute on this then you can put it in blocked stock. Later when the dispute or problem is resolved then you can put the blocked stock in the unrestricted use stock and use it as per your requirement.

Quality stock:-

Material in quality stocks is a quantity of material which is sent for quality inspection and this quantity can not be used unless and until it is released or accepted by quality department.

Blocked stock:-

Material in blocked stock is a quantity of material which is blocked due to some reason. This stock can not be used and in some cases this quantity is not even counted for inventory stock status check.

Unrestricted use stock:-

Unrestricted use stock is stock which may be withdrawn can be used, consumed and sent to the customer.

In goods movement processing there are several terms which are used from time to time.

• Goods Receipt/Issue Slip Number

This field is on the goods movement screen. This Specifies a number, which uniquely identifies a goods receipt /issue slip. This number can be assigned both internally and externally.

Chapter 12

GOODS RECEIPT

Introduction:-

Goods receipt is a term which means receiving of goods. It may be from any vendor or it may be previously uncounted stock. You can receive goods as per specific reason against specific movement types. When vendor sends you any quantity or volume of material stock you have to count it properly. With the goods vendor also sends you a document which is a delivery document which will contain all the information regarding the stock. After counting it you have to match this information with the details in the document.

Menu path:-

To receive goods you follow a particular process. The menu path is mentioned below.

SAP Easy Access > Logistics > Materials Management > Inventory Management > Goods Movement > MIGO

Alternatively you can also enter transaction code MIGO in the command line.

Initial screen:-

On inputting the movement type you can see the initial screen as below. Now we will get into the goods movement transaction screen.

As per documents creation screen, you can see the header and item detail screen here also.

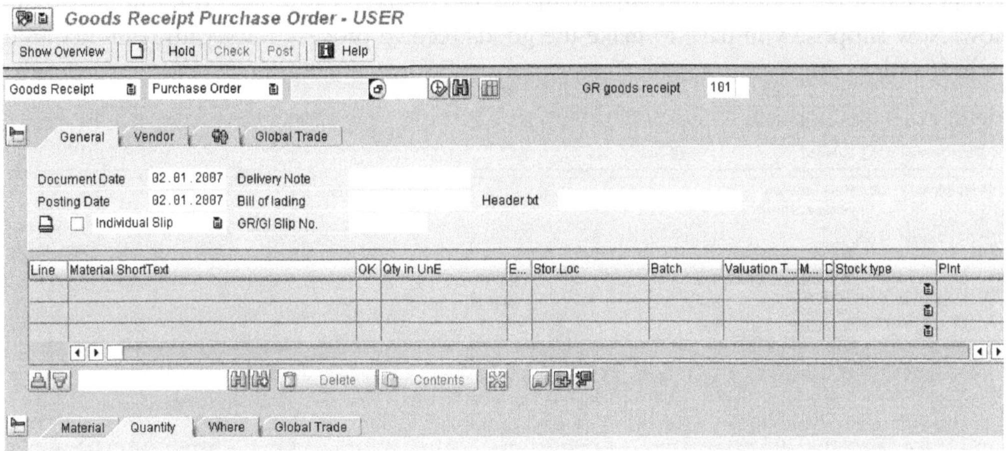

In last a few chapters you have learned about purchase order creation. As in the picture above you can see in details. We will do a goods movement step by step. In this we can take reference to an already created purchasing document as we have done in the last chapter of purchasing.

Select transaction:-

In this field you have to select the type of transaction that you are willing to do, as it is shown below in the picture. As in the current process you have to select Goods Receipt movement process.

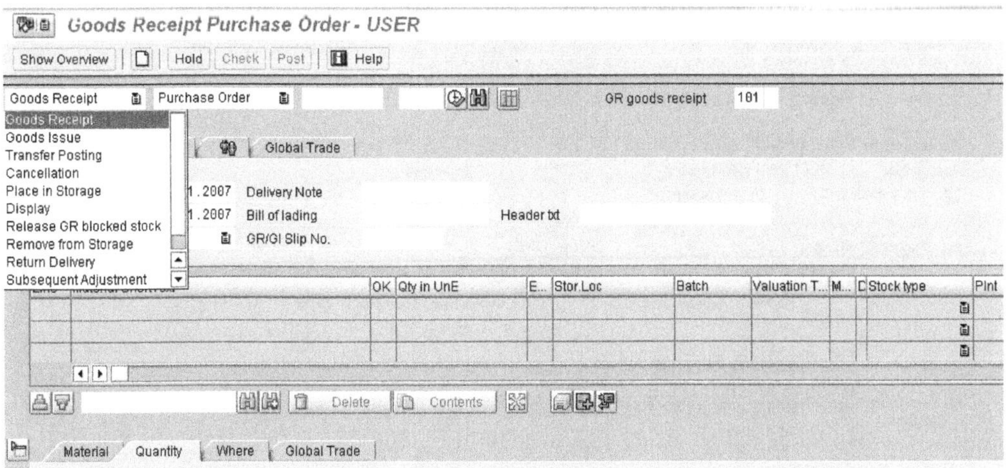

Reference document:-

After selection of transaction type as goods receipt you have to choose whether you are willing to do the transaction with reference to any prior document or without any reference. This you can see the process in the picture below that how to select the reference document from the drop down list in the reference field. This is because some goods movements may happen as per purchase order, some be happen as without any reference as others. You can see as sown below. Now suppose you have to make the goods receive process entry with reference to the purchase order.

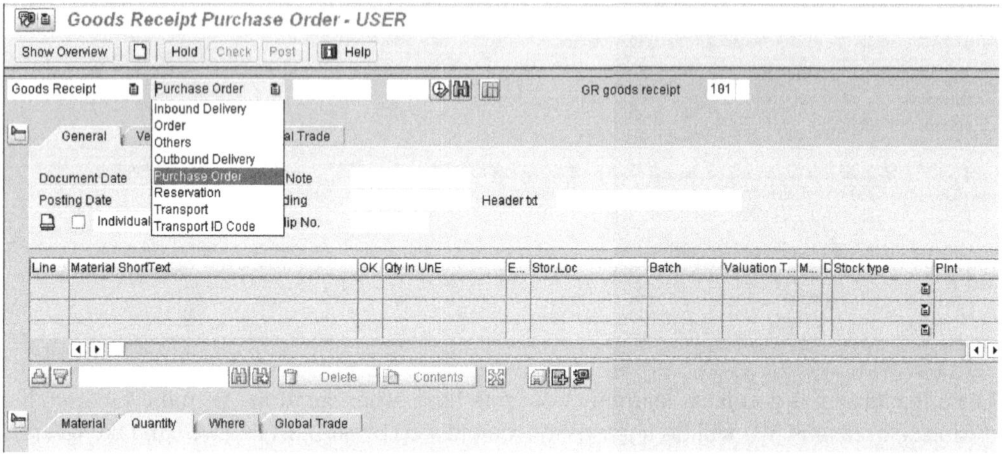

Near to the field of reference document you can see a blank field here you can enter the document number if you know the document number against which the movements should take place. This is shown in the picture blow. If you do not know the document number then you can select the icon of binocular which will take you to the purchase order search screen.

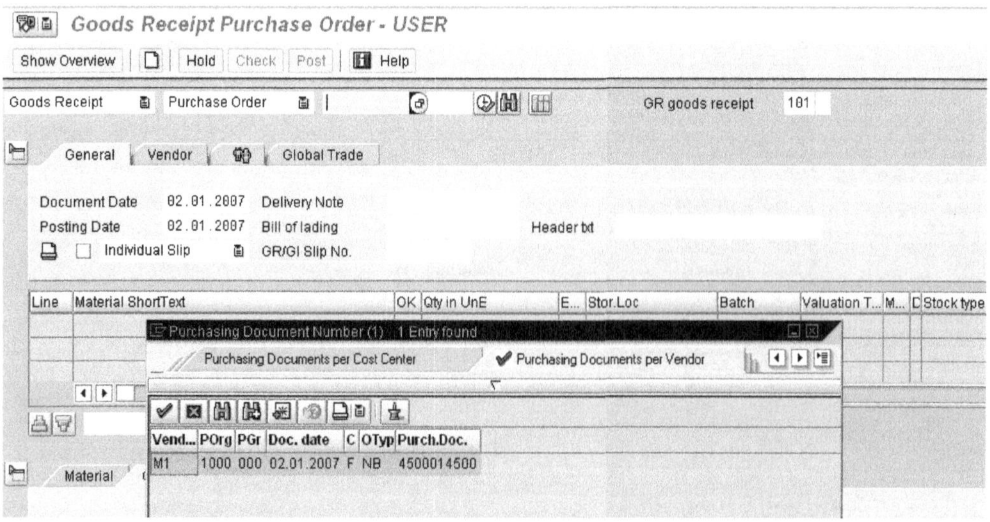

According to the transaction and reference document you will have to select the movement type. As in this picture you can see that as 101 movement type. After selecting the purchase order document number you will have to press enter to confirm the movement.

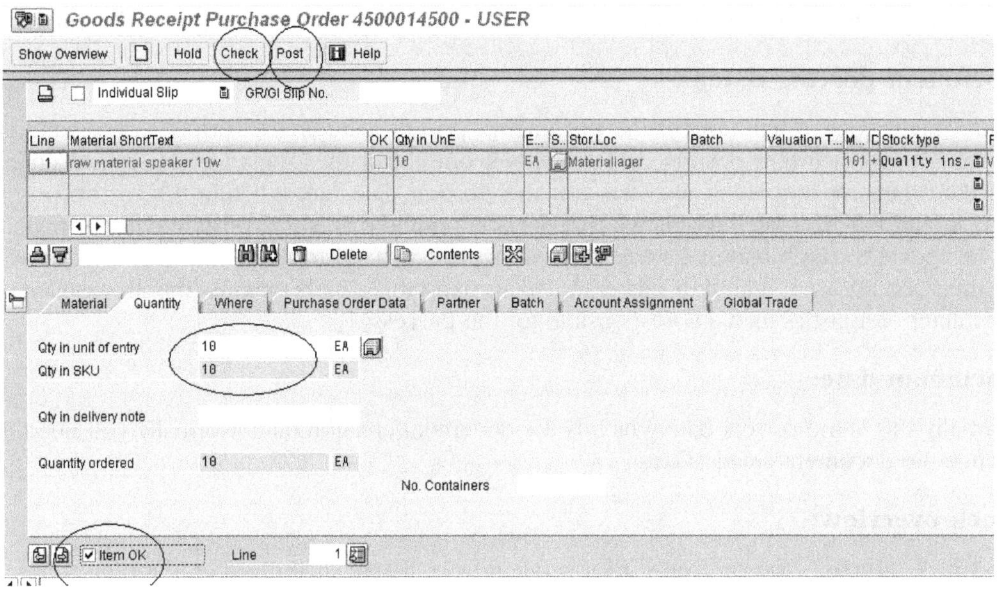

Now you can see that the information from the purchase order is copied in this movement screen. On quantity tab page you can change here the quantity if you need, enter the delivery note which is on the delivery sheet that is coming with the goods from the vendor. In where tab page you can see the information as where this stock should be kept or in which plant and storage location. If purchase order is created to fulfill the requirement of direct consumption then the account assignment field should be filled up with the information as per the account assignment category selected in the purchase order. In the above scenario we can see the document creation only with reference to the standard purchase order without any account assignment category.

Item OK:-

You can see on the screen of goods movement a check box at the footer of the page. You have to check the item ok field. You can see this in the picture below. This will make the document ready for the document checking process.

Quantity:-

You can see in quantity tab page the total quantity is captured from the reference purchase order quantity. If you are going to receive any quantity other than purchase order quantity then you need to change this quantity in the qty in unit of entry field and press enter.

Check:-

You have to press the icon on the menu bar on the header of the page named "Check". Pressing this will check the document whether all the required information is entered or some information is missing if any information is missing then system will prompt for the entry.

Document posting date:-

There might come some error if the document's posting date is not correct as normally this document takes current posting date as default one. So if the prompt error says to change the date then the error will also tell you the posting date range within which the posting date should fall. You need to change that. Reason behind this is that posting date for material value update through material stock change in plant is fixed for 1 month. And all the stock postings should occur within this date. In real scenario this date is updated month wise by MM consultant or logistics manager responsible for the process.

Document date:-

Normally this is the current date which is the document creation date. Normally you need not change the document creation date.

Stock overview:-

On where tab page you can see stock overview field. If you click this icon then this will take you to the MMBE transaction for stock overview check.

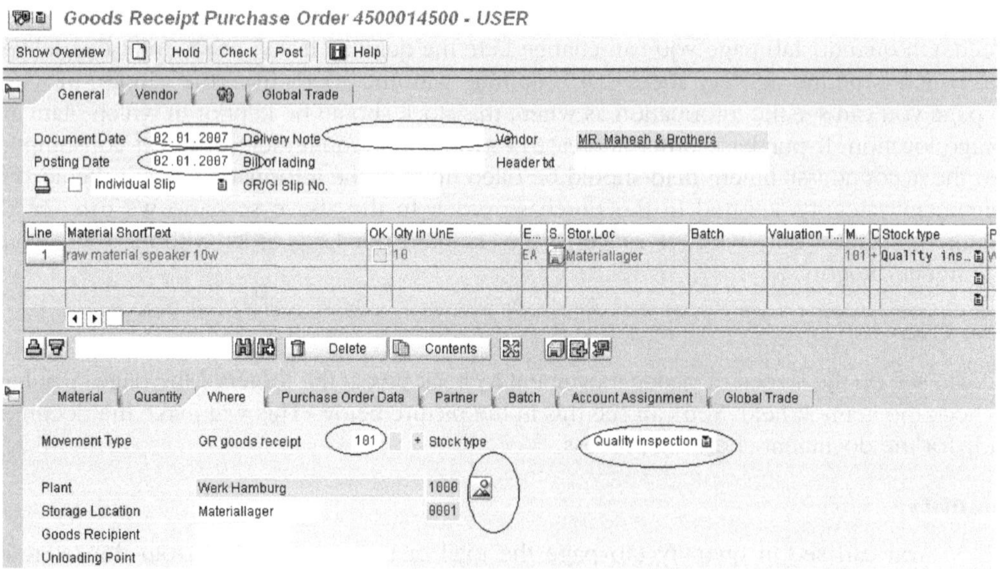

Stock type:-

On the same where tab page you can see stock type as quality inspection or blocked stock or unrestricted use stock. You can set this stock type as per your business process or requirement.

If other requirement is not set then unrestricted use stock is automatically selected or else you can select that.

Purchase Order Data

On the above screen you can see that there is purchase order data tab page. Here is the Del Completed Ind. Field. In this field you will be able to see following options.

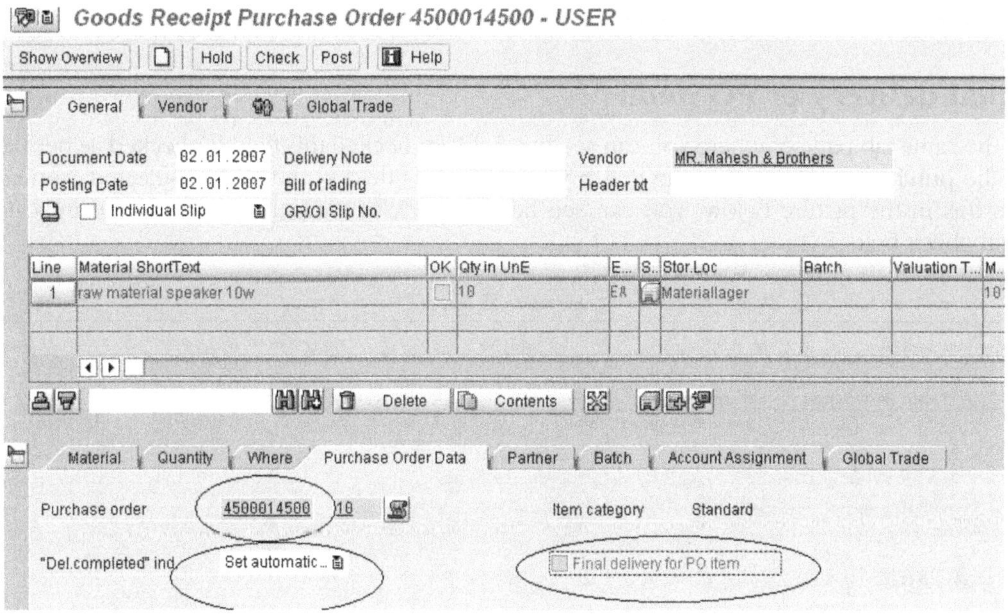

Purchase order document number:-

This is the purchase order document number to which this goods movement is referred. If you double click on this document number then this will take you to the purchase order document display screen there you can see all the details of purchase order.

Delivery completed indicator:-

This is the indicator which confirms that no further goods will be received against the reference document mentioned. You can see this option in the screen above. On the purchase order data tab page you can set this indicator.

Set:-

This field is set manually if you want to select delivery of this purchase order quantity as complete whatever quantity is delivered.

Set automatically:-

If this option is selected which is a default one then system will count this purchase order as completed one when total ordered quantity is delivered. Until the quantity is not delivered in total system will keep the purchase order open and expect further goods receipt.

Do not set:-

If this option is selected then system will not set the purchase order as complete.

Final delivery of PO item:-

In the same tab page of where you can see this field as checked this field is checked as because in the purchase order itself in the delivery tab page this field is checked as selected. You can see this in the picture below. You can see here a check in the delivery completed indicator field check box.

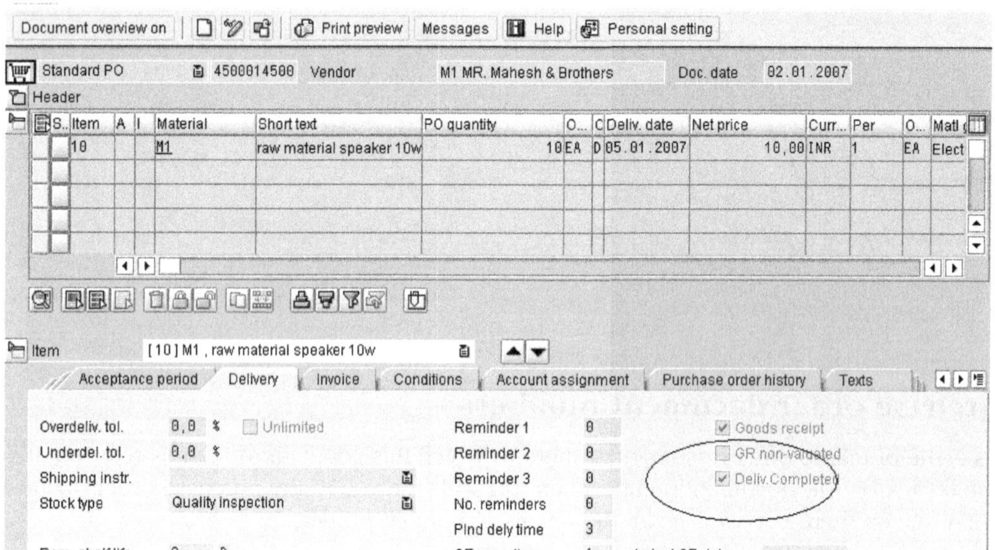

Now once all these details are entered check the document and save/post it.

While saving this material document any document number range related error comes then you can follow under mentioned process path.

Open a new session

Enter command /NFBN1 OR /OFBN1

Enter

Enter company code that you are working in.

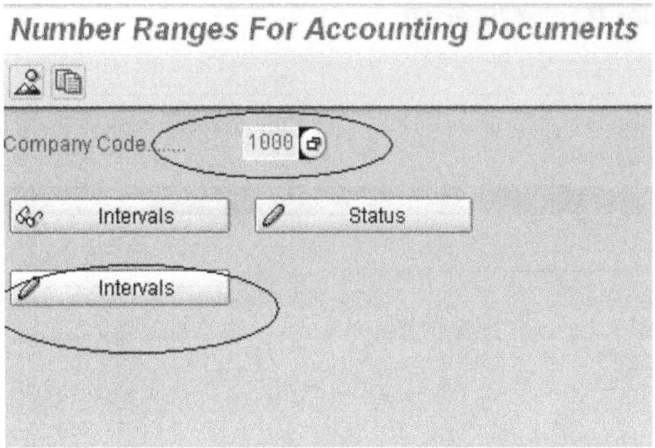

Click on change interval.

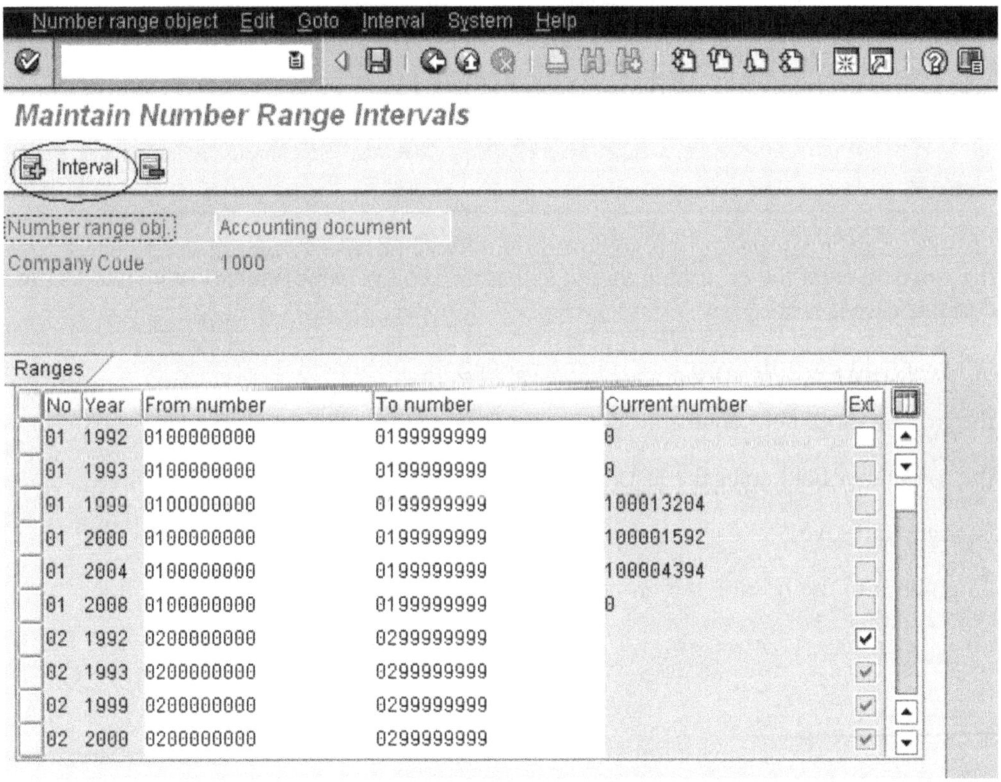

As in the above screen shot click on interval or insert interval.

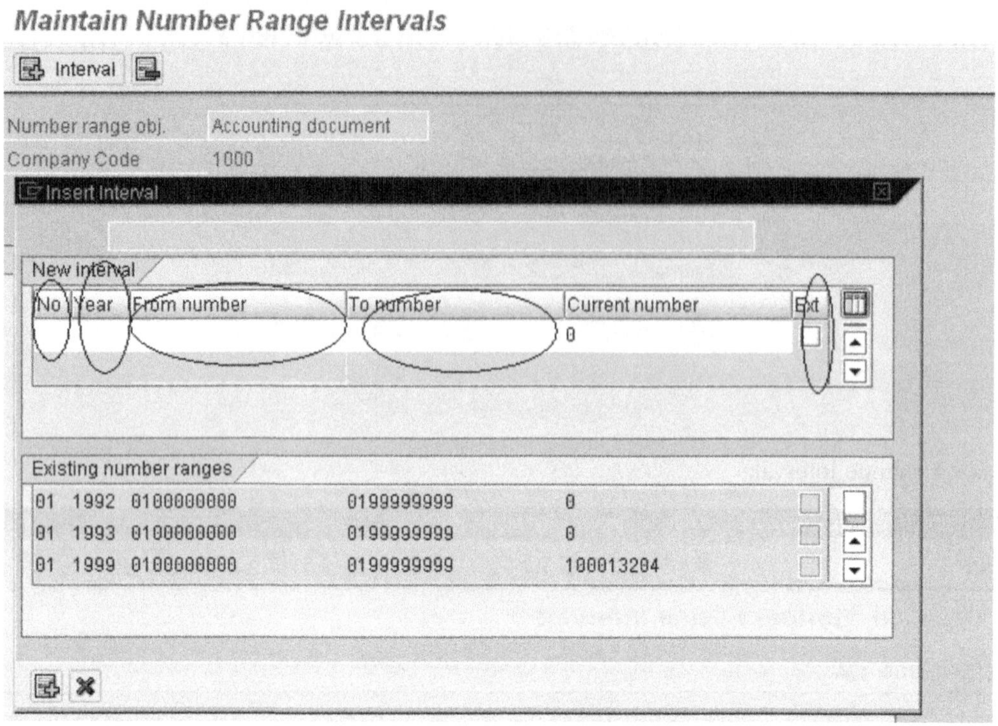

In the No. field enter the error number range that the prompt came while posting the document and in this case it is 50.

In the year field enter the year that you are posting the document.

In the from number field enter the start number as “5000000000”.

In the to number field enter the last number as “5999999999”

Press enter and save.

Then go back to the posting screen of MIGO. Save the document.

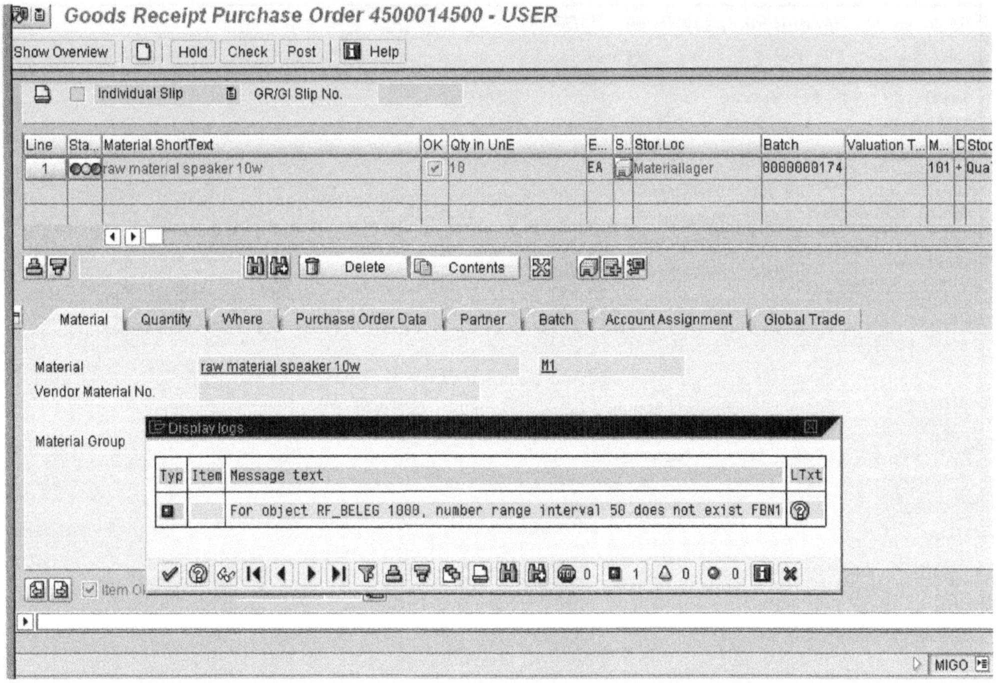

On the status bar you can see the document number generated.

Displaying a Material document:-

After you have posted the document, you can see the material and financial document which is generated from this transaction. Once you have selected the transaction Display from the drop down list you can see a different screen. Here you can see in reference document field as material document and right to this you can see a field where last posted material document number is entered and if this field is blank then you cal search for the proper document to display with the help of some criteria.

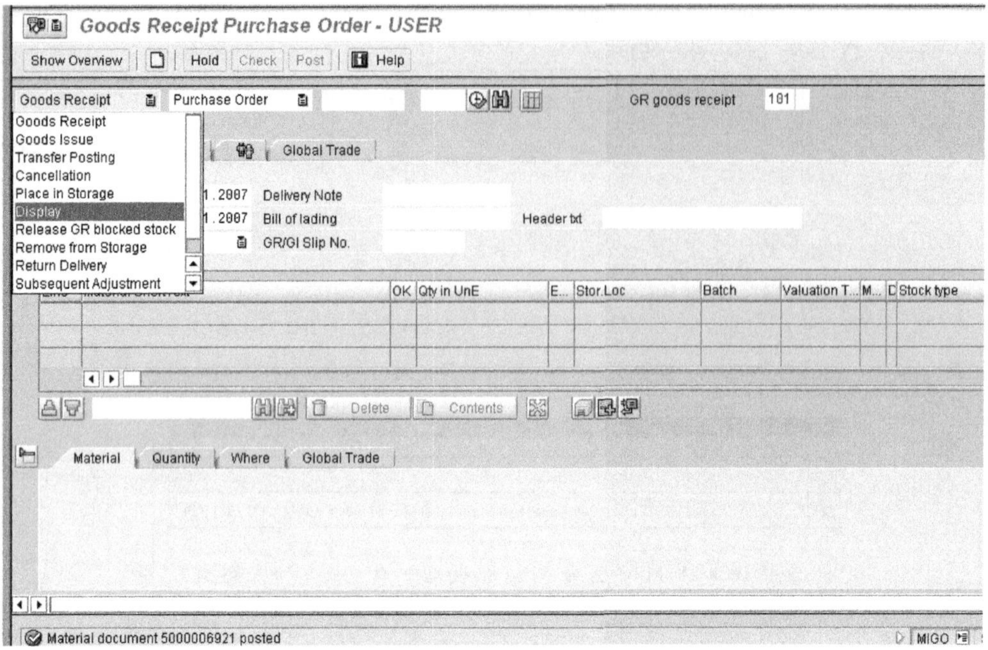

Press enter and you will be able to see the goods movement document. From here you select the Doc info tab page where you will be able to see an icon for FI document. Once you double click on this document you will be able to see the financial document.

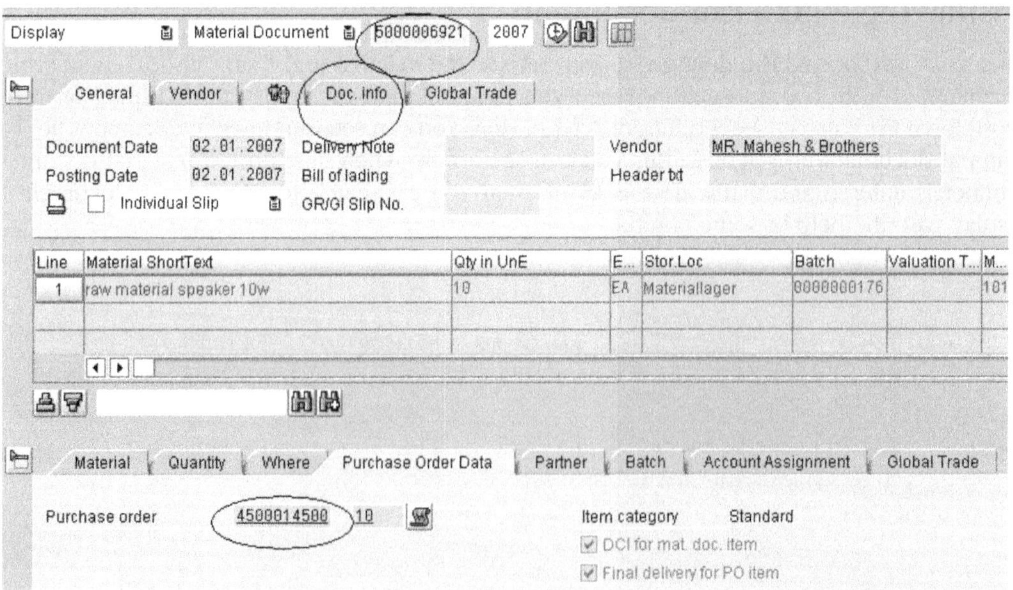

On clicking this document icon you will be able to see the FI document tab page.

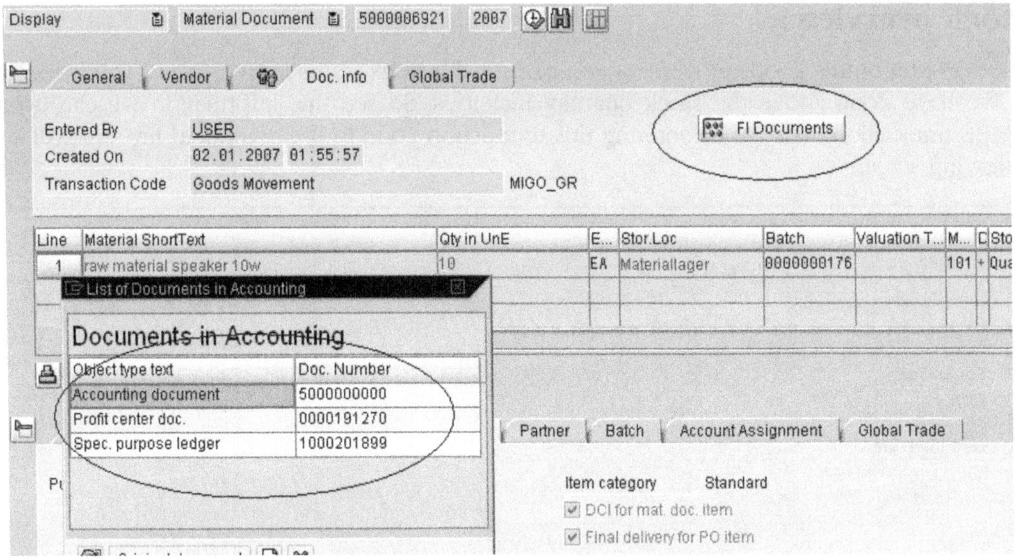

Here you can see accounting document with a number, Profit center document with a number and special purpose ledger with document number.

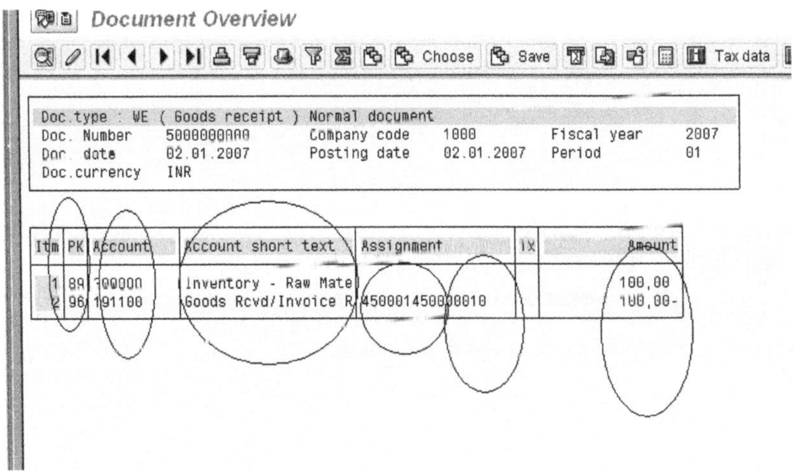

These are the documents which are proof of entries posted in different G/L accounts. You can see these documents in details as below in the picture.

PK = posting key this defines whether this amount and GL account is posted as debit or credit.

Account= this is the General Ledger number to which the amounts are being posted in this process.

Assignment is the PO number and item number

Stock overview:-

After posting of this goods movement you can see the stock status as after every goods receipt as we have done above the stock quantity increases. So see this information we can go to MMBE transaction code. After entering this transaction code in the command line we will see following screen.

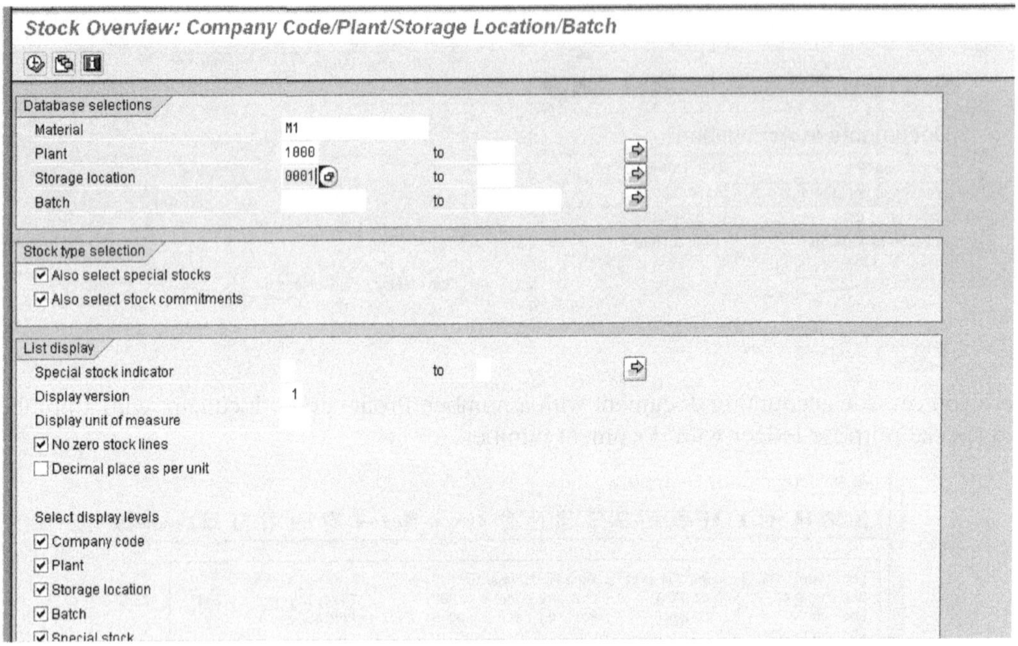

We can see in the above screen different selection criteria. Also we can see that this stock over view screen can display only one material's stock status.

In the screen you can see that material is posted to quality inspection stock in our scenario. Other wise it is normally posted to unrestricted stock.

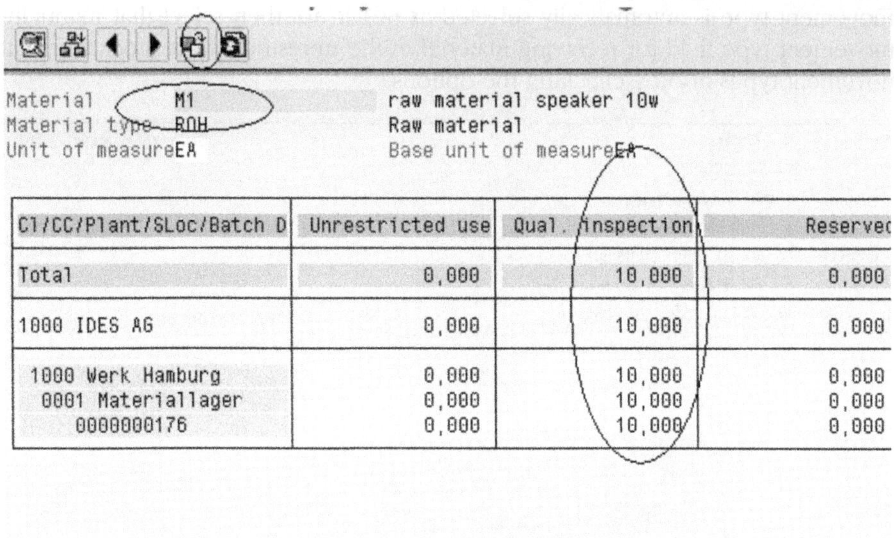

In the above screen you can change the material number from M1 to any other and then press new selection. You can see the new selected material's stock details

In the above screen we can see the stock overview of material M1. we can see different company codes and their respective

Goods receipt without any reference document:-

You can either receive goods with reference to any document or without any reference material. If you need to receive goods without any reference material then you can do it as following process.

Select transaction as goods receipt.

Select "other" in the reference field.

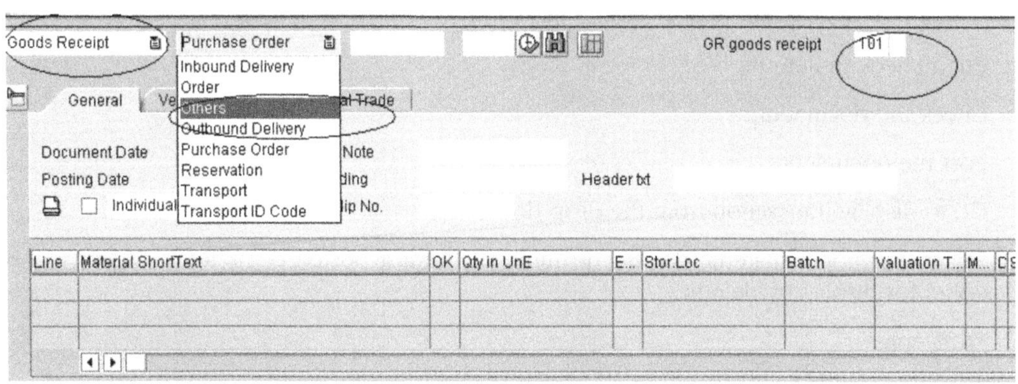

Select movement type is automatically selected as 561 if not then select that manually as 561 in the movement type field for receiving material in the unrestricted use stock. You can select other movement types also by checking the options.

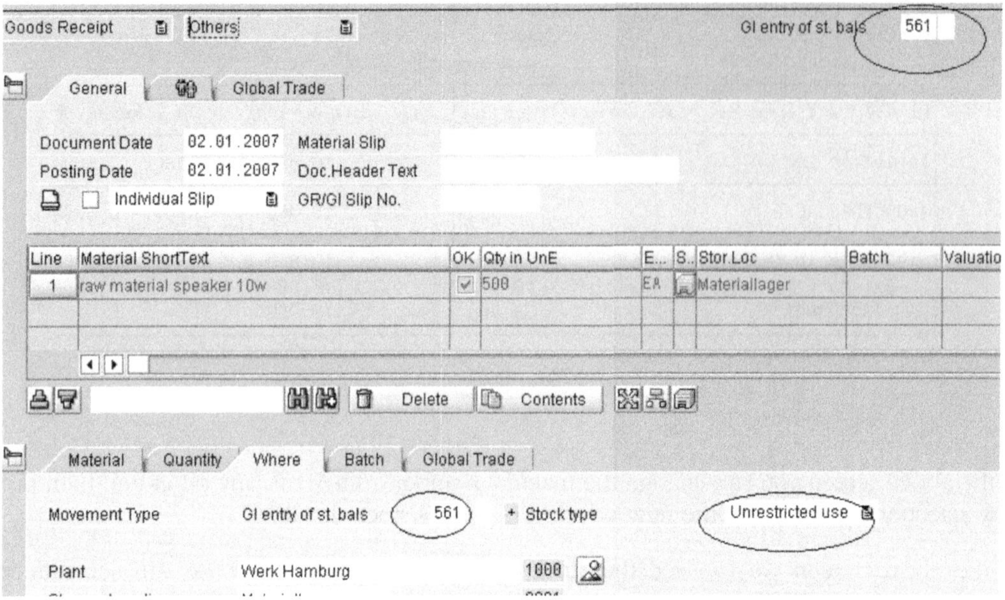

Movement types should be same as in the field above and on the where tab page.

Enter plant as 1000.

Enter storage location as 0001

Enter material that you are willing to record as initial stock entry.

Enter the initial stock entry quantity on the quantity tab page.

Confirm that stock type is selected as "unrestricted use" stock.

Check the posting date which should fall within the posting period.

Put a check in item ok field.

Check the document.

Post the document.

Go to display transaction from the drop down list.

Select the proper material document number. The last posted document number will be opted for display by default.

Press enter.

Go to doc info tab page.

Double click on the FI document icon.

Select the accounting document number.

View the accounting document and amount posting.

Go to MMBE transaction code to view the material stock status.

So in the process mentioned above you can easily receive material stock with or without any reference document.

In MB51 you can see the material document list.

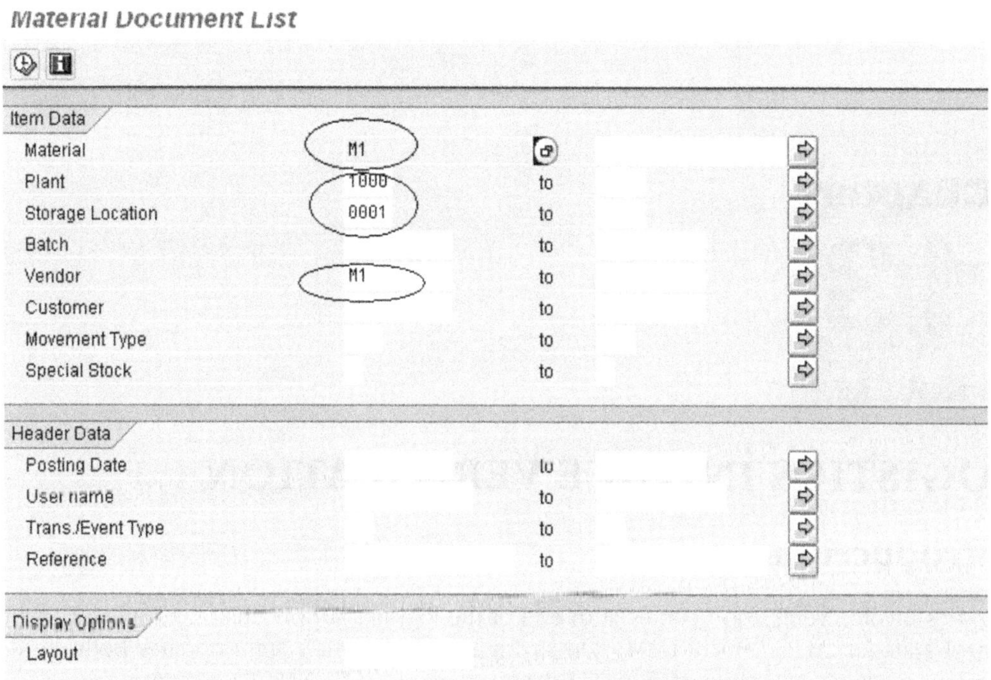

So in the above mentioned process you can receive stocks as per your requirement with reference to the document or without reference to the document.

Chapter

13

LOGISTICS INVOICE VERIFICATION

Introduction

Logistics Invoice Verification comes at th end of the logistics supply chain and it is a very vital part of Materials Management (MM). On saving this document system updates both the data materials management data and financial data.

You know the complete procurement process flow. If you are a purchaser then you generate a requirement in the required division. Then with reference to that you create a purchase order and send it to the vendor that informs the vendor that you require material or service specified. The vendor then supplies the material or performs service. You receive the material from the vendor. Along with this vendor also sends a invoice with all the information details of the sent material or performed service with pricing details and taxes applied. In logistics invoice verification you receive this paper of invoice and enter that in your system.

An invoice can be processed in Logistics Invoice Verification in following ways:-

- **Invoice Verification Online**
  - In this process you receive an invoice. You have to enter the very same information in the system that you have got in the invoice. Then you will compare the these information

with the rference document for its correctness and if required do the corrections and save the document. On posting the invoice multiple financial documents are generated in the system and multiple G/L accounts are updated.

- **Invoice Verification in the Background**
  - After receiving the invoice you only enter the total amount of the invoice and match the invoice up with another system document. The system then checks the invoice in the background and saves. If errors do occur, the system saves the invoice and you then have to process it in a separate step.

- **Automatic Settlement**
  - o Evaluated Receipt Settlement (ERS)
    - This type of invoice settlement happens where you have to pay to the vendor on regular interval without getting any request for payment from the vendor. Without receiving any invoice you post them yourself based on information contained in purchase orders and goods receipts.
  - o Consignment and Pipeline Settlement
    - You are not expecting a vendor invoice because stocks are kept at your place only liability lies with the vendor. Now vendor does not comes to know when you are going to use it. Instead you settle posted withdrawals yourself and send the vendor a statement of the settlement.
  - o Invoicing plan
    - In this process you do not receive the invoice instead you create invoices based on the dates scheduled in the purchase order and these trigger the payment to the vendor.
  - o Revaluation
    - In this process You determine difference values based on retroactively valid price changes and create the associated settlement documents. You send these documents to the vendor.

- **Invoices Received via EDI**
  - In EDI the invoice information enters the SAP R/3 System via electronic data interchange and the system tries to post the invoice automatically. If errors occur, you have to process the invoice manually.

When an invoice is posted folloing doucment numbers are generated.

Document number of the accunting document

Displays material document number

Document number of the invoice reduction.

Transaction codes:-

Below there is a list of some Invoicing related transaction codes.

Transaction	Activity
Document Entry	
MIRO	Enter Invoice
MIR7	Park Invoice
MIRA	Enter Invoices for Invoice Verification in the Background
Further Processing	
MIR4	Display Invoice Document
MR8M	Cancel Invoice Document
MRBR	Release Blocked Invoices
MIR6	Invoice Overview
MR90	Output Messages
Automatic Settlement	
MRRL	Evaluated Receipt Settlement (ERS)
MRKO	Consignment and Pipeline Settlement
MRIS	Invoicing Plan Settlement
MRNB	Revaluation
GR/IR Account Maintenance	
MR11	Maintain GR/IR Clearing Account
MR11SHOW	Display/Cancel Account Maintenance Document
Archiving	
MRA1	Create Archive
MRA2	Delete Documents
MRA3	Display Archived Document
MRA4	Manage Archive

Incoming Invoice

An incoming invoice can be an invoice or a credit memo.

An invoice contains information, such as:

- The invoice issuer
- Prior reference document
- Tax amount
- Total expected amount to be paid

If the vendor invoice contains different information, you can change the data proposed. The system checks whether your entries are allowed and are within allowed limit. It may display a warning or error message if anything is incorrect.

An invoice is related to following data bases.

Master Data

This is a permanent data on objects, for example materials.

- Material Data:-

  Material master data contains information on the materials bought by or produced in the company. You will find material number, material name, units of measure, stock data, over delivery and under delivery limits and other related important information which are used in different processes.

- Vendor Data

  This provides supplier's information. Address bank data, terms of payment, currency and other information.

- Accounting Data

  The accounting data is maintained in Financial Accounting. It includes all general ledger related information and defined process.

Transaction Data

When we record any process step in the SAP system it generates a document for that. This is Transaction data. It may be purchase order, scheduling agreement, goods receipt, or invoice. The document data of a transaction depends on the application area that the transaction belongs to. Every document receives a document number by which it can be uniquely identified.

• Purchasing Document

Example of a purchasing document may be purchase order, request for quotation, quotation contracts and other documents.

• Material Document

When there is any change of quantity based changed in material stock or service level in the SAP system a material document is created.

• Accounting Document

An accounting document is created on goods receipt of a valuated material or an invoice is posted. It contains details of the individual postings with the account number, posting key, and the amount. It documents the value-based changes.

Displaying the MM and FI Document Number

You can display materials and financial documents with the help of the following transactions:

- Enter Invoice (MIRO)
- Park Invoice (MIR7)
- Cancel Invoice (MR8M)
- Invoice Overview (MIR6)
- Evaluated Receipt Settlement (MRRL)
- Revaluation (MRNB)
- Invoicing Plan (MRIS)
- Invoice Verification in the Background
- In the status message, EDI invoices also receive the accounting document number

Chapter 14

INCOMING INVOICE ENTRY

Invoice entry

Invoice entry is a step in which you enter the information contained in the incoming invoice in to your SAP system. This may be entered with a reference document or for a direct entry.

In the picture below you can see the menu path to perform all the logistics invoice verification related transactions.

Menu path:-

SAP Easy Access > Logistics > Materials Management > Logistics Invoice Verification > Document entry > Enter Invoice

Transaction code:-

Other wise than following menu path you can also enter MIRO transaction code in the command line.

Initial Screen of MIRO:-

Initial screen of incoming invoice entry will look like a screen as in the picture below.

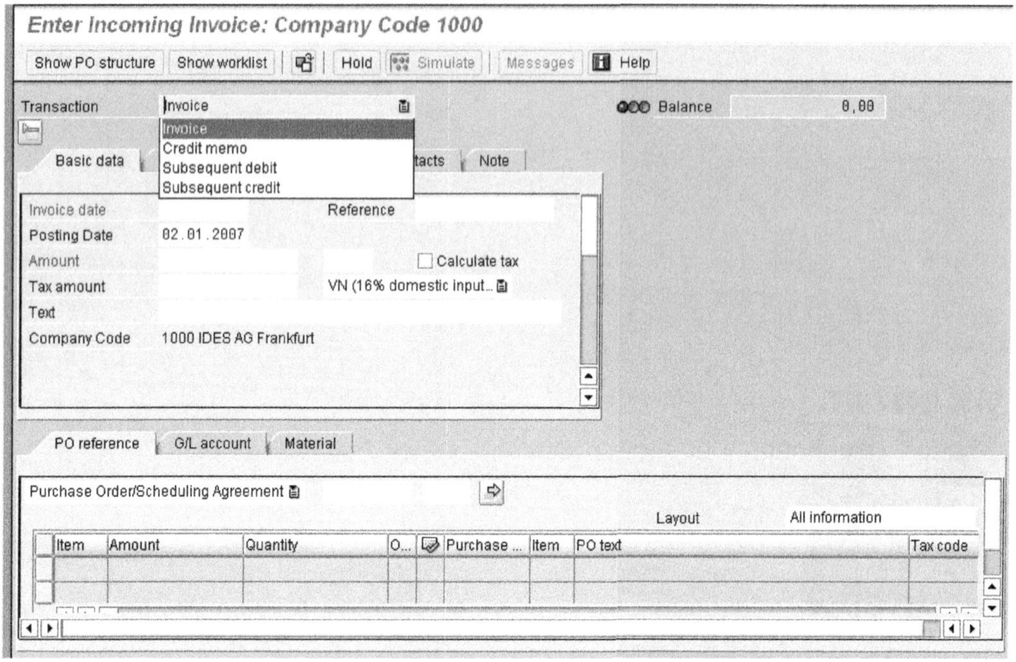

In the picture you can see the transactions in the drop down. These are followings.

- Invoice
- Credit memo
- Subsequent debit
- Subsequent credit

Invoice:-

Invoice is a document that is sent by the seller to the buyer. Invoice entry is a process in which this received document is entered by the buyer in his own SAP system. This may be verified with reference to any previously created document.

Credit memo:-

Credit memo refers to a credit memo from a vendor. The posting a credit memo always leads to a debit posting on the vendor account. It reduces the balance of receivable or payable.

For example, you had ordered for a material quantity of 100 pieces.

- Ordered quantity 100 pieces
- Goods received 100 pieces
- Fault founded in 30 pieces
- Goods returned 20 pieces
- Vendor receives back 20 pieces
- The vendor sent a debit memo.
- It becomes credit memo for you.
- Further you expect another goods receipt of 20 pieces.
- If goods are not sent then amount is to be paid is to be reduced.

The vendor creates a debit memo for 20 pieces and sends it to the buyer. For buyer it becomes a credit memo that the buyer enters in his system. When you post a credit memo, the total quantity in the purchase order history is reduced by the credit memo quantity.

Subsequent Debit/Subsequent Credit:-

A subsequent debit/credit exists when an additional invoice or credit memo is received for a transaction that has already been invoiced.

Invoice Entry Processing:-

In SAP system you already have multiple documents ready that may be used as a reference document in invoice entry process. When you created purchase order you sent it to your vendor. When you received goods there should be a document that will have delivery related information. This delivery document number is enter in the system in delivery not. You can take this as reference document. You can also take vendor as a reference then all the goods receipt that has not been invoiced will be displayed.

When you had accepted the performed service in service a document was created for the service entry sheet. This can also be taken as reference document.

As you can see in the picture below you can select PO as reference documents. In the reference document field which is blank PO reference tab page press F4.

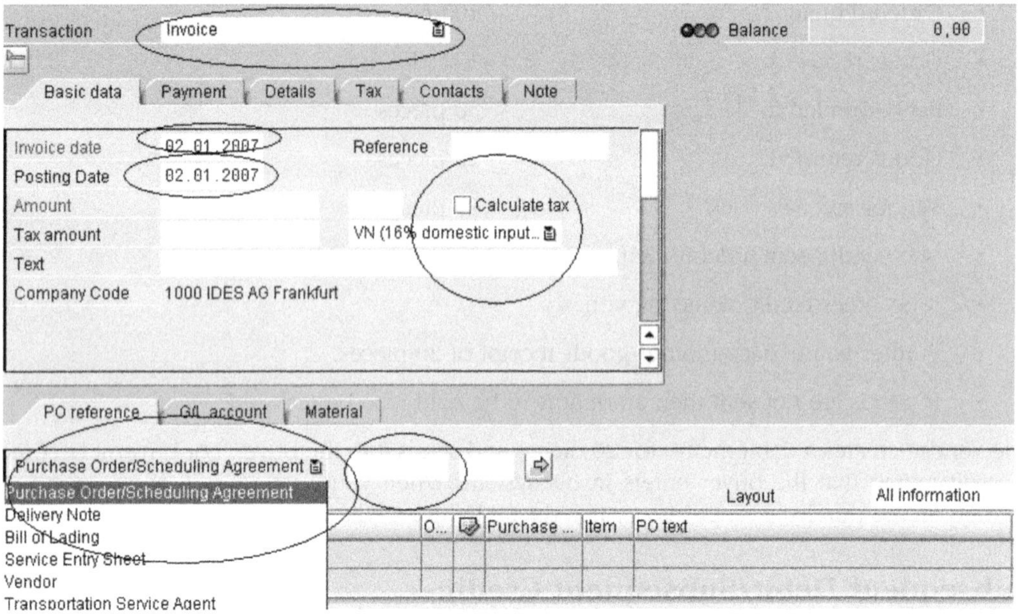

On selection of Purchase order as reference document following initial screen will be displayed.

Enter vendor number and company code.

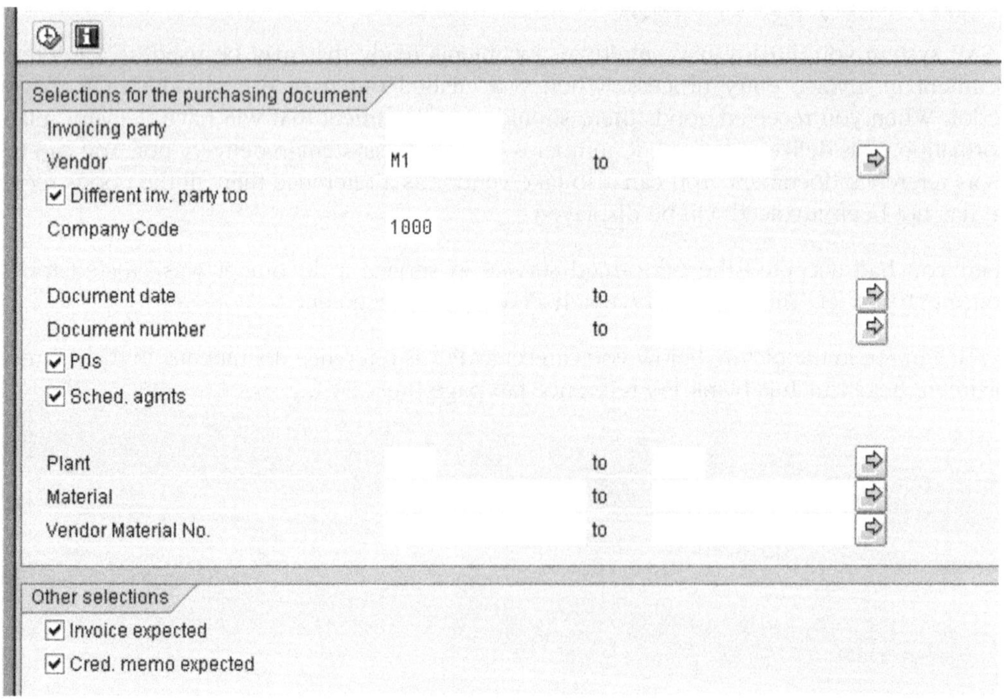

Execute.

This will display all the purchase order for vendor number entered.

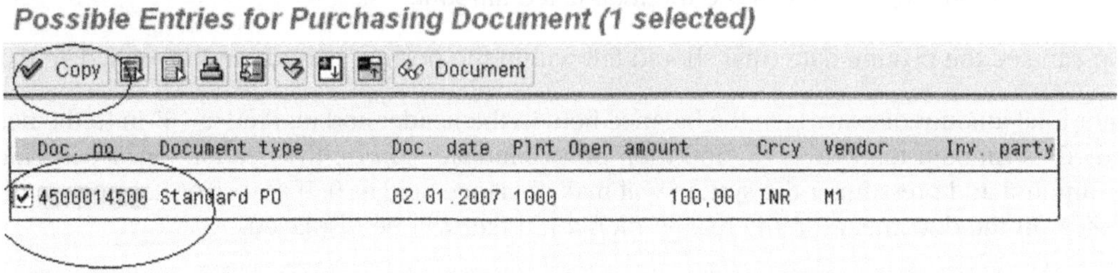

There it may display a number of purchase orders for that vendor but select a purchase order that you wish to process.

Go to copy or press F9. Document will be selected at the main screen and then press enter.

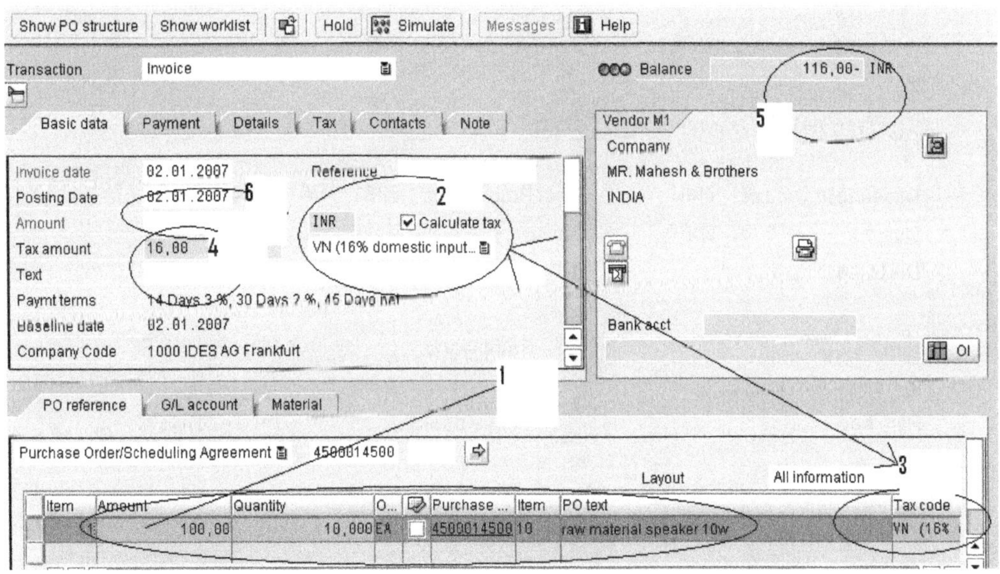

The number will be copied.

Press ENTER and following screen will be displayed.

On the screen you can see that purchase order number and details. This amount is a total of goods receipt.

You can see one more amount on the top right of the screen. This is the total amount to be paid to the vendor. If tax is applicable then this will be base amount + total taxed amount.

The field in the picture above mark number 2's field and mark number 3's field for tax code should be similar for smooth processing.

In the tax amount field you can see the total taxed amount.

You can see the posting date (that should fall within the posting period) and invoice date that.

Enter total amount displaying in the balance field in the header and marked as "5" in to the field named as Amount marked as "6" and then press simulate icon on the header. Once you enter the amount and press Enter the system will make balance field as 0. If any error happens in this process in the document for any reason then a red flag will be displayed.

On this screen on line item select tax code as VN in this case. Same tax code on the header as VN to apply 16% domestic input tax on purchase. Along with this also enter a check in the field calculate tax. You can see this in the screen below.

Baseline date:-

This is the start date of the due date calculation. You have to enter this as per decided rule. Or enter the posting date.

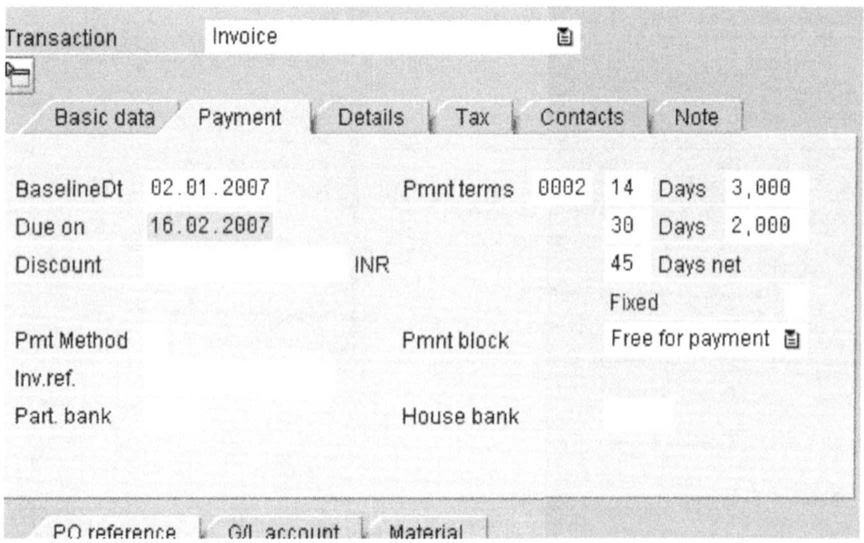

Simulation:-

Once you have entered all the information correctly simulate the document. You can see on the top of the screen simulate icon. This will check and calculate the information entered in the document with the reference material information. If no error is found then system will display a red flag and show the preview results in a pop up screen. This is shown below in the picture.

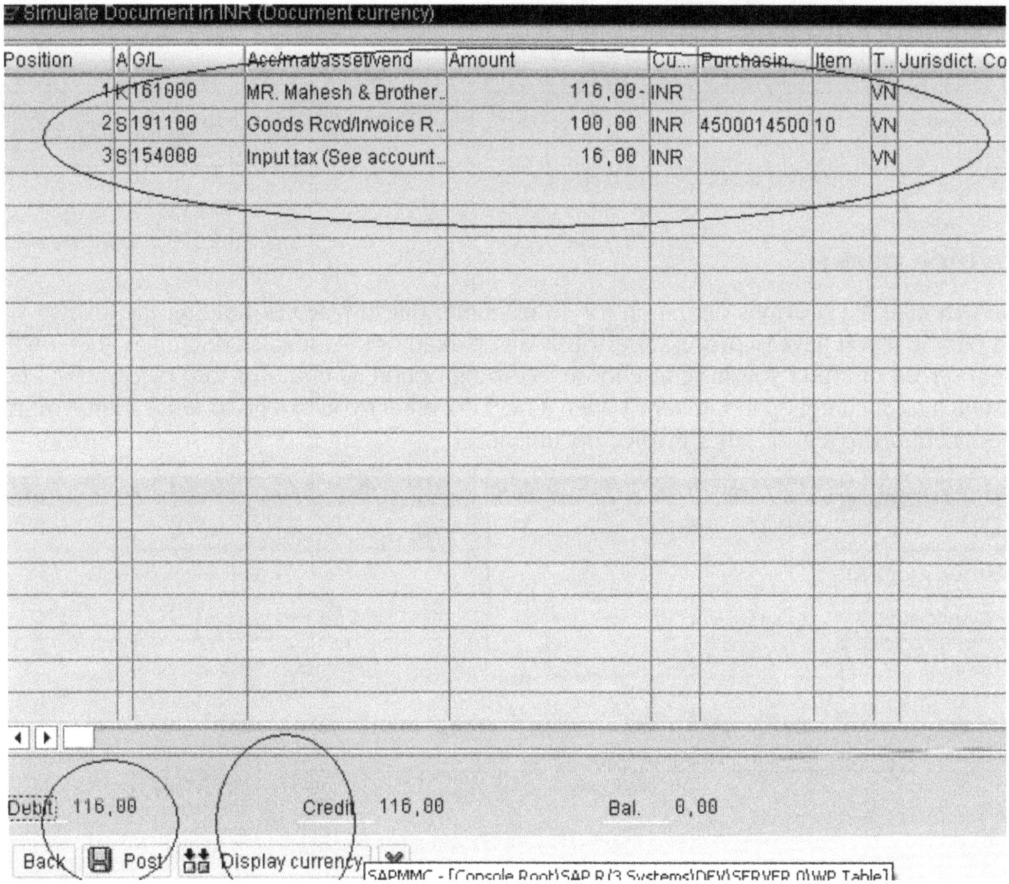

From this status you have four options:-

Hold the invoice

Park the invoice

Keep the document as save as complete

Post the document

Hold invoice:-

Invoice hold is a stage where you have made initial entry of information. But you have not checked any information, you have not verified and information, you have not calculated any tax code or any amount or you have performed all of these. But still there is a need to be checked by the higher authority before invoice posting. In this case you will keep the document as hold. This will just create a document number, but this will not create any financial document. Below in the picture you can see the hold button.

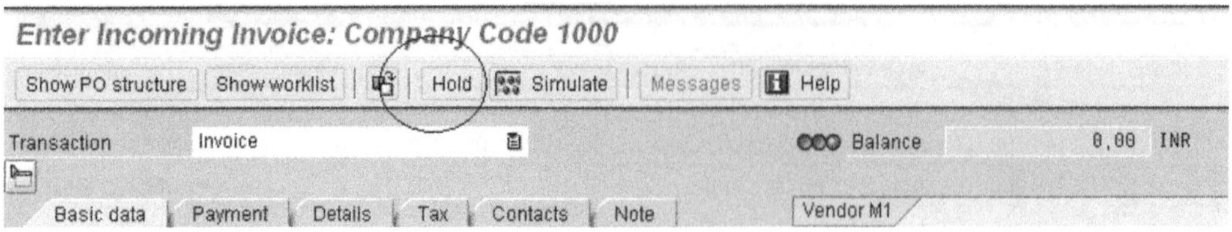

Invoice park:-

You can take the previous operation for an example. But in place of holding the invoice you can park it. If you have to process previously any parked or held invoice document then on the initial screen of MIRO you have to choose following option as in the picture below. From Edit to switch to document parking. Or to open a held document you can go to MIR4. Here you can select held document or other invoice document.

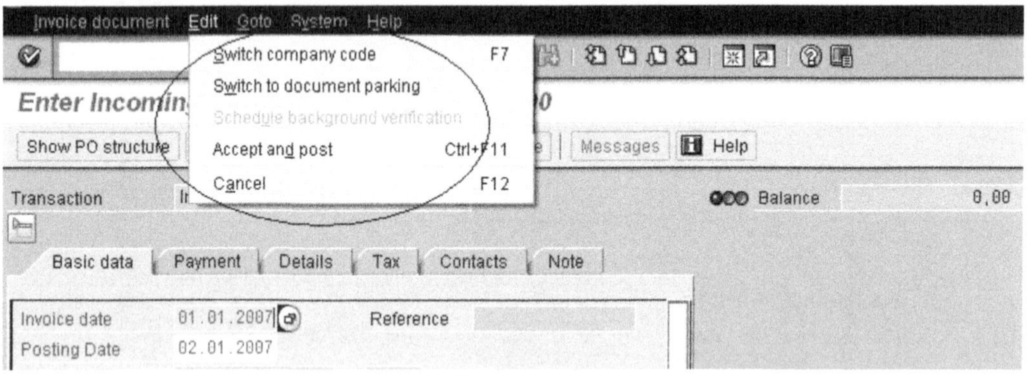

You can work on the invoice document and in this step making some corrections if needed you can post the document if every thing is ok or if there is any error then it will not be posted. So in this case you can either hold the document again for correction or you can park it.

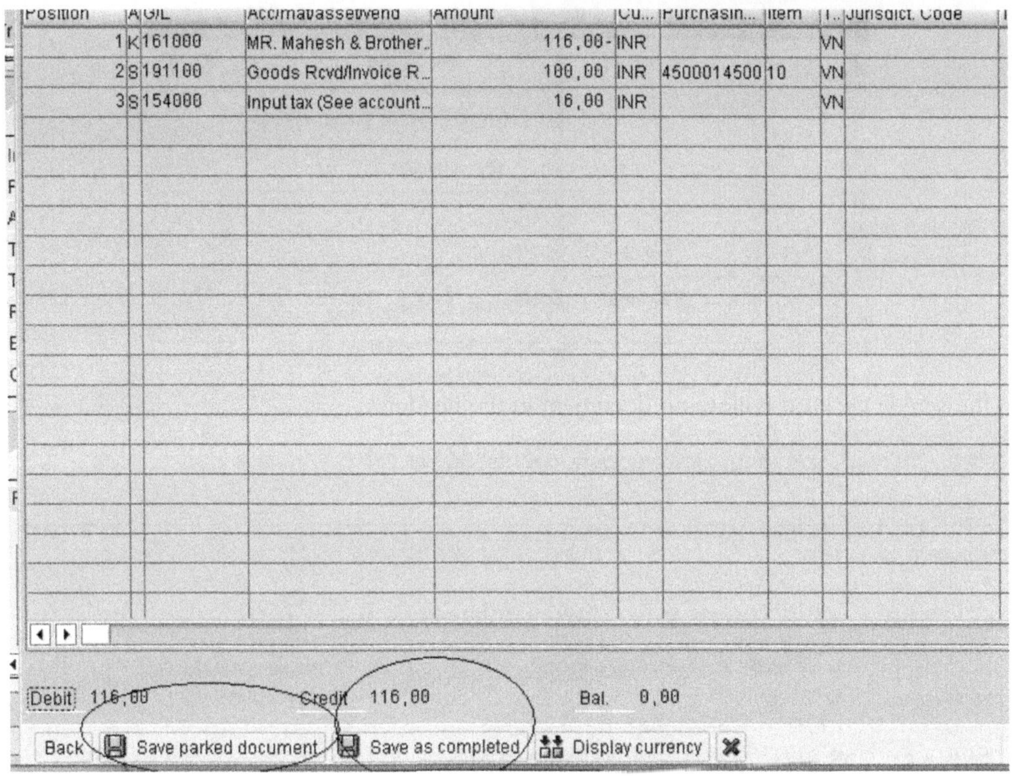

While processing the invoice with the same held invoice of one specific purchase order in simulation mode you will see following options as shown in the picture above.

Save Parked document

Save as complete

You can also go back to the main screen and post it direct.

If you hold the document then no FI document will be generated.

If you park the document then FI document will be generated but no account postings will take place. You can see this in the picture below.

Displaying the Document

Open MIRO transaction code

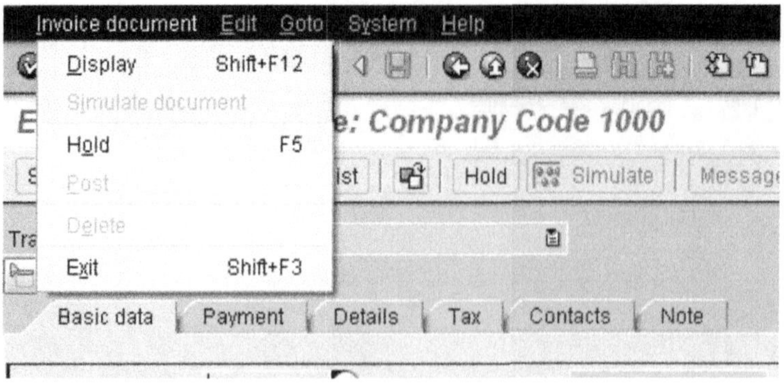

On the screen click on Follow on document in the header

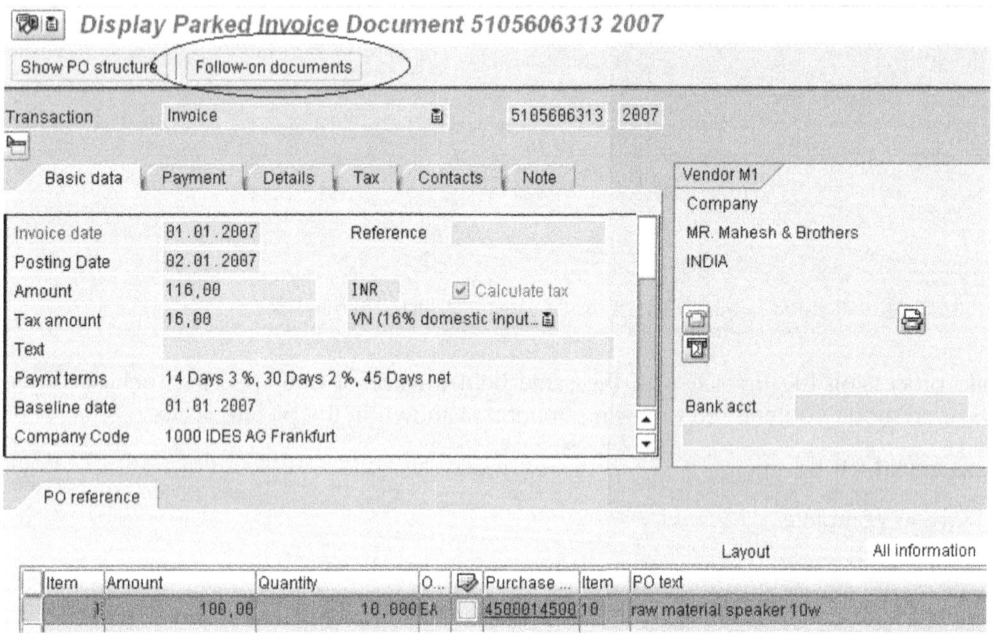

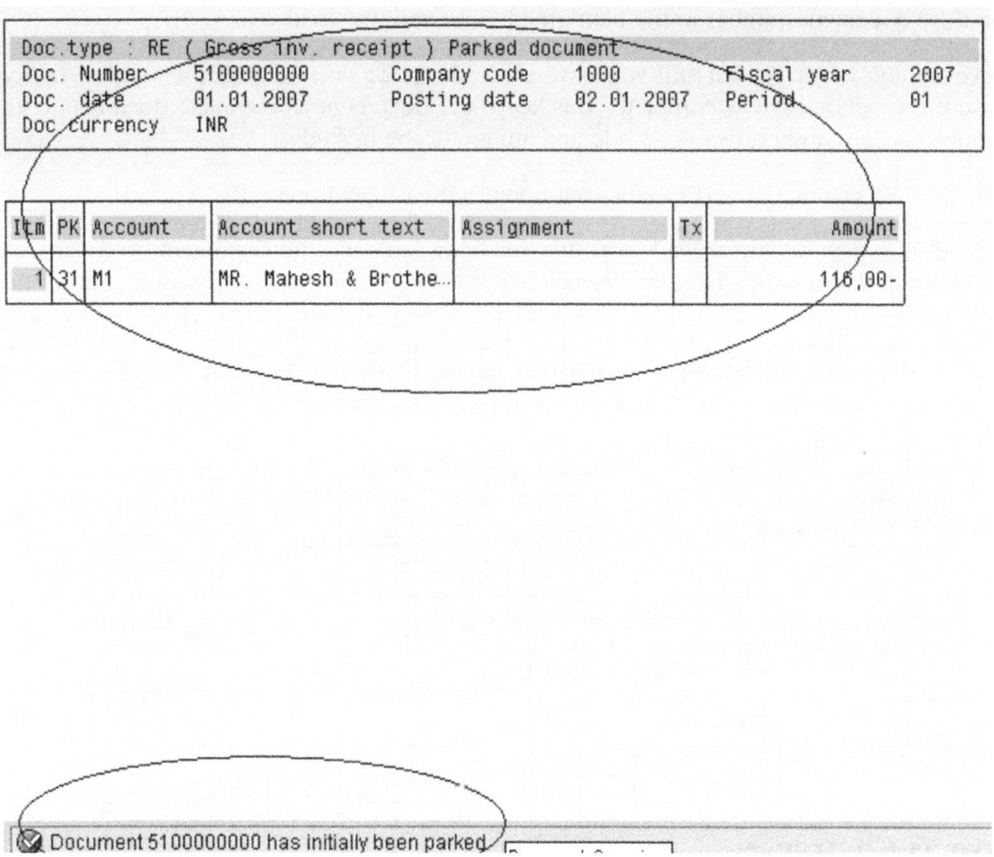

You can see the details and the information status as of parked document.

Other document:-

If you need to select the other document than system is showing then you can select it via icon other document as shown in the picture below.

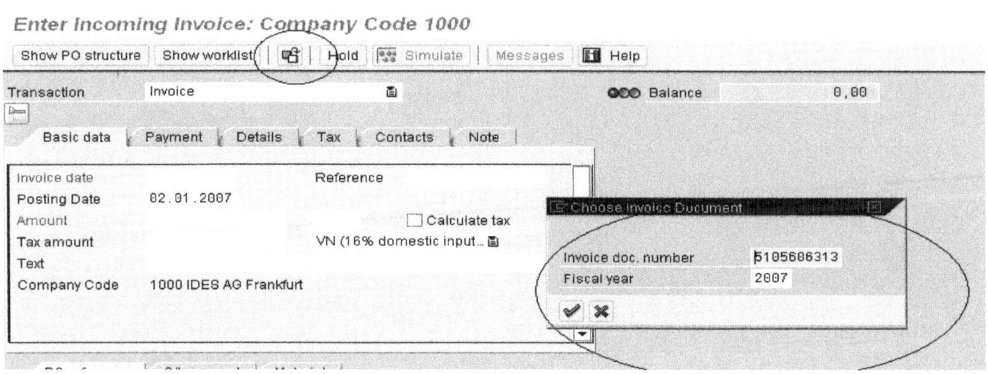

Enter the document number in the blank field there and the fiscal year.

If every thing is correct but still you have some doubt or dispute with the vendor then you can use the option save as complete. This keeps the document as complete document correct amount postings and correct tax c ode and amount to be posted.

This does not create a new document but updates the original one only.

After all the disputes are solved, you or your boss can save the document. You can select document as display document then select display-change document and post it after properly checking it.

After the document is posted you can display the document and similarly you can also check the posted FI documents too, as it is shown in the picture below.

Doc. Number	5100000000	Company code	1000	Fiscal year	2007
Doc. date	01.01.2007	Posting date	02.01.2007	Period	01
Doc.currency	INR				

Itm	PK	Account	Account short text	Assignment	Tx	Amount
1	31	M1	MR. Mahesh & Brothe...		VN	116,00-
2	86	191100	Goods Rcvd/Invoice R	450001450000010	VN	100,00
3	40	154000	Input tax		VN	16,00

Save as Complete:-

This is a step in which you check the document and make all the verifications. Save the document. You can go to MIR4 Screen to select previously held or parked document. Select the document and do all the corrections. After all the corrections are done you can again simulate the document. In the picture you can see this.

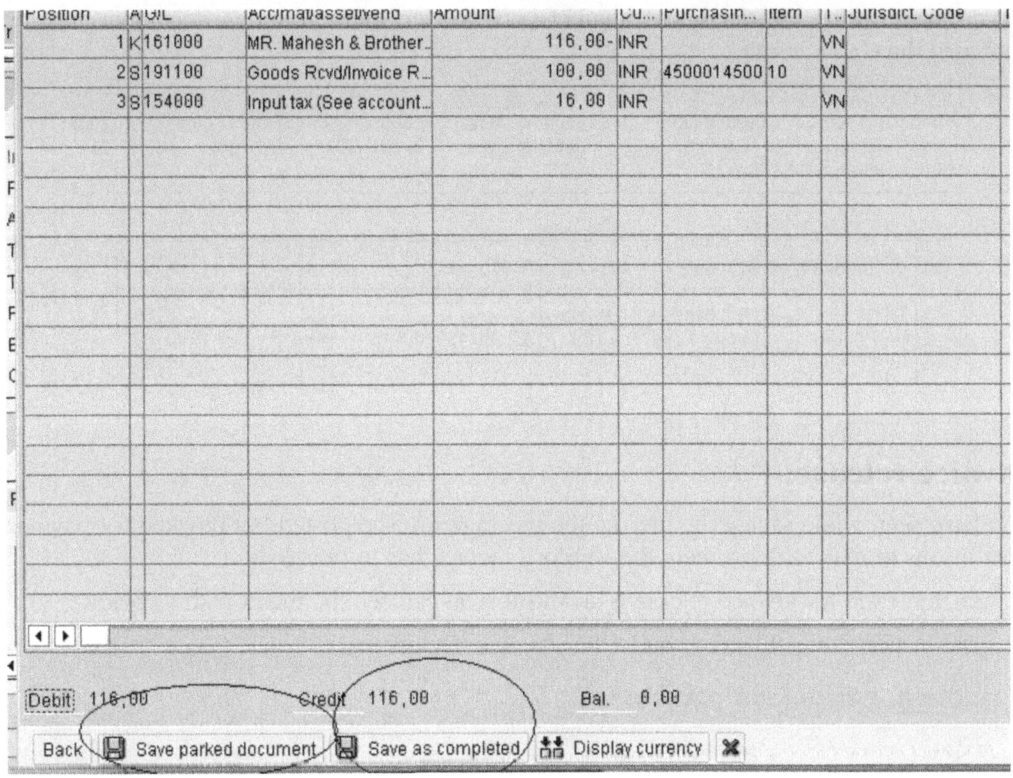

From here you can park the document, put the document as save as complete or simple post the document. The posting will do the G/L entries.

Blocked document:-

After you have posted the document after so many changes the status of the document will be as posted but blocked for payment. This blocking may be due to multiple reasons. One reason may be that though the document is correct but due to so many changes system has blocked it for payment. Second reason may be that there is some variance in the amount, quantity, price, or any other variance in the document with respect to the purchasing document. These variance rules and limits are fixed by the consultants as per the company's policy.

On the document display screen the document will be shown as below. Here you have option of reversing the invoice. This is done if there was wrong entry in any of the field but it was within the allowed limit so the system allowed the document to be posted. But on invoice posting entries have posted to FI and information has been transferred to FI domain. If you reverse the invoice document after invoice post then two documents will have to be reverse without any delay other wise on due date in spite of invoice reverse the vendor will get the payment. So reversal has to be in FI domain also that will be done by finance people. On posting of the document you can see a field as Follow on document. You can see this in the picture below.

On double clicking the document number you can see the accounting document and their entries in the G/L accounts.

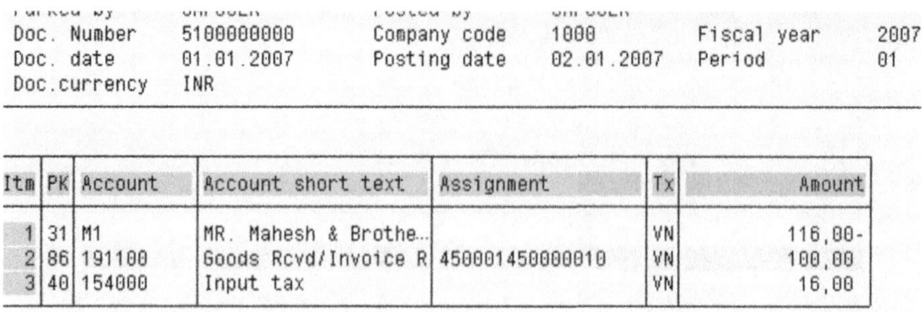

Doc. Number	5100000000	Company code	1000	Fiscal year	2007
Doc. date	01.01.2007	Posting date	02.01.2007	Period	01
Doc.currency	INR				

Itm	PK	Account	Account short text	Assignment	Tx	Amount
1	31	M1	MR. Mahesh & Brothe...		VN	116,00-
2	86	191100	Goods Rcvd/Invoice R	450001450000010	VN	100,00
3	40	154000	Input tax		VN	16,00

Invoice release:-

You have seen while saving the invoice the message invoice posted but blocked for payment. That means to make the payment the vendor's invoice has to be released.

Transaction code for invoice release is as MRBR. You can see the menu path as below.

This transaction code will take you to the screen as below.

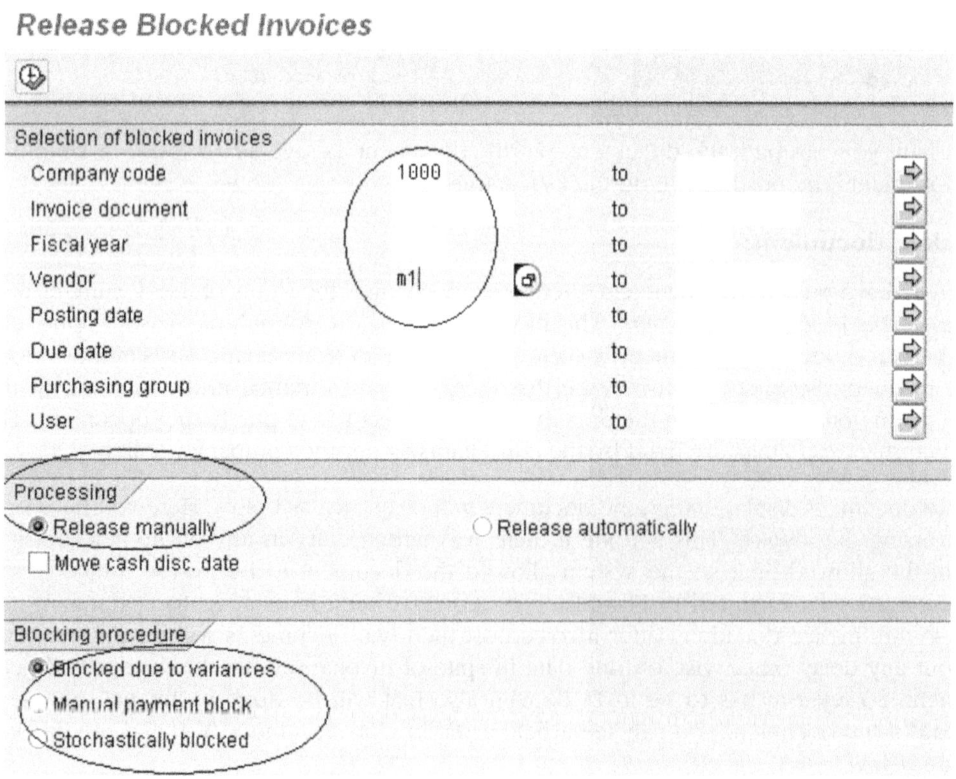

Company code:-

On this screen enter company code 1000.

Document number:-

Enter invoice document number if you know that or enter vendor code.

Release Manually:-

In processing you must select Release manually if you have to release any specific blocked invoice.

Release Automatically:-

If you select release automatically then all the related blocked invoices will be released for payment that might not be expected.

Blocking procedure:-

In this option you have to select the reason which blocked the invoice.

Normally first option of blocked due to variances are taken into account because that happens to be the frequent reason for blocking. Now question may arise why, how and who blocks these invoices for payment. Answer is that these settings are customized and defined in the system for different blocking reasons. For each and every reason there is an option for upper limit and lower limit of tolerance or variance to settle the account. You can see these configurations in SPRO. Transaction code is OMR6

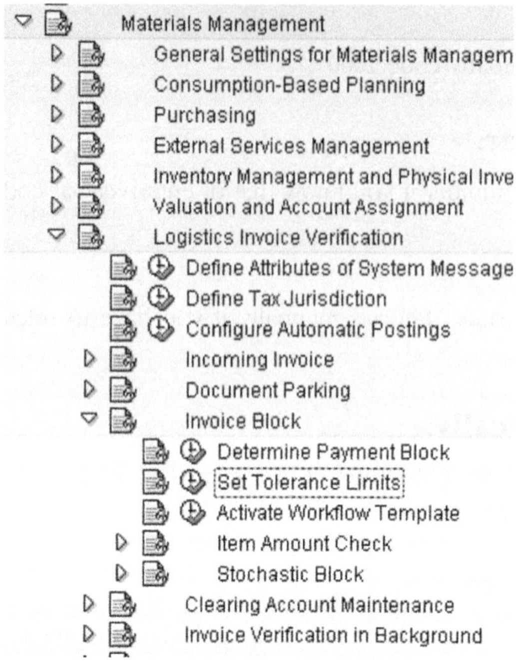

The reasons are as follows or you can create new reasons also.

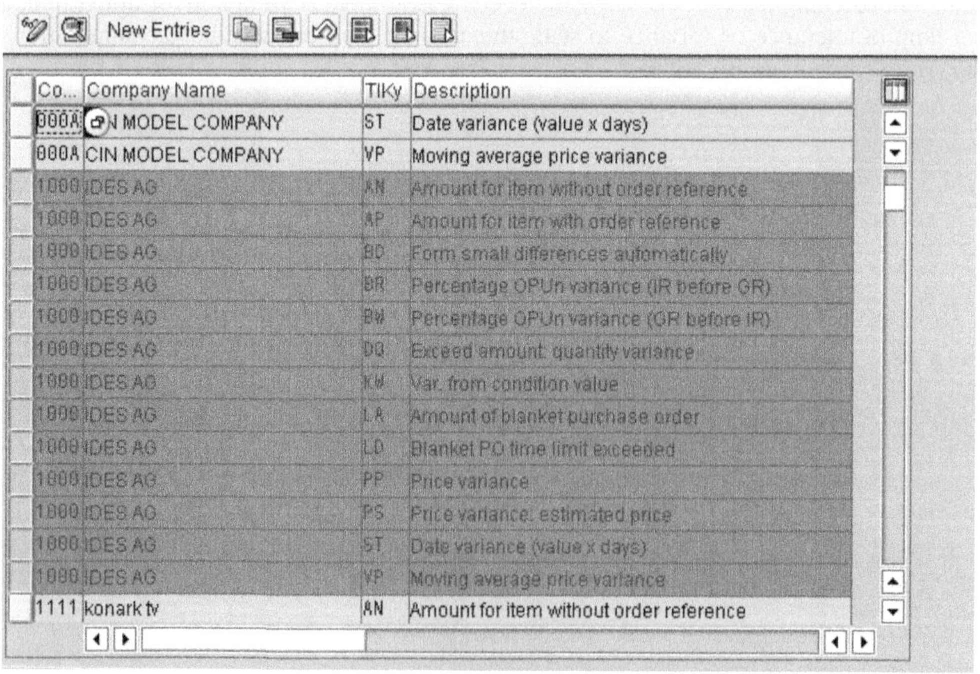

Change View "Tolerance Limits": Overview

New Entries

Co...	Company Name	TlKy	Description
000A	N MODEL COMPANY	ST	Date variance (value x days)
000A	CIN MODEL COMPANY	VP	Moving average price variance
1000	IDES AG	AN	Amount for item without order reference
1000	IDES AG	AP	Amount for item with order reference
1000	IDES AG	BD	Form small differences automatically
1000	IDES AG	BR	Percentage OPUn variance (IR before GR)
1000	IDES AG	BW	Percentage OPUn variance (GR before IR)
1000	IDES AG	DQ	Exceed amount: quantity variance
1000	IDES AG	KW	Var. from condition value
1000	IDES AG	LA	Amount of blanket purchase order
1000	IDES AG	LD	Blanket PO time limit exceeded
1000	IDES AG	PP	Price variance
1000	IDES AG	PS	Price variance: estimated price
1000	IDES AG	ST	Date variance (value x days)
1000	IDES AG	VP	Moving average price variance
1111	konark tv	AN	Amount for item without order reference

Double click on any item and enter the allowed values as per your need. This will make the system authorized for blocking.

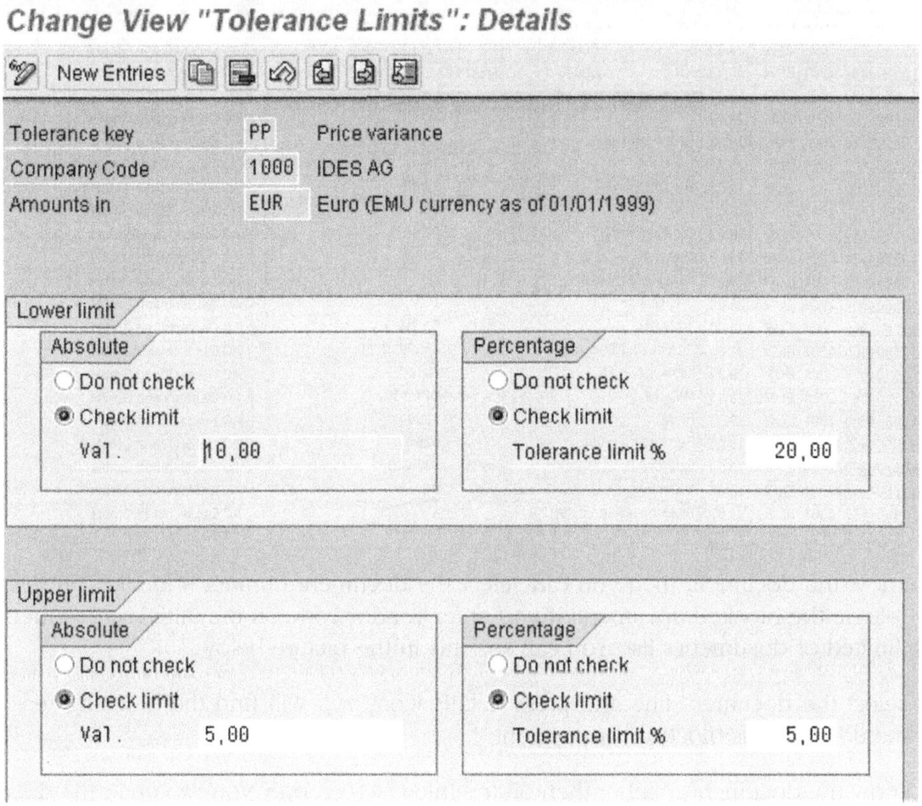

Execute the document:-

If you execute the process after entering the required input, a huge list of invoice documents will be displayed which are blocked. Now you have to find the document and select the line.

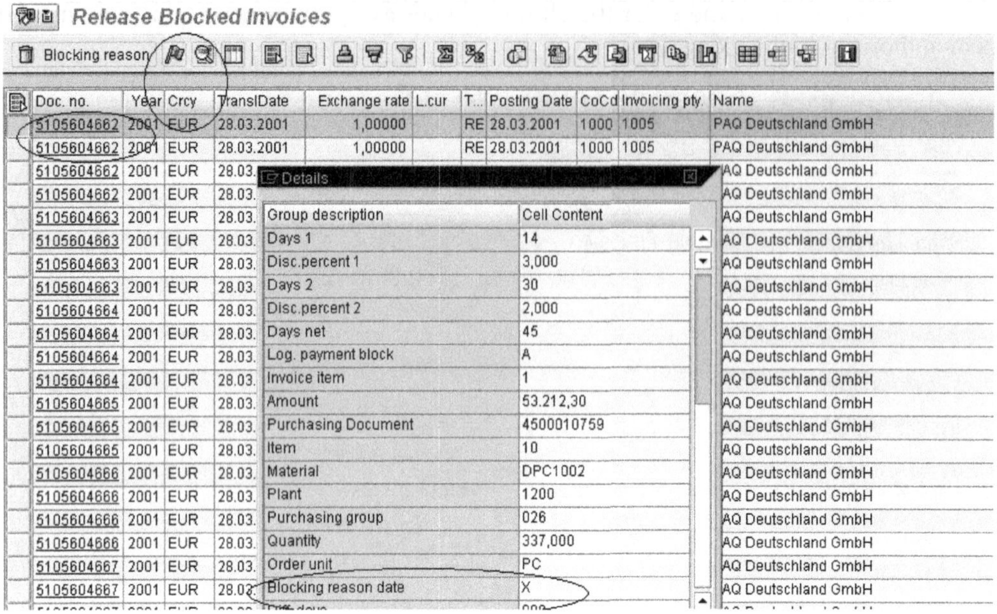

If you know the document then you can select the document number and click on the green flag to release the blocked document. If you enter vendor code on the initial screen then there will be limited of document's list. You can see this in the picture below.

If you select the document line and press details icon, you will find the blocking reason for which the document is blocked for payment.

If you know the document number then on the initial screen only you can enter the document number and execute.

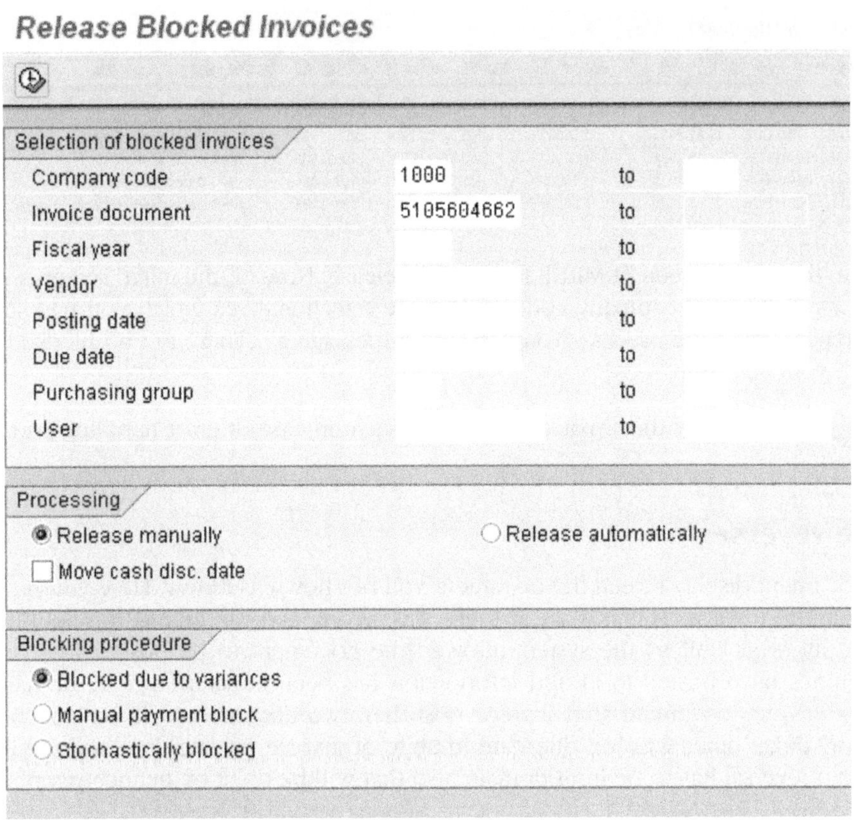

On this screen select the line and press the green flag icon for release invoice.

In the picture below you can see that the invoice document is having 4 line items so all four line items were displayed. You can select the line number and click green flag to release it.

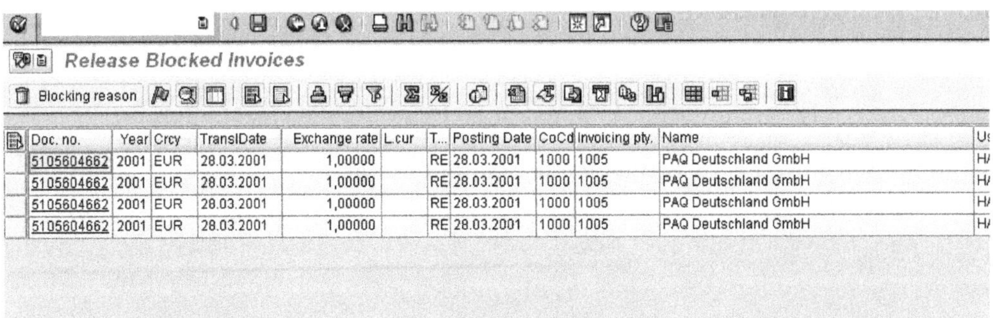

The invoice line will become green, save the document.

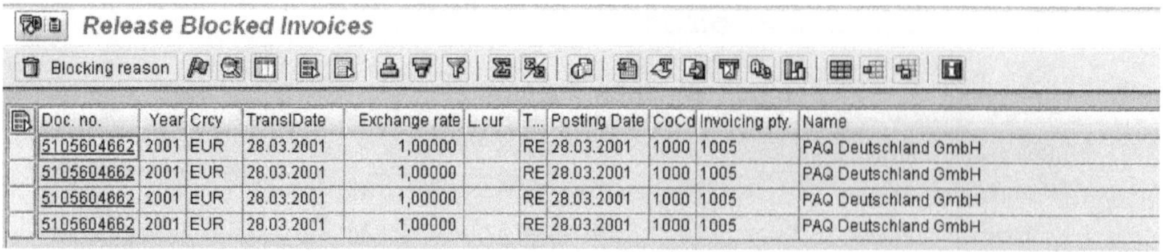

Release Blocked Invoices

Blocking reason

Doc. no.	Year	Crcy	TranslDate	Exchange rate	L.cur	T...	Posting Date	CoCd	Invoicing pty.	Name
5105604662	2001	EUR	28.03.2001	1,00000		RE	28.03.2001	1000	1005	PAQ Deutschland GmbH
5105604662	2001	EUR	28.03.2001	1,00000		RE	28.03.2001	1000	1005	PAQ Deutschland GmbH
5105604662	2001	EUR	28.03.2001	1,00000		RE	28.03.2001	1000	1005	PAQ Deutschland GmbH
5105604662	2001	EUR	28.03.2001	1,00000		RE	28.03.2001	1000	1005	PAQ Deutschland GmbH

Go back to the initial screen of MRBR for invoice release. Now on the initial screen again enter the vendor number and company code and all the selection steps which you had selected in the last step. Execute the process. You will find a message as "There are no blocked invoices that match your selection"

So thus you can see how this invoice block is effective in case of error handling and payment procedure.

Invoice reverse:-

On the document display screen the document will be shown as below. Here you have option of reversing the invoice. This is done if there was wrong entry in any of the field but it was within the allowed limit so the system allowed the document to be posted. But on invoice posting entries have posted to FI and information has been transferred to FI domain. If you reverse the invoice document after invoice post then two documents will have to be reverse without any delay other wise on due date in spite of invoice reverse the vendor will get the payment. So reversal has to be in FI domain also that will be done by finance people.

There are two ways to reverse the invoice posted wrongly or for any other reason. One process is shown in the picture below.

In the invoice entry screen select other invoice.

Find your desired invoice number to be reversed.

Select the document number by entering it.

This will take you to MIR4 screen.

Here you can see invoice reverse icon in red or go to invoice document > reverse.

Here on this screen you have to enter the reason for reversal.

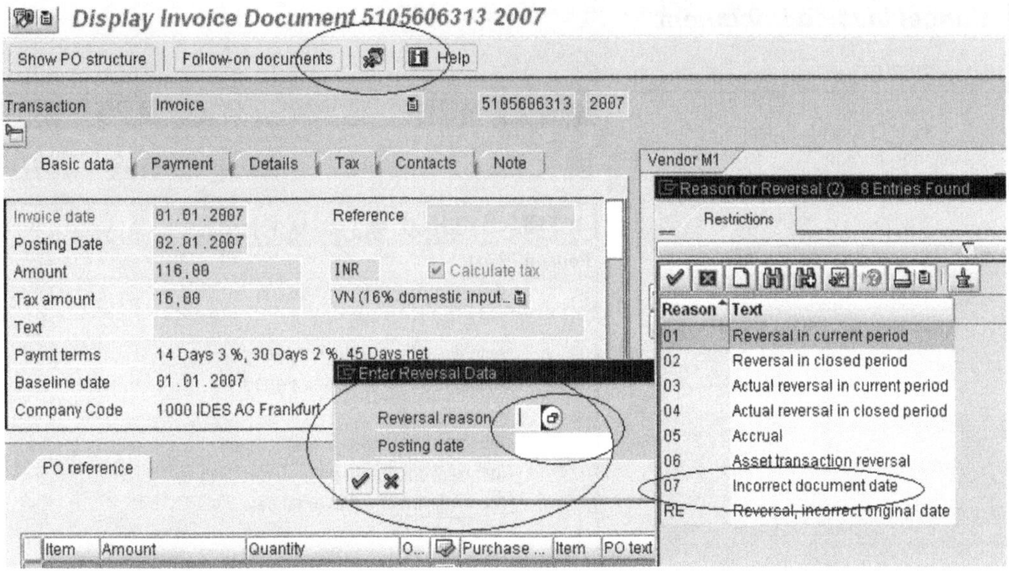

Enter posting date. This date should fall within the allowed posting date interval.

Save the document. When you save the document following message will come and if you double click on the message there will be shown a link to transaction code F-44 to clear the financial document manually in the FI domain. You can see this in the picture below.

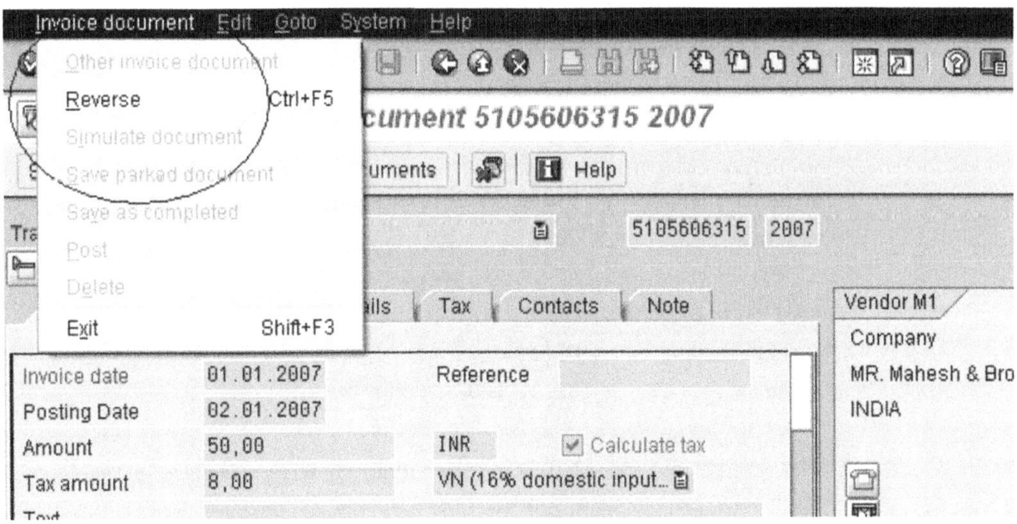

Other process to reverse the invoice document is to follow MR8M transaction.

In this screen select the reason for reversal and posting date.

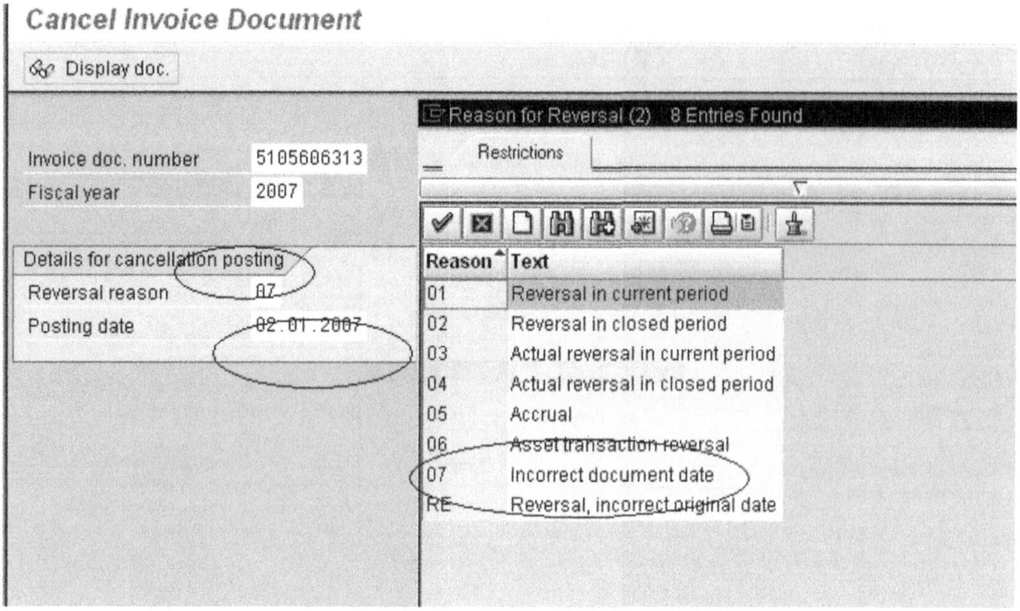

Go to invoice document. Select Reverse or simply save the document. The document will

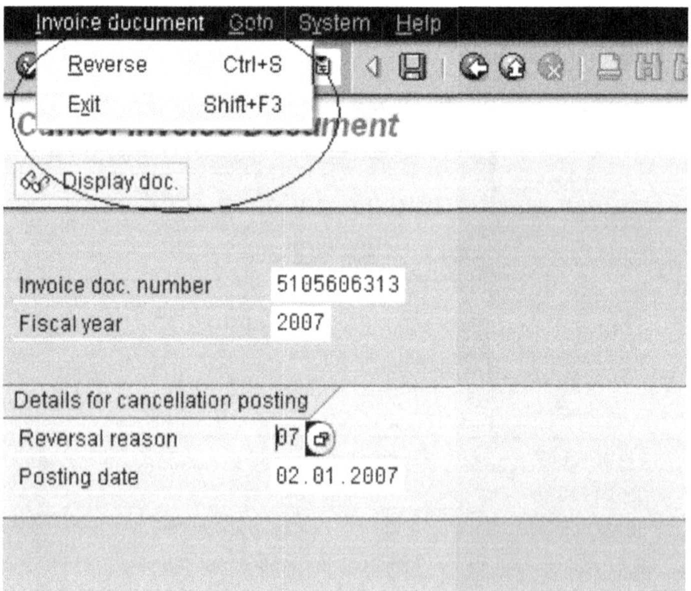

Invoice reverse document:-

If you reverse any invoice document a separate invoice reverse document is created automatically. On the message status bar you can see following message as in the picture below. Please manually clear FI document. Double click on the message. This will take you to display message screen. Here you have to click proceed hyperlinked text. This will take you to F-44. Basically this FI domain's reversal procedure is to be processed by the FI people and as the MM invoice document is reversed they should be informed about the reversal.

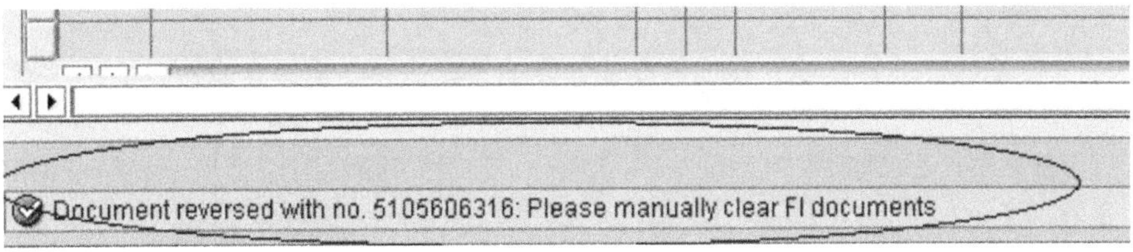

Go to F-44 and reverse the amount of the reversed invoice document. You have to reverse the amount which will appear against the financial document number which was generated while posting the invoice document.

PART-4

RELATED PROCESSINGS

Chapter 15

GOODS ISSUE

Introduction:-

We know that Goods movement is a transaction which results in a change of stock and stock value which affects financial statement. We have also seen in the last chapter about Goods Receipt. In the current chapter we will discuss about Goods issue.

What goods issue is:-

A goods issue (GI) is a goods movement in which material is taken out of inventory stock for material consumption, or sent to a customer. A goods issue leads to a reduction in warehouse stock. Goods issue reduces the stock status in inventory.

Types of goods issue:-

In the Inventory Management system we mainly use following types of goods issue:-

- Withdrawal of material for production purpose
- Withdrawal of material for sampling
- Return deliveries to vendors

- For internal consumption
- Deliveries to vendors without the involvement of the SD Shipping component

Reference document:-

Reference document is a document which is created as per requirement and further based on which processing will happen. In case of goods issue reference document may be any material document, order (which may be production order or any internal order), purchase order, reservation.

Goods Issue with Reference:-

If any document preexists in the process for the determination of requirement out of material document, order (which may be production order or any internal order), purchase order, or reservation, then goods issue may be performed as goods issue with reference.

Goods Issue without Reference

If no reference document exists, as mentioned above because the goods issue is not planned (for example, urgent request of a material), then you can enter the goods issue without any reference.

Menu path:-

Following picture can give you an idea about the menu path for goods movement. As in the last chapter we have seen and the transaction code is MIGO.

Transaction:-

While you enter this in the command line, the goods movement screen will be opened. You can see the screen below. In that screen in the transaction field select Goods issue from the drop down list.

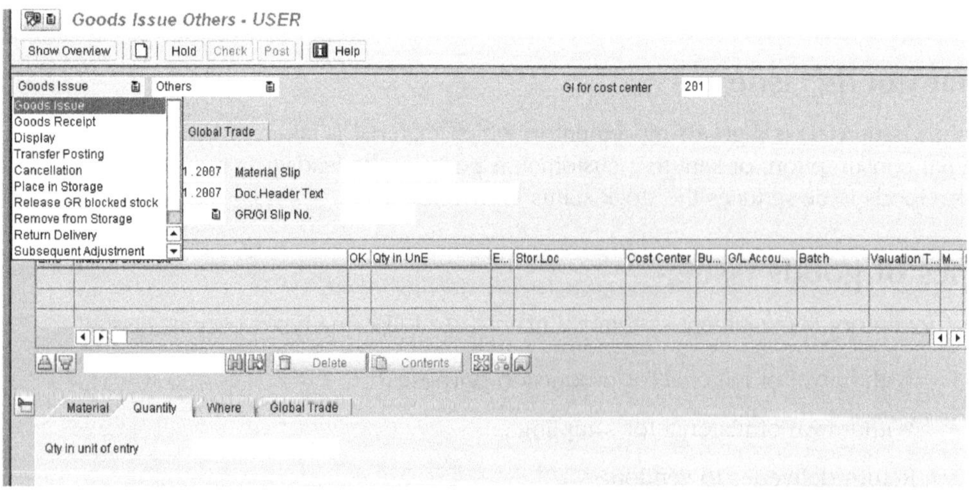

Reference document:-

After this from the reference field select the reference document as against which you wish to do the goods movement. In the case now select others as for without reference document. If you wish to issue goods for reference document then select relevant reference document. You can see this procedure in the picture below.

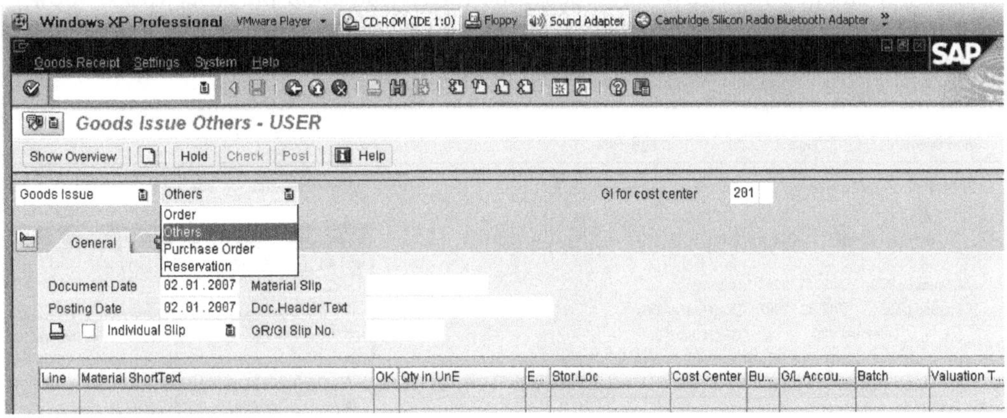

Here you can see how to select others in the reference field.

Posting Date:-

This is the date on which posting for goods movement is done. This date should lie within the allowed posting period.

Document Date:-

This is the date on which this document for goods movement is being done. Normally this date is set as default current date.

Material:-

On the material tab page enter the material number that is to be issued. Then ENTER.

Quantity:-

Enter Quantity of the material that is to be issued to the reason.

Plant:-

In this field enter plant from where you are going to issue the material.

Storage location:-

Enter the storage location from where the goods will be issued.

Movement type:-

Enter the movement type as 201 for goods issue for consumption purpose. This is shown as how it is to be selected. The movement types should be same in the header movement type field and the movement type field on where tab page.

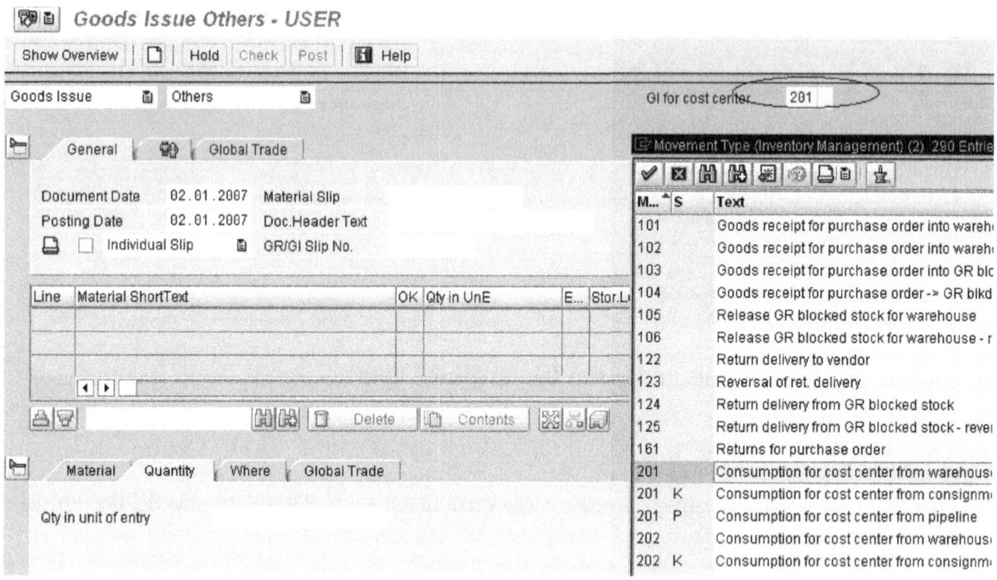

Stock type:-

Apart from this you can also see a field as with the options unrestricted use, Quality inspection and blocked stock. Check that this field should be selected as unrestricted use stock.

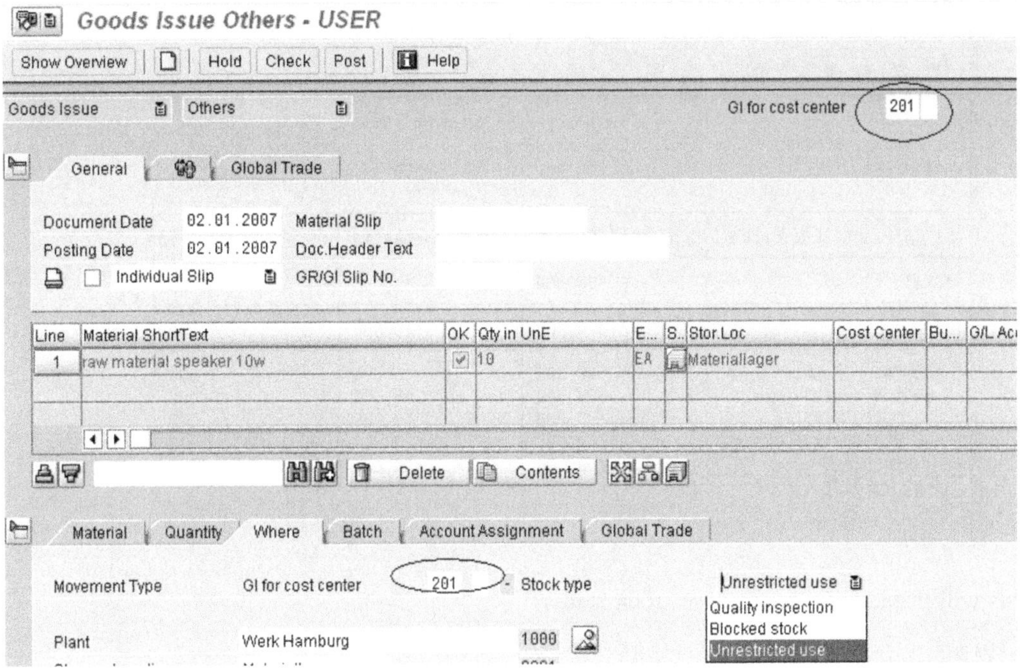

Account assignment:-

On the account assignment tab page select the relevant cost center for which the goods will be issued.

Batch number:-

If batch management is selected for the material then you have to choose the proper batch number from which material is to be issued.

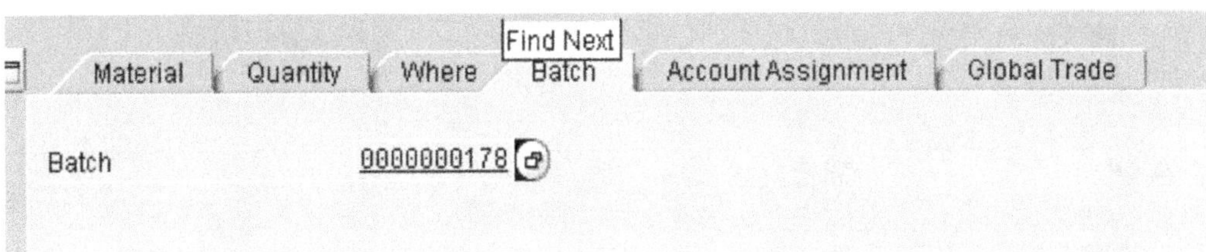

To know the correct batch and stock status you can use the t-code as MMBE.

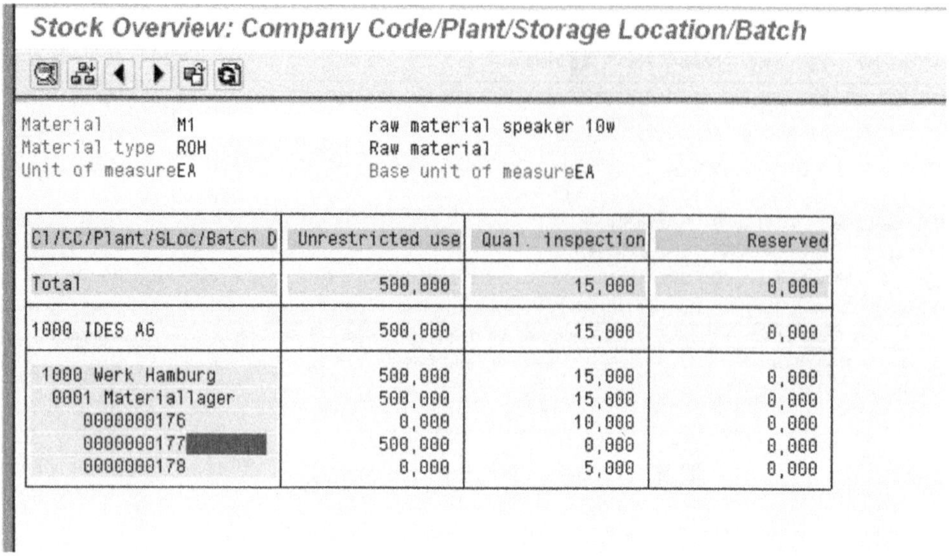

This will display you batch wise stock status.

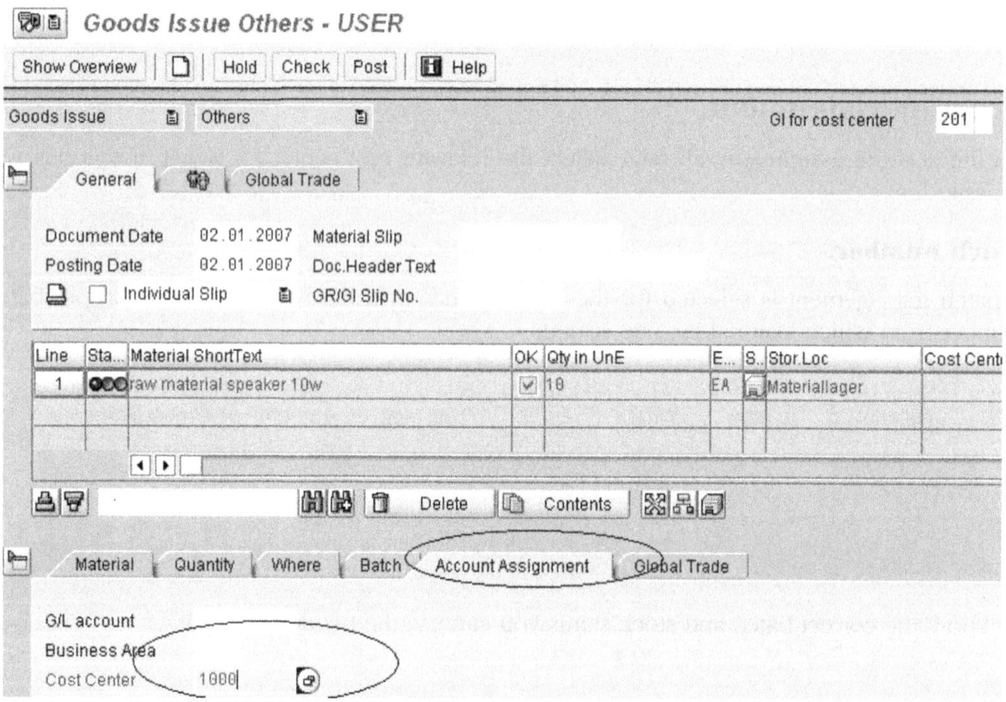

Cost center:-

In account assignment tab page in this field enter cost center as 1000. A cost center is a consumption point where consumption for any specific purpose occurs. It is a cost object which collects costs that we spend.

Press ENTER to confirm the entries.

Check the document by pressing Check entries (F7).

If message is like Document is ok then post the document shift+F11

A document number with all these information will be generated.

Display:-

From transaction field now select Display. Last material document number will be shown. If not, you can find the relevant material document to five from the icon search for material document.

In this screen you can see that after post system has traced the relevant and applicable G/L account as 400000, business area as 9900, and profit center as 1402. System could find this information as because it has been already configured in customization.

FI document:-

Go to Doc info tab page and press FI documents. Here you will be able to see the transaction amount detail which has updated the values in the Finance department.

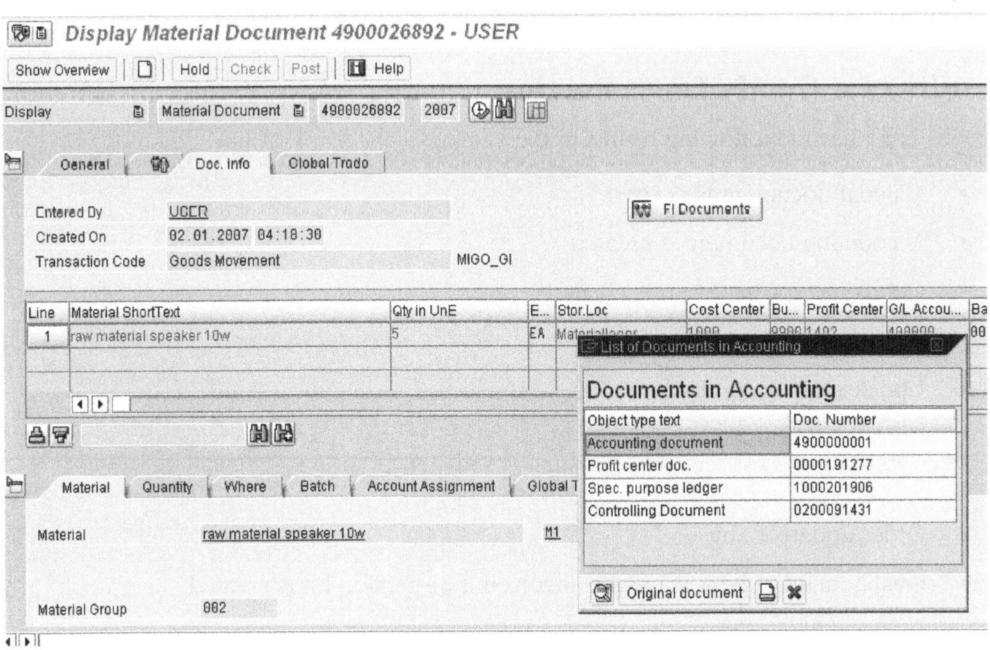

Here you can see multiple FI documents.

So now you know what goods issue is and how it may be done. If some other goods issue without reference you can select other movement types. Some of them are enlisted below.

Entry of Account Assignment Data

MvT	For Consumption in	Data to be entered
201	Cost center	Cost center
221	Project	WBS element/networks
231	Sales order	Sales order no., sales order item
241	Asset	Main asset number, asset sub-number
251	Sales	Cost center
261	Order	Order number
281	Network	Network or operation
291	All account assignments	Any account assignment

Now if you need to issue goods for sampling purpose then from the following picture you can get an idea about this movement and movement type.

With all the movement types the odd numbers of movement type are for the movements and the even movement types are for the reverse of the documents posted.

Results of a Goods Issue Posting

A goods issue has the following results in the system:-

- Material document is created
- Accounting document is created
- Goods receipt/issue slip is created
- Stock is updated
- Updates G/L accounts
- Consumption updates
- Reservation updates if any
- Order update if any.
- Quality management team gets involved if inspection lot is created

Creation of a Material Document

After any goods movement at least one material document is created automatically. This can not be changed but only canceled or reversed. This is a proof of the goods movement.

Creation of an Accounting Document

Along with the material document creation system also creates an accounting document. This document contains amount posting related information.

Creation of a Goods Receipt/Issue Slip

After entering goods issue transaction you can also print this document as goods issue slip.

Update

On creation of goods issue document the following stocks are reduced by the issued quantity:

- Total valuated stock
- Unrestricted-use stock
- Reserved stock if the goods issue is entered with reference to a reservation or an order.

Update of G/L Accounts

When the goods issue is posted, the system automatically creates posting lines on the accounts of the accounting system.

Consumption Update

You can also see the consumption updated in the Material Master itself. For this follow the following process to see the consumption tracking.

Go to material master display screen by entering transaction code MM03.

Enter material number.

Select plant stock and storage location stock views only.

Enter organization structure as plant 1000 and storage location 0001.

In the plant stock view following screen and tab page will be shown.

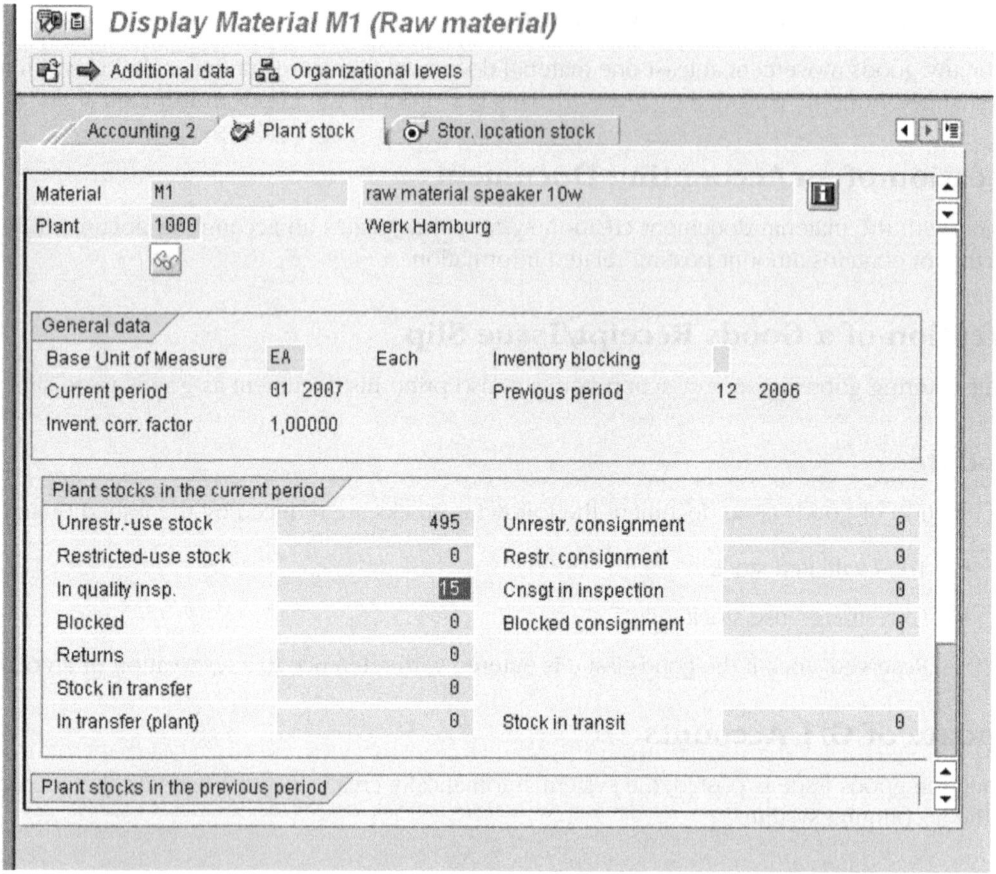

On this screen select additional data icon field. This will take you to the following screen.

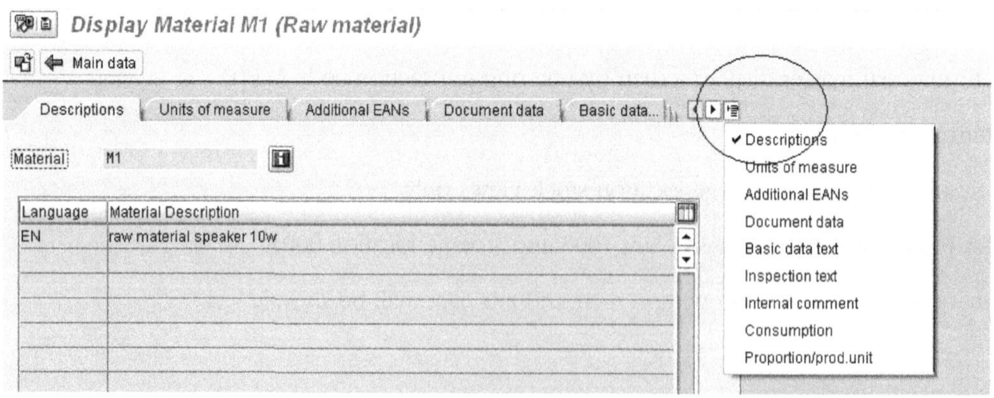

In Consumption tab page you scroll down the items, this will show you the total stock consumed.

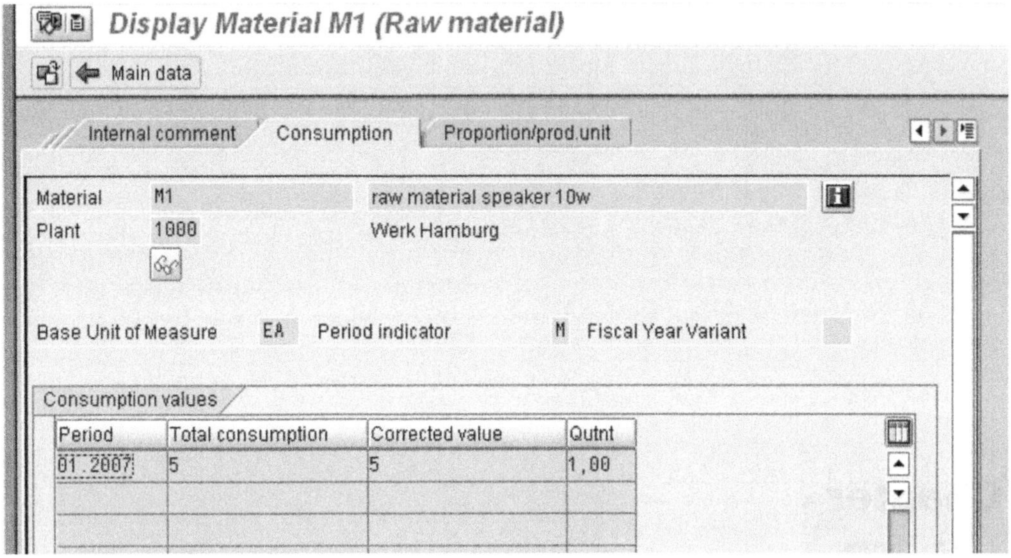

On this screen select consumption tab page. Here you can see the total goods issued for consumption purpose.

This consumption statistics are used by MRP for forecasting. In this process planned and unplanned withdrawals are taken into account.

If the withdrawal is planned, total consumption is updated. If the withdrawal is unplanned, both total consumption and unplanned consumption are updated.

The system does not update the consumption statistics in the material master record, if you post goods movements using the special stock types Sales order stock and Project stock.

Reservation Update

If any goods issue is performed with reference to a reservation or a sales order, the quantity withdrawn is updated in the reservation item. When the total reservation quantity has been withdrawn or when the final issue indicator is set manually at goods issue the reservation item is completed.

Order Update

If goods are issued with reference to an order, then the quantities withdrawn for the components are updated in the order.

Update in Other Applications

If goods are issued for consumption purpose then respective consumption center and accounts are updated by the value consumed.

Chapter 16

TRANSFER POSTING AND STOCK TRANSFER

Stock Transfer:-

This component of SAP Materials Management is used to record physical movement of stock. It may be of following types.

- **Within Same company code**
  - o Stock transfer Storage location to storage location (same plant)
    - One step procedure
    - Two step procedure
  - o Stock transfer plant to plant or Storage location to storage location (from one plant to another plant)
    - One step procedure
    - Two step procedure
- One Company code to another company code
  - o Stock transfer Storage location to storage location (different plant)

        - One step procedure
        - Two step procedure
    - o Stock transfer plant to plant or Storage location to storage location (from one plant to another plant)
        - One step procedure
        - Two step procedure

Transfer Posting:-

Assume an example where you have enough stock at plant 1000's storage location and now due to some reason you have a requirement at plant 1200's storage location. So in this case you have two options, one is that you will procure extra stock only for storage location 1200 from any external vendor or you have another choice to get that usable stock from plant 1000. In this kind of business process you need to use the process of transfer posting.

In transfer posting physical movement of material stock may or may not happen. Or only the status of the material may change. It usually refers to a change in a material's stock (for example, release from quality inspection, accepting consignment material). The transfer posting usually changes in stock type, batch number, or material number.

Stock Transfer Procedures

There are three different procedures to transfer stock.

- Stock transfer via stock transfer posting using the one-step procedure
- Stock transfer via stock transfer posting using the two-step procedure
- Stock transfer using stock transport order

Prerequisites:-

You have to create material within multiple organization levels in which you will do the movements.

- Create material for plant 1000 & storage location 0001
- Create material for plant 1000 & storage location 0002
- Create material for plant 1200 & storage location 0001

All these plants and storage locations should be assigned in a single company code because transfer posting will be done within a single company code.

Transaction code:-

You can use MIGO or MB1B to perform transfer posting. Following screen will come for transfer posting.

If you do transfer posting in MIGO then following screen will appear.

As reference document you can also select either "others", any "material document" or "reservation".

If you do transfer posting in MB1B then following screen will appear.

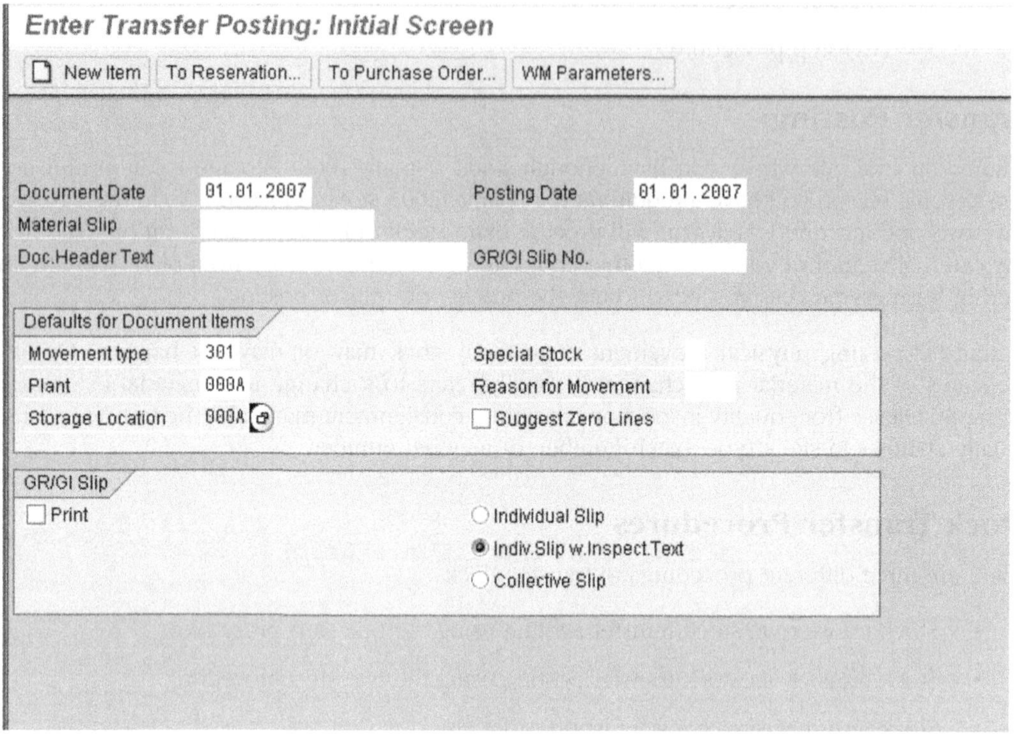

Enter movement type for respective transfer posting nature. For example:-

301 for transfer posting plant to plant (one step)

303 for transfer posting plant to plant (remove from storage)

305 for transfer posting plant to plant (place in storage)

309 for transfer posting material to material

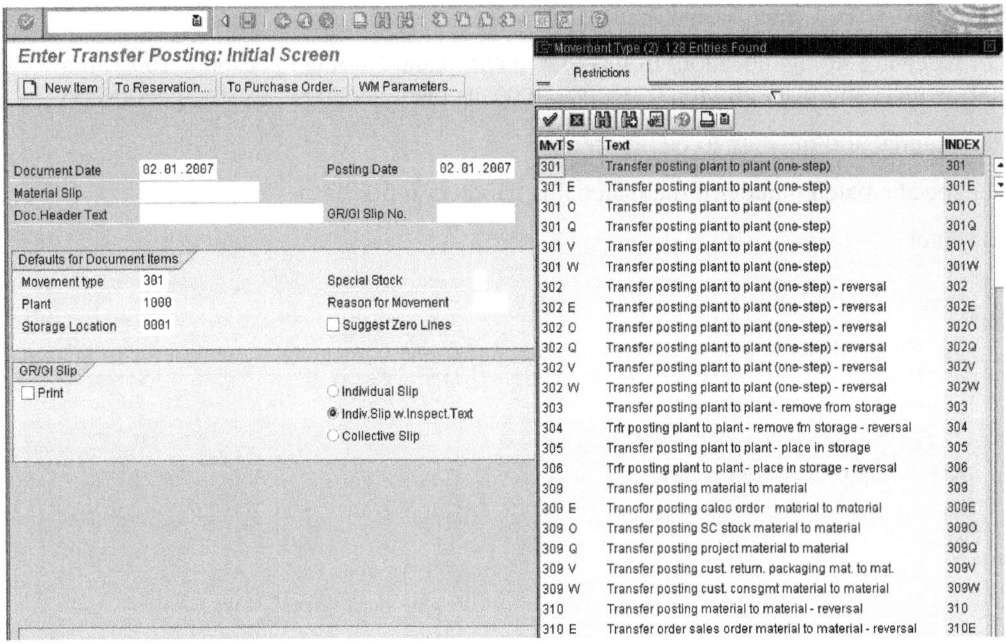

Enter plant and storage location.

Enter correct posting date.

Press ENTER.

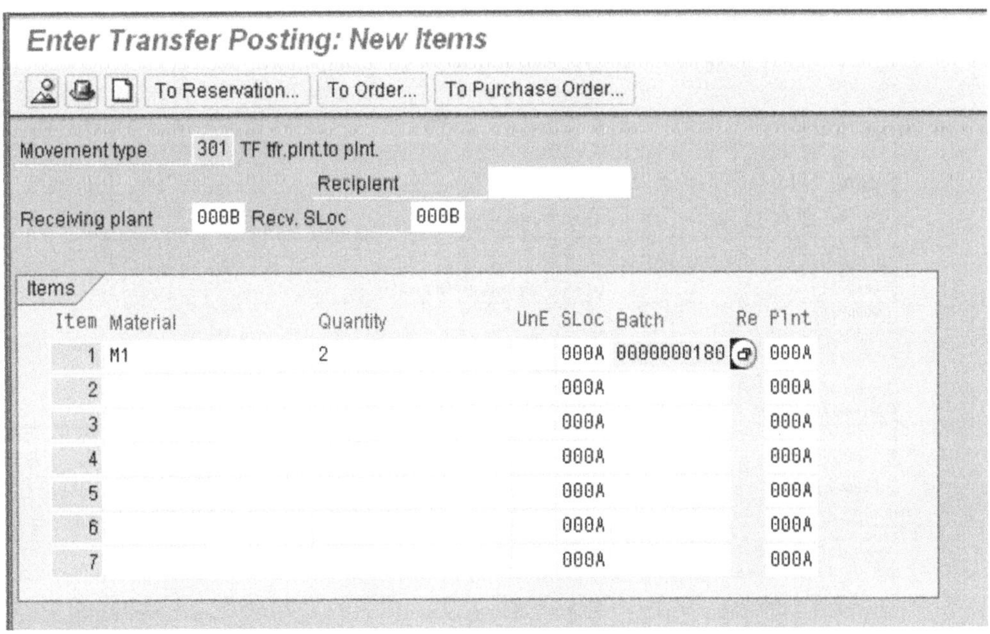

On the next screen enter receiving plant.

Enter receiving storage location. In place of '000B' plant 2 storage Location. You can also use '1200' as receiving plant and for '000A' use '1000' as plant and '0001' as storage location.

Enter material and quantity to be transferred.

Enter specific batch number if the material is handled in batches.

Press enter.

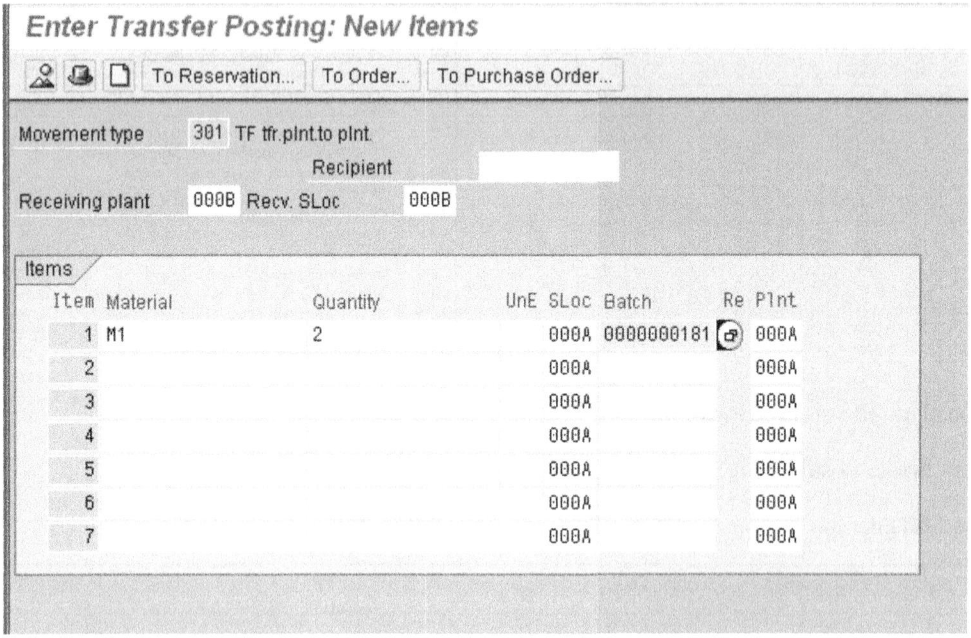

Enter multiple times

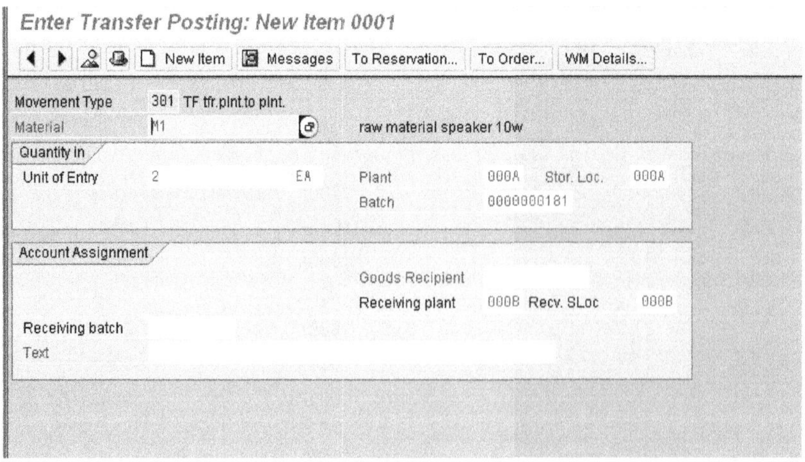

Save the document.

Display Material document of transfer posting

Choose t code MB1B.

Select display option from dropdown menu of Transfer Posting.

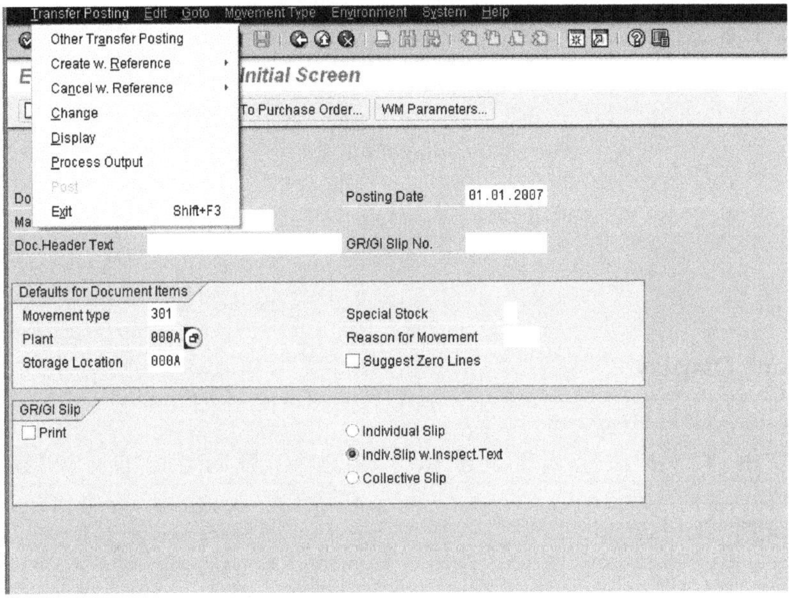

Select the proper document number of find and enter document number of transfer posting.

Enter.

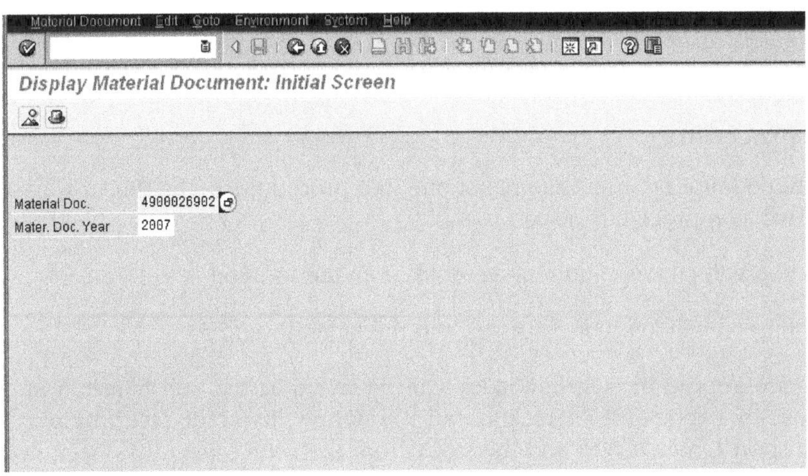

If you press accounting document then following screen will be shown.

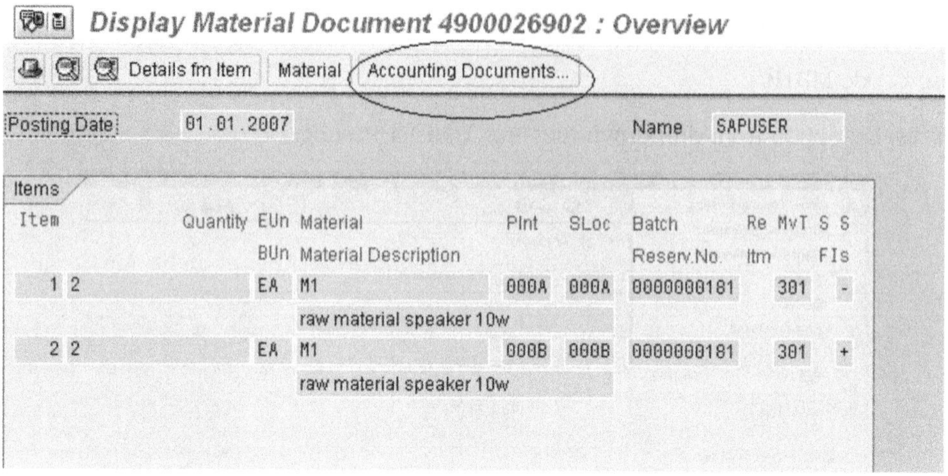

FI Document Display

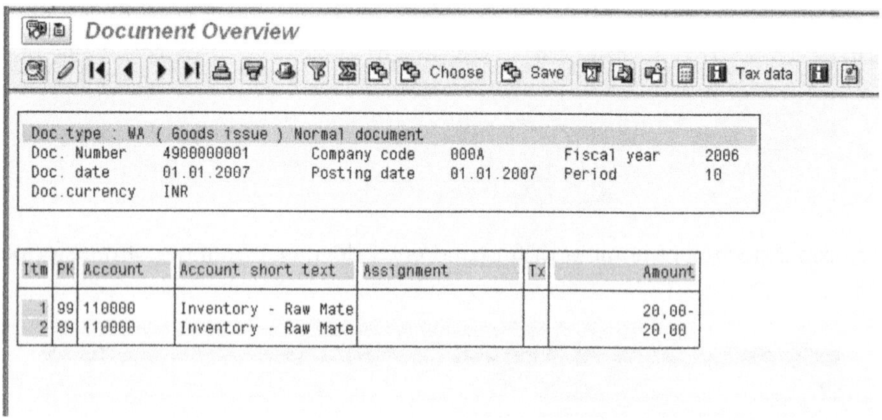

Two step procedure

Above mentioned process is an example of one step procedure. In the similar way you can also perform in two step procedure also.

In first step you will pick up and remove stock from the location.

In second step you will keep or place stock in the target location.

Until stocks are kept in the location stock will be called as stock in transit. You can see the stock in transit by t code MB5T (Stock in transit) but only if you the receiving plant has issued a Stock Transport Order (STO), and the stock from the source plant has been issued against this STO document. You can see the stock status in MBE stock over view. There you will have to double click in the target location for placement.

MIGO:-

Same transaction you can also do in MIGO transaction also. Effect and use is the same only the process is different.

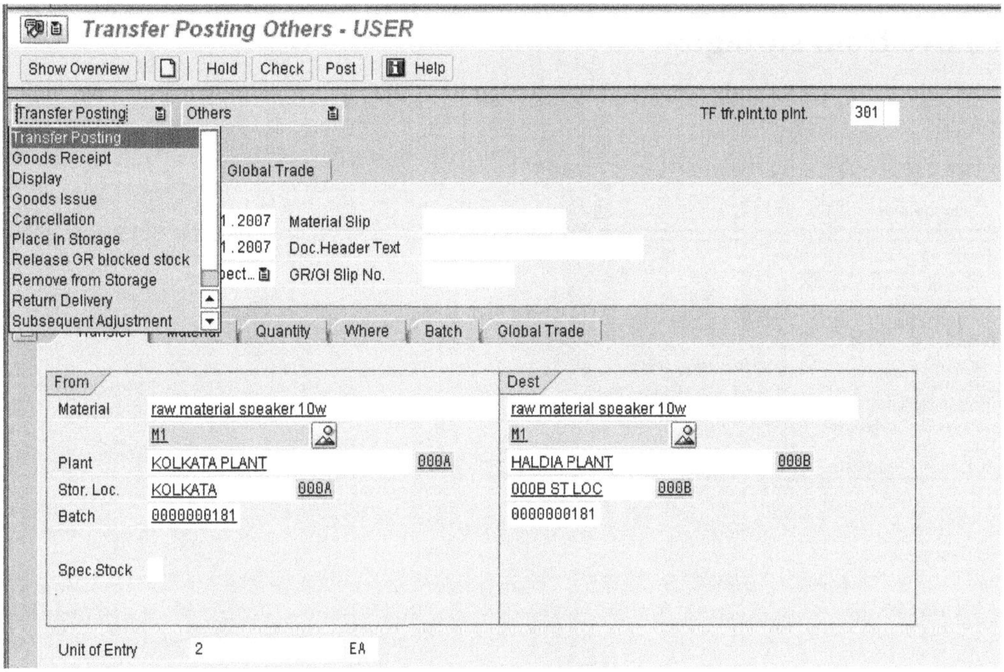

As you can see that in the transaction drop down you can select transfer posting for one step procedure and relevant movement type. You can see this in the picture blow.

Storage location to storage location (within plant):-

In this procedure you can see that the target plant is kept in display mode. See in the picture below.

Enter material, plant, source storage location on the left and target storage location on the right and post the document after check.

If in display document you check FI document then you will not find any account document.

Storage location to storage location (one plant to different plant):-

In this procedure you have to select movement type 301 for transfer posting plant to plant.

Two step procedure for one plant to another plant:-

In two step procedure 1st you have to pick stocks from one plant or storage location and then put that in the target plant and storage location.

Screen will change as per your selected movement type.

Remove from storage:-

If you select the transaction remove from storage then the option of movement types will be reduced.

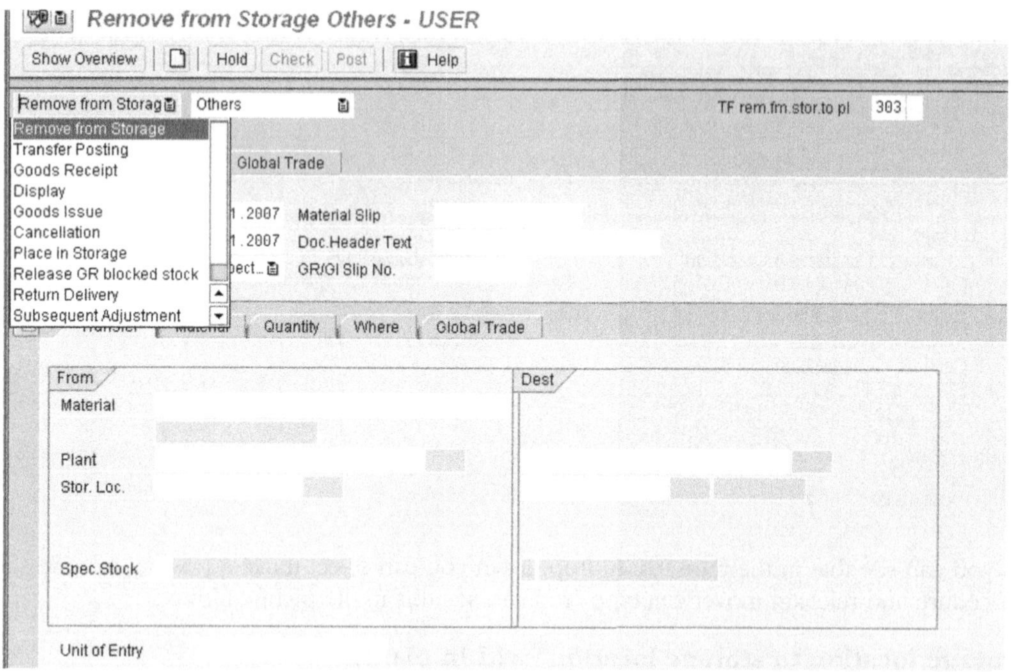

As in case of removing from storage location from plant to plant the movement types are limited and if you select 303 then as destination system will ask only the destination plant name and not any storage location name.

You have to put name of the destination storage location when you will place in storage. With respect the any material document or any stock in transit material that will reach to the destination storage location

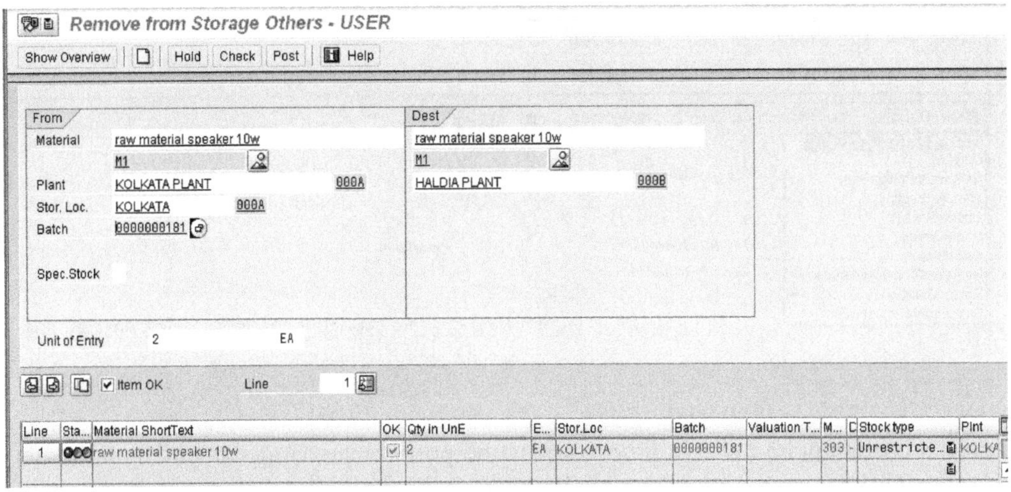

In this removal step fill all the entries and post the document after checking it. Note if the material is a subject to be maintained in batches then batch number is to be assigned and that too only of issuing plant and not of receiving plant.

In display document you will material document and FI document for this transaction.

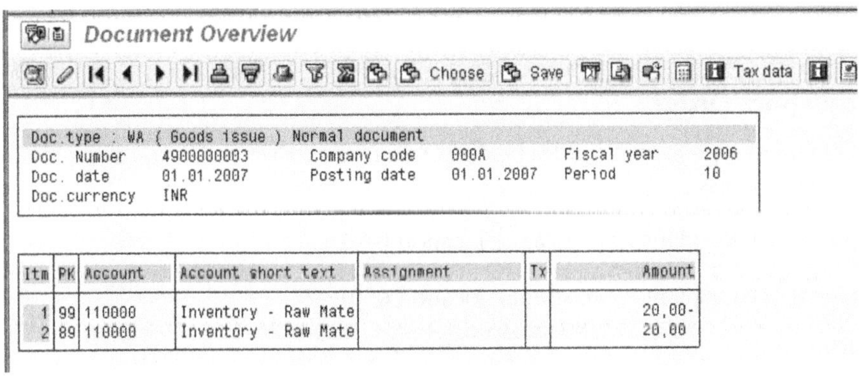

Place in storage:-

In this step select transaction place in storage and reference document as material document. Change any quantity if need to change. This time system may ask you to enter storage location but system will automatically input batch number for the transaction.

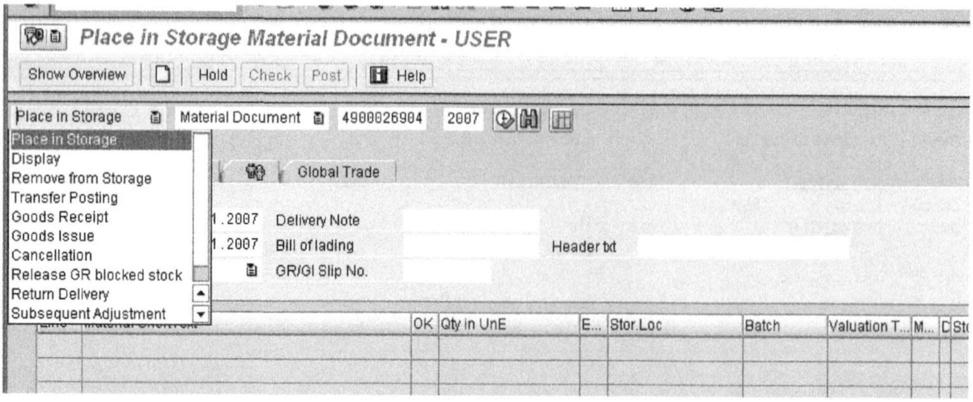

Check the document and post it. If you display the posted material document, then there will not be any FI document as no FI posting happens in the 2nd step.

Stock in transit:-

This stock status is displayed if the transfer posting is being done through any stock transport order (STO).

To follow this process you have to create a stock transport order. You can follow the steps as mentioned below.

Stock Transport Order

This is a document type for with order type STO. You can follow following steps to completely understand the process.

Create material M1 for plant 1000, storage location 0001

Create material M1 for plant 1200, storage location 0001

Procure material initially for plant 1000 and 0001storate location in MIGO

Goods receipt – others – movement type (561)

Check stock in MMBE for plant 100, storage location 0001 and plant 1200, storage location 0001.

Create Purchase order ME21N

Order type UB

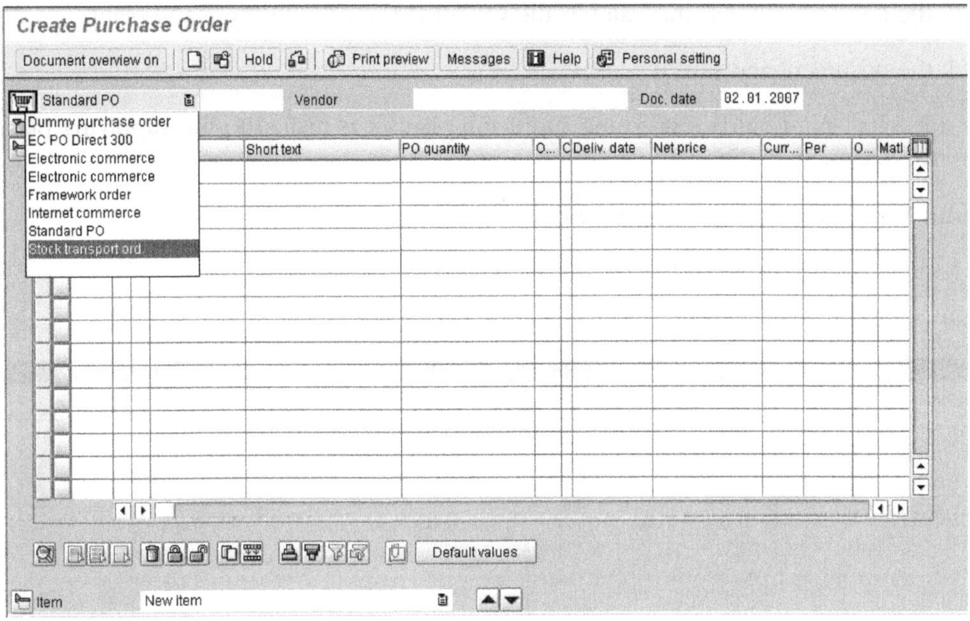

In this purchase order type you need to enter the supplying plant from where material will be procured in the field vendor.

Check item category is U for stock transfer.

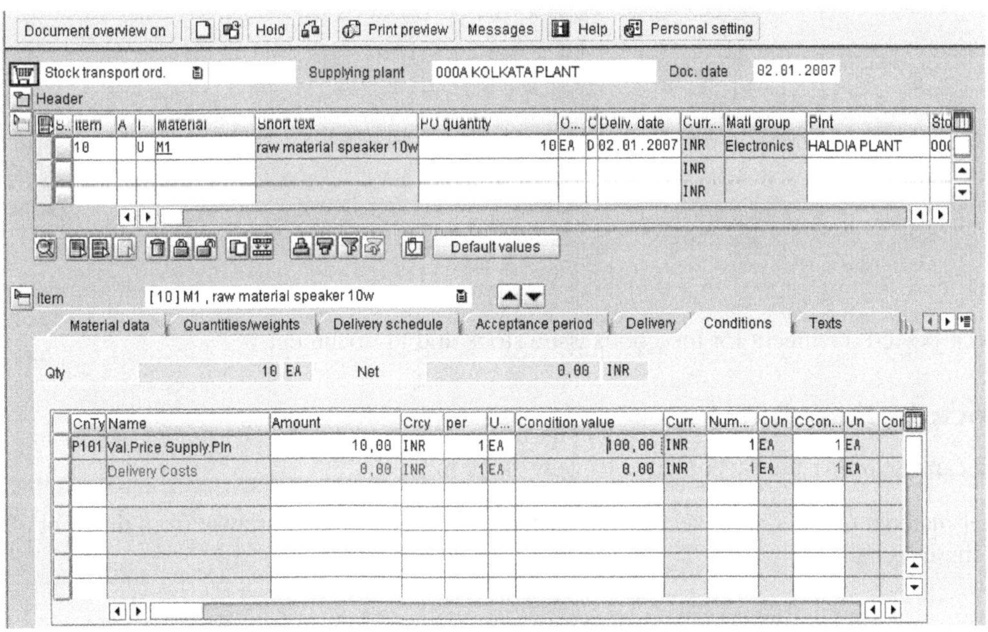

Check the item condition as this value is the valuation price of the supplying plant.

Check the document and save it.

This document print out is sent to the supplying plant or is mailed to the supplying plant as reference document.

Goods Issue for Stock transport order:-

The supplying plant's end user issues goods against this document.

MIGO – Stock Transport Order – movement type 351

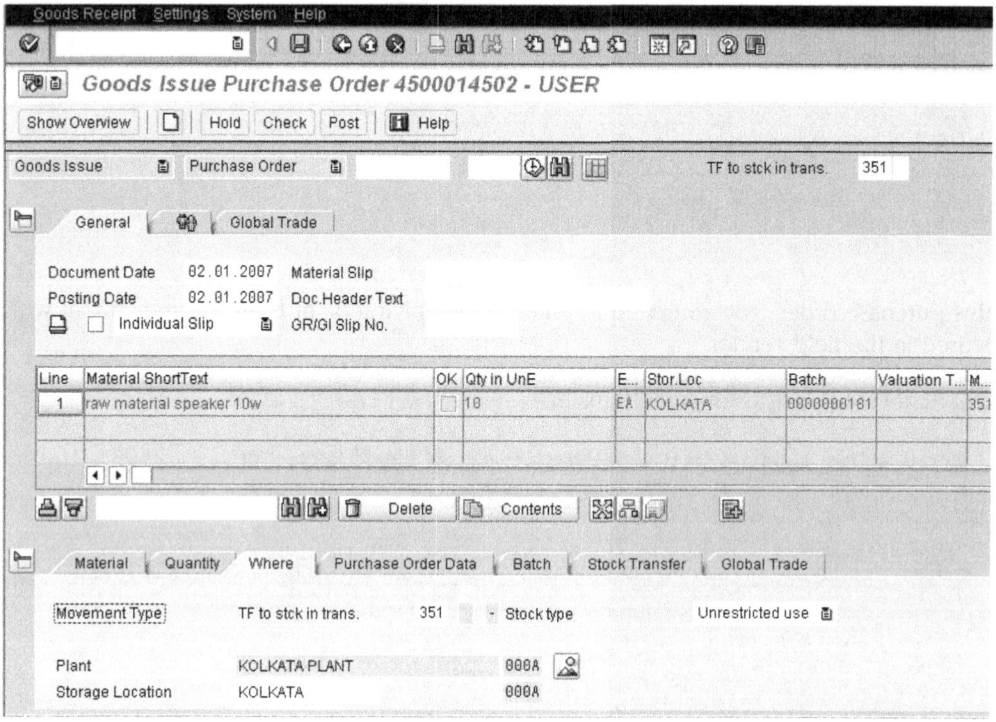

Check posted document for the goods issue stock and FI document.

Stock in Transit:-

You can use MB5T transaction code to view stock in transit.

Enter material number and execute. This will display all the stock in transit from different plant for the material.

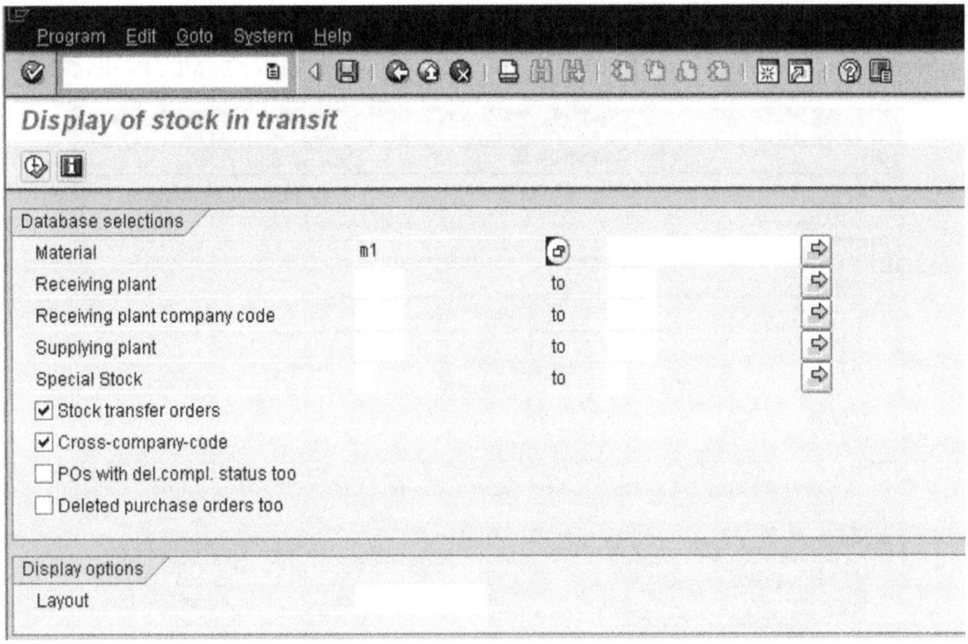

Goods Receipt at Receiving Plant against Stock Transport Order

While goods receipt do just the normal good receiving process in MIGO transaction code. You can see this process in the picture below.

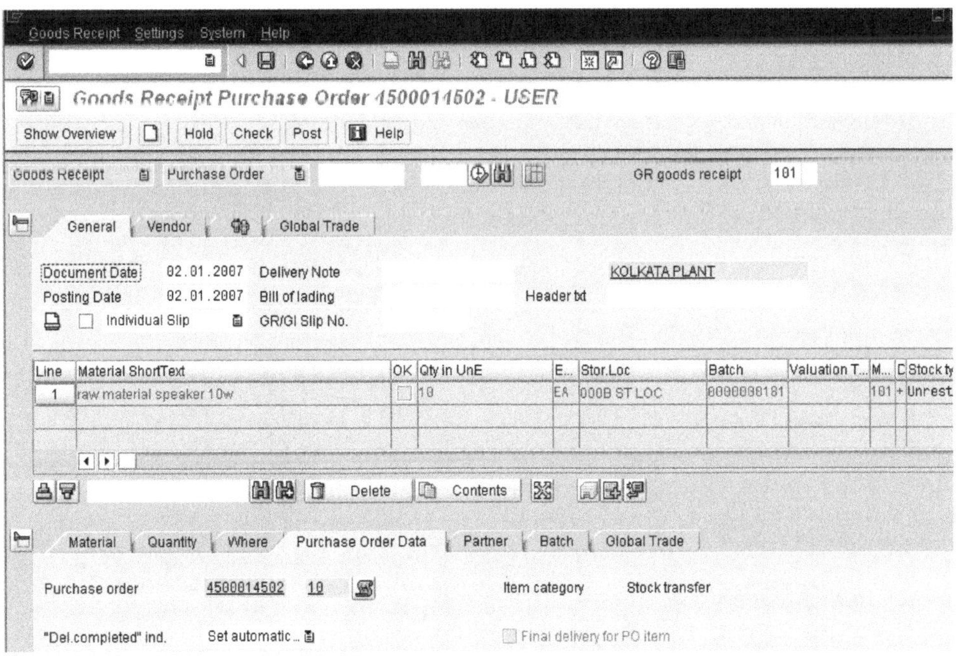

Purchase order history:-

You can also see purchase order history for the stock transport order in ME23N item details.

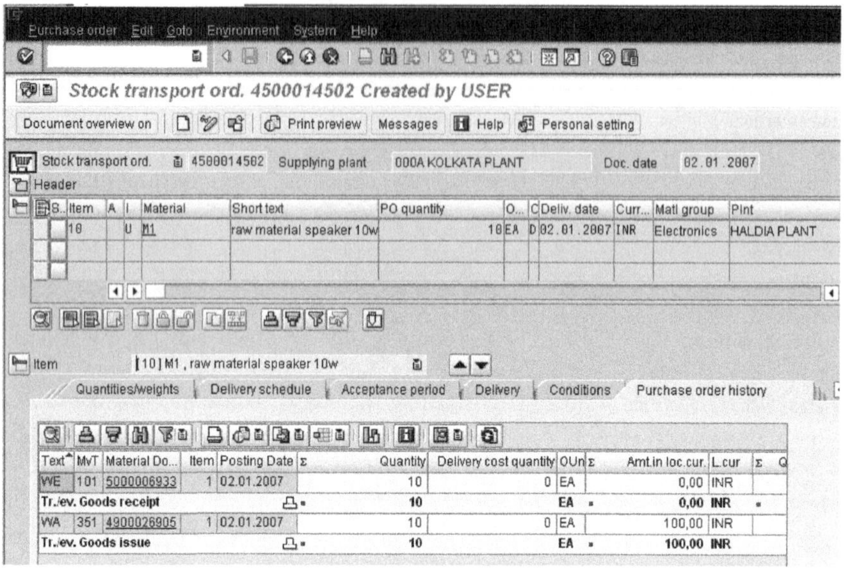

Stock overview:-

Check stock status in different plants after goods movements.

Chapter

17

REQUEST FOR QUOTATION

Introduction

It is a purchasing document in an invitation form. This contains information about material that buyer is willing to procure. It is sent to the vendor by the purchase department to know the willingness and potentiality of the vendor. Request is made through this invitation to the vendor to submit a quotation (bid) for the supply of materials or performance of services.

Think about an example. You are a buyer willing to procure a material of a quantity 1000 pieces. You know that in the market there is more than one vendor who can supply the material. But there are possibility that price of the material may be same or vary from vendor to vendor. So you are willing to ask for price and conditions first. Then you need to compare for best possible price taking all the condition and discount factors into account. Based on comparison system will prompt for the best potential vendor who should be awarded with the purchase order. So this is the whole process of request for quotation and quotation processing.

We will proceed with a process flow of procurement to understand the use and importance of these purchasing documents.

Create Material:-

Create material which you are willing to procure. This is to be created in a normal way with all the relevant basic details.

Create Vendor:-

Create vendor from whom you are going to procure the material. This is to be created in a normal way with all the relevant basic details. In the current processing you will have to create vendor master data for more than 1 vendor. So create vendor master record for 3 vendors.

Create Purchasing Info Record:-

Create purchasing info record for each vendor who is in the marked dealing in that material and from whom you might be willing to procure the material. In the current case this master data maintenance is not a compulsory but an optional one. This is optional because info if you do not maintain purchasing info record initially then it will be created automatically during the process.

Create source list:-

This master data will have a list of all the vendors who are in the market and from whom you can procure the material. One thing is to be noted that not a single vendor line item should be checked for Fixed vendor or Blocked vendor. This is as because if you check fixed vendor in source list then vendor will be adopted in the purchase requisition automatically. If blocked vendor is the set status in the source list then that vendor will not be able to participate in the procurement process. So take a note of these things.

Create Purchase Requisition:-

Create purchase requisition as a normal process with a required quantity of 1000 pieces. Do not assign any vendor in the purchase requisition.

Create Request for Quotation:-

In the process below we will make entry without reference to purchase requisition

For RFQ creation you can follow the following menu path as shown in the picture below. Or alternatively you can enter ME41 as transaction code in the command line.

Create RFQ transaction's initial screen will look something like as in the picture below.

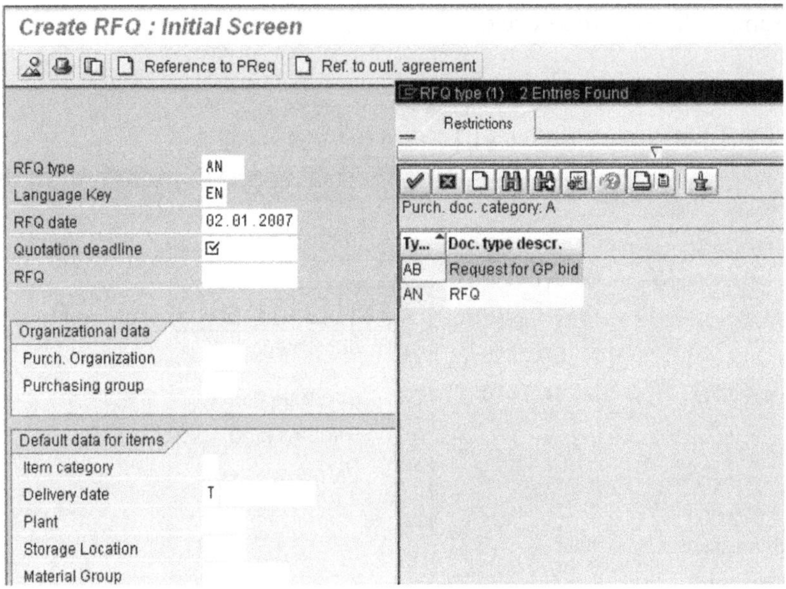

RFQ type:-

In the picture above you can see RFQ type as AB for biding, AN for Request for quotation document.

RFQ Date:-

This is a default current date of the system that you will be working on.

Quotation Dead line Date:-

Enter this date as a date within which you wish all your vendors should submit their offer in the quotation form to you for further processing.

Purchase Organization:-

Enter purchase organization as 1000.

Purchase Group:-

Enter purchase group as 000.

Delivery date:-

This is the date on or within which you wish your vendor should supply you the materials procured.

Plant:-

Check that plant is already pre-selected.

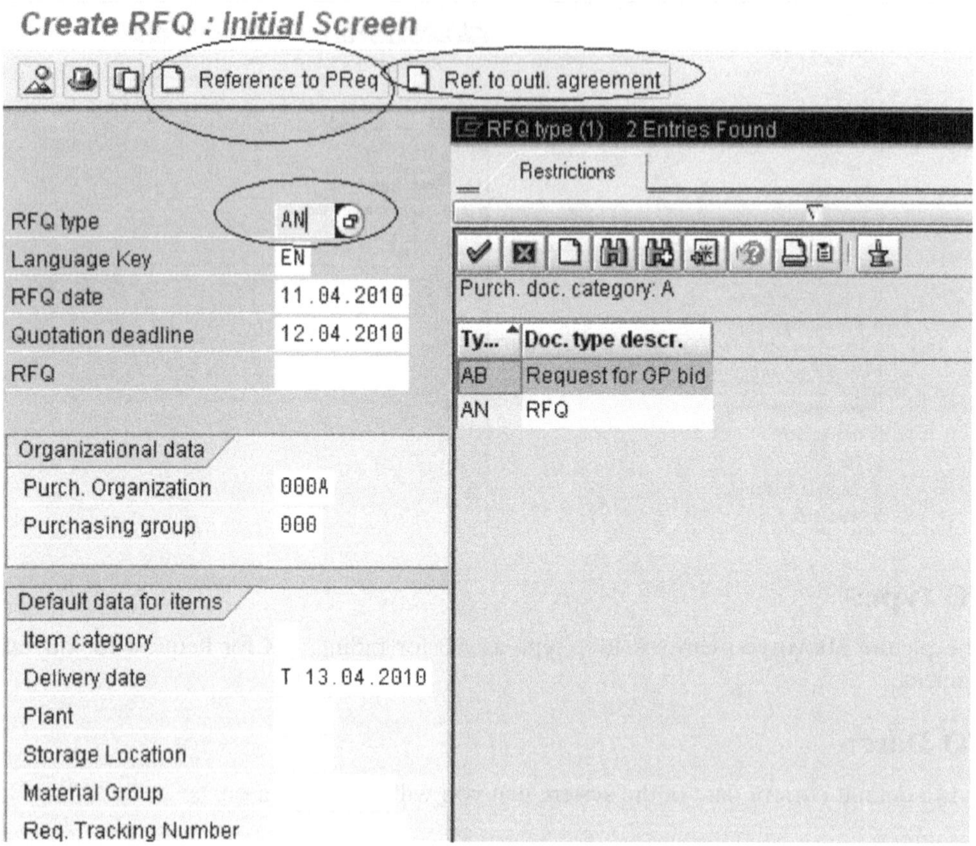

On pressing Enter you will get inside of this document as below.

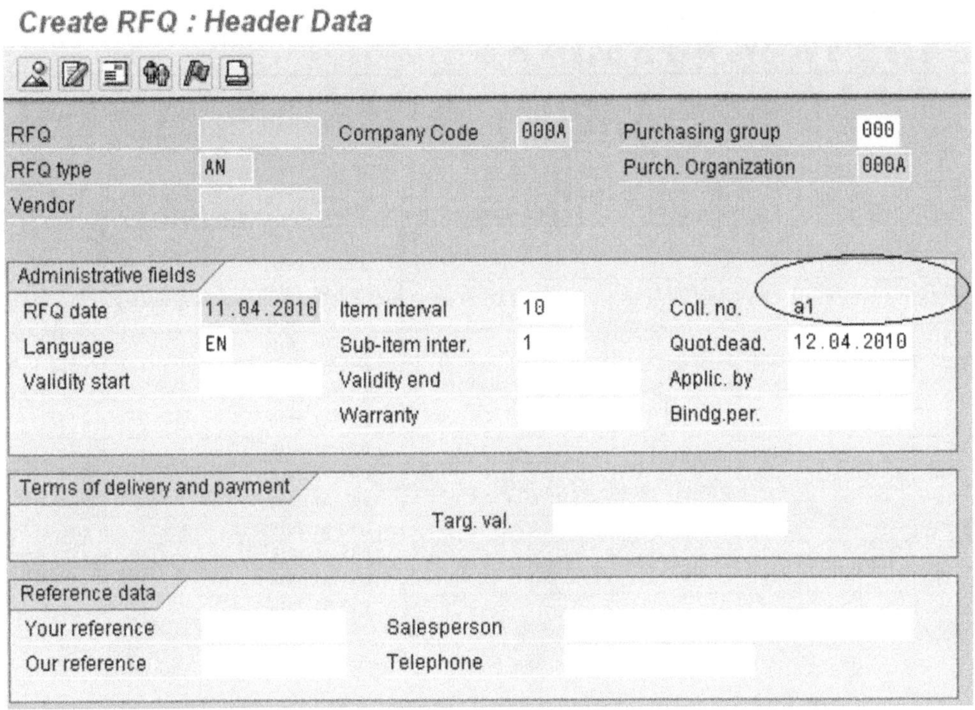

Coll. number (Collective number):-

On this screen you will have to enter Coll. number. This is a number which bundles all similar requests for quotation documents which should be taken into account for one particular processing. This is just a kind of grouping process. If collective number is assigned with the RFQ then it will become possible to list and process all the individual RFQ /inquiries that are grouped under this number.

Item overview:-

Select item overview field as on the screen you can see on the header data screen. Here enter material and required quantity in the relevant field.

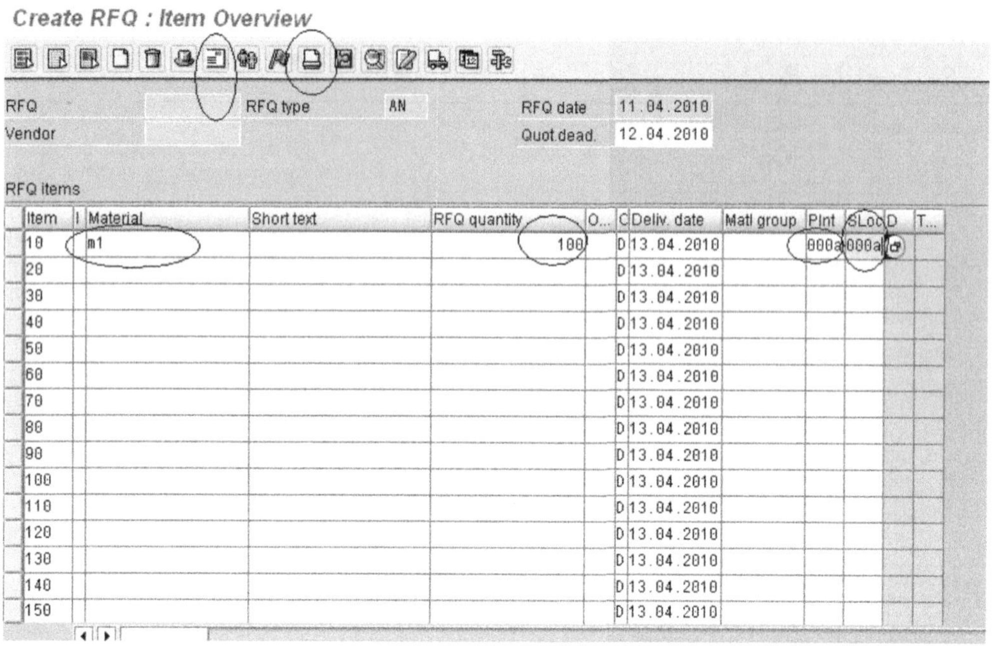

Vendor number:-

On this item overview screen select Vendor Address. Here enter vendor number as A in this processing. You can see this in the picture below.

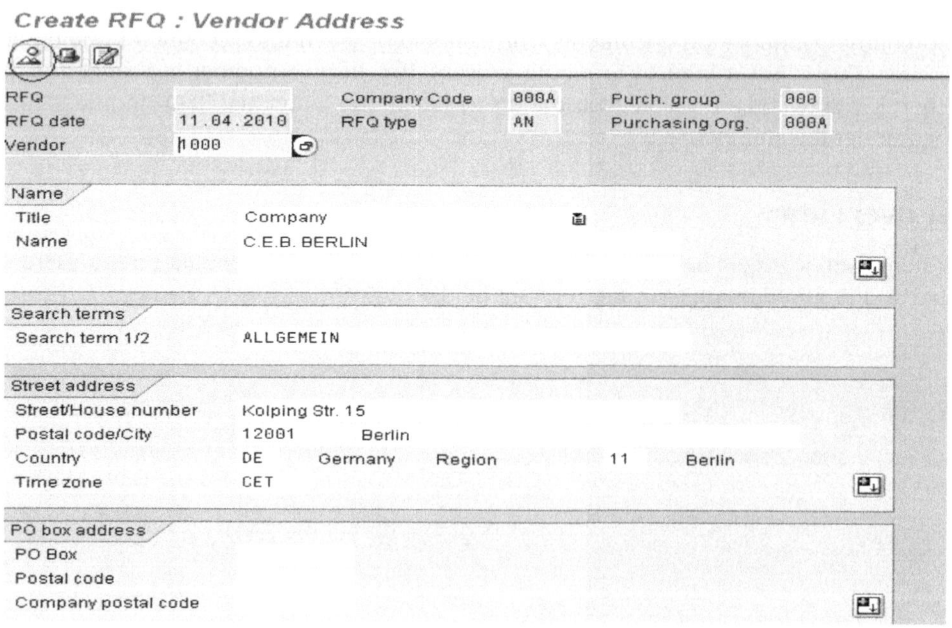

Again go back to overview tab page. Here select messages (Shift+F1)

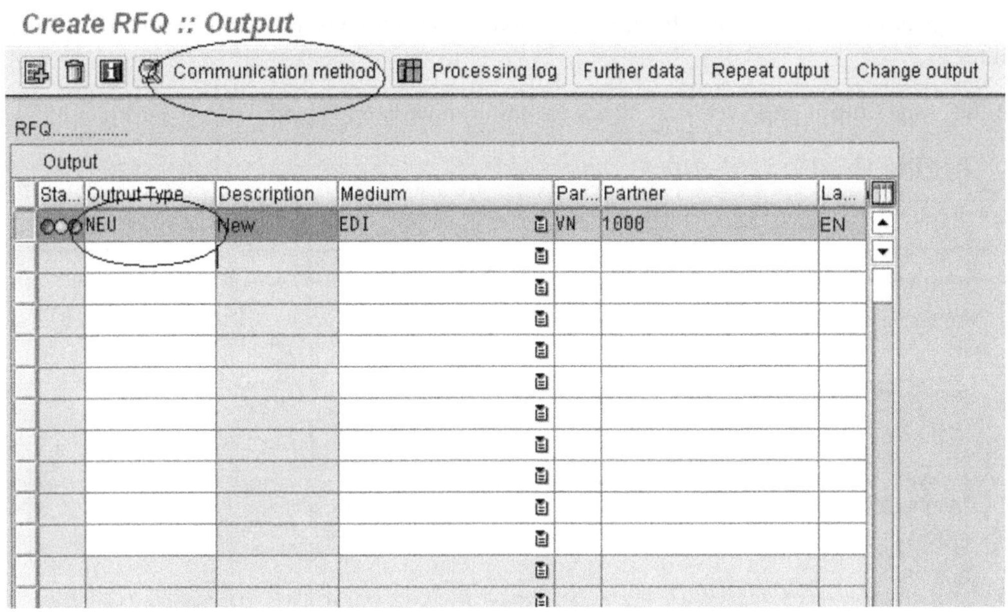

On pressing this option following screen will come. Here enter NEU in the output type field. This setting is required for input as to get printout of the documents.

Select the line and click on communication method.

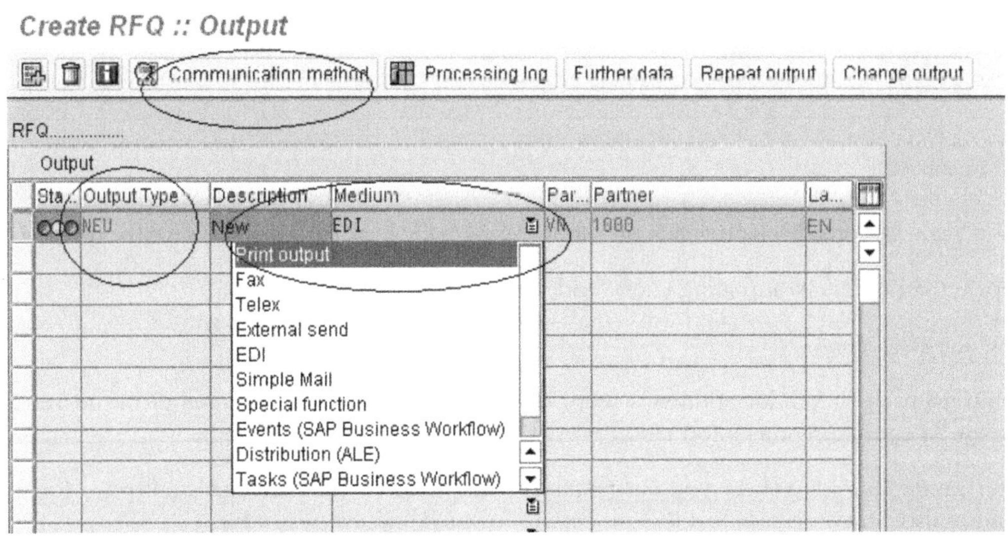

In medium select print output.

After this select the line item and go to communication method.

Here logical destination. Enter from search option A000 for virtual printer or LP01 as virtual printer.

On the same output page you can check for print immediately check box.

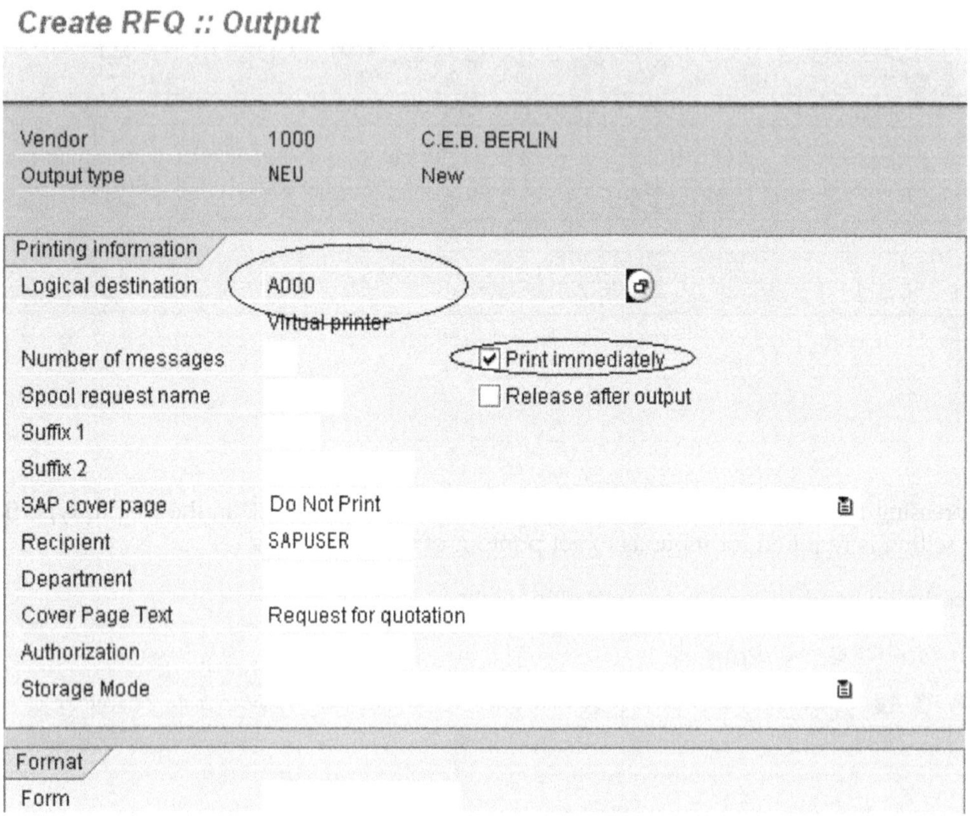

Then again go back, back and click on vendor icon on the header menu and save the document.

Repeat the process by inputting each vendor's number

Save the document.

Again go back to Vendor address screen. Here you can enter vendor number in the vendor screen. After entering this information press ENTER and save the document.

After saving this RFQ sheet you can enter another vendor's number and again save for that vendor also. So you can repeat this procedure for each and every vendor.

Print RFQ:-

You can also enter ME9A for the document printing. Following screen will come.

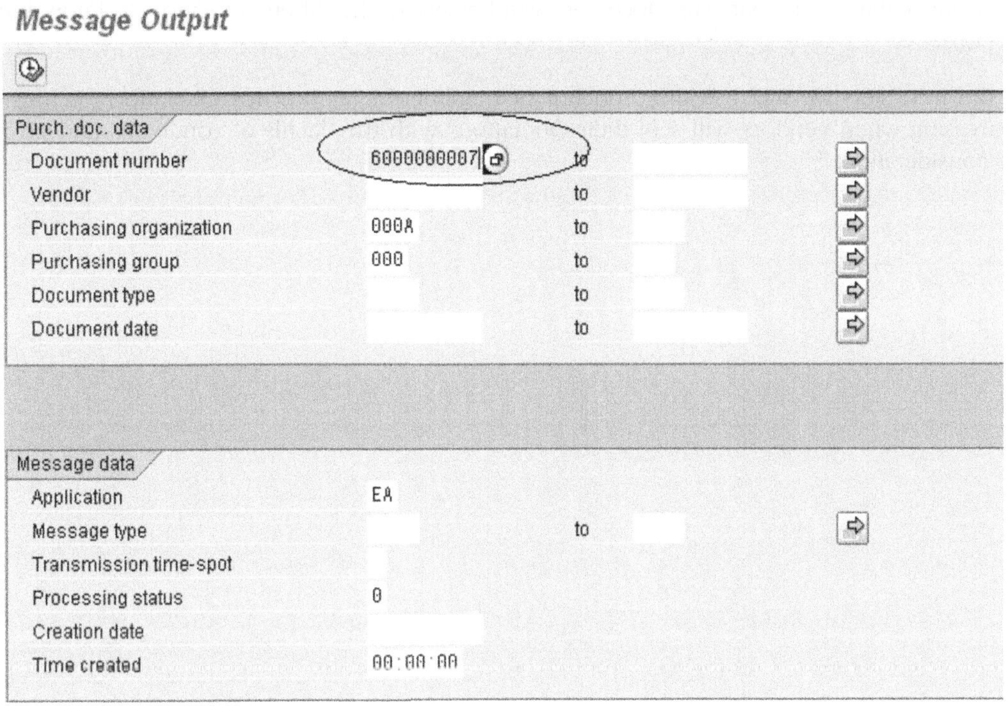

Here you enter your RFQ document number and execute. You also have option of keeping the document number field blank.

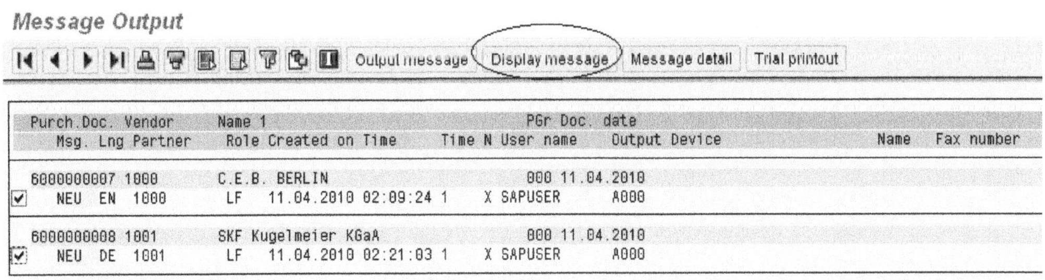

Select any one document number line item check box.

Click on display message.

You can see the document in the letter form and save it.

Now you will need the purchase document as RFQ will be printed out on the hard copy of document and will be sent to the respective vendor.

If no specific document number is entered then all the RFQ documents as initial selection parameter entered will be displayed. Select the required document number and go to output message or Display message this will show you a printout of the RFQ document. Take the print out of that document. This document will be sent to the different vendors to know their response.

In the next step we will use these document numbers of Request for Quotation for further processing when vendors will sent their Quotations with the details of conditions and prices for consideration.

Chapter

18

QUOTATION

Introduction:-

A quotation is an offer which is sent by a vendor to a purchasing organization regarding the supply of materials or performance of services on specified conditions.

It is a legal document for a certain period. The quotation is the vendor's response to a request for quotation which was issued and sent by a purchasing organization to the vendor.

A quotation consists following information.

Containing all the information of a Request for Quotation it also contains information regarding applicable conditions.

You can also set info record update indicator so that info record is updated as per quotations of the vendor respectively.

Menu path

SAP Easy Access > Logistics > Materials Management > Purchasing > RFQ/Quotation > Quotation > Maintain.

Transaction code:-

You can also use transaction code ME47. here on this screen you have to give the Request for quotation as reference document number.

Alternatively you can also enter transaction code ME47.

RFQ number:-

The initial screen will ask you the RFQ number. This should be the RFQ number that was sent to the vendor for consideration. If you can not remember then you can find by pressing F4.

Press ENTER.

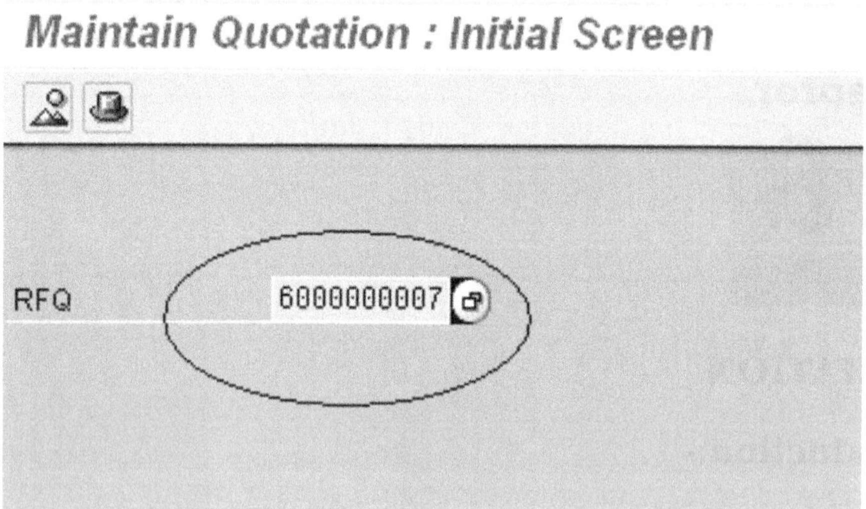

You can see following screen which will look same like the screen of RFQ with some changes. The Net price is added in the line item for price entry.

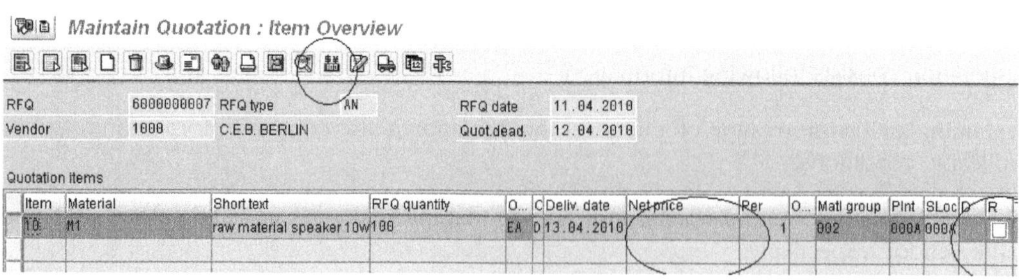

Item conditions:-

You can select the line item and go to item conditions by pressing Shift+F6.

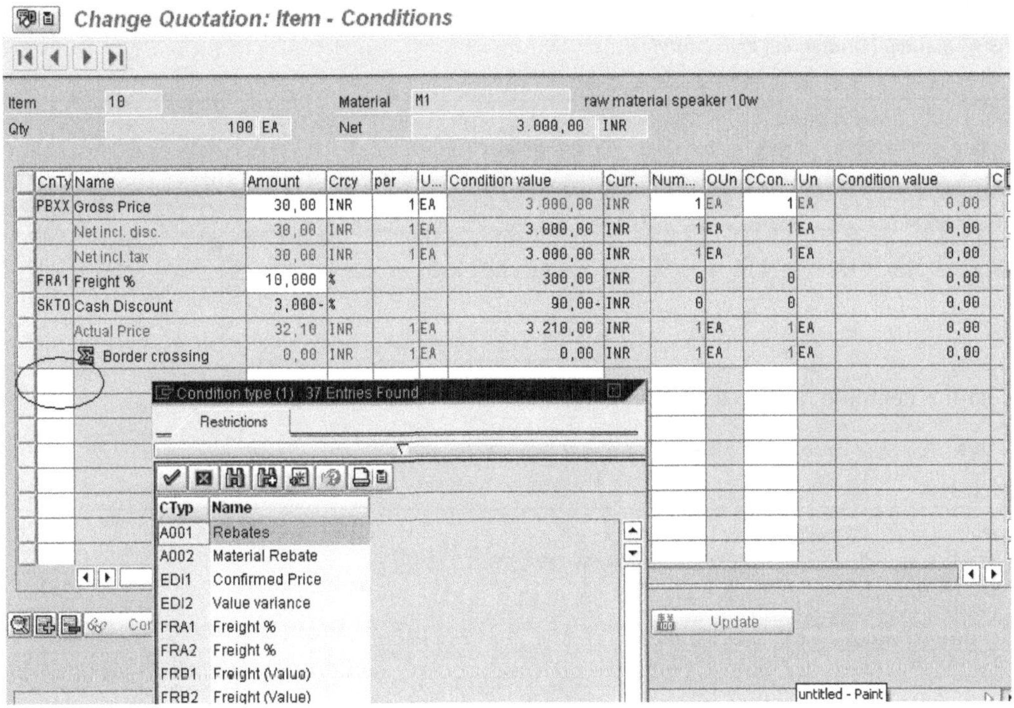

As in the picture above here you can add some other conditions in cnty field and respective amount in the amount field. The net amount applicable will be automatically counted by the system.

Quotation Rejection Indicator:-

You can also reject the quotation if it does not match your criteria by selecting a check in the indication on the right side for Rejection ind. If needed by the system you can also print this rejected Quotation for vendor information or reporting purpose.

Delivery schedule:-

You can also set different delivery schedules as per your need. This is shown in the picture below.

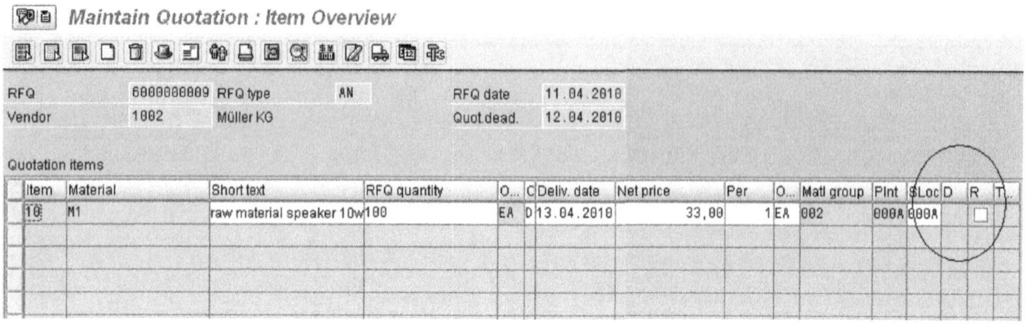

Select the item line and go to delivery schedule (shift+5)

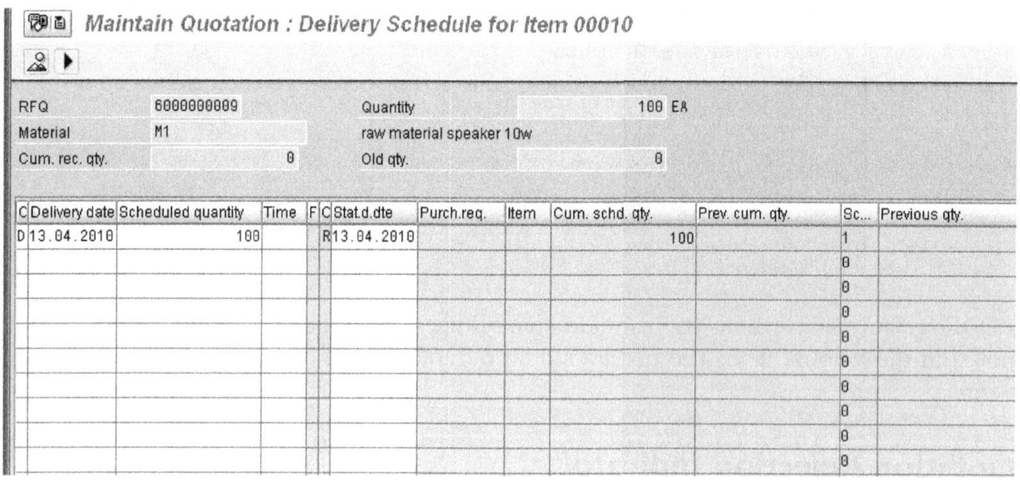

On this screen you can set different delivery dates and scheduled quantities along with time details.

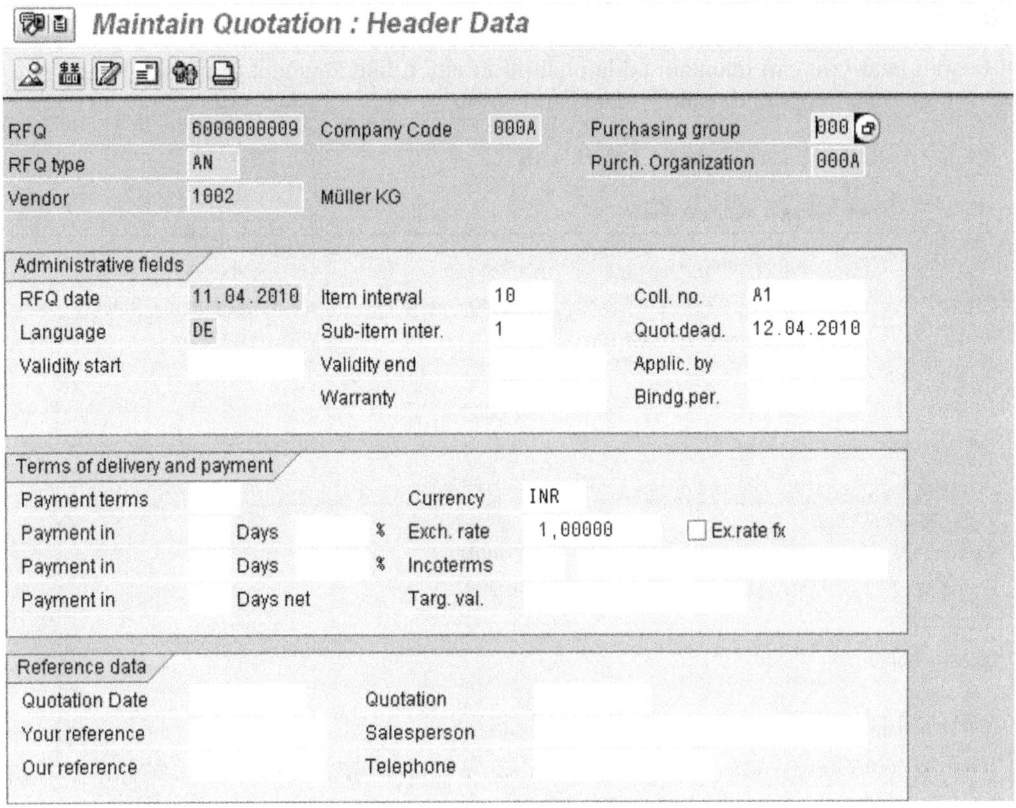
Maintain Quotation : Header Data
RFQ 6000000009
Company Code 000A
Purchasing group 000
RFQ type AN
Purch. Organization 000A
Vendor 1002
Müller KG
Administrative fields
RFQ date 11.04.2010
Item interval 10
Coll. no. A1
Language DE
Sub-item inter. 1
Quot.dead. 12.04.2010
Validity start
Validity end
Applic. by
Warranty
Bindg.per.
Terms of delivery and payment
Payment terms
Currency INR
Payment in Days %
Exch. rate 1,00000
Ex.rate fx
Payment in Days %
Incoterms
Payment in Days net
Targ. val.
Reference data
Quotation Date
Quotation
Your reference
Salesperson
Our reference
Telephone

Additional data:-

On header data you can maintain additional information like Payment terms, exchange rate if any changes has happened, validity dates and so on.

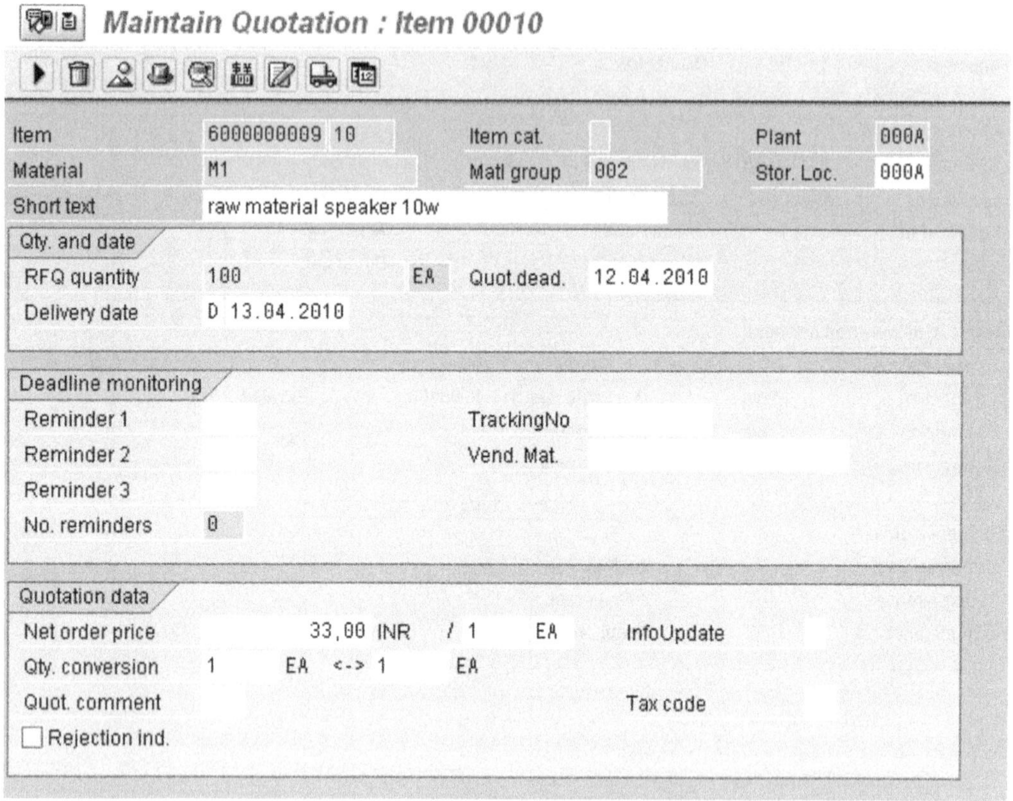

On item details screen you can enter tax code so that it will reflect in the purchase order and through the process up to invoice entry. Along with these all you can also maintain deadline reminders if any delay in delivery happens. In the info update field you have options based on that purchase information record will be updated. If the quotation is to be stored in a purchasing info record, fill the *InfoUpdate* field on the item detail screen.

In additional data you can also maintain if any additional information regarding material is to be changed or to be newly entered, if needed then you can do that.

After entering these details go back to the main screen and save the Quotation. Same RFQ number will be updated.

Repeat same procedure against each related RFQ document number as per your need for each vendor from whom you have got the quotations.

Chapter
19

PRICE COMPARISON

Introduction

This is a processing component by which we decide which vendor's price quote is best suitable for your company or procurement requirement. This procedure is performed based on the documents of Quotations which again is based on Request for Quotations.

Menu path

SAP Easy Access > Logistics > Materials Management > Purchasing > RFQ/Quotation > Quotation > Price comparison

Transaction code:-

Alternatively you can also use transaction code ME49 for this. Following initial screen will be displayed.

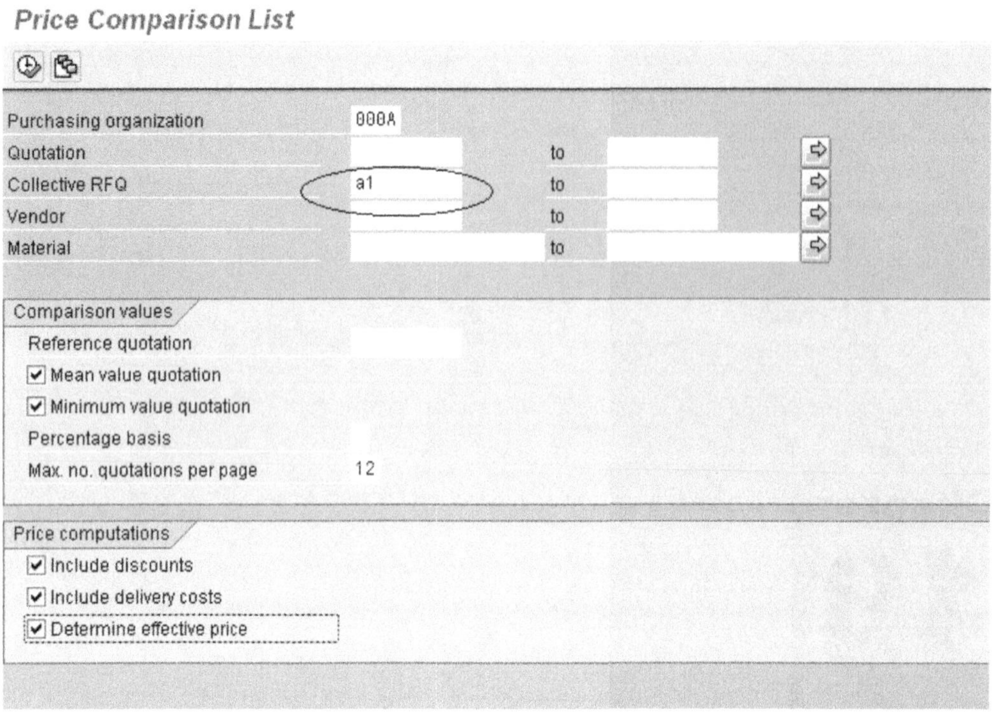

Purchasing organization:

On this screen enter Purchasing Organization. The purchasing organization should be as you have mentioned in request for quotation.

Collective RFQ:-

Enter Collective RFQ number. This is a grouping number for all related Request for Quotations for a particular procurement requirement on a particular time. Remember what number or character you had assigned in the Collective RFQ field while creating RFQ.

Minimum Value Quotation:-

Select minimum value quotation as deciding element.

Include Discounts:-

While calculating effective price this factor will be taken into account if you select this option.

Include delivery costs:-

If you select this option then delivery costs will be taken into account and if you do not select then whatever be the delivery cost it is not going to affect the effective price.

Determining effective price:-

If you select this option then discounts and delivery costs will be taken into account while price simulation for vendor selection.

Execute the process.

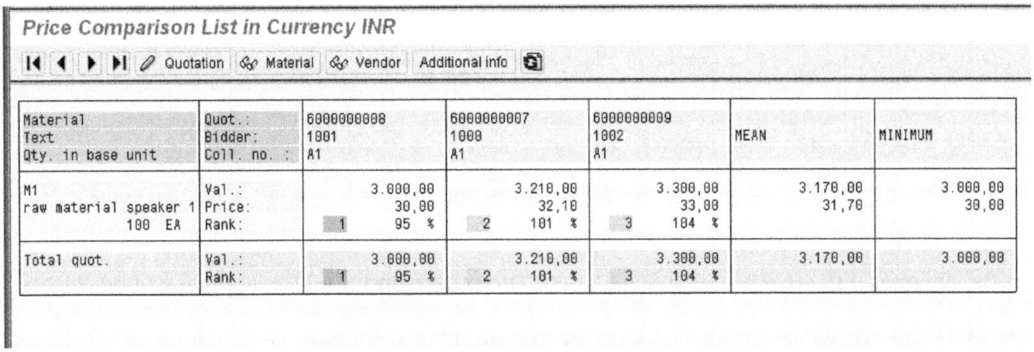

Price Comparison List in Currency INR

Material / Text / Qty. in base unit	Quot.: / Bidder: / Coll. no.:	6000000008 / 1001 / A1	6000000007 / 1000 / A1	6000000009 / 1002 / A1	MEAN	MINIMUM
M1 raw material speaker 1 100 EA	Val.: Price: Rank:	3.000,00 30,00 1 95 %	3.210,00 32,10 2 101 %	3.300,00 33,00 3 104 %	3.170,00 31,70	3.000,00 30,00
Total quot.	Val.: Rank:	3.000,00 1 95 %	3.210,00 2 101 %	3.300,00 3 104 %	3.170,00	3.000,00

In the next screen you can see the vendor's price evaluation. You can see a column of MINIMUM, in which minimum price is calculated as per set criteria and conditions entered in the quotations.

Here you can see minimum priced vendor's name is in green line.

Experiment Change:-

Now for learning process and see the effect you can do one thing. Just double click on any of the quotation document number.

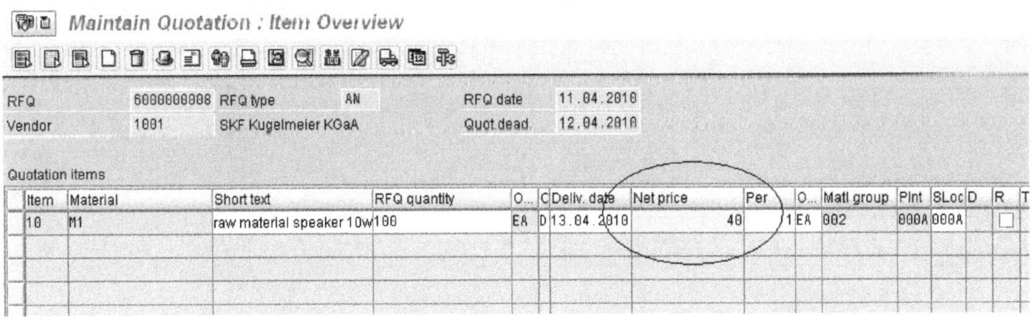

Maintain Quotation : Item Overview

RFQ 6000000008 RFQ type AN RFQ date 11.04.2010

Vendor 1001 SKF Kugelmeier KGaA Quot.dead. 12.04.2010

Quotation items

Item	Material	Short text	RFQ quantity	O...	C	Deliv. date	Net price	Per	O...	Matl group	Plnt	SLoc	D	R	T
10	M1	raw material speaker 10w	100	EA	D	13.04.2010	40	1	EA	002	000A	000A		☐	

This will take you to item over view screen. Here you can see price as in display mode.

Select the line item.

You can change price here in this page or go to item conditions and change value of any of the condition type so that price changes.

Save the document.

Saving will take you back to the same price simulation screen.

Refresh the screen.

Price Comparison List in Currency INR

Quotation | Material | Vendor | Additional info

Material Text Qty. in base unit	Quot.: Bidder: Coll. no.:	6000000007 1000 A1	6000000009 1002 A1	6000000008 1001 A1	MEAN	MINIMUM
M1 raw material speaker 1 100 EA	Val.: Price: Rank:	3.210,00 32,10 1 92 %	3.300,00 33,00 2 94 %	4.000,00 40,00 3 114 %	3.503,33 35,03	3.210,00 32,10
Total quot.	Val.: Rank:	3.210,00 1 92 %	3.300,00 2 94 %	4.000,00 3 114 %	3.503,33	3.210,00

See the changes. Effective price is recalculated. The other vendor with low price will be selected.

So this is the whole procedure of Request for quotation, Quotation maintenance and price comparison.

Now you know the vendor name whose price is the lowest. In the next process go to purchase order creation and create it as required with the selected vendor. While creating purchase order you can select the RFQ number in the field RFQ. System will fetch all the detailed data of RFQ into the purchase order screen.

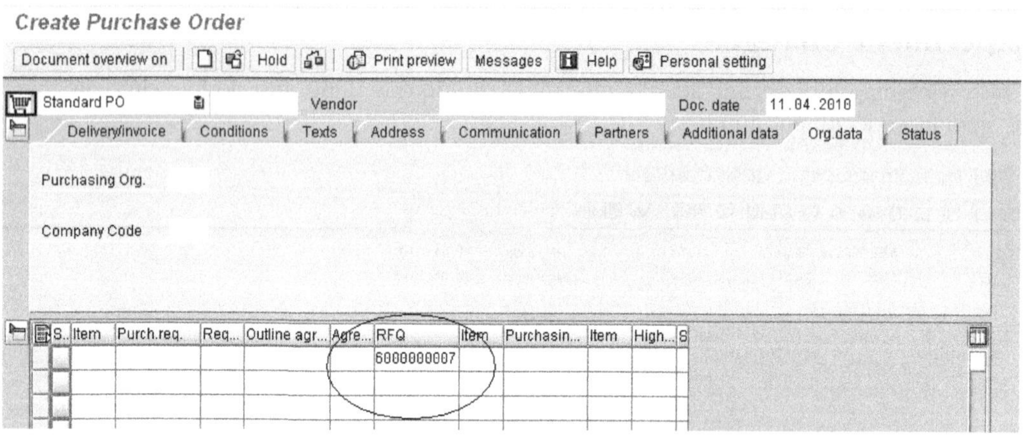

Save the purchase order and then do goods receipt for purchase order as usual.

PART-5

OTHER PROCUREMENT PROCESSES

Chapter 20

SUBCONTRACTING

Introduction:-

Subcontracting procurement is a process in which a material which may have one or more components is procured from an external vendor and vendor is paid for his assembly services provided. In this process components are provided to the vendor and the vendor supplies back the finished or processed end product is supplied back the purchasing company.

In subcontracting procurement process flows like as follows.

1. Requisition of some end product is raised as per requirement.
2. There is a subcontracting vendor to supply the end product.
3. The end product may have components.
4. A Bill of Material is maintained for the tracking the composition of the components for the end material.
5. Components are provided to the component materials vendor for processing.
6. Vendor starts processing with the for the end material.
7. A purchase order for the end product is raised and is sent to the subcontracting vendor.

8. End product is taken back from the subcontracting vendor.
9. Vendor sends an invoice to the purchasing party for payment of service.
10. Vendor is paid for his work done.

Stock of Material Provided to Vendor

You can see the stock status of the components in the system.

- You can check the status report of subcontracting stock in the transaction *SC Stock Monitoring for Vendor (RMO6ELLB*; transaction code *ME2O*
- *From this transaction code you can also provide further required components' quantity to the subcontracting vendor.*

Pre requisites:-

We will follow this subcontracting procurement process step by step.

Create material:-

For any procurement process of material, this is a must. You have to create material master for the materials. Here one major difference is with other processing. In the subcontracting process you have to maintain a minimum of two raw materials and one either semi finished or finished material. You can even create other material types too provided that should contain multiple components. So you will have to create raw material C1 and C2 as components and F as finished material for end product to be procured. This F material you will be procuring from the subcontracting vendor. While creating a finished material for the process you have to note that on the MRP 2 view the special procurement field should be selected for subcontracting procurement.

Create Material F (Finished product)

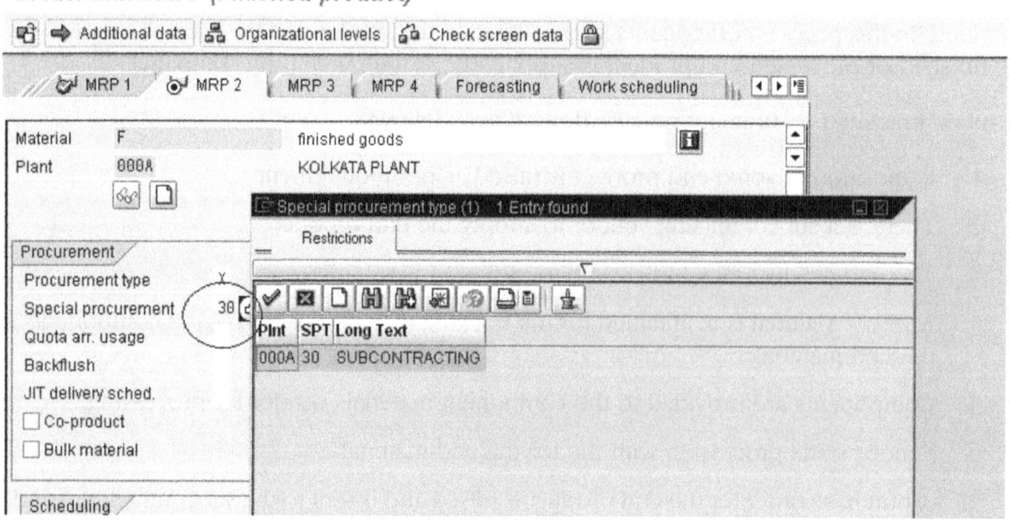

Apart from that enter the valuation class on the Accounting 1 view from the drop down list. Enter S in the price control for standard price and enter amount for the standard price as any amount.

Create Vendor:-

Vendor creation process will remain same as in the other processes. This will be a subcontracting vendor.

Create info record:-

Info record should be created for each and every material. If you do not create for each and every material then it must be created at least for finished material F. But in case of info record creation for subcontracting material one thing is to be noted that the info type on the initial screen should be selected for Subcontracting. You can see this in the picture below.

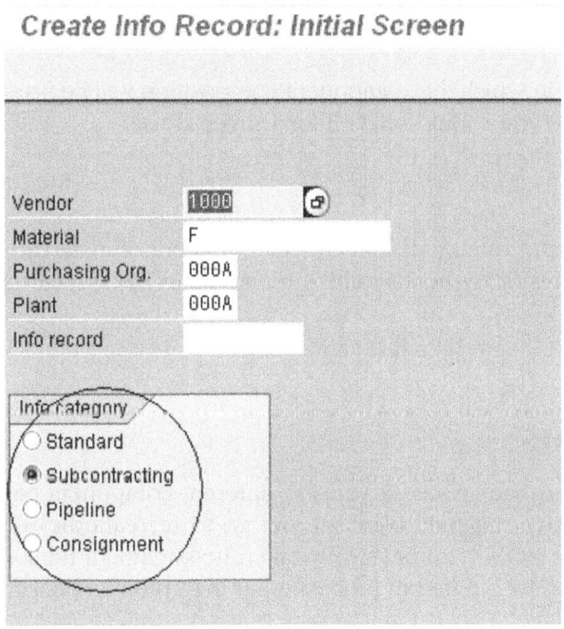

This will provide the rate on which vendor will do the assembly work for finished material.

Source List:-

Create a source list for each and every material whether be it a component or a finished material.

Bill of Material:-

Create a Bill of material with the transaction code CS01 or if you want to follow the menu path then follow as in the picture below. SAP Easy Access > Logistics > Production > Material Data > Bill of material> Material BOM > Create

Initial Screen:-

Initial screen of Bill of material will look something like as in the picture below.

Material:-

On the initial screen you will have to enter end material which will be created from components.

Plant:-

Enter plant code in which this finished material is created and the components will be assigned with the material.

BOM Usage:-

BOM Usage is the area in which this component composition will be used. It may be production or any other area. Here you should select 3 for Universal use.

Validity Date:-

You should also enter the validity date from which this bill of material will be used. If you do not enter any date in this field, then system will automatically take current date as default start date.

Enter:-

Alternative BOM:-

Alternative BOM is used and created if you use different component composition for different time and purposes. Leave this field blank. If you go to recreate the BOM 2nd time then you will see that alternative BOM is automatically taken it assignment thinking that you will create some other composition for a different process other than pre-composed composition for BOM.

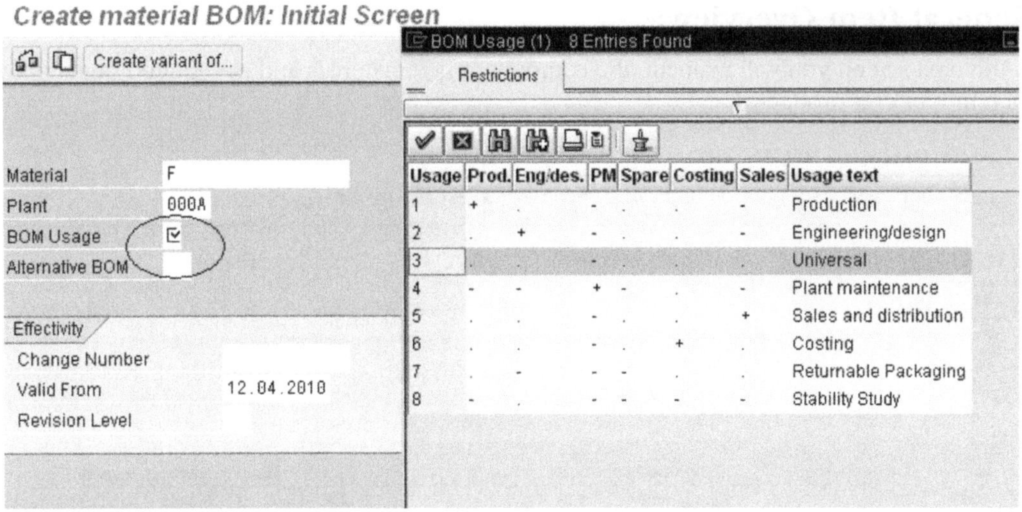

ENTER.

Alternative BOM:-

Alternative BOM is used and created if you use different component composition for different time and purposes. Leave this field blank. If you go to recreate the BOM 2nd time then you will see that alternative BOM is automatically taken it assignment thinking that you will create some other composition for a different process other than pre-composed composition for BOM. You can see this automatically generated number below in the picture.

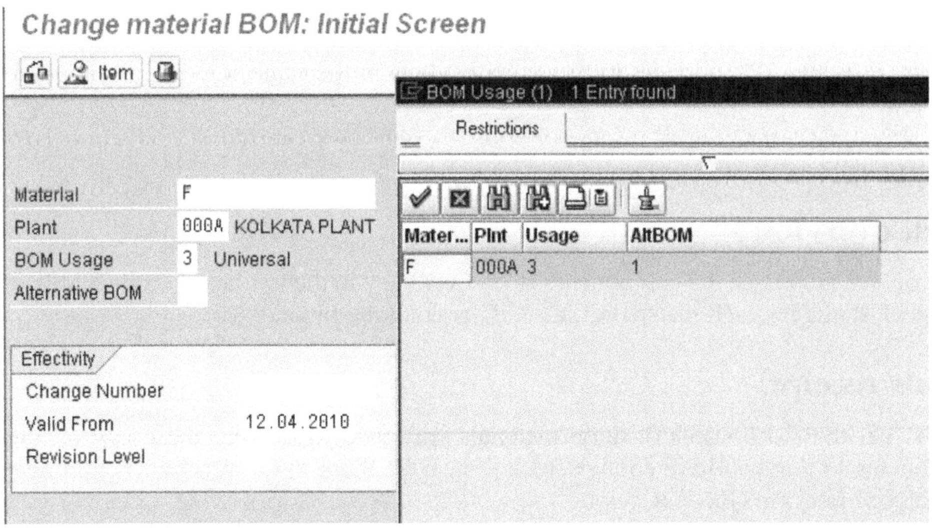

General Item Overview:-

In the next screen you will maintain the component raw materials and its required quantity for each unit of end product.

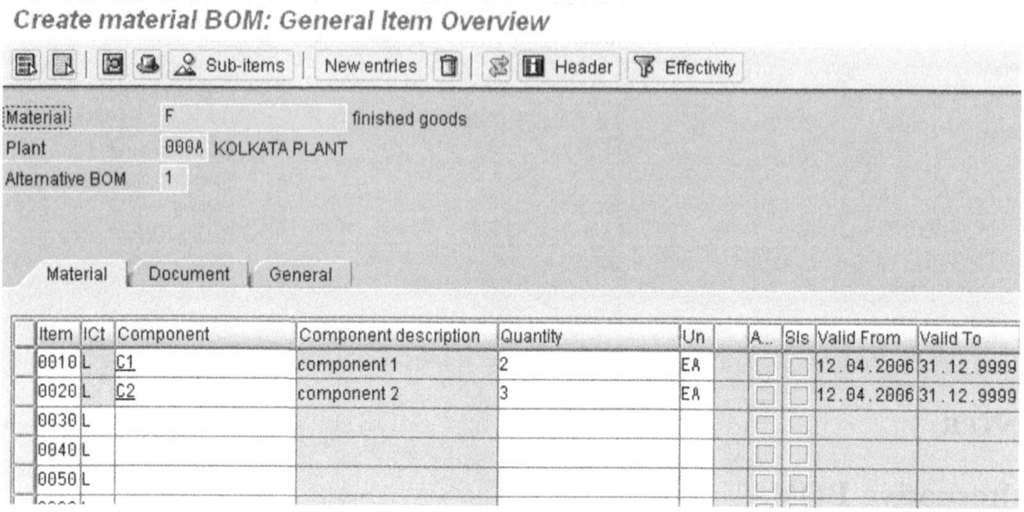

As you can see in the above picture that component c1 and component c2 is maintained with the required component quantity 2 & 3 respectively. That means for production of F material, component c1's 2 unit quantities and component c2's 3 units quantities are required. You can enter as many components are required.

Sub item Overview:-

You can also enter component's further compositions in the same way by selecting Sub item Overview.

Save the BOM.

Stock overview:-

Next you need to check the component's stock over view in the transaction code MMBE. Check here stock status for each material c1, c2 & F material one by one.

Goods receipt:-

Next as per the stock status of these materials you need to procure these raw materials or components so that you have enough stock to provide these to the vendor when in need. For this purpose perform Goods Receipt.

We already know how to procure material from a standard external procurement process. This time in this chapter we will procure goods as initial entry of stock. This process is used when you have enough stock in your stock point but you have not yet entered this into your system.

So to perform these processes go to the transaction code MIGO.

Here from the drop down of operation or movement select Goods Receipt. This is shown in the picture as below.

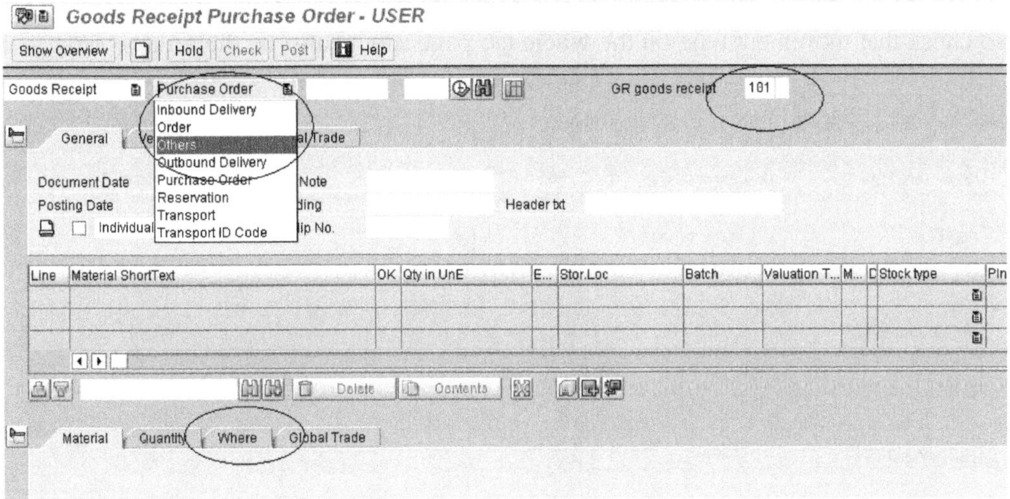

Then from the reference field select others as we are not going to intake goods against any reference document.

Check the movement type on the right hand field should show as 561. This is a movement type for initial entry of stock for unrestricted use. You can see this in the picture below.

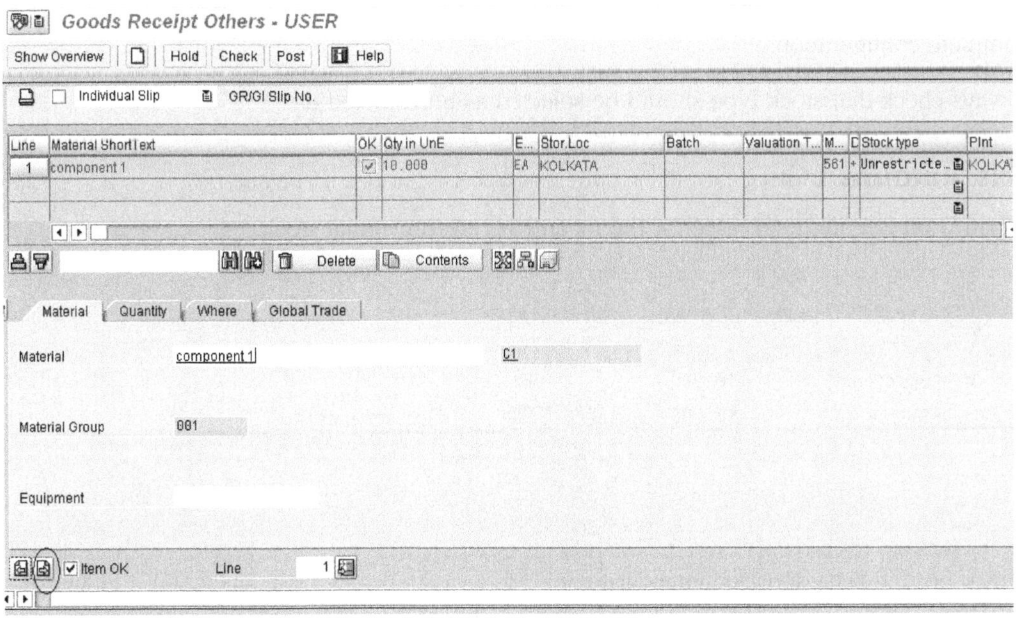

In the material tab page enter material c1 in the material field.

On the quantity tab page enter quantity 10000.

Then on the where tab page enter plant code and storage location in the respective fields.

Also check that movement type on the where tab page should also be the same as 561.

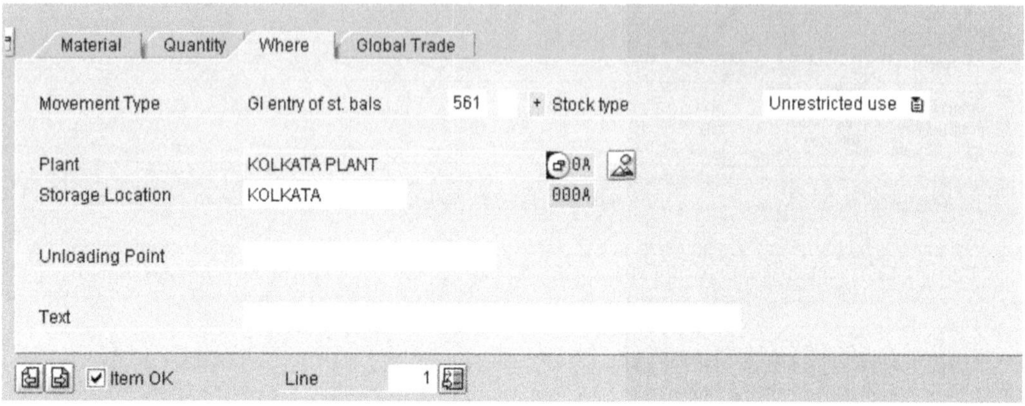

If it is not that change this to 561.

You can see in the picture below that just bear text and item OK field there is an arrow icon. This is to enter another material in the same material document. Press the right arrow icon and enter material c1, quantity 10000, plant 1000 and storage 0001 location in the same way as it was done in the last step. In the screen shot I have used 000A plant and 000A storage location some times you can use 1000 plant and 0001 storage location as per your IDES system's existing complete configuration.

Always check that stock type should be selected as unrestricted use.

Ext. amount LC:-

If you want to enter total price for the initially received material stock

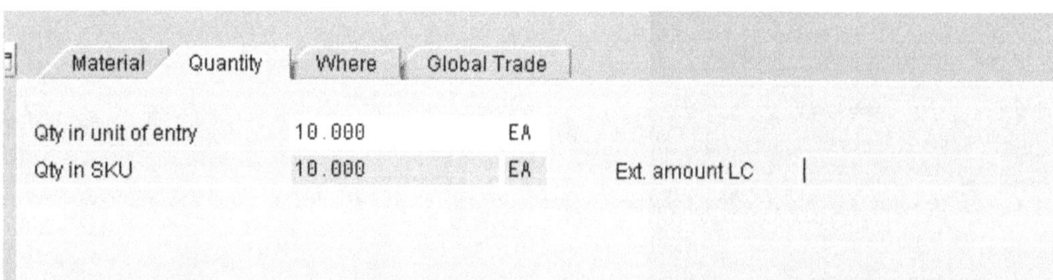

Check posting Date and Document date.

Post the document.

Display the material document as usual.

Stock overview:-

Check the stock in the transaction code MMBE as usual and see there increased stock level.

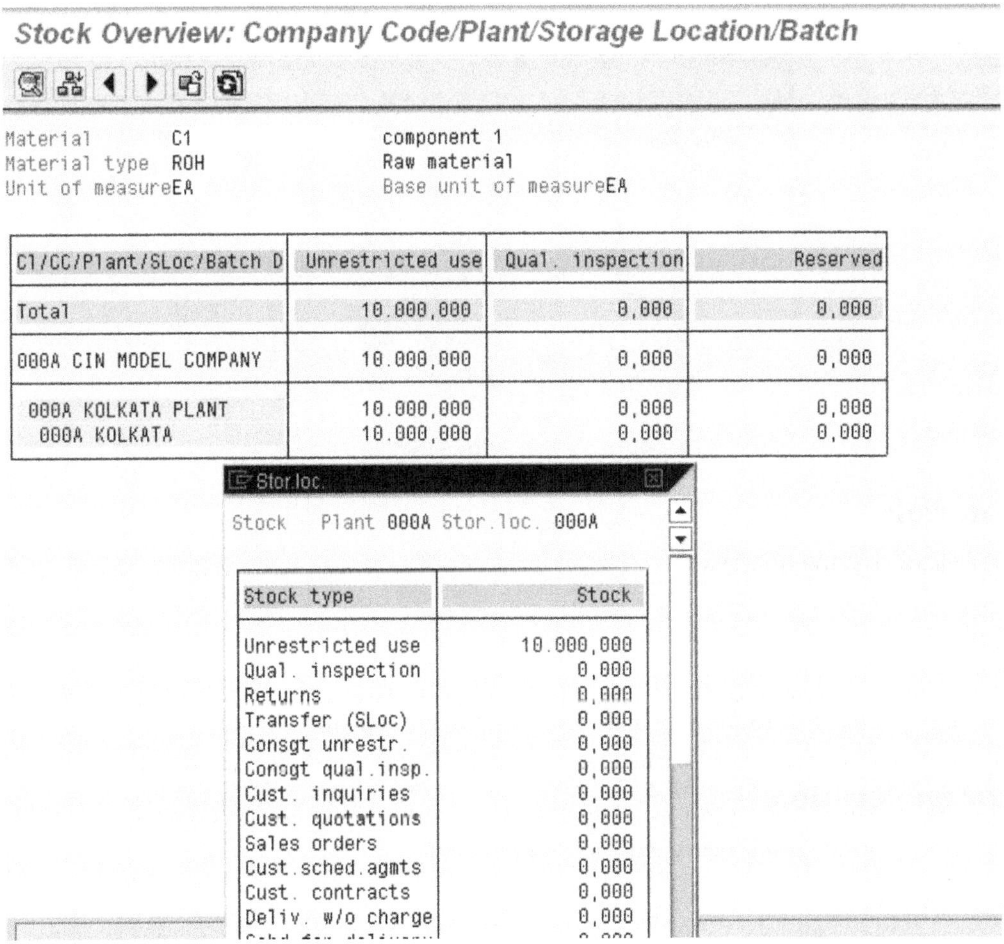

Transfer posting:-

In this step you will provide material to your subcontracting vendor. Go to transaction code MIGO. Here select movement transfer posting. In the reference field select others. Movement type should be as 541.

Movement type:-

Enter movement type as 541.

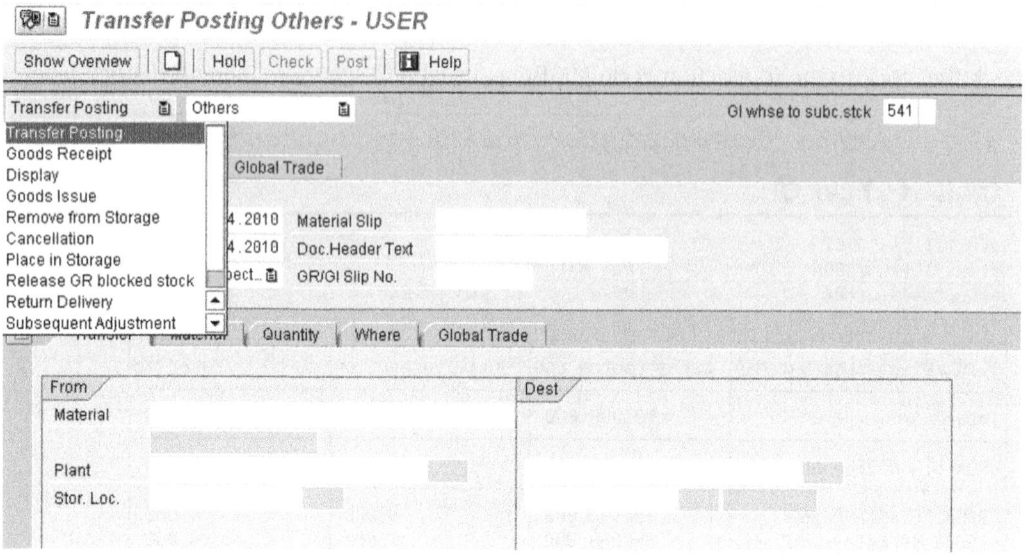

Material:-

Enter material in the usual way.

Plant:-

Enter plant on the material tab page or where tab page. This is the plant from where you will give away the material to the subcontracting vendor. Enter plant as 1000.

Storage location:-

Enter storage location respective storage location 0001.

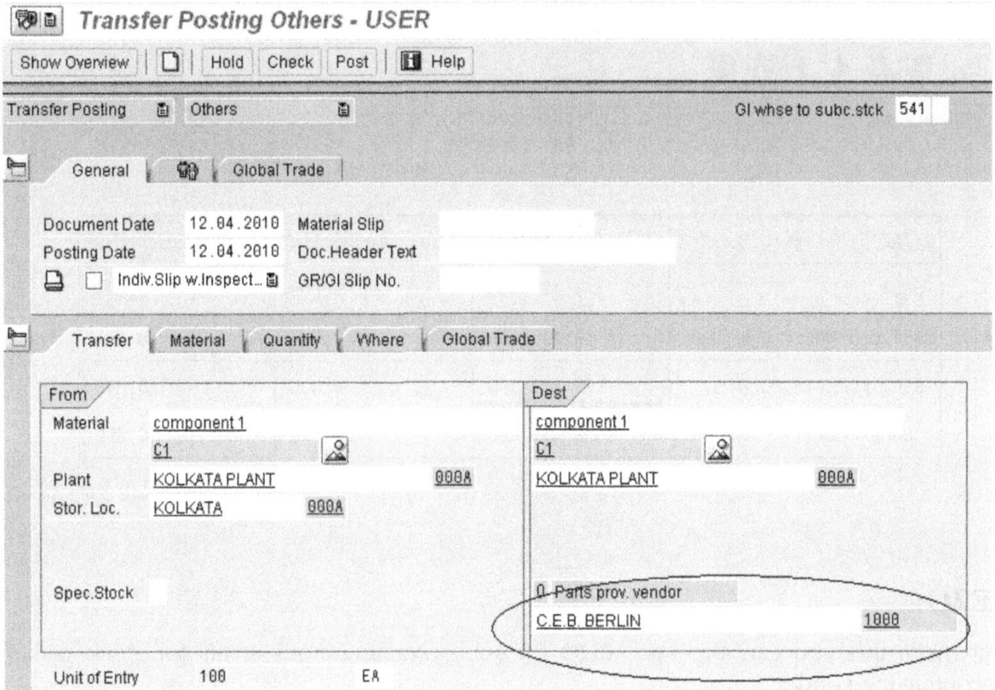

Unit of Entry:-

Enter quantity of material that is being provided to the vendor.

Parts provided vendor:-

This is the field where you have to enter the subcontracting vendor's name, you are providing the material.

Enter both the material on the same material document or you alternatively you can provide material one by one in different material document to the vendor.

Check the Posting date.

Check the document date.

Check the stock status in the MMBE transaction code by entering components. If you double click one the quantity line this will popup the break up of stock status. Here you can see SC stock unrestr. as stock with subcontractor.

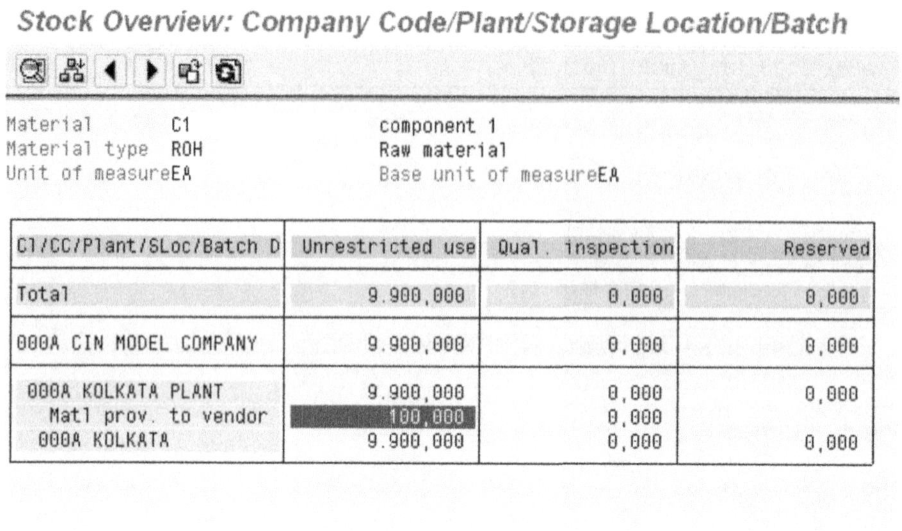

ME2O:-

Apart from this you can also see ME2O for subcontracting stock status for stock with the subcontracting vendor.

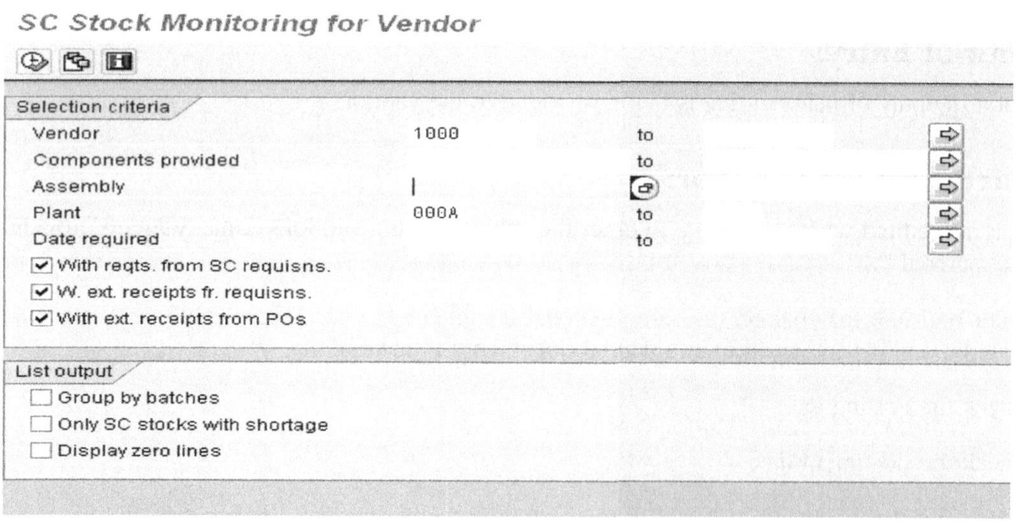

While displaying report you can select the material line check box and you can click on post good issue then further required quantity against any purchase order will be posted to the vendor.

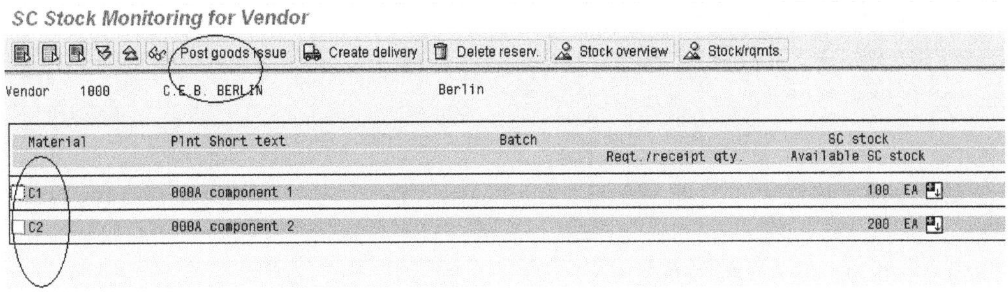

Purchase Requisition:-

Create the purchase Requisition as usual. But note that you have to enter L in the item category field to make it a subcontracting purchase requisition. You can see this in the picture below.

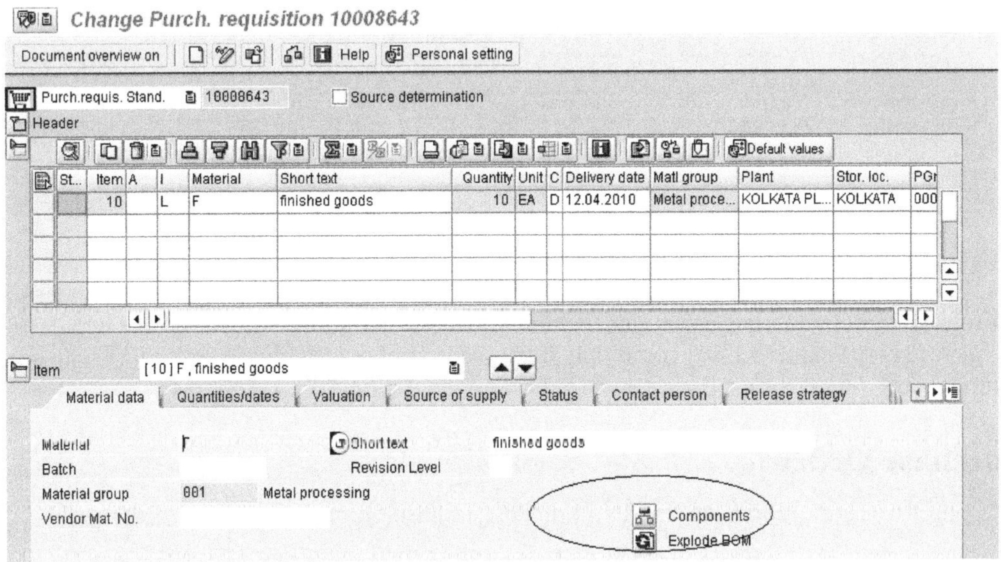

Enter material F for the material that you are going to procure from the vendor. You can click on components or explode BOM icon.

If release procedure is activated in your number then go to ME54N.

Select purchase requisition number.

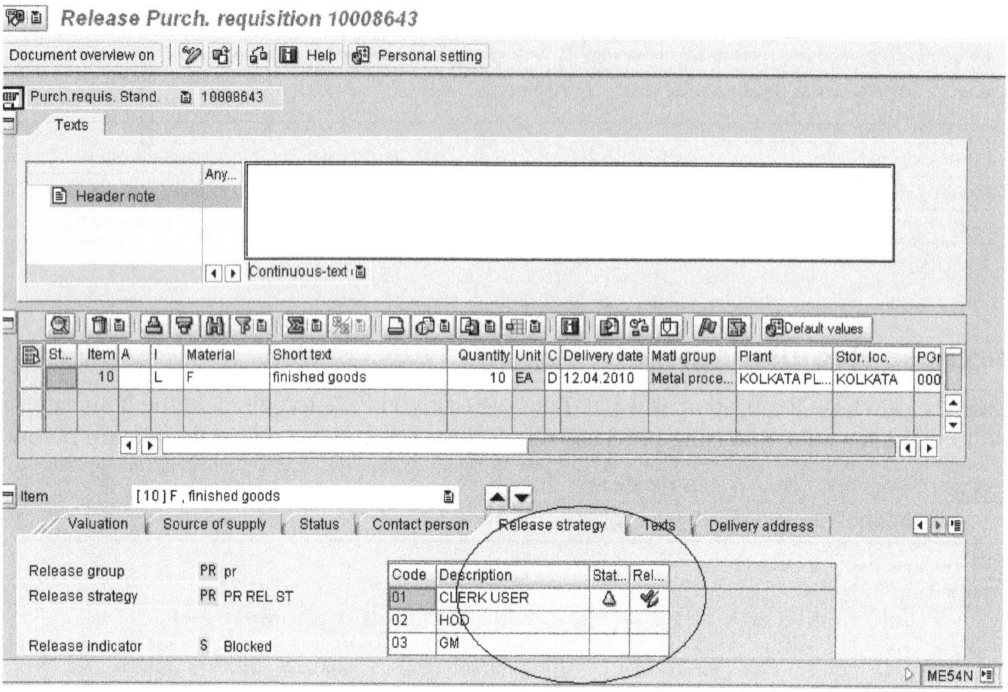

Click on display change icon.

On release strategy tab page you can see a few icons which normally you do not see. Like in the picture below, and this will come only if you have configured release procedure with some criteria.

Purchase Order

Pick purchase requisition from the field purchase requisition in the purchase order page.

Here also you can check components and total components involved in the process for this purchase order document number.

Components:-

On the material data tab page you can see components icon. This is for component tracking. If you double click on this then a screen for component overview will be displayed as it is shown below in the picture.

Explode BOM:-

By pressing this icon you can get details of the bill of material line item details for the total quantity entered in purchase order item quantity.

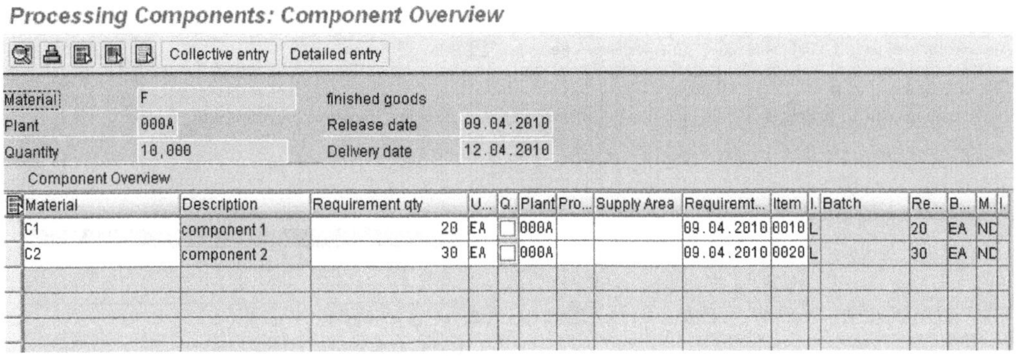

Check the purchase requisition and save this.

Purchase Order:-

Now go to purchase order creation screen ME21N. Go to the field Purchase requisition. From this field find the respective purchase requisition number by pressing F4 and then finding it with respect to material. This is shown as below in the picture.

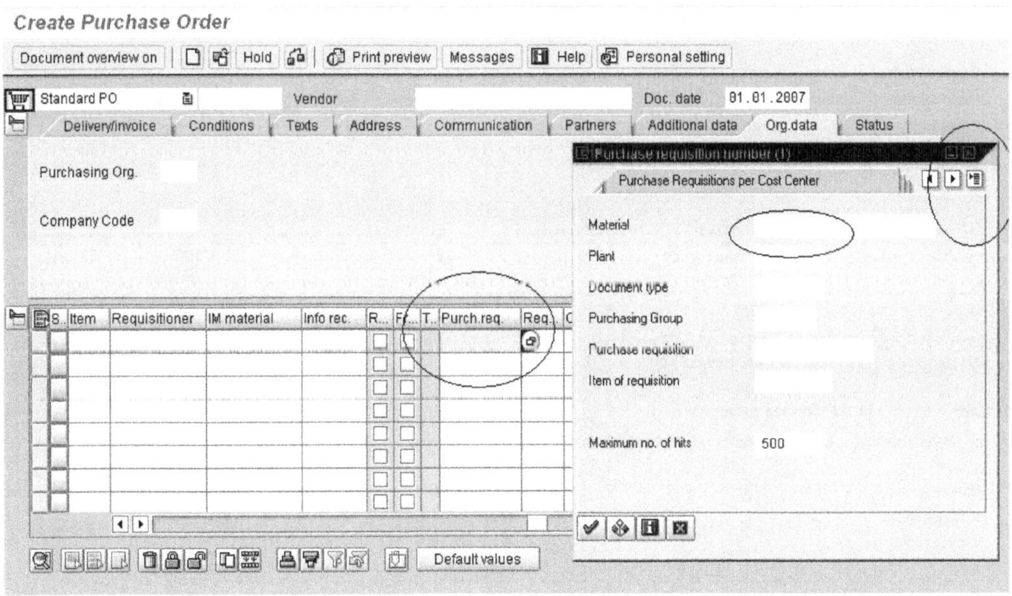

Find the purchase requisition number.

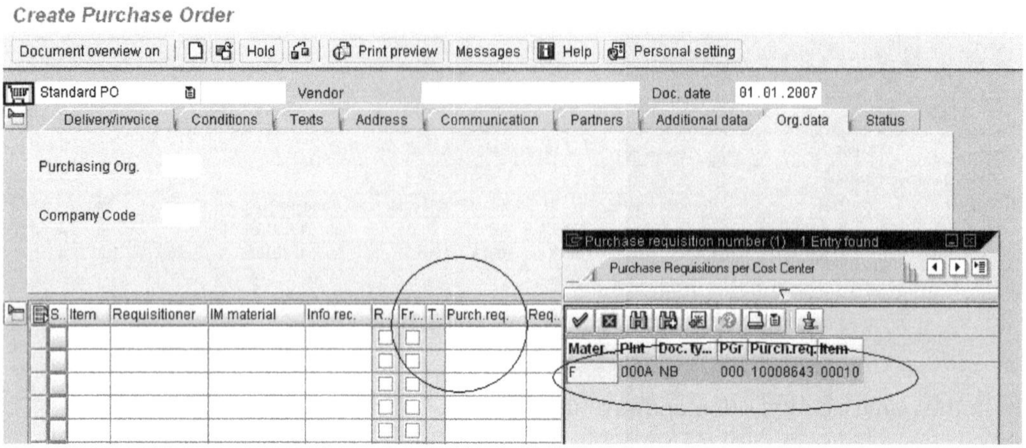

ENTER.

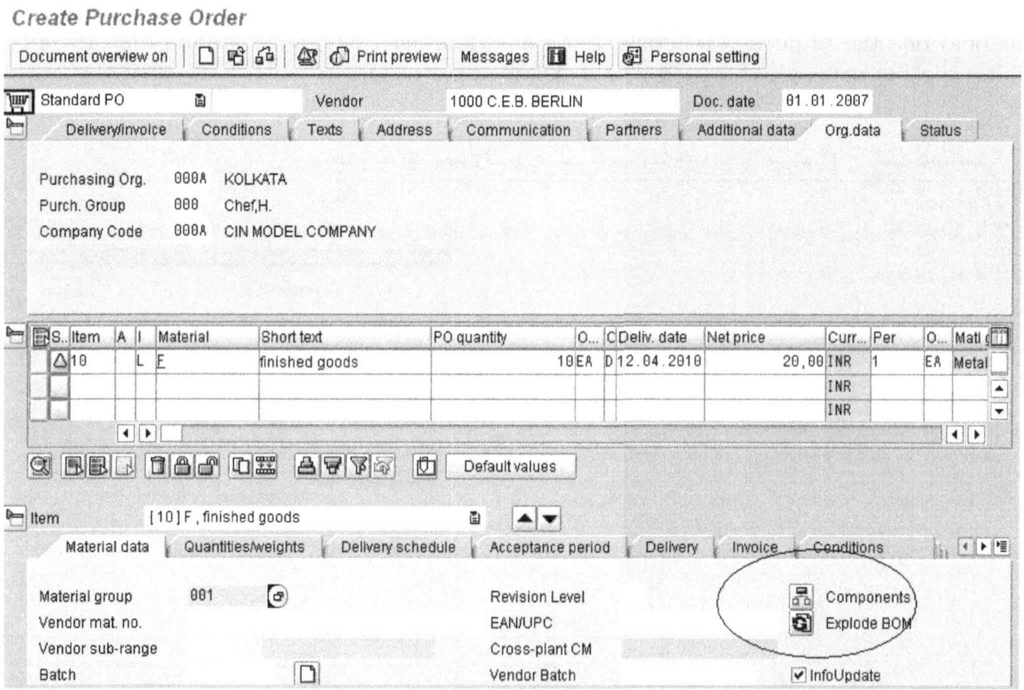

Check the document.

Save the document.

Enter it and save the purchase

Goods receipt:-

In this step you accept goods from the subcontracting vendor as goods receipt transaction. You had provided the components to the vendor. He has assembled it and now you will take the assembled or final product from him. Do this step as you have done usually with reference to the purchase order. Check that with the finished material you are also getting back the components as bundled in the finished material.

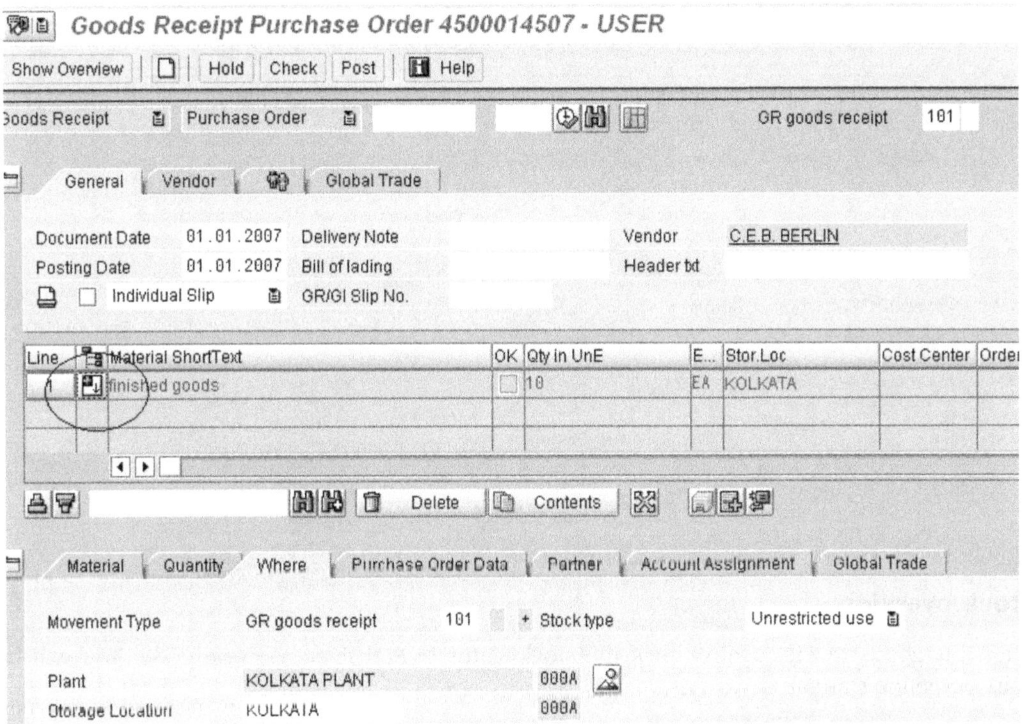

In the next screen you can see that the components are being received against movement type 543.

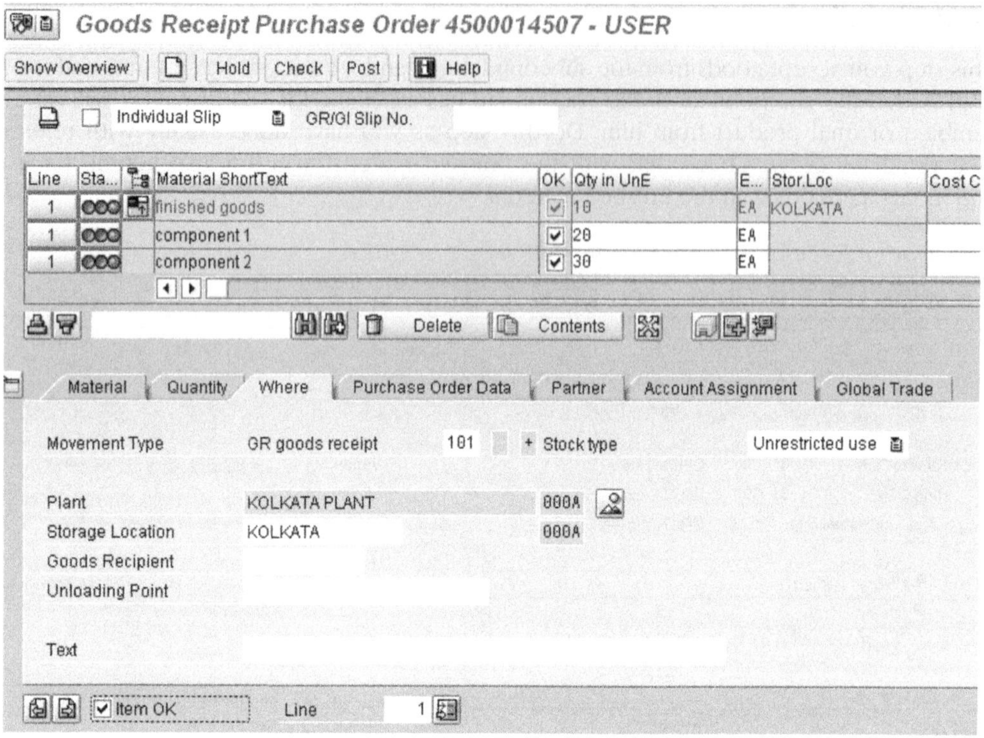

Check the document and post the document.

Stock overview:-

After this goods receipt again check the stock status in MMBE transaction code. You will be able to see the status.

Display:-

In this step you should check the material document that was generated on goods receipt and also the FI document.

SC stock with Subcontractor:-

You can check the subcontractor's stock status at any point of time in the transaction code ME2O.

Invoice entry:-

You have received material from the subcontracting vendor. Along with goods delivery vendor has also sent you a document that is invoice. This is a bill for the service that this vendor has done for your material creation or assembly. In this step you make the invoice entry, check the invoice document and post the document as usual so that vendor gets payment from the finance department for his invoice. This step is done as usual that we have done in the standard procurement process.

Chapter 21

PIPELINE

Introduction:-

Pipeline Procurement

A pipeline material is a type of material that is already available at into the production process or a consumption center through a pipeline (for example, oil), from a pipe (for example, water supply), or through wire (like example, electricity). This type of material can be consumed at any time and in any quantity. Apart from that this also can not be stored.

Material Type PIPE:-

Material type for this kind of material is defined as PIPE in the SAP system. There are certain characteristics of this type of material procurement.

- o Pipe line material can only be consumed.
- o No purchase order is possible or Pipe line material.
- o No procurement planning is possible for this material.

- o Liability of the material lies with the vendor only unless and until material in not consumed
- o Vendor will be paid only after this material is consumed and the level or extent it is consumed.
- o It can be procured any time as required.
- o It can be procured any time when required.
- o It can not be stored or kept in stock.
- o No physical inventory or counting is possible.
- o In goods movement pipeline materials can only be consumed and no other movements are possible.

For other Material Types:-

For other material types also you can configure pipeline movement's possibility. As

- o Mandatory for specific valuation area.

  In this case only pipe line movements are possible for procurement of that type of material.

- o Allowed for specific valuation area.

  In this case pipeline and other movement can also be posted. Along with that other movement type's features can also be used like stock keeping, inventory controlling etc.

Creating a Pipeline Material:-

Now we start creating a new pipeline material. In the screen below you can see that with the material type pipeline material selection when select view is selected there are only a few views are optioned.

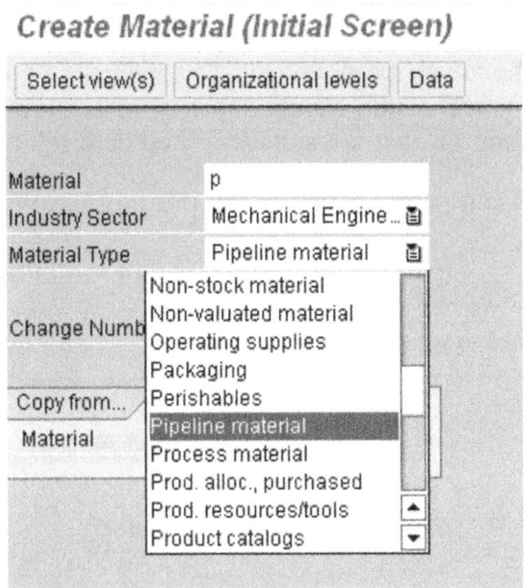

In material initial screen you have to select material type as pipeline.

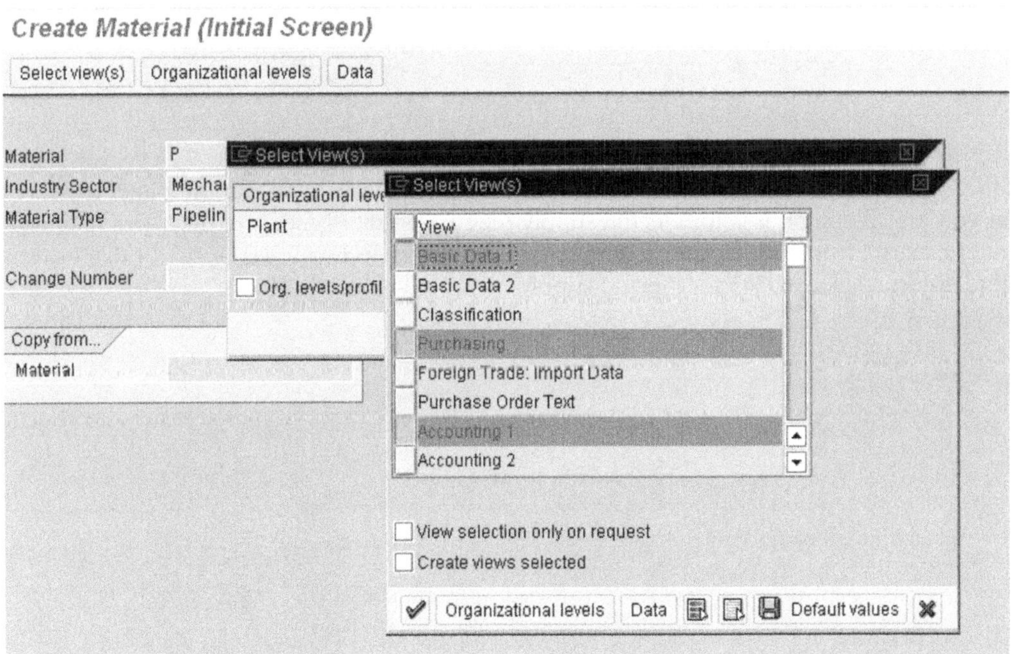

Out of these, select basic data1, Purchasing, and accounting 1 as mandatory selection views. Other than that you can select all the views but one thing should be noted that there are no MRP related views or Storage related views.

Organization level:-

Once you have selected the views, press ENTER. This will take you to the organization level screen where you will also see a little change. That is system is not asking for any storage location data. This again confirms that not storage related data will be available.

After entering plant 1000 again press ENTER. In the picture I have used plant 000A, so please do not get confused.

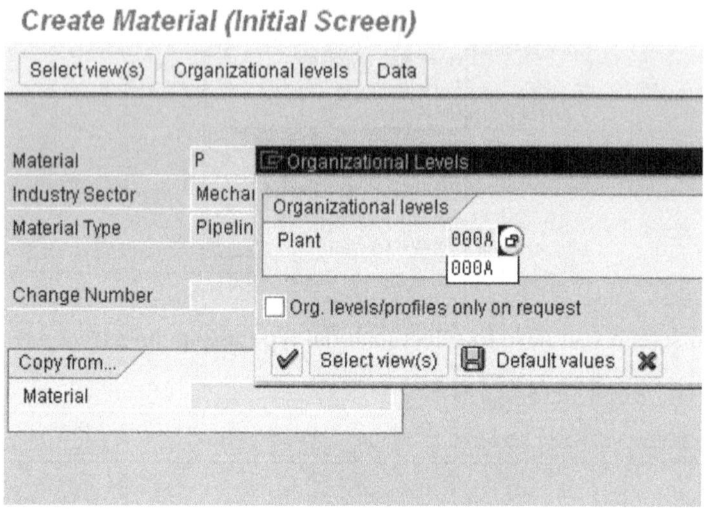

In the basic data tab page you have to select Base unit of measure as per the pipeline material that you are creating if it is for electric supply then base unit of measure may be KW or other unit of measure from the selection. After that you have to select material group for that material. There you can select 00203 for Electric supply.

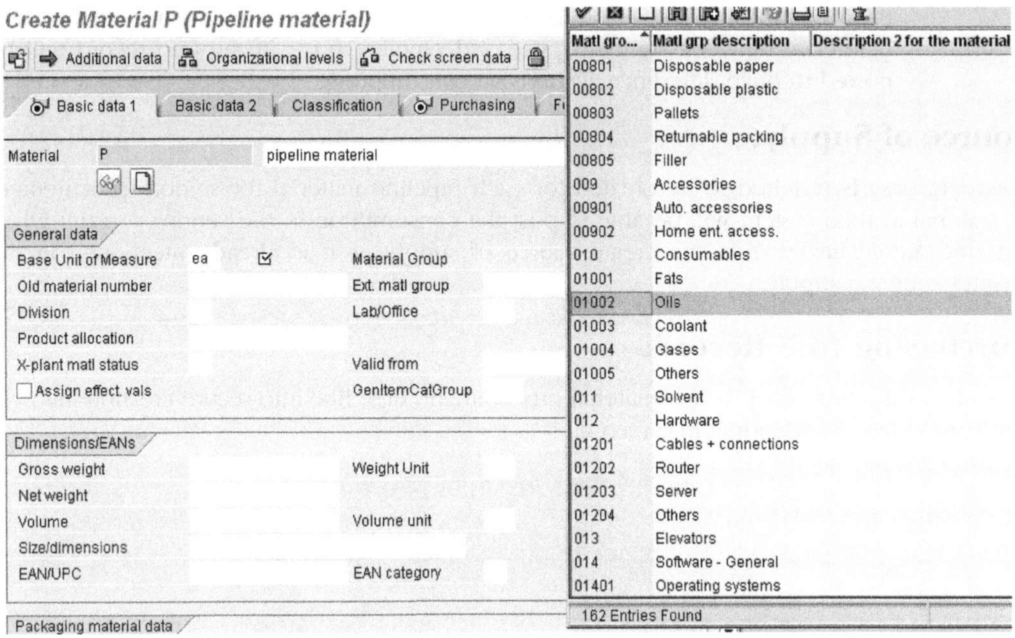

Other than that this material can be created as already discussed in the material creation chapter. So the minimum information that you require to input are enlisted below.

- Material – E1
- Industry sector as required
- Material type – Pipeline.
- Basic Data
    - Material - E1
    - Description – Electric Supply
    - Base unit of measure - KW
    - Material group - 00203 or electric supply
- Purchasing data
    - Purchase group
- Accounting data
    - Valuation class
    - Price control:-

      Choose price control V (moving average price), So that any pipe line consumption is posted to the consumption account.

Price control choose S (standard price), if this selection is taken then the price difference between standard price and pipeline price in the info record will be posted to price difference account on consumption.

Source of Supply:-

This data base is required to be created for each pipeline material for smooth procurement of material as then system will be able to post the consumption to the vendor account when required automatically. You can create source of supply as it is already mentioned in the chapter source o supply.

Purchasing Info Record:-

This master is a must for pipeline material procurement. Pipe line info record creation involves a little deviation from normal info record.

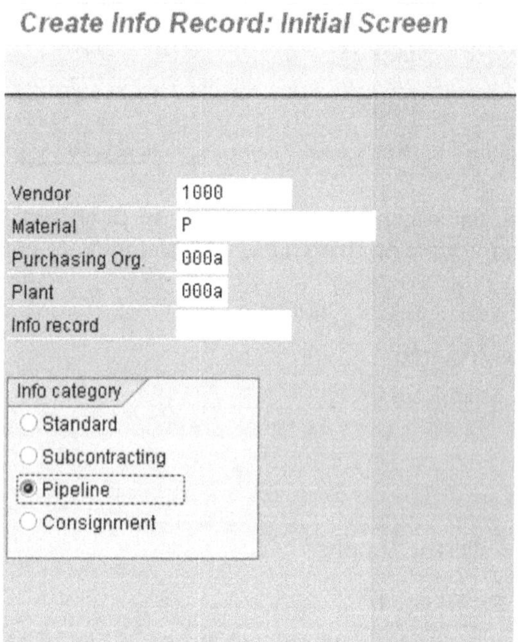

As you can see in the above picture in the create info record you enter .

- The vendor number from which you will procure the pipeline material,
- Enter pipeline material number,
- Purchase organization 1000, and
- Plant 1000,
- Then below in the same initial screen you see the info category. There select Pipeline button,

- Enter.

  This will take you to the next screen. There you enter data as required in the same way as we have already discussed in the info record chapter.

- Tax Code - Only change will be in the Purch. Organization Data 1 tab page. Here in the Tax Code field you will have to select a tax code which will be applicable. You can select any input tax as shown in the picture below.

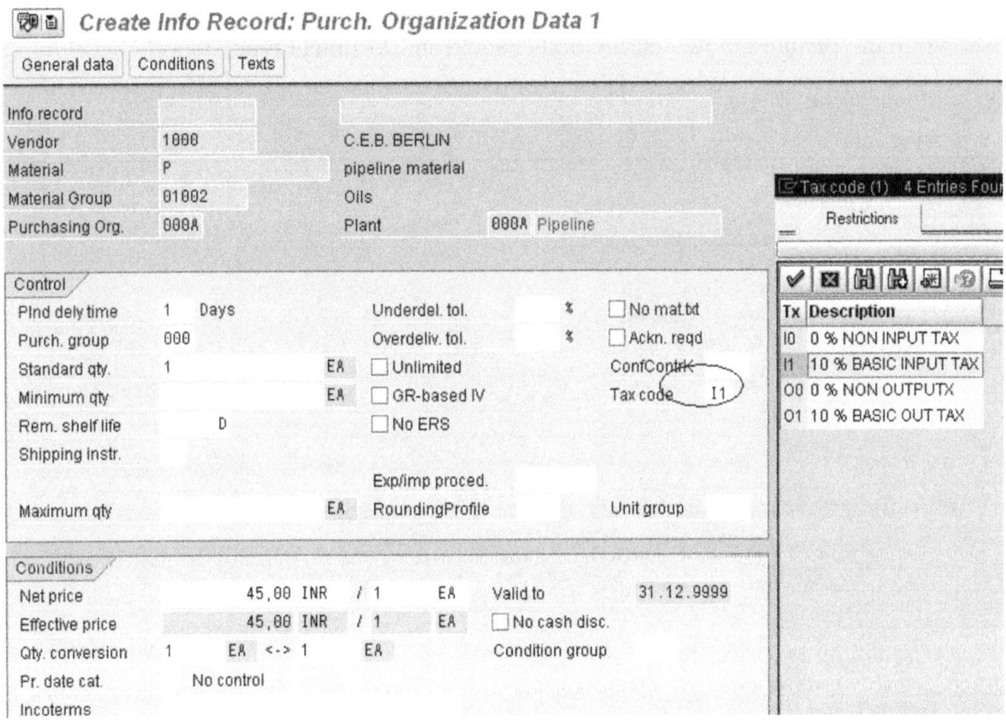

(Note:- The valuation of withdrawal is valuated at the price already defined in the pipeline info record. Tax is already mentioned in the pipeline info record as because there is possibility of entering tax information while entering or settling an invoice for pipeline material.)

After completing this save the info record.

Requirement of purchase order in pipeline process:-

In the next step you simply go to the transaction code ME21N. As we know this transaction code is used to create purchase order. As we have already discussed in the purchase order chapter try to create the purchase order. After entering all the details like material, plant, purchase organization, purchase group, company code etc. you will come to know that there is a red flag below at the status bar. There you will be able to see the message that No procurement is defined for the material as you can see in the picture or material P. So this only confirms that procurement via purchase order is not possible for pipeline material.

Goods Issue:-

After creating all these required master data now you need to consume the material and you have started consuming it. As you keep on consuming the material you also keep on making a document entry for the consumption and that is done via Goods Issue.

Transaction code is MIGO. We have already discussed about this transaction code which is basically for goods movement.

As shown in the picture below, select Goods issue from document type.

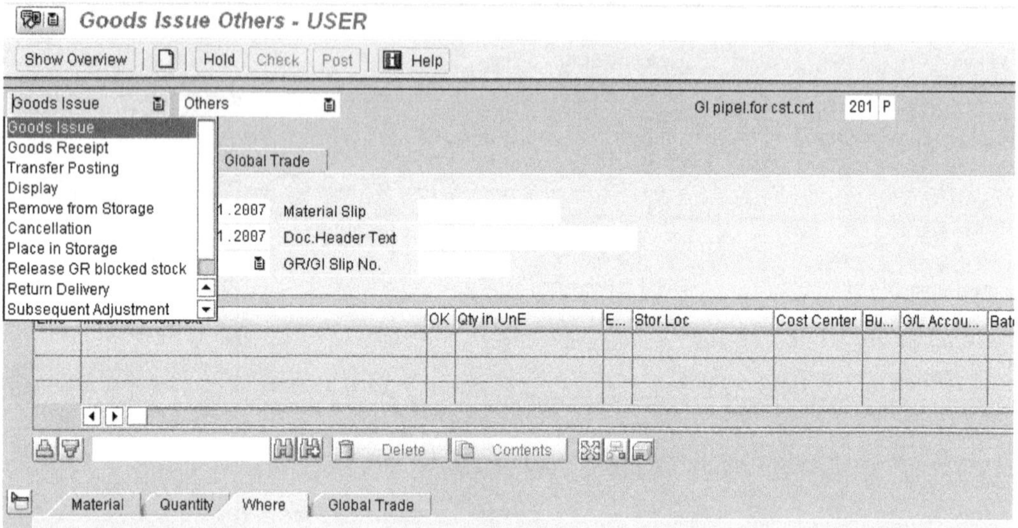

Here you will be able to see the following screen.

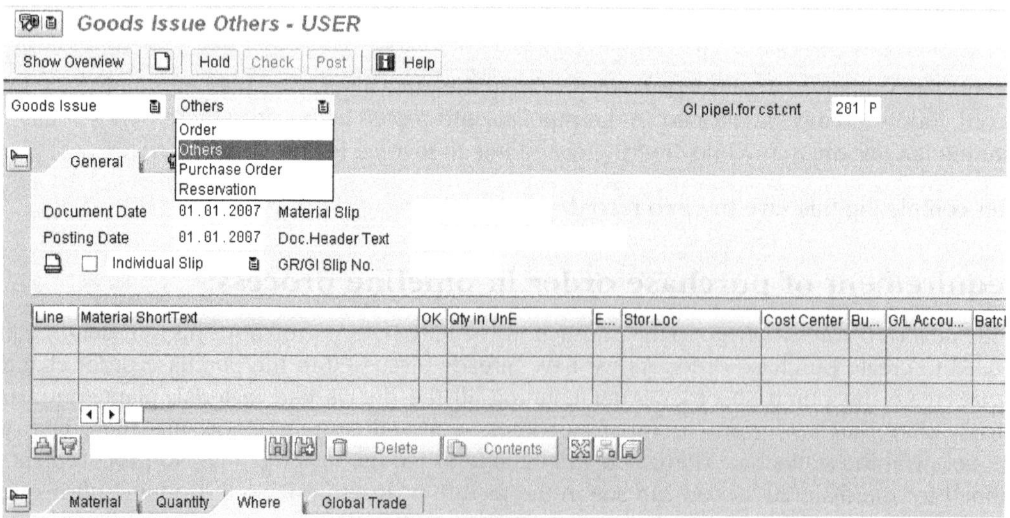

In the movement option select Goods as shown in the picture and in the reference option select others from drop down list.

After selecting this you will be able to see at the right hand side on the screen movement type field. From there pressing F4 select movement type 201 P for goods issue for consumption from pipeline material. This is shown below in the picture.

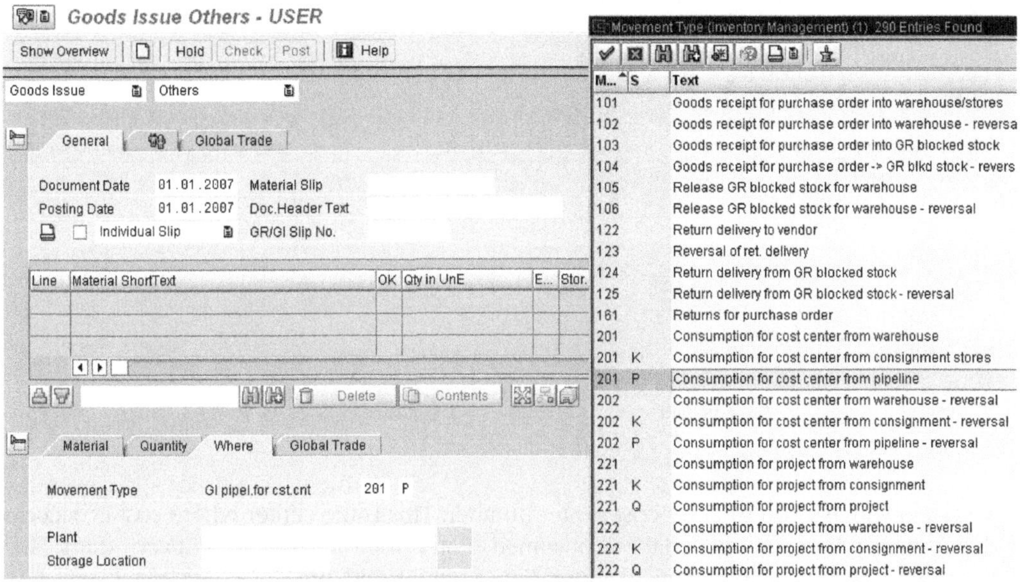

After selecting movement type enter pipeline material, quantity consumed, Plant. Here on difference you will see, is that system will ask you to enter vendor number. This should be the vendor who is supplying you the pipeline material. Enter your vendor number. Make sure Info Record and Source List for the material is already created in the system and also tax code in the Info Record is mentioned.

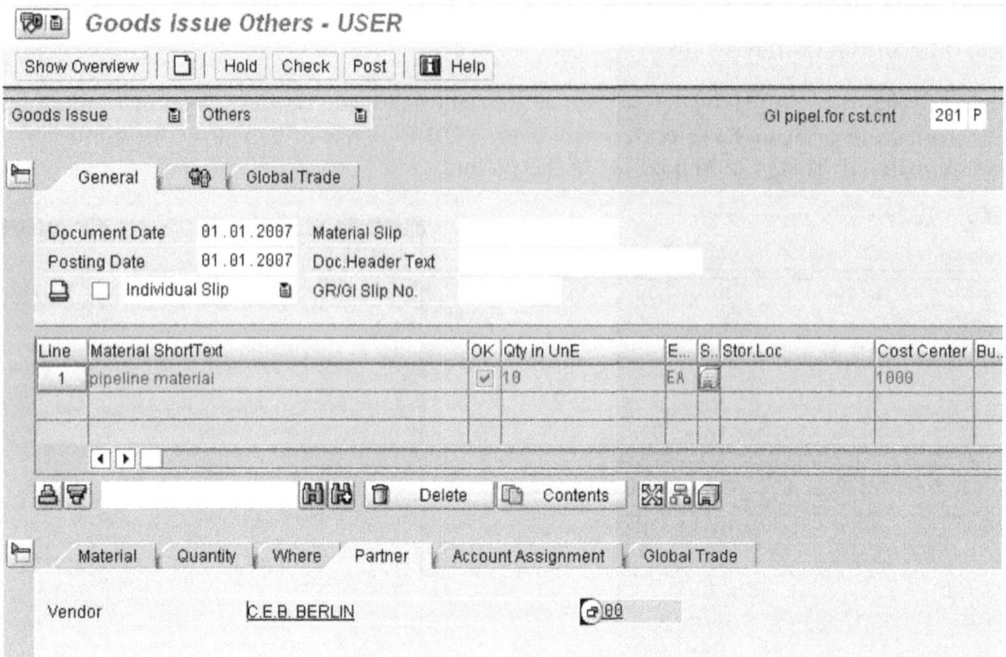

Now system will ask you to enter cost center number. This is the center where cost is occurred or department where this material is consumed. Enter 1000 here. Now is every thing is ok then system will not prompt you to enter G/L Account and business area but it will fetch automatically.

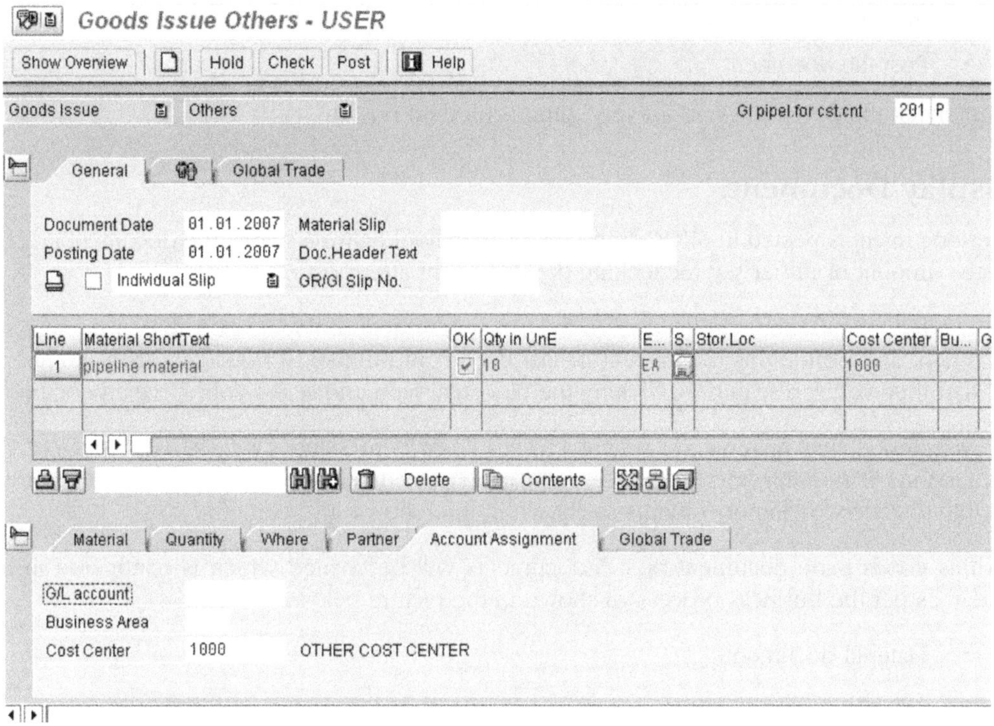

To simplify the process you can refer the following list.

- Transaction- Select Goods issue
- Reference document- Select reference document as others
- Movement type – 201 P
- Posting date – Allowed posting period
- Document date – System taken current date
- Material – E1 or any pipeline material
- Quantity – 100 or any quantity
- Plant – 1000
- Vendor – Your vendor
- Cost center – 1000
- General Ledger Account – Auto selected (as configured in customization)
- Business Area - selected (as configured in customization)
- Select Item Ok check box
- Check the document

- See the message if any
- Post the document

Then check the document and if every thing is ok then post it.

Display Document:-

After document is posted in MIGO transaction, you should always check the document and the posted amount or rather say rechecking the document after post.

In the MIGO transaction you have to go to Display transaction. You will be able to see material document and beside this the current or last document number. If your document number is not that then you can search by clicking the binocular icon and select your targeted document.

You are inside that material document screen. From here select Doc. Info tab page at the header. On clicking this you can see on right side FI Documents icon. Click that. Here you will be able to see following documents as shown in the following screen.

On this goods issue document post 5 documents will be created which is configured in the system as per the business process as shown in the picture below.

- Material document
- Accounting Document
- Profit Center Document
- Special Purpose ledger
- Controlling Document

So to simplify the process follow the enlisted process.

- MIGO – Transaction code in command bar
- Display – Transaction type
- Reference Document – Material document
- Document Number – Enter in the field for that
- ENTER
- Document Info tab page – Select.
- FI document – Click on the icon
- See the FI documents by double clicking it.

Automatic Settlement of Consumption:-

After this you need to enter invoice for the vendor for the material quantity that you have consumed the material. For this you enter MRKO. This a transaction code for Automatic

Settlement of invoice. For the consumption invoice is not entered in the system via MIRO, which is basically for invoice entry.

On entering this transaction code MRKO following screen will come.

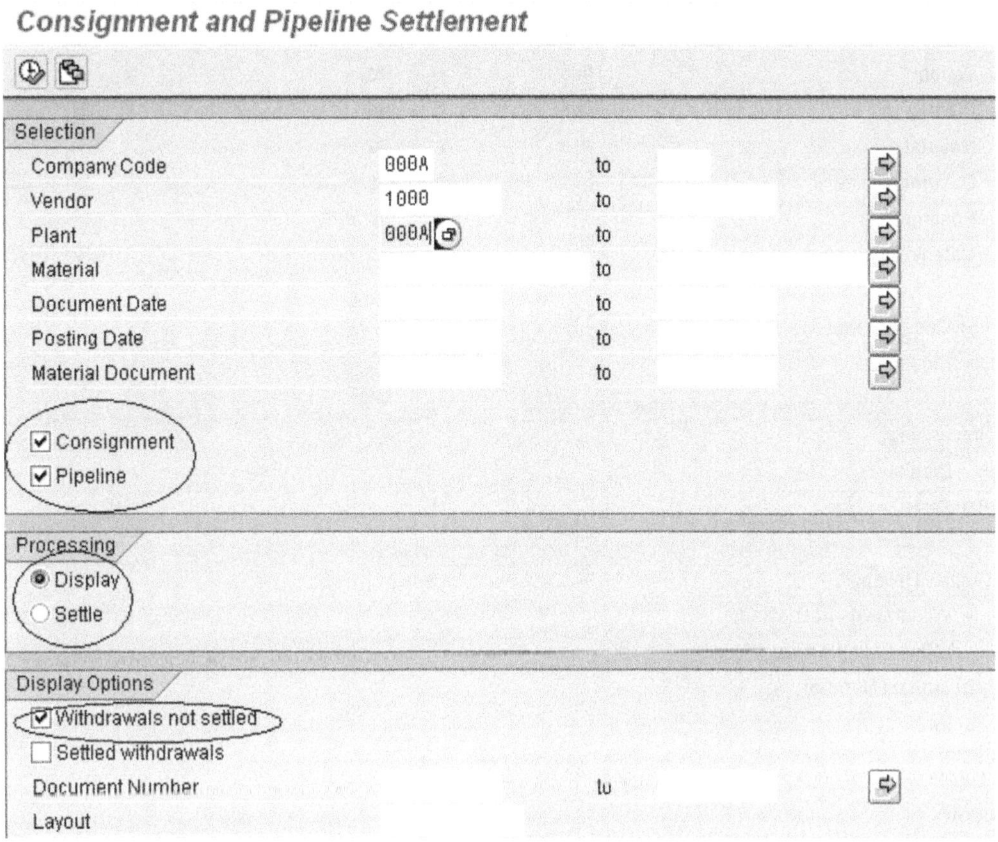

Here you will have to enter company code, vendor number whose material is consumed, plant at which material is consumed and material that is consumed. Apart from this please pay attention that you have to select pipeline option below there as material is pipeline so settlement should be for pipeline consumption.

After this again pay attention about processing option. There you will be able to see 2 options, Display and Settle. You will have first select Display option as first of all you would like to see the documents to be posted to be confirmed. Apart from this select in the Display option for Withdrawals not settled. This will enlist all the withdrawal documents which are not settled and due to be settled, because without this settlement vendor will not get any payment for consumption.

As a result you will be able to the pipeline documents due to be settled.

After this again go back to the initial screen. Here keep al the details as same but just change the Processing option as settled and select that.

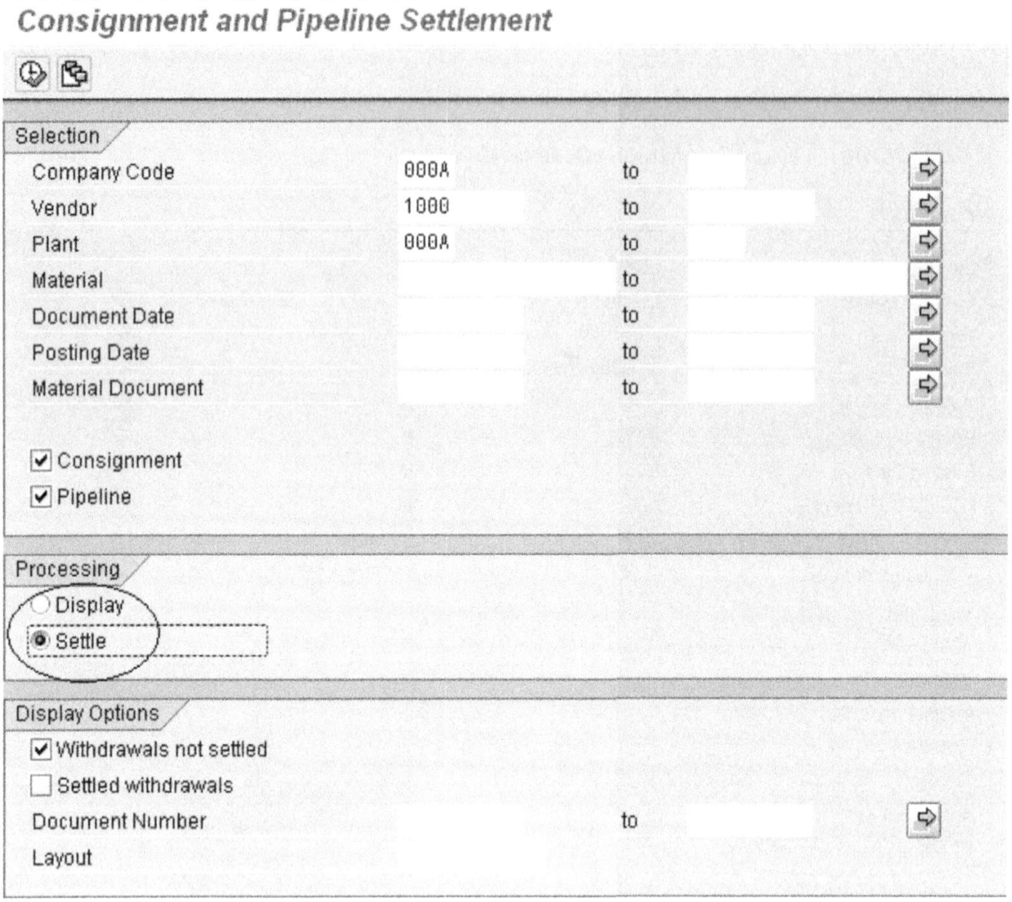

Execute.

If configuration settings in the IMG is perfectly done then document will be posted and document created message will be shown as it is shown in the picture above.

To simplify the process follow the path as enlisted below.

Transaction code – MRKO

Company code – 1000

Plant – 1000

Vendor – Your vendor

Material – Your Pipeline material

Posting Date – As allowed in your system

Select Pipeline Check Box

Processing - Select Display button

Display option – Select Withdrawals not settled.

Execute.

See the document and check find the document number to be settled. After this again go back to the process of MRKO.

Transaction code – MRKO

Company code – 1000

Plant – 1000

Vendor – Your vendor

Material – Your Pipeline material

Posting Date – As allowed in your system

Select Pipeline Check Box

Processing – This time select Settle option

Display option – Select Withdrawals not settled.

Execute.

See the message that document is posted. By double clicking this FI document you can see the amount and the General Ledger accounts which is updated by this transaction.

Remarks:-

Pipeline withdrawals can be made for an order or for a cost center. Note that indicator P denotes for Pipeline.

The valuation of withdrawal is valuated at the price already defined in the pipeline info record.

Tax is already mentioned in the pipeline info record as because there is possibility of entering tax information while entering or settling an invoice for pipeline material.

Pipeline material does not affect warehouse stock status any way.

Chapter

22

CONSIGNMENT PROCUREMENT

Introduction:-

Consignment procurement process is a kind of process in which an external vendor provides and supplies material to the buyer organization and is kept in the buyer organization's consignment stock point. But only condition is that legal ownership is not transferred to the buyer unless until it is consumed and ownership will be transferred only to the extent of stock consumed. That means liability lies with the vendor only till it is consumed or withdrawn for consumption. Only then vendor is required to be paid for the material procured. This payment may be on monthly consumption basis or after a certain time period.

Features

- Consignment stock is not a separate type of material but same material may be treated as consignment material as per requirement and specific process.
- It may be inventoried and taken into counted stock.
- Separate Consignment Info type is maintained.
- Consignment stocks are not valuated. Its valuation is updated only when it is consumed or withdrawal happens.

- A consignment material can be allocated to any of three stock types:
    - o Unrestricted-use stock
    - o Quality inspection stock
    - o Blocked stock

Prerequisites for Consignment Procurement:-

Consignment procurement is slightly different from normal procurement process. For consignment process you need to maintain following prerequisites.

- Material master
- Vendor master
- Source of supply
- Purchasing Info Record

Material master:-

In this step you have to create material as you have already created. You can refer to the chapter material creation. Only difference that is to be made is that while creating material or changing material Select MRP 2 view. And there select special procurement as consignment and in the standard system it is defined as 10 for consignment material. This defines and allows the material to be procured through consignment procurement and also stock can be maintained in the special stock consignment category. The same selection procedure is shown in the picture below.

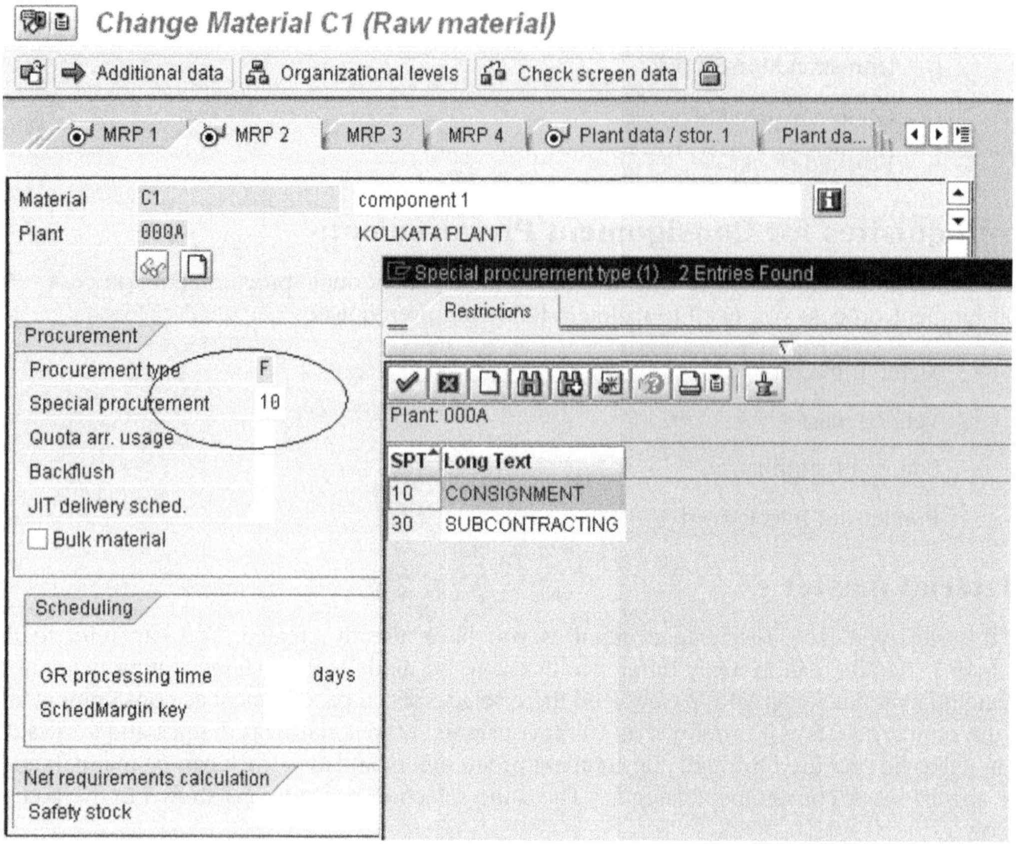

Source of supply:-

This data base is required to be created for each material for which consignment procurement process may or may not be followed. You can create source of supply in the same process as it is already mentioned in the chapter source o supply.

Purchasing Info Record:-

This master data is a must for Consignment procurement process. Pipeline info record creation involves a little deviation from normal info record.

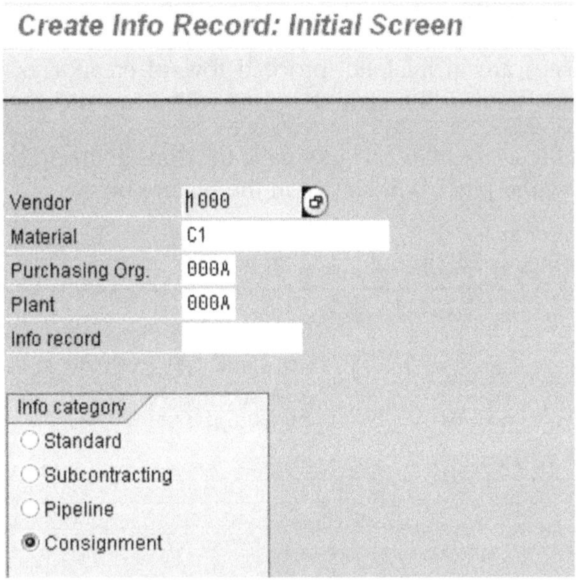

As you can see in the above picture in the create info record you enter

- The vendor number from which you will procure the Consignment material,
- Enter Consignment material number,
- Purchase organization 1000, and
- Plant 1000,
- Then below in the same initial screen you see the info category. There select Consignment button,
- Enter.

  This will take you to the next screen. There you enter data as required in the same way as we have already discussed in the info record chapter.

- Tax Code - Only change will be in the Purchase Organization Data 1 tab page. Here in the Tax Code field you will have to select a tax code which will be applicable. Yu can select any input tax.

(Note:- The valuation of withdrawal is valuated at the price already defined in the Consignment info record. Tax is already mentioned in the Consignment info record as because there is possibility of entering tax information while entering or settling an invoice for Consignment material.)

After completing this save the info record.

Purchase Requisition:-

After all the prerequisites are maintained, proceed toward creation of purchase requisition. Process of purchase requisition will remain the same with a few differences.

In this process first of all select Item category as K for Consignment procurement type. Then enter to confirm. Follow the process as shown in the picture below.

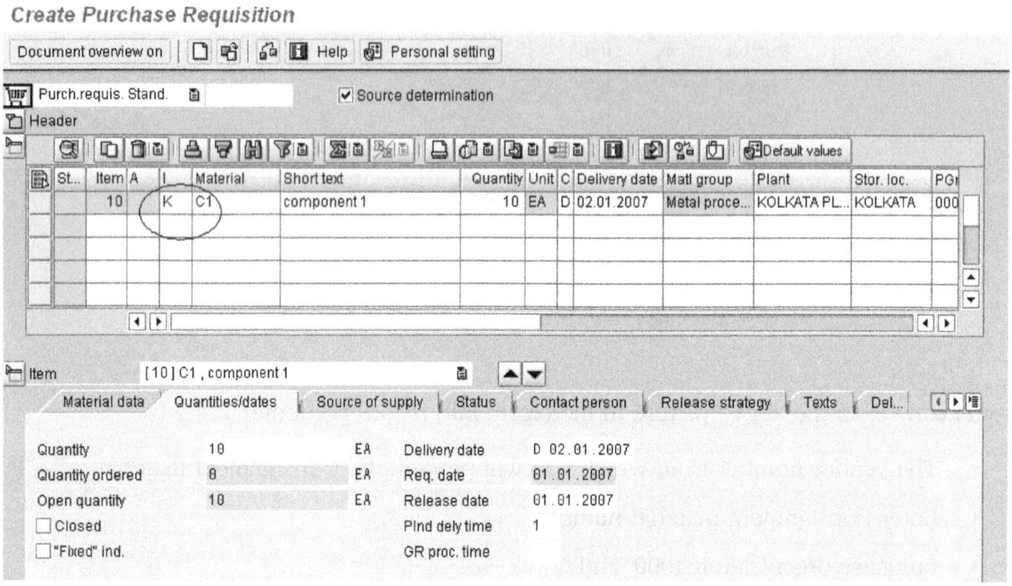

After this enter material which is configured as consignment procurement. Then enter plant after entering plant system will fetch all the relevant information. If vendor is confirmed then assign the vendor as consignment vendor. Enter quantity to be procured. Enter purchase group.

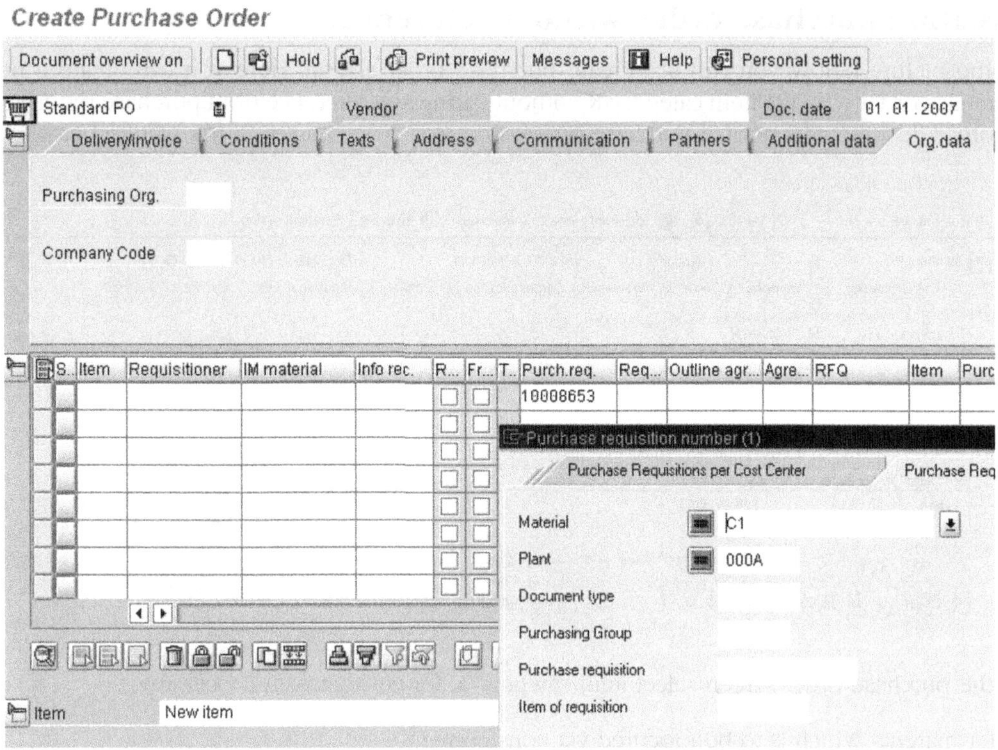

In the picture above you can see that for subcontracting material C1 item category K is selected and quantity 10 is to be procured. Also you can see that in the purchase requisition only the vendor is selected and assigned. Below vendor code on the Source o supply tab page you can also see Info Record number. Check this document and save it. On the status bar you can see the purchase requisition document number generated.

Creating purchase order without reference:-

In the picture below you can see create purchase order screen. Here you can create a new purchase order with the item category K without taking any reference from purchase requisition or other document as normal purchase order is created. You can see in the picture below.

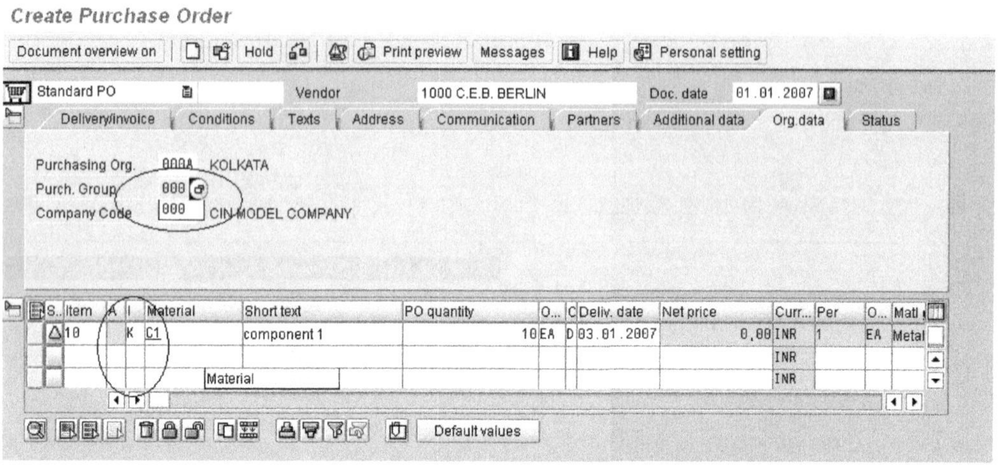

In the purchase order screen select item category K for consignment processing.

Enter material which is to be procured via consignment.

Enter plant.

Enter storage location if the storage location is known.

Enter quantity that is to be procured.

Enter vendor code in the vendor field at the header level.

On the organization data tab page at the header level enter company code and responsible purchase organization.

Press ENTER.

Enter purchase group.

You can see that price field is either in display mode with grey color with not changeable mode. Apart from that if you check the condition tab page at the header data you can see that no condition is taken. You can see in the picture below.

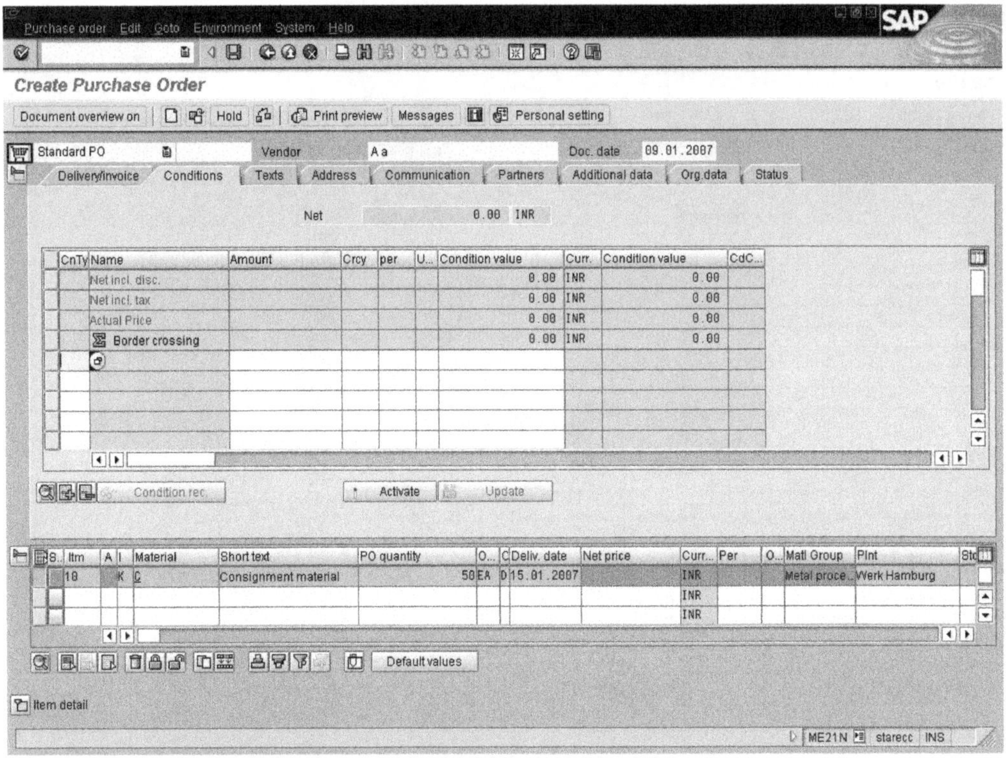

Apart from that there is no condition tab page at the item details tab pages.

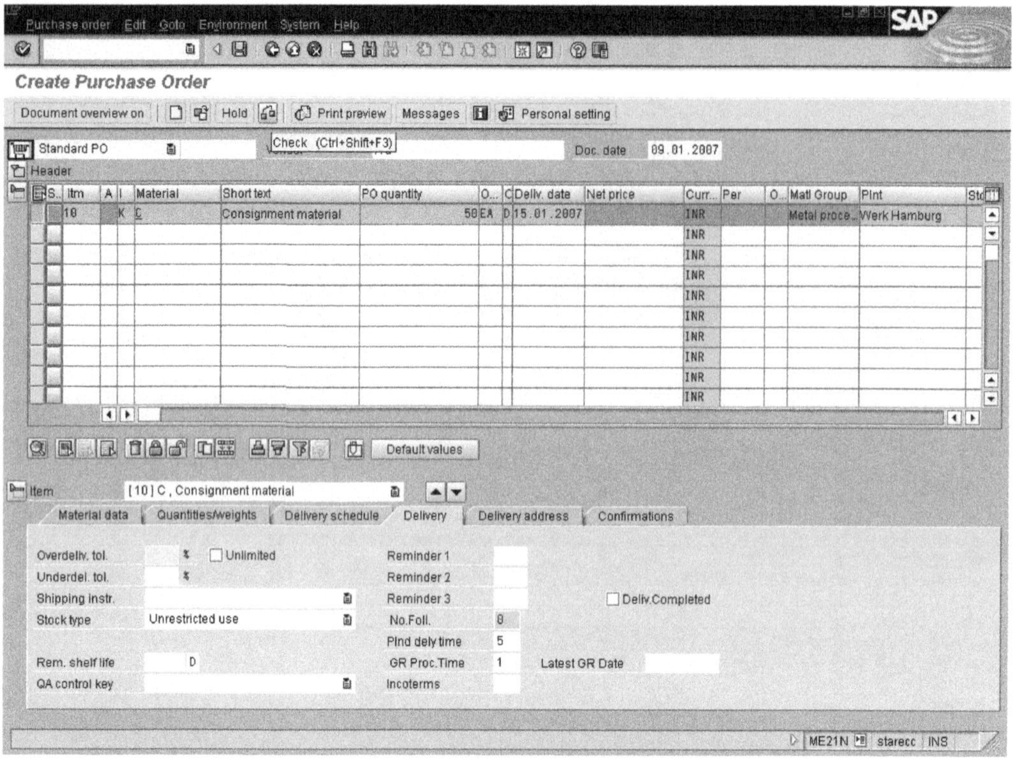

Check the purchase order (Ctrl+Shft+F3) and Save it.

Creating purchase order with reference to purchase requisition:-

Alternatively you can use previously created purchase requisition as a reference document and create purchase order based on that. Process of creation purchase order will remain same but with a little difference.

First of all go to the create purchase order screen. On this screen on item line move right and select F4 in the purchase requisition field. Select the appropriate purchase requisition number and press ENTER.

The system will adopt all the details of that purchase requisition.

Now enter purchase organization.

Enter purchase group.

Enter company code if required. Normally it is taken from the link of plant as it was entered in the purchase requisition.

Enter vendor number if it was not entered in the purchase requisition.

Check the document and save it.

Goods Receipt

This is a step in the procurement process in which we receive and accept goods after physically counting and entering details in the SAP system. You can see in the picture below. In the transaction field goods receipt movement is selected from the drop down. Purchase order is selected from the reference document field. After that you can see a field for purchase number field. Press here F4 and select purchase order number from the options with reference to material. You can see in the picture below.

Check the movement type above, you can see 101 for goods receipt with reference to purchase order.

Check the movement type below on details data. On the Where tab page you will find 101 K movement type for 'goods receipt for consignment stock'.

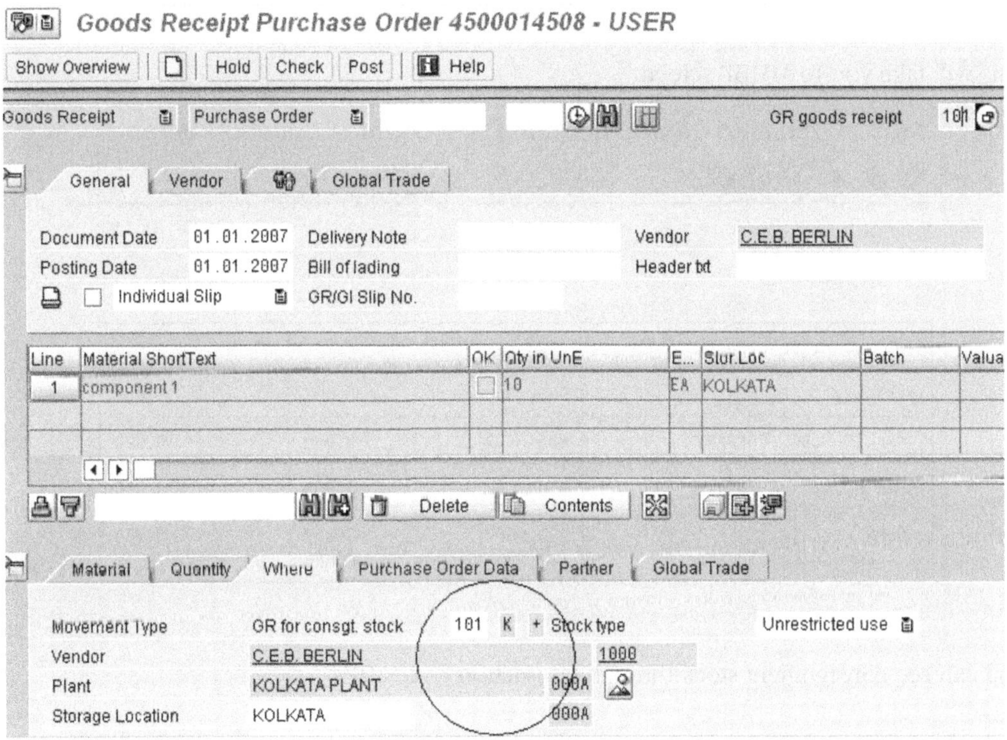

Enter delivery note number on in the Delivery note field.

Check the document and Post the document.

Check the material stock status:-

Enter transaction code MMBE in the command line. Enter material number and execute. It will show the material status in consignment stock.

Alternatively you can also see stock overview in the consignment stock. T-code is MSk3.

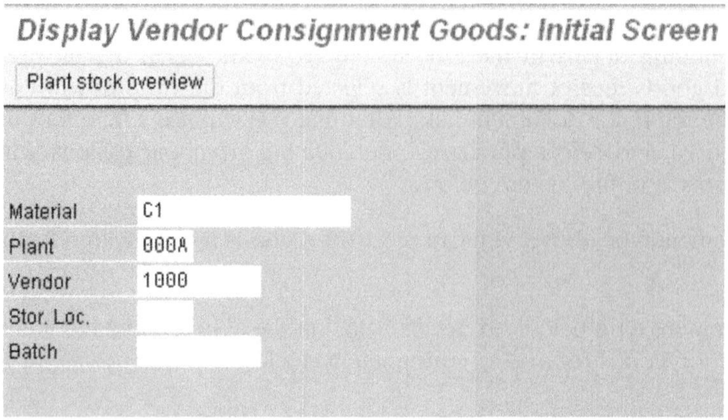

This will take you to MMBE screen.

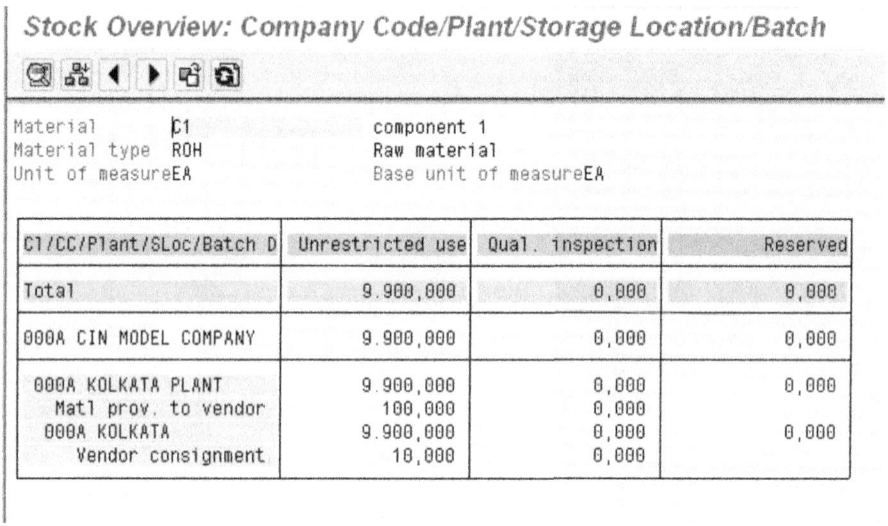

Cl/CC/Plant/SLoc/Batch D	Unrestricted use	Qual. inspection	Reserved
Total	9.900,000	0,000	0,000
000A CIN MODEL COMPANY	9.900,000	0,000	0,000
000A KOLKATA PLANT	9.900,000	0,000	0,000
Matl prov. to vendor	100,000	0,000	
000A KOLKATA	9.900,000	0,000	0,000
Vendor consignment	10,000	0,000	

You can see consignment stock through transaction code MB54.

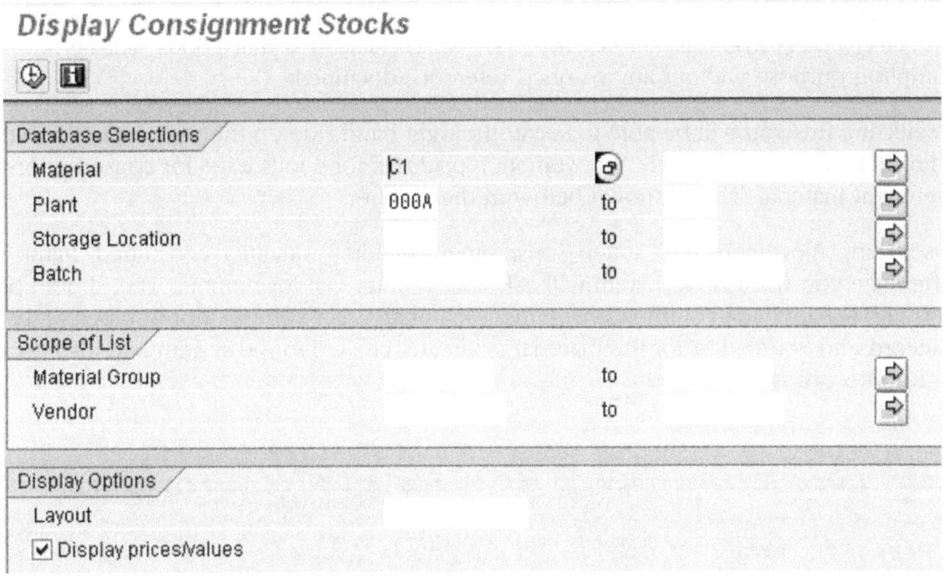

Enter the consignment material code and plant.

Execute.

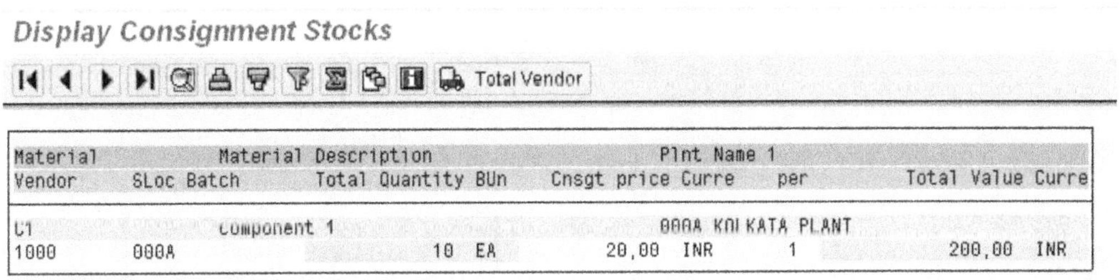

It should be noted that there was no price in the price field in consignment PO. Display the material document and check for FI document. You will find no subsequent document found in Accounting.

Goods Issue:-

After creating all these required master data and having stock in your stock point now you might need to consume the material and you have started consuming it. As you keep on consuming the material you also keep on making a document entry for the consumption and that is done via Goods Issue.

Transaction code is MIGO. We have already discussed about this transaction code which is basically for goods movement.

In the movement option select Goods Issue as shown in the picture below and in the reference option select others from drop down list. Why other? Reason is that goods will be issued for consumption purpose without any planned reference document.

After selecting this you will be able to see at the right hand side on the screen movement type field. From there pressing F4 select movement type 201 K for goods issue for consumption from Consignment material. This is shown below in the picture.

After selecting movement type enter Consignment material, quantity consumed, Plant. Here on difference you will is that system will ask you to enter vendor number. This should be the vendor who is supplying you the Consignment material. Enter your vendor number. Make sure Info Record and Source List for the material is already created in the system and also tax code in the Info Record is mentioned.

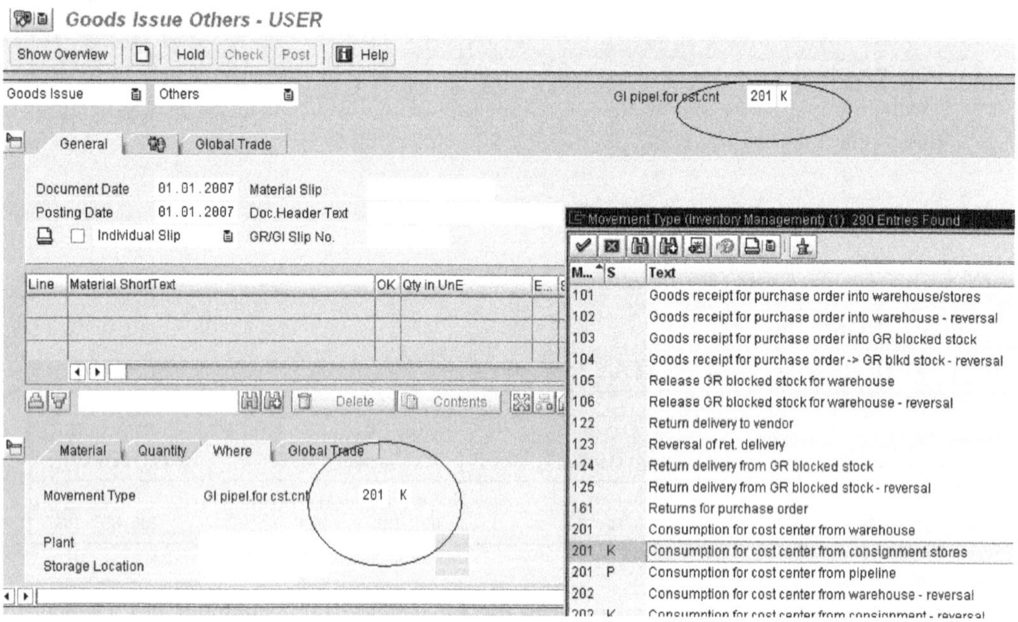

Now system will ask you to enter cost center number. This is the center where cost is occurred or department where this material is consumed. Enter 1000 here. Now is every thing is ok then system will not prompt you to enter G/L Account and business area but it will fetch automatically.

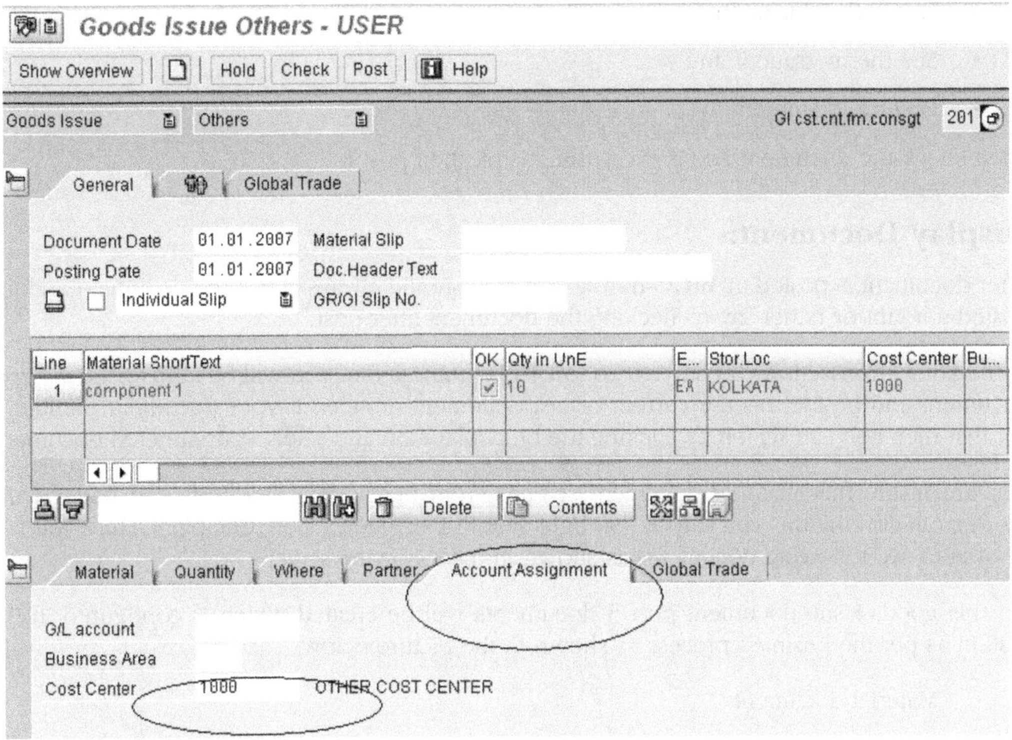

To simplify the process you can refer the following list.

- Transaction- Select Goods issue
- Reference document- Select reference document as others
- Movement type – 201 K
- Posting date – Allowed posting period
- Document date – System taken current date
- Material – E1 or any Consignment material
- Quantity – 100 or any quantity
- Plant – 1000
- Vendor – Your specific vendor whose stock is consumed and who is to be paid.
- Cost center – 1000
- General Ledger Account – Auto selected (as configured in customization)
- Business Area - selected (as configured in customization)
- Select Item Ok check box

- Check the document
- See the message if any
- Post the document

Then check the document and if every thing is ok then post it.

Display Document:-

After document is posted in MIGO transaction, you should always check the document and the posted amount or rather say rechecking the document after post.

In the MIGO transaction you have to go to Display transaction. You will be able to see material document and beside this the current or last document number. If your document number is not that then you can search by clicking the binocular icon and select your targeted document.

You are inside that material document screen. From here select Doc. Info tab page at the header. On clicking this you can see on right side FI Documents icon. Click that. Here you will be able to see following documents as shown in the following screen.

On this goods issue document post 5 documents will be created which is configured in the system as per the business process as shown in the picture below.

- Material document
- Accounting Document
- Profit Center Document
- Special Purpose ledger
- Controlling Document

So to simplify the process follow the enlisted process.

- MIGO – Transaction code in command bar
- Display – Transaction type
- Reference Document – Material document
- Document Number – Enter in the field for that
- ENTER
- Document Info tab page – Select.
- FI document – Click on the icon
- See the FI documents by double clicking it.

Automatic Settlement of Consumption:-

After this you need to enter invoice for the vendor for the material quantity that you have consumed the material. For this you enter MRKO. This a transaction code for Automatic Settlement of invoice. For the consumption invoice is not entered in the system via MIRO, which is basically for invoice entry.

On entering this transaction code MRKO following screen will come. Here you will have to enter company code, vendor number whose material is consumed, plant at which material is consumed and material that is consumed. Apart from this please pay attention that you have to select Consignment option below there as material is Consignment so settlement should be for Consignment consumption.

After this again pay attention about processing option. There you will be able to see 2 options, Display and Settle. You will have first select Display option as first of all you would like to see the documents to be posted to be confirmed. Apart from this select in the Display option for Withdrawals not settled. This will enlist all the withdrawal documents which are not settled and due to be settled, because without this settlement vendor will not get any payment for consumption.

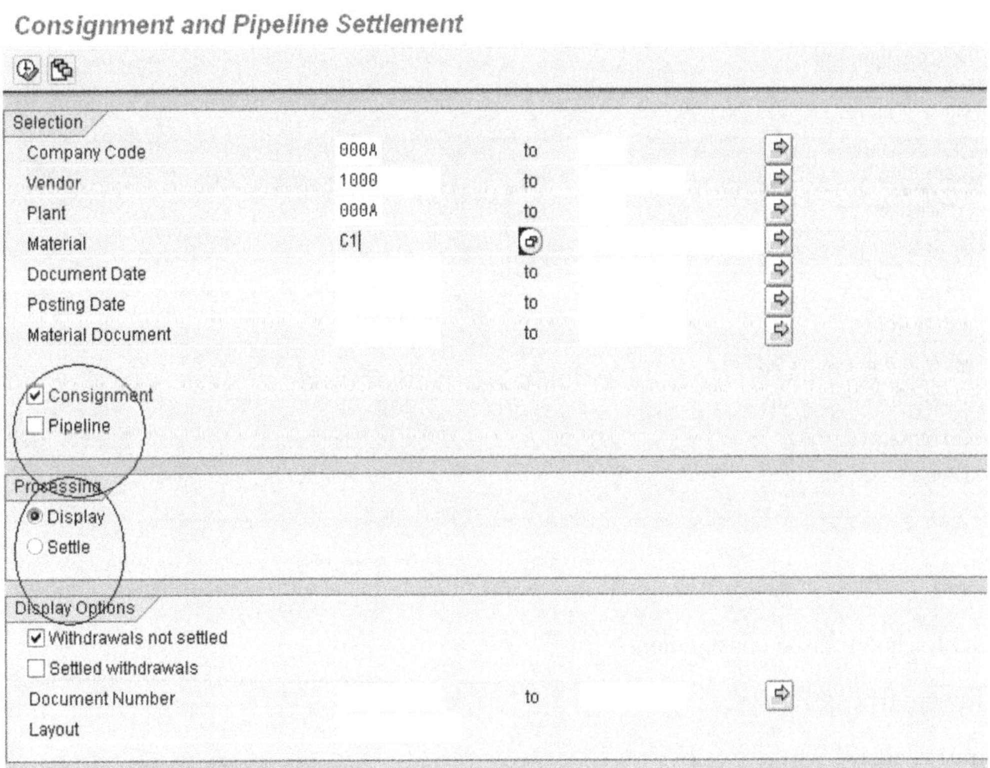

As a result you will be able to the Consignment documents due to be settled. As shown in the picture below.

After this again go back to the initial screen. Here keep al the details as same but just change the Processing option as settled and select that.

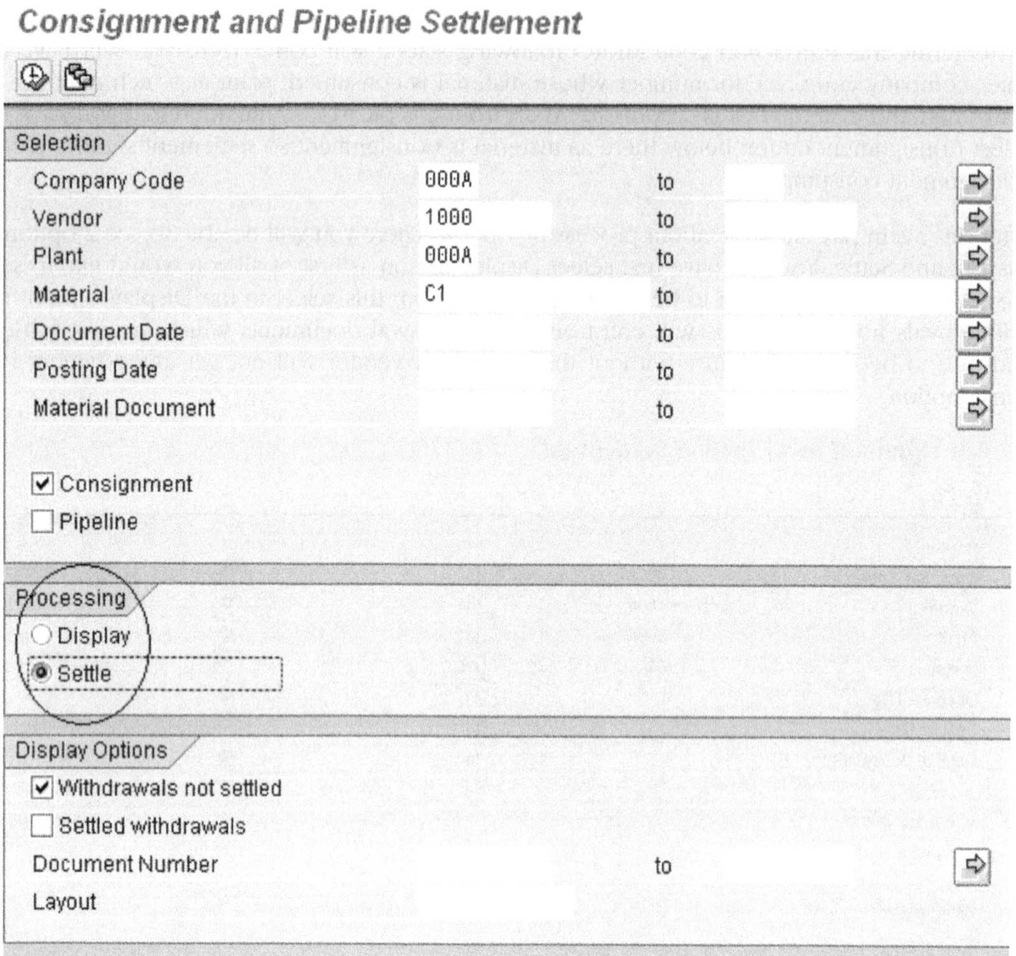

Execute.

MIGO for goods issue consignment

Movement type 201 k

Partner vendor

Account assignment cost center

In goods issue you will be able to see FI document

If configuration settings in the IMG is perfectly done then document will be posted and document created message will be shown as it is shown in the picture above.

To simplify the process follow the path as enlisted below.

Transaction code – MRKO

Company code – 1000

Plant – 1000

Vendor – Your vendor

Material – Your Consignment material

Posting Date – As allowed in your system

Select Consignment Check Box

Processing - Select Display button

Display option – Select Withdrawals not settled.

Execute.

See the document and check find the document number to be settled. After this again go back to the process of MRKO.

Transaction code – MRKO

Company code – 1000

Plant – 1000

Vendor – Your vendor

Material – Your Consignment material

Posting Date – As allowed in your system

Select Consignment Check Box

Processing – This time select Settle option

Display option – Select Withdrawals not settled.

Execute.

See the message that document is posted. By double clicking this FI document you can see the amount and the General Ledger accounts which is updated by this transaction.

Remarks:-

Consignment withdrawals can be made for an order or for a cost center. Note that indicator P denotes for Consignment.

The valuation of withdrawal is valuated at the price already defined in the Consignment info record.

Tax is already mentioned in the Consignment info record as because there is possibility of entering tax information while entering or settling an invoice for Consignment material.

Consignment material does not affect warehouse stock status any way.

Chapter

23

OUTLINE AGREEMENT

Introduction:-

An outline purchase agreement is a longer-term agreement between a purchasing organization and a vendor regarding the supply of materials or the performance of services within a certain period according to predefined terms and conditions. (Outside SAP, such agreements may be referred to by a number of terms, including "blanket", "master", "framework" or "umbrella" agreements). --SAP Definition

Outline Purchase Agreements are subdivided into following types In the SAP System.

- **Contracts**
    - **Centrally agreed contracts**
    - **Distributed contracts**
- **Scheduling agreements**
    - **Scheduling agreement referencing a centrally agreed contract**

Structure

An outline agreement consists of a document header and Items (it may be one or more items).

- **Document header:-**

  It contains information relating to the entire agreement.

- **Items:-**

  It contains information which is not related to the entire agreement but only a part of that and is specific to the relevant material or service in the item line.

Texts

You can also enter different kinds of text for the agreements you can create your own texts from scratch or change a text that has been suggested by the system.

Texts are of two kind header text and item text. Texts are further subdivided into text types. These are mentioned as a tree. Text type determines the print sequence on the print out document.

- **Header text**
  - **Shipping instructions text type**
  - **Delivery instructions text type**
- **Item text**

In next section of Contract and Scheduling agreement we will discuss how these agreements are created and how these are utilized in SAP system.

Chapter 24

CONTRACT

Introduction:-

A contract is a type of outline purchase agreement against which release orders (releases) can be issued for agreed materials or services.

Contract terms:-

Some times a contract may also be referred to by a number of other terms, such as

1. "Systems contract",
2. "Blanket order agreement",
3. "Blanket contract", and
4. "Period contract".

Types of contracts:-

Contracts can be based on following options.

- Quantity contracts

This type of contract is used if the total quantity to be ordered is known and fixed writhing a specific validity period.

- **Value contracts**

  This type of contract is used if the total Value of all the release orders issued against the contract is not to exceed a predefined value within a specific validity period.

- **Centrally Agreed Contract**

  Some times requirement of a certain material or service may not be limited to just one particular receiving plant. So in this case, a centrally agreed contract is created without specifying any plant. Plant is specified only when contract release order is created.

A centrally agreed contract is useful if

- A single purchasing organization procures for an entire group of companies, or
- Or a contract between a reference purchasing organization and the vendor is created. Later as per requirement the other purchase organizations create contract release order against this centrally agreed contract.

Contract release order:-

For the procurement with reference to contract, a contract release order is required to be created. A contract release order is nothing but a standard contract but which is created within the boundary of a contract. Such purchase orders are thus termed as

- "Contract release orders" or
- "Simply "release orders".
- "Call-off orders" (Outside SAP, particularly in the UK)

Structure of a contract:-

A contract consists of a document header and Items (it may be one or more items) and texts.

- Document header:-

  It contains information relating to the entire agreement.

- Items:-

  It contains information which is not related to the entire agreement but only a part of that and is specific to the relevant material or service in the item line.

- Texts

  You can also enter different kinds of text for the agreements you can create your own texts from scratch or change a text that has been suggested by the system.

  Texts are of two kind header text and item text. Texts are further subdivided into text types. These are mentioned as a tree. Text type determines the print sequence on the print out document.

- Header text
  - o Shipping instructions text type
  - o Delivery instructions text type
- Item text

  You can assign an item category with a contract. This will define the type of procurement.

  You can also assign account assignment category with the contract as per cost bearing ratio.

Release documentation:-

In release documentation release orders issued are logged.

Over the contract validity period, certain quantities of the materials or services covered are released (called off) against the contract as and when required through the issue of purchase orders referencing the latter.

Creating a Contract

You can create a contract as follows:

- **Manually:-**

  You enter all data relating to the contract manually.

- **Using the referencing technique:-**

  You can create a contract using a reference document as enlisted below.

  - o Purchase requisitions
  - o RFQs/quotations
  - o Other contracts

- **Combining both the options:-**

  You can create a contract by combining both the options. First adopt data from any a reference document and then change and add data as required.

Prerequisites

Before you create a contract, following data must be in your system.

Material:-

You should know what material is to be procured.

Account assignment

You should have knowledge whether procurement will be with any particular account assignment category or a standard one.

Plant

You should know for which plant contract for the specified material or service will be applicable..

But in centrally agreed contract you need not enter specify any plant code.

A centrally agreed contract can be used for

- All plants assigned to the responsible purchasing organization
- All plants of other purchasing organizations for which the responsible purchasing organization has been defined as reference purchasing organization in Customizing

MPN material number

If you wish to order a material with a manufacturer part number (MPN), you need the MPN material number. A manufacturer part number is the details of the manufacturer whose material the vendor is going to supply you. Apart from that it will also give information about the part number used by that manufacturer.

Purchasing organization:-

A purchasing organization is to be specified.

Purchase group:-

A purchasing group is to be specified.

Source list:-

There should be source list master data for the specified plant. You can also create it when maintaining the contract by choosing *Environment ®Source list*.

Vendor:-

There has to be a master record for the vendor subject to contract.

Create contract:-

You can create contract by entering transaction code ME31K in the command line or by following the menu pate as below in the picture.

SAP Easy Access > Logistics > Material Management > Purchasing > Outline Agreement > Contract > Create

Transaction code:-

Transaction code for contract creation is ME31K. for change contract it is ME32K and for display contract it is ME33K.

On choosing this transaction following initial screen will appear.

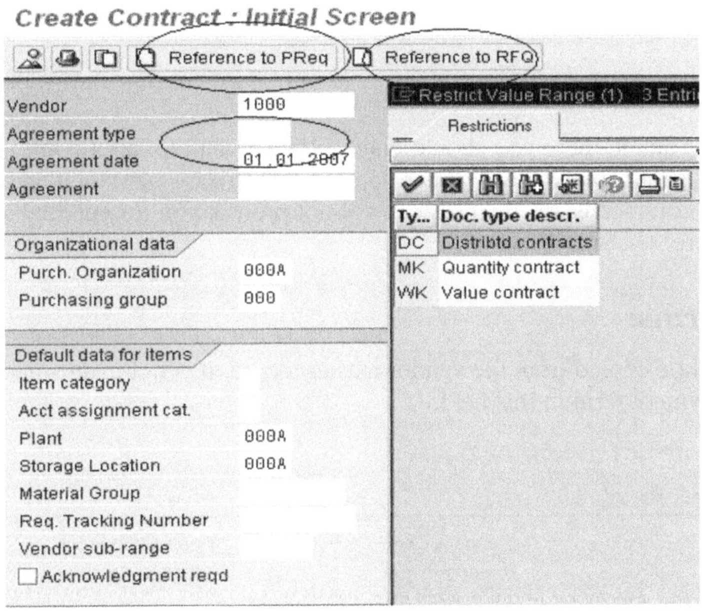

Contract with reference to document:-

On the top of the screen you can see 'Reference to PReq' and 'reference to RFQ'. So here you can decide whether you want to create contract with reference to any reference document or without reference to any document.

Vendor:-

Here first enter the vendor code with whom you are going to create the contract.

Agreement type:-

Here you can choose the type of contract you are going to create. Enter either MK or WK.

Agreement date:-

Enter the date on which you are going to create the contract. If you do not enter then system will take current date.

Purchase Organization:-

Enter purchasing organization name under which this contract is being created. Enter here 1000.

Purchase group:-

Enter here 000.

ENTER.

After you enter following header data screen will appear. We have already discussed on header data.

Target Value:-

In case of value contract here you should enter the total value of all the release orders which will be created against this contract. Enter here 100000 in case of value contract. If you have chosen quantity contract as MK then system will not prompt you for entering any value in this field or any where.

Payment terms:-

This field should be copied from the vendor master record. If is not maintained there then you can maintain payment term in this field.

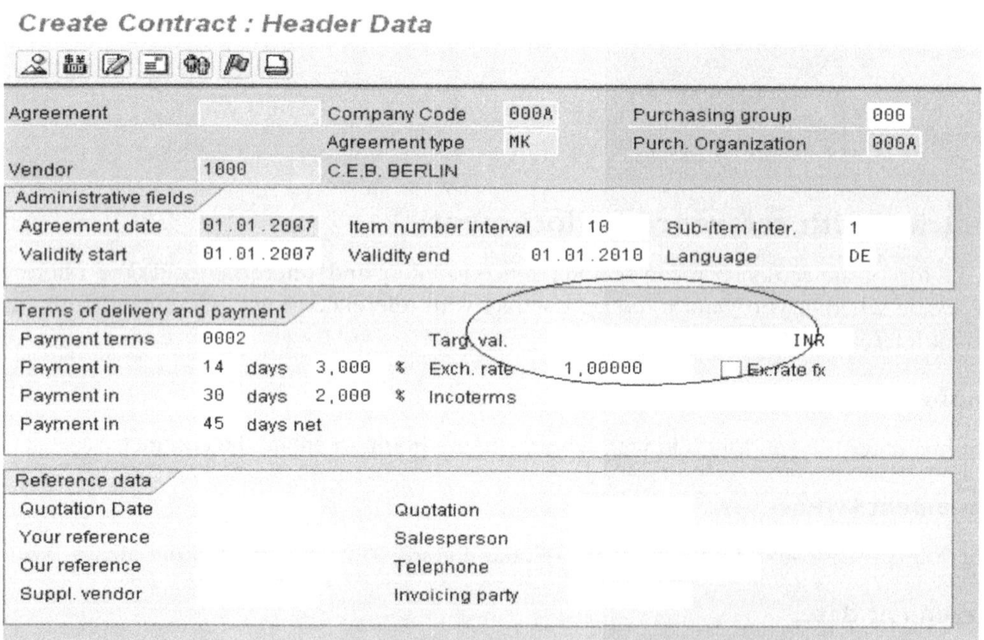

ENTER to confirm the entries on the header data page.

If the contract is a value contract then enter target value in this page other wise you can leave this field blank and enter quantity in line item.

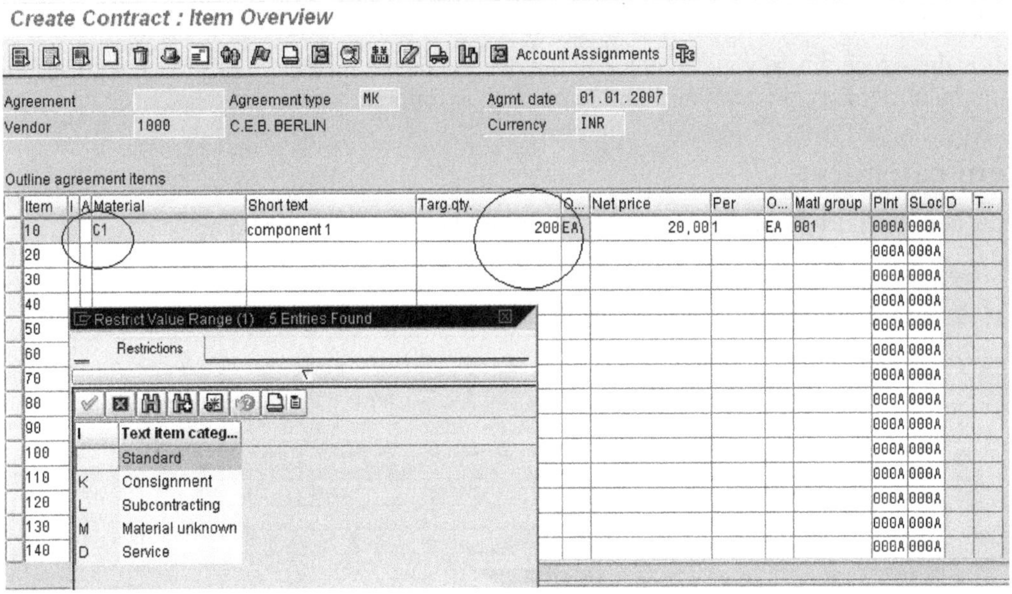

In case of value contract if you press enter without entering any value in the target value field then system will move into the next screen without any error prompt. This is evident in the last screen shot.

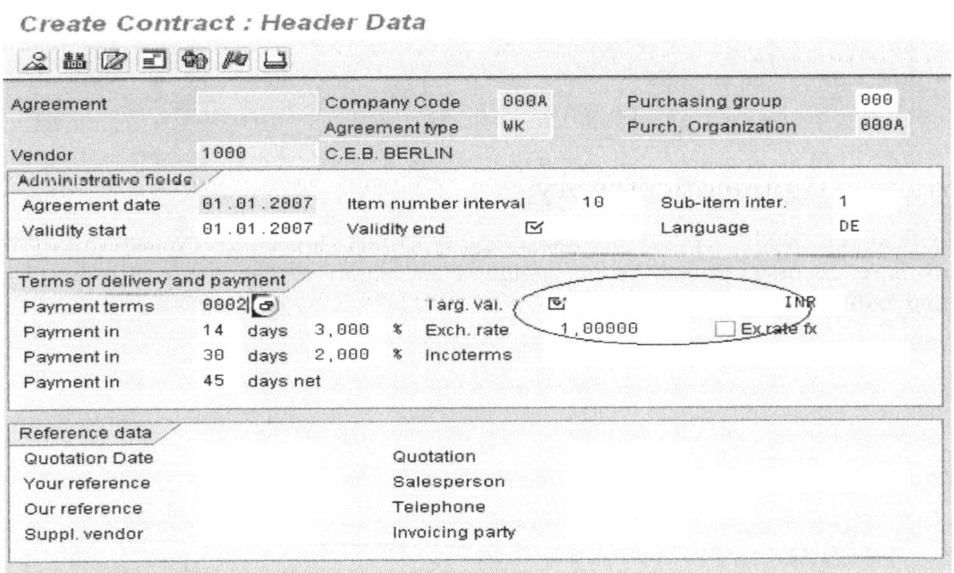

But in case of value contract if press enter without entering any value in the target value field on the header data page, system will prompt to maintain the target value. This is evident in the screen shown above.

Item Overview:-

This is the screen where you can enter all the details about a material or a service with account assignment category on item level and item category on item level.

Item category:-

Enter item category as per your choice or leave it blank for a standard one.

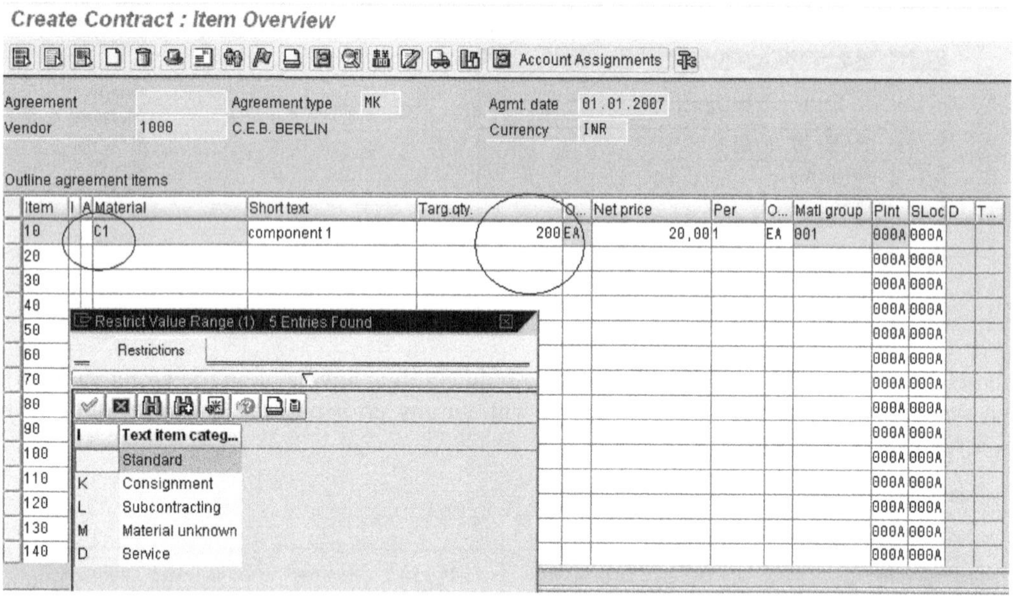

Account assignment category:-

In this field you need to specify account category as you can see in the picture below. We already have discussed about account assignment category in the purchase order chapter. Meaning and uses are the same.

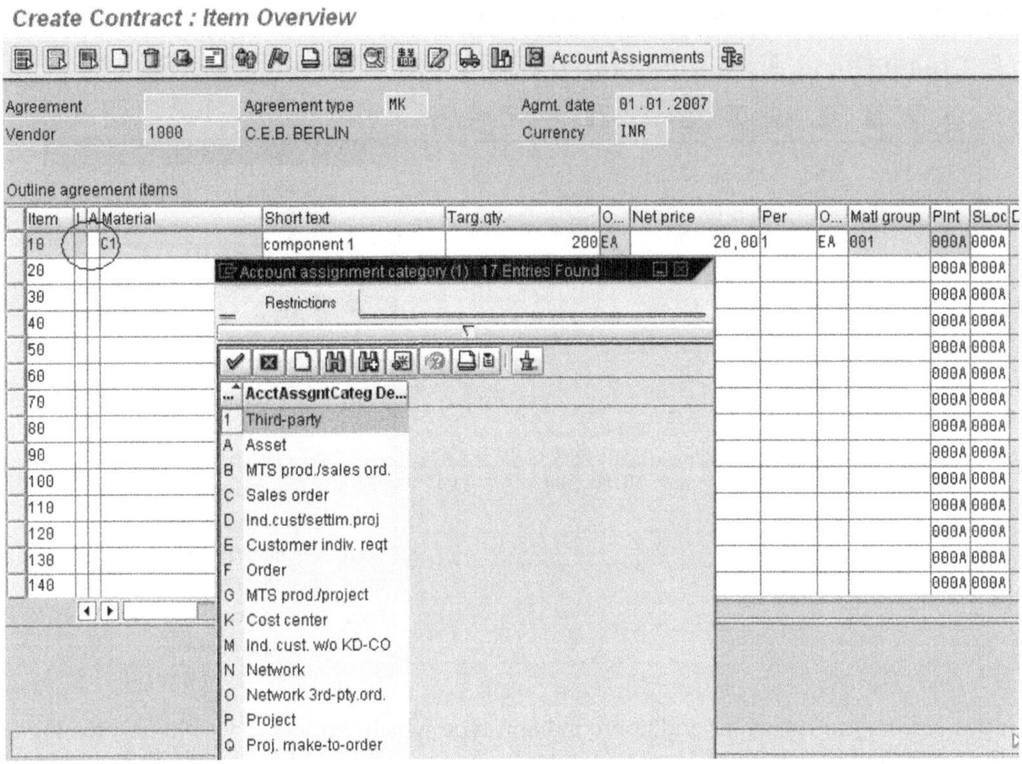

Item conditions:-

Select the line item of the material and go to item condition. You can see in the picture below where you need to click on the icon.

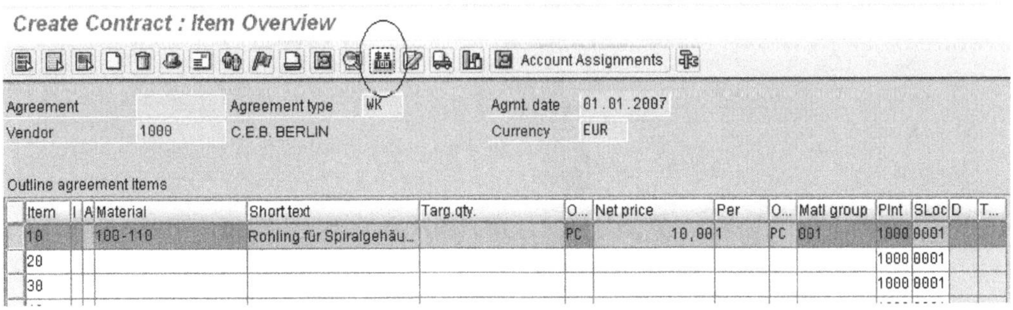

Next picture will show you the item condition screen.

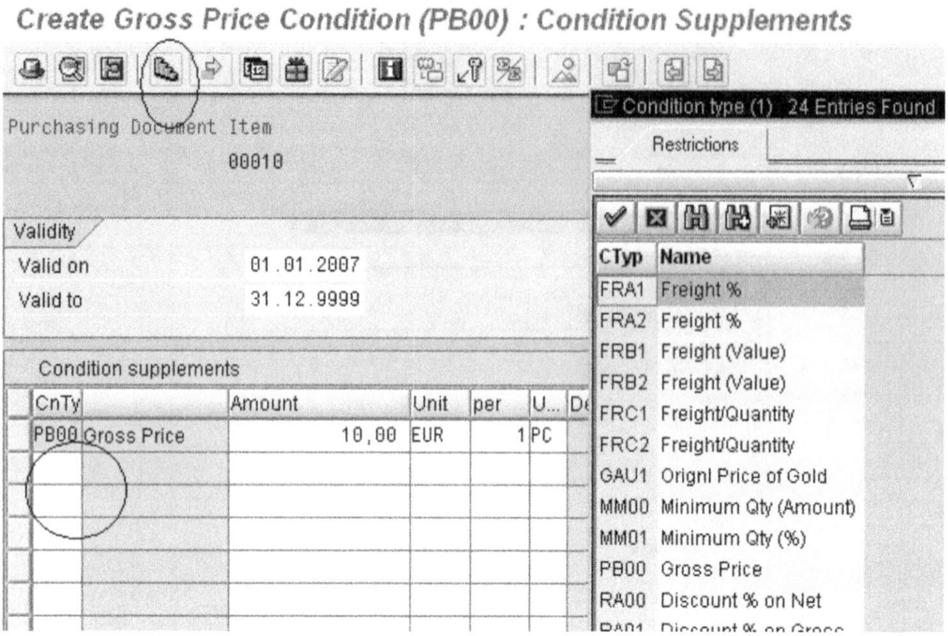

On this screen you can enter addition condition type which will come visible on pressing F4 in the CnTy field below PB00. Here you enter for an example FRA1 for freight in % and in the amount field enter 20 to result as 20% freight applicable.

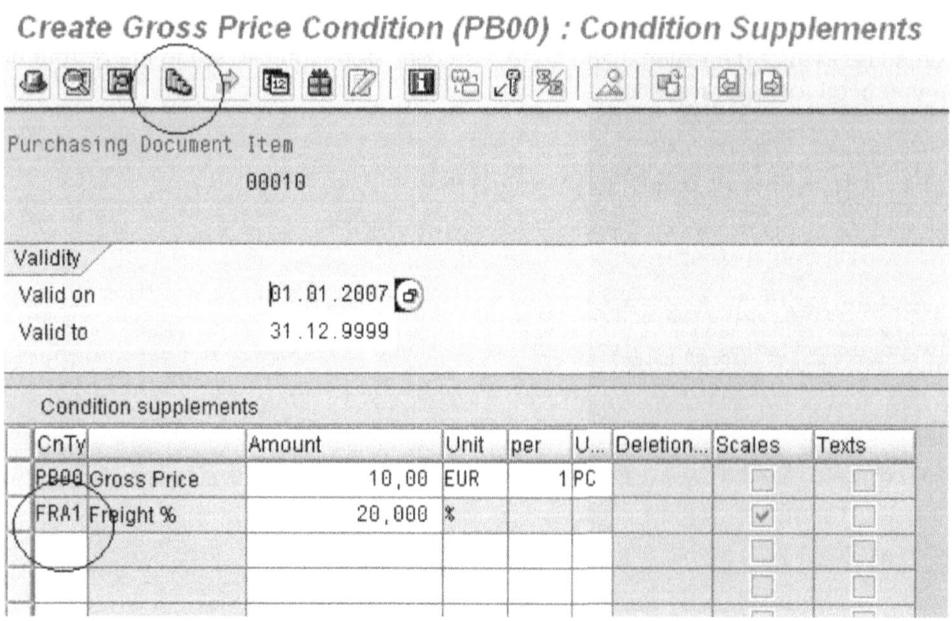

Validity period for condition:-

In the item condition supplement page you can also see the validity date for the item conditions.

Scales:-

You can also maintain scales for the condition type. Select the line of the condition and go to scale as in the picture above or press F2.

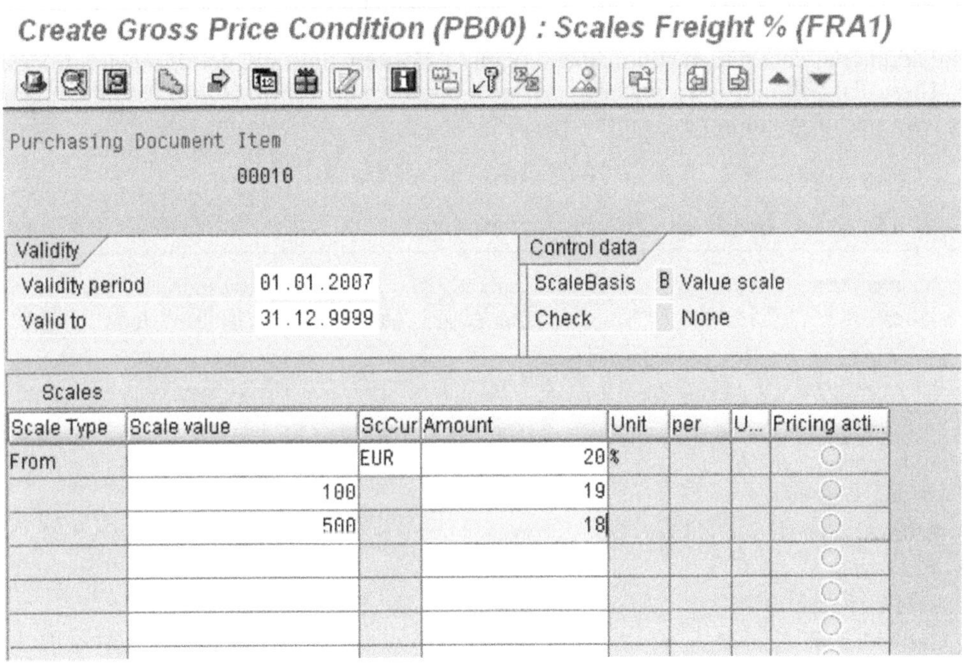

Here maintain scale for the item condition type. You can follow as it is done below.

Blank in the Quantity field & in the price field 20 (That means from 0 to 99 pieces quantity in the purchase order system will calculate @ 20 EUR each)

100 in the quantity field and in the price field 19 (That means from 0 to 99 pieces quantity in the purchase order system will calculate @ 20 EUR each and from 100 to 499 pieces it will calculate @ 19 EUR each)

500 in the quantity field and in the price field 18 (That means from 100 to 499 pieces quantity in the purchase order system will calculate @ 19 EUR each and from 500 and onwards it will calculate @ 18 EUR each)

(Note: It may be EUR or INR depending upon the vendor's currency.

It the item condition is base value or price then amount field will be in currency and if the condition is other then base price then according to the condition type this value will be either in amount or in %.)

This whole process is called scaling of condition. This process is same as this is in the purchasing information record.

From the item overview screen you can again navigate to the header details page. You can see in the picture below.

Additional Data:-

By selecting icon as below you can move to additional data page or by pressing Shift+F5.

On the additional data screen you maintain planned delivery time and goods receipt processing time. These data should from material master record. Apart from that you can also maintain other relevant information here on this page.

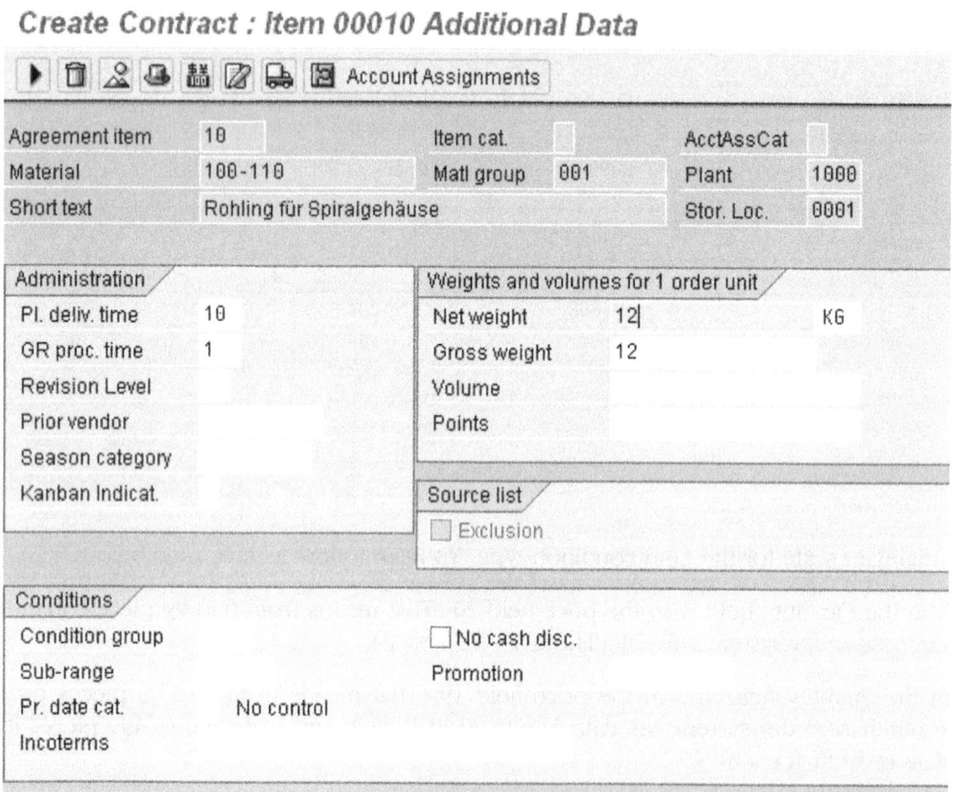

Messages:-

By pressing Shift+F1 you can move to messages page where you can set this contract for printing purpose.

After you have done all these entries, save the document.

Contract Release Order:-

A contract release order is like a purchase order. Only difference is that this purchase order is created taking reference from a relative contract.

To create this type of purchase order, go to ME21N to go to purchase order screen.

Outline agreement document number:-

Here on the item line go to the field Outline agreement. Here press F4. In the search popup page enter material or vendor, and in the order type enter K for quantity contract.

Press ENTER. The reference contract document number will come.

Adopt that document.

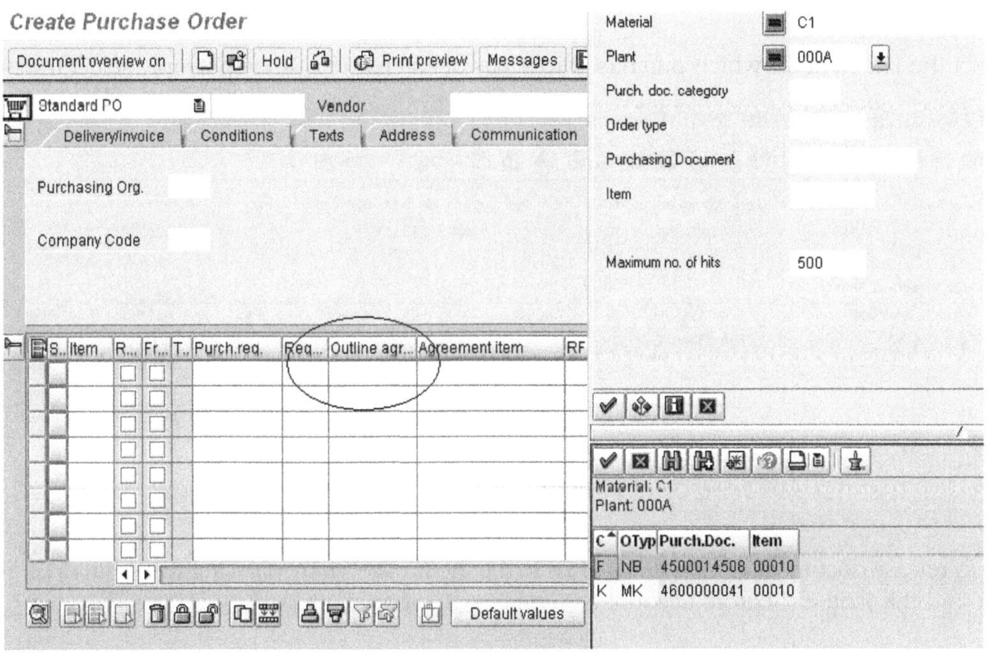

Plant:-

In the purchase order you will have to enter plant to make it plant specific.

If you have not maintained release procedure for contract then you can straight create purchase order by saving that.

Release Order document:-

Release order document is a document which enlists purchasing document which has been created with this reference document. You can see this document. To see this follow the procedure as mentioned below.

Go to ME32K transaction code. This is a transaction code to change the contract document.

On the initial screen enter the purchasing document number of the contract.

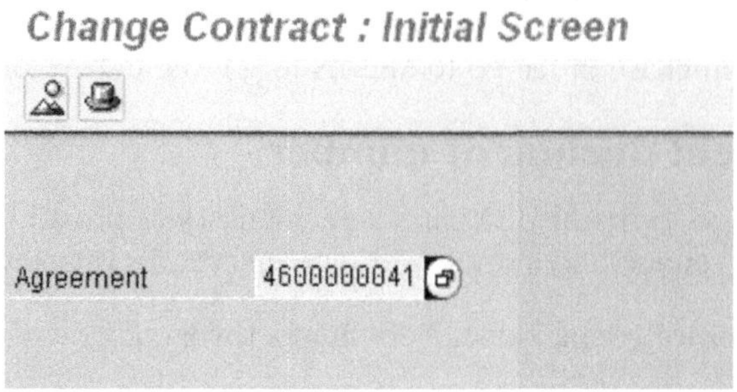

ENTER.

Select the line item for which purchase order has been created. Or even simply select the line.

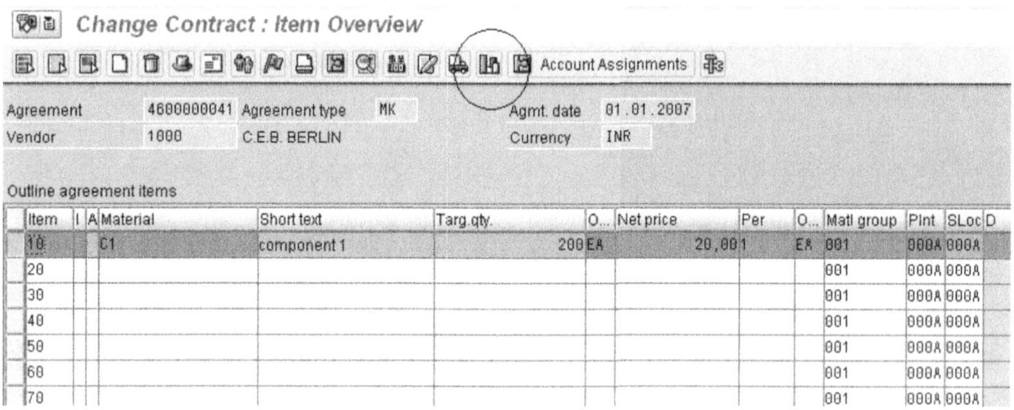

Go to release documentation as it is shown in the picture above by pressing Ctrl+Shift+F12. You can find this icon just before account assignment on the menu bar.

On selection this you can see the release document as it is shown in the picture below.

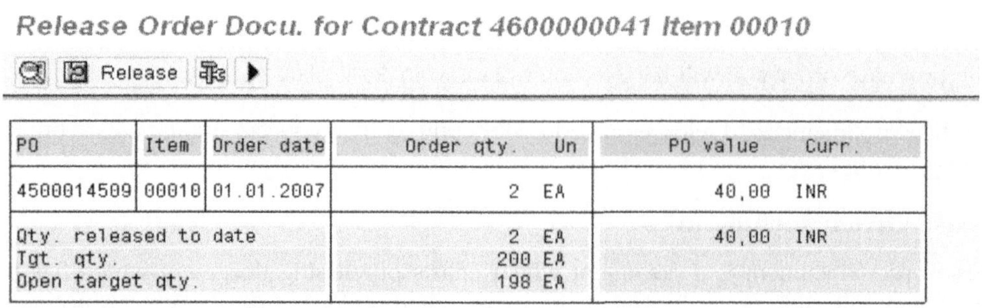

In the document above you can see that purchase order quantity of 2units have been updated and total value as per contract condition price is updated as per quantity ordered. Now you can procure only the balance quantity in the further purchase order with reference to this contract item as maximum limit is up to 200 units as target quantity.

Open order quantity is as 198 units.

After creation of purchase order following process will be performed in the materials management domain.

- After this you can simply send the purchase order to the vendor.
- Vendor will send you the ordered quantity.
- You will count the quantity and record it in the SAP system under Goods receipt.
- Along with this vendor will also send you the invoice for the delivery.
- You have to enter this invoice in the system under logistics invoice verification.
- After release of the invoice vendor will get payment from the finance department.

So After creation of purchase order the whole follow on procedure will be maintained as normal procedure. We have already covered these procedures in other relevant chapters. You can refer those chapters for complete the process.

Change (ME32K):-

In the transaction code you can change the contract document.

Display (ME33K):-

In the transaction code you can display the contract document.

Release (ME35K):-

If you have maintained and configured release procedure for contract then you will have to release this document before this is used form purchase order processing.

Print the contract (ME9K):-

By this transaction code you can get the printout of the contract.

But for that you have to maintain condition as printable and have to follow these steps while creating contract or while changing contract select message output.

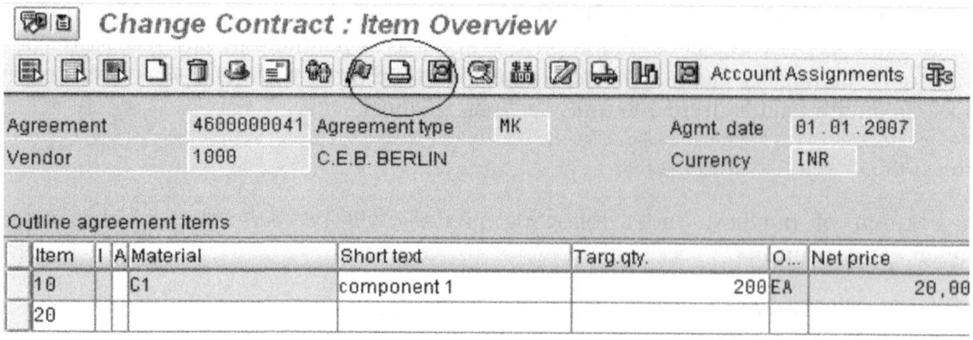

Set printer location and printer id.

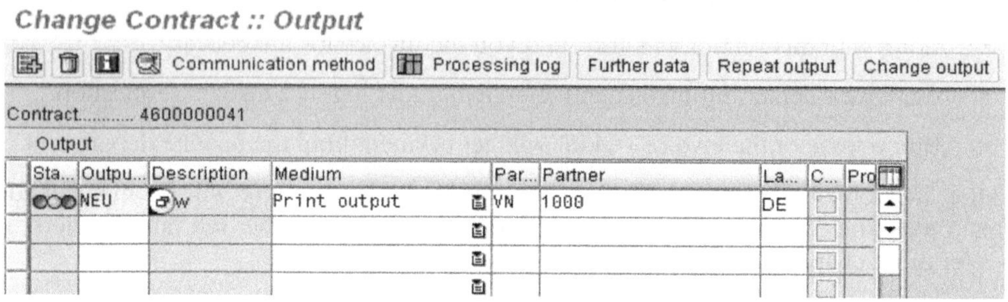

Set print output.

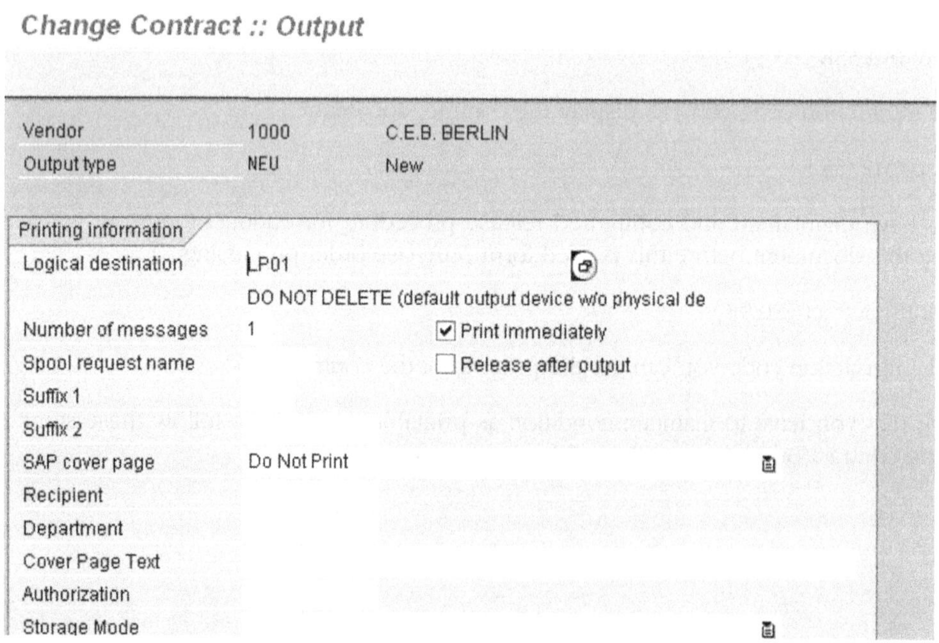

In document print option select document to be printed.

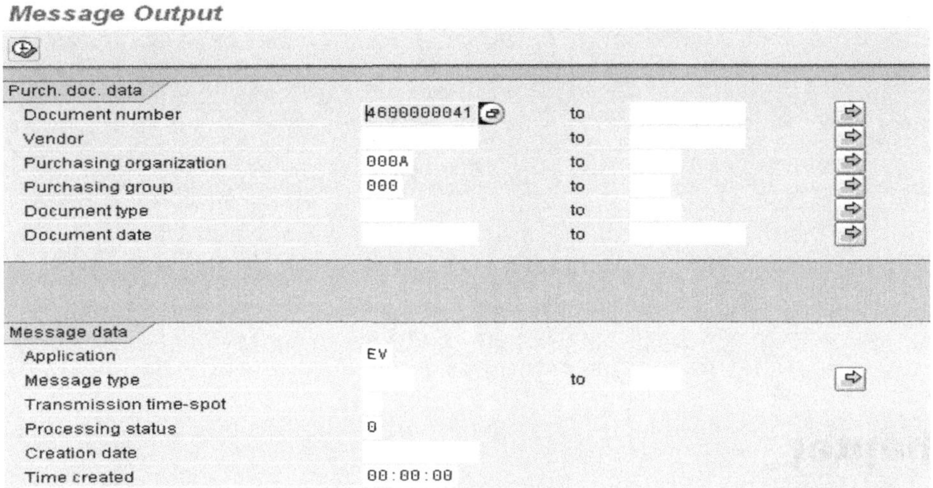

Select the document number and click on display message.

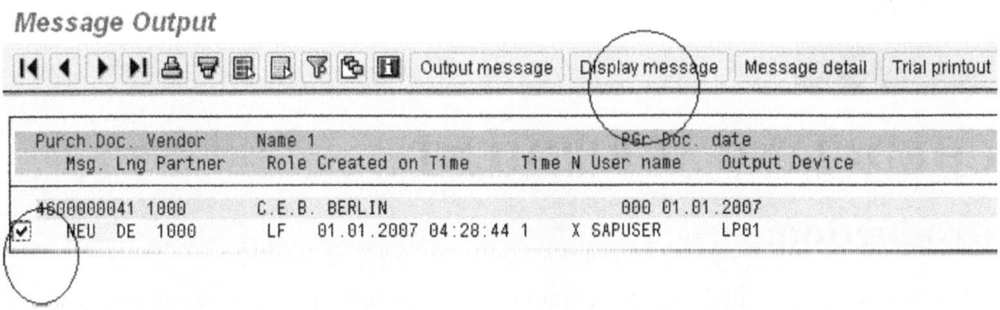

You will be able to see the printout.

Chapter

25

SCHEDULING AGREEMENT

Introduction:-

This is a type of outline purchase agreement in which materials are procured on predetermined dates within a certain time period.

Structure

A scheduling agreement consists of a number of items, for each of which a procurement type is defined. The following item category you can assign with the scheduling agreement.

- Standard
- Subcontracting
- Consignment
- Stock transfer

Delivery of the total quantity of material specified in a scheduling agreement item is spread over a certain period in a delivery schedule, consisting of lines indicating the individual quantities with their corresponding planned delivery dates.

For scheduling agreement items involving subcontracting, you can specify the materials or components to be provided to the subcontractor with respect to each scheduled delivery of the ordered item.

Conditions in scheduling agreement at header level:-

Conditions can apply to the entire scheduling agreement.

Conditions in scheduling agreement at item level:-

Conditions at item level apply specifically to the material to be supplied in each case.

Scheduling agreement releases:-

Scheduling agreement releases (comprising a header and the actual delivery schedule) are issued to the vendor, instructing the latter to effect deliveries of the relevant material on the dates shown.

Create scheduling agreement:-

A scheduling agreement is created with the help of ME31L in the same way as a contract is created with the help of transaction code ME31K. Even the initial screen will also look the same. But there is a little difference between these two initial screens. On the scheduling agreement creation screen you can see that a scheduling agreement can be created with reference to contract also. So we can see that scheduling agreement can be created in the following way.

In the picture below you see the menu path. SAP Easy Access > Logistics > Material Management > Purchasing > Outline Agreement > Scheduling Agreement > Create > Vendor known.

Transaction code:-

Transaction code is ME31L.

- ## Manually:-

You enter all data on the scheduling agreement manually.

- ## Using the referencing technique:-

As reference document is a document which is already created and which you can copy from. Following are the reference documents.

- o Purchase requisitions
- o RFQs/quotations
- o Other scheduling agreements

- o Centrally Agreed Contracts
- o You can combine the two processes. In the first step you copy from a reference document and after manually change that.

In the picture below you can see that in details. On the initial screen you have to enter following information.

Vendor:-

You have to enter Vendor number from whom you are going the material.

Agreement type:-

In this field you have to enter LPA for scheduling agreement.

Purchase organization:-

Here enter the responsible purchase organization such as 1000.

Purchase group:-

Enter responsible purchase group in the field.

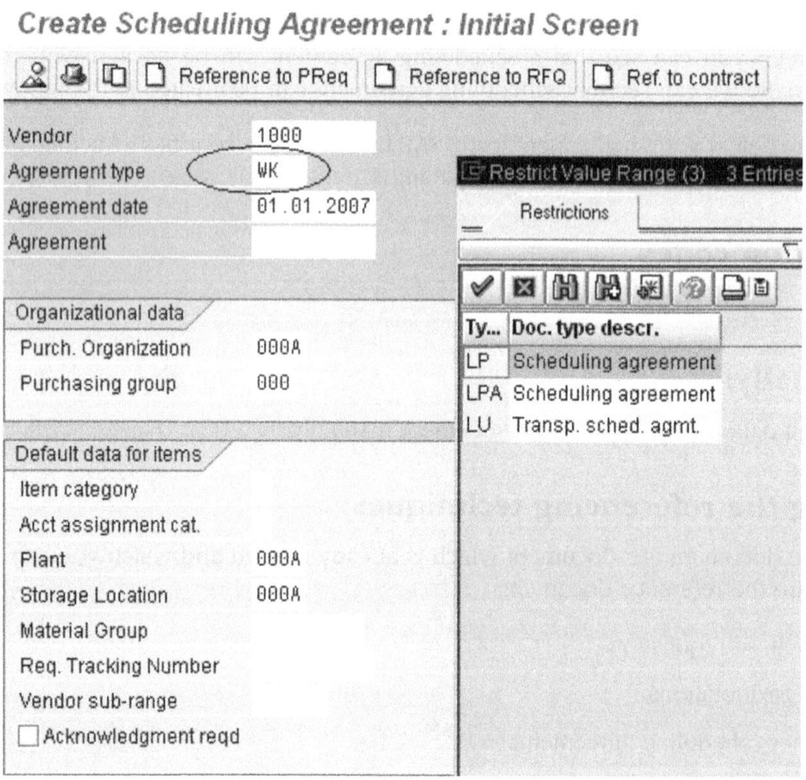

Header data:-

On the header data screen you have to enter validity start date and validity end date. You can see that this screen is same as create contract screen. Same details are to be maintained here also.

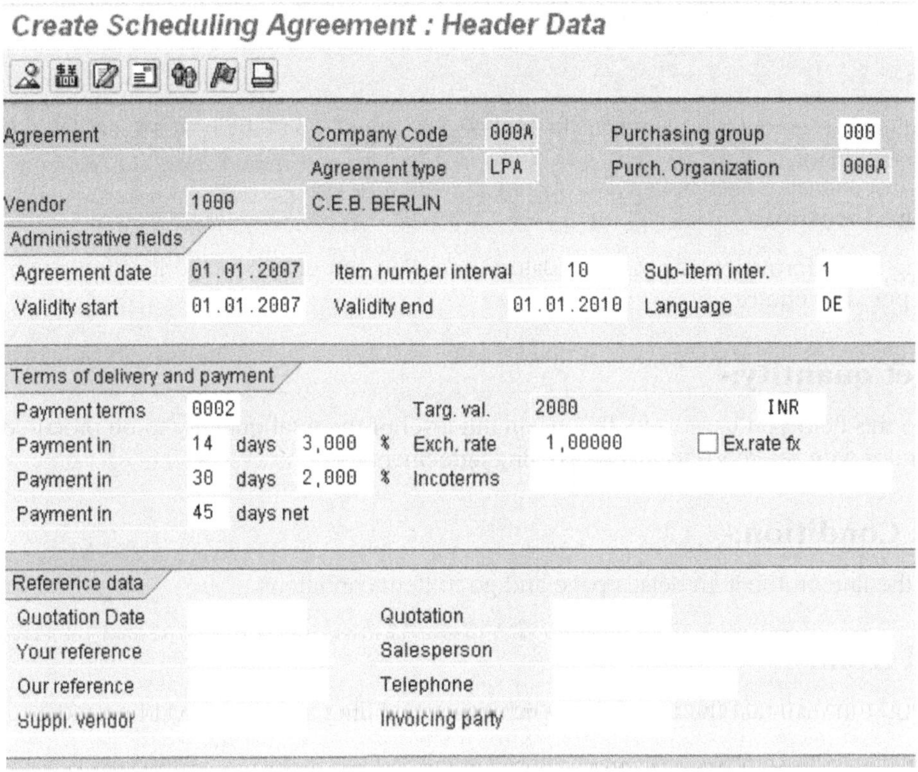

Payment terms:-

You can maintain payment terms in the field as mentioned in the screen below.

Item overview:-

Following information is required in different field in the item overview screen. You can see that as in the picture below.

Material:-

You have to maintain materials for which you are going to create the scheduling agreement.

Item category:-

You may choose item category as per your requirement. You can see the item category options as below in the picture.

Account assignment category:-

In this field you can enter account assignment category from the options available. You can see this in the picture below as per your requirement.

Neither the item categories M and W nor the account assignment category U (account assignment Unknown) are allowed in scheduling agreements.

Plant:-

Scheduling agreement is a plant specific outline agreement. So in the next screen you will have to maintain plant.

Storage location:-

Entering this information is not a mandatory one. You can enter storage location or you may not as per your choice.

Target quantity:-

Here in this field you have to fix the maximum level of the total quantity to be procured from the vendor with reference to this scheduling agreement.

Item Condition:-

Select the line on the item details page and go to item conditions.

Valid from:-

Here you can maintain the date from which this scheduling agreement will be valid.

Valid to:-

This is the field where you maintain up to which date this scheduling agreement will be valid.

Cnty:-

In this field you can maintain addition conditions if you have come to any resolution such as RA00 for discount % on net. In the value field maintain 5 to result as 5% discount on net price.

Scales:-

Select the line and go to scales where you can maintain multiple price stages.

Here maintain scale for the item condition type. You can follow as it is done below.

Blank in the Quantity field & in the price field 30 (That means from 0 to 99 pieces quantity will be calculated @ 30 EUR each)

100 in the quantity field and in the price field 29 (That means from 0 to 99 pieces quantity will be calculated @ 30 EUR each and from 100 to 499 pieces it will be calculated @ 29 EUR each)

500 in the quantity field and in the price field 28 (That means from 100 to 499 pieces quantity will be calculated @ 29 EUR each and from 500 and onwards it will be calculated @ 28 EUR each)

This whole process is called scaling of condition. This process is same as this is in the purchasing information record.

Additional data page:-

Additional data information is adopted from the material master and if it is not maintained automatically then you can maintain manually as per your need.

Below in the picture you can see that additional data screen in this scheduling agreement is asking more information than the information in the additional data screen of a contract. You can compare both by opening these to in different sessions.

You can get help about these fields by putting cursor in the field and pressing F1 for help.

Item details:-

On item details screen you will find following relevant information to input.

Info Update:-

In this field you can select from options whether price information will be updated in the info record from this scheduling agreement or not.

Acknowledgement required:-

This field is to be checked if you want that the vendor should inform you by an acknowledgement letter about receipt of purchase order or purchasing document so that you can proceed with smooth procurement process.

Stock type:-

From this item details screen only you can maintain stock type on goods receipt of the specified material from the vendor. For this you have to specify stock type in the stock type field whether goods will be received in the quality inspection, blocked stock or unrestricted use stock as a default at the time of goods receipt.

You can fix whether invoice receipt will base on goods receipt quantity wise or purchase order wise. There are more than these a few important control indicators in this screen.

After entering all these information you can save the scheduling agreement document.

Change (ME32L):-

In the transaction code you can change the scheduling agreement document.

Display (ME33L):-

In the transaction code you can display the scheduling agreement document.

Release (ME35L):-

If you have maintained and configured release procedure for scheduling agreement then you will have to release this document before this is used form purchase order processing.

Print the scheduling agreement (ME9L):-

By this transaction code you can get the printout of the scheduling agreement.

Chapter 26

PO BASED INVOICE VERIFICATION

Introduction:-

PO Based Invoice Verification is a kind of verification which is not based on goods receipt quantity. It is based on purchase order and invoice is received for total quantity received. You do not have any option of rejecting any invoice amount. You will have to accept total quantity whether you are willing to accept for any low quality or delivery in dispute or not. But you will have to accept all of these. To understand this process and it's complicacy we will have to take a look on the whole procurement procedure which starts from material creation. We will discuss on this step by step. We will discuss on this step by step.

Prerequisites

Material master:-

Create material with all the details.

Vendor Master:-

Create Vendor mater as it is created normally. On the purchase data screen pay attention that the 'GR based inv. Verify.' field is not checked. This is shown in the picture below. You can see that field in the picture as checked. Uncheck that and save it.

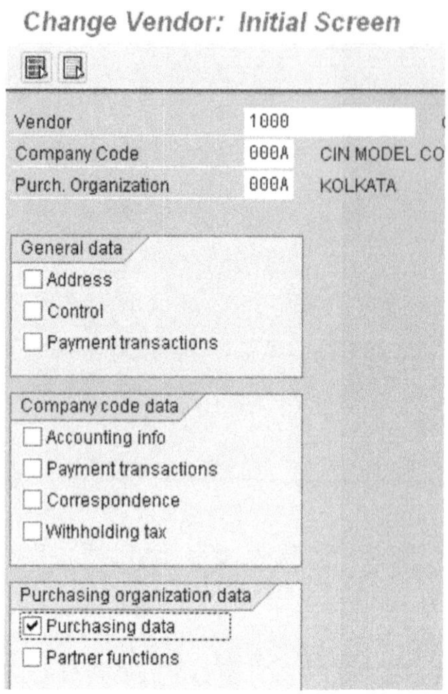

You can create vendor and while creating vendor you can maintain whether in purchasing data tab page invoice verification should occur based on purchase order or based on goods receipt.

If you have already created or processing from any existing vendor then you can go to change option and maintain same feature.

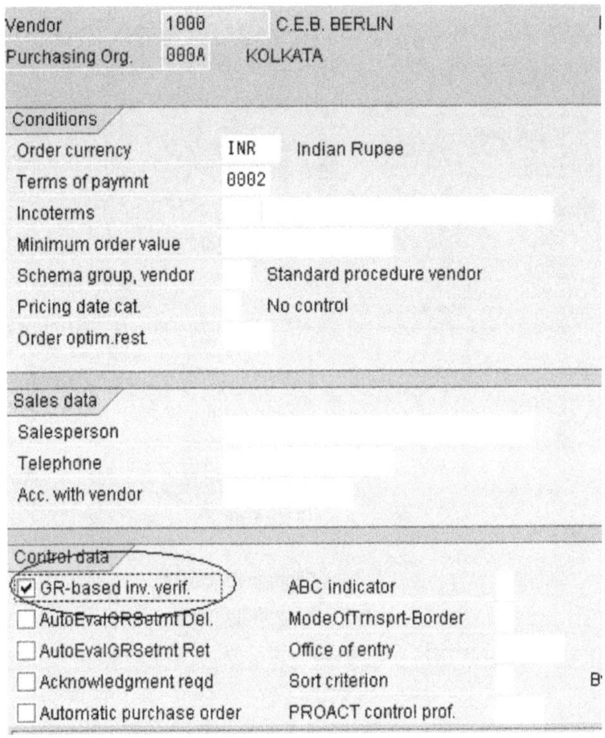

Source List:-

Create Source list as normally it is created.

Purchase Info Record:-

Create purchasing info record normally but pay attention on the purchasing organization data. The field GR Based IV field should not be checked. It is checked in the picture below. Uncheck that and save it.

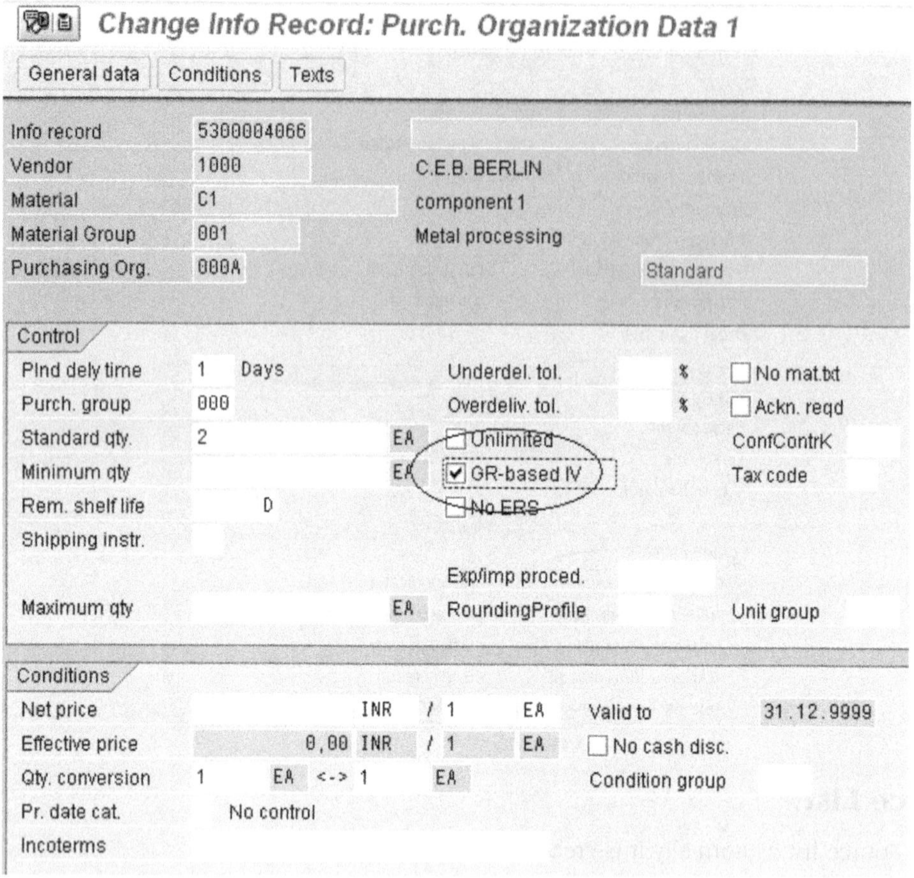

This data is adopted from Vendor master record.

Purchase order:-

Create purchase order as usual. Again here you have to pay attention on the Invoice tab page as there you will see information on GR Based IV. It is shown in the picture below.

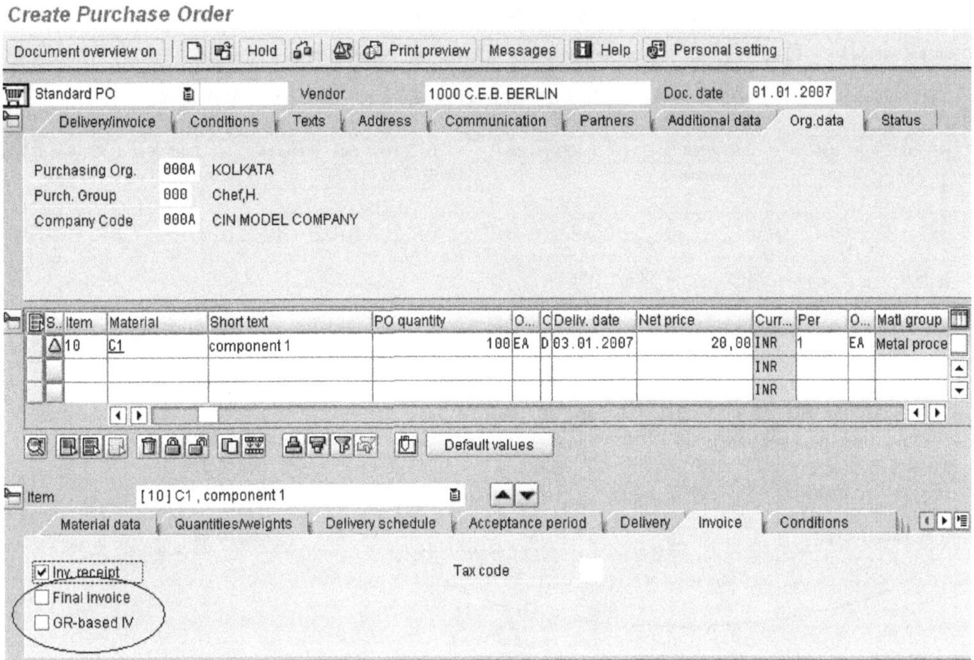

In the quantity field input quantity as 100. Save the purchase order after checking it.

Goods Receipt:-

Now go to MIGO screen. There receive goods as usual. There check on the quantity screen. There you will find quantity as 100 as total quantity. In this field check and change the quantity and input there as 10 as quantity. Check the document and save it. Check the material document and FI document. Check quantity received in the transaction MMBE in stock overview.

Repeat same transaction twice with receiving quantity 20 and 30. This time also goods receive should be with reference to purchase order. When entering goods receipt 2nd time check total quantity left to be received. It should show as 80 pieces. Change the quantity as 30, check it and save it

Repeat again goods receipt with reference to purchase order third time. This time quantity should show as 50. Change the quantity as 40. Check quantity and save it.

Purchase Order History:-

Go to transaction code ME21N. Go to other purchase order. Enter the purchase order number that you are procuring. Go to Purchase order history tab page. Here you will be able to see the processing that has happened with this purchase order. Multiple goods receipt with reference to this purchase order is tracked in and recorded here. You can see in the picture below.

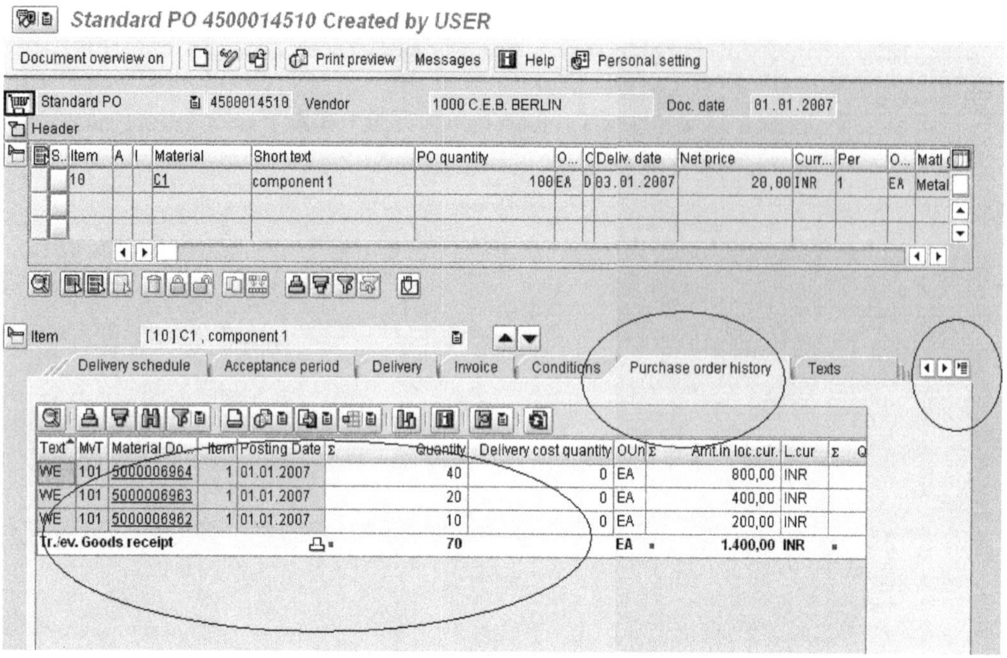

On the Delivery schedule tab page you can see total SL quantity (scheduled quantity) and in the Delivered field you can see total delivered quantity as 90. In open quantity you can see quantity as 10.

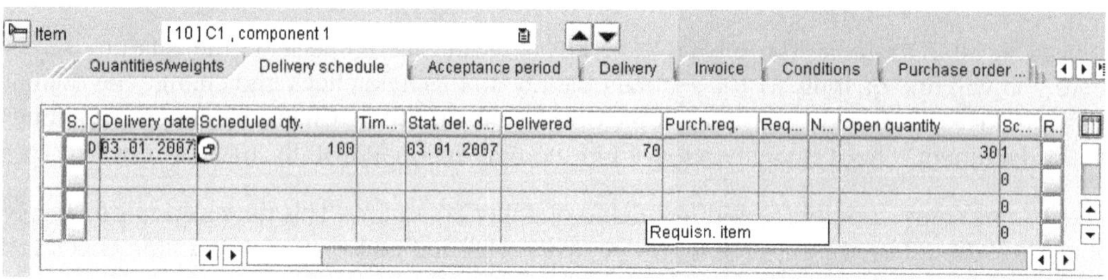

Incoming Invoice Verification:-

Enter invoice in the transaction code MIRO in the command line. There take purchase order as reference document. Enter document number and adopt that.

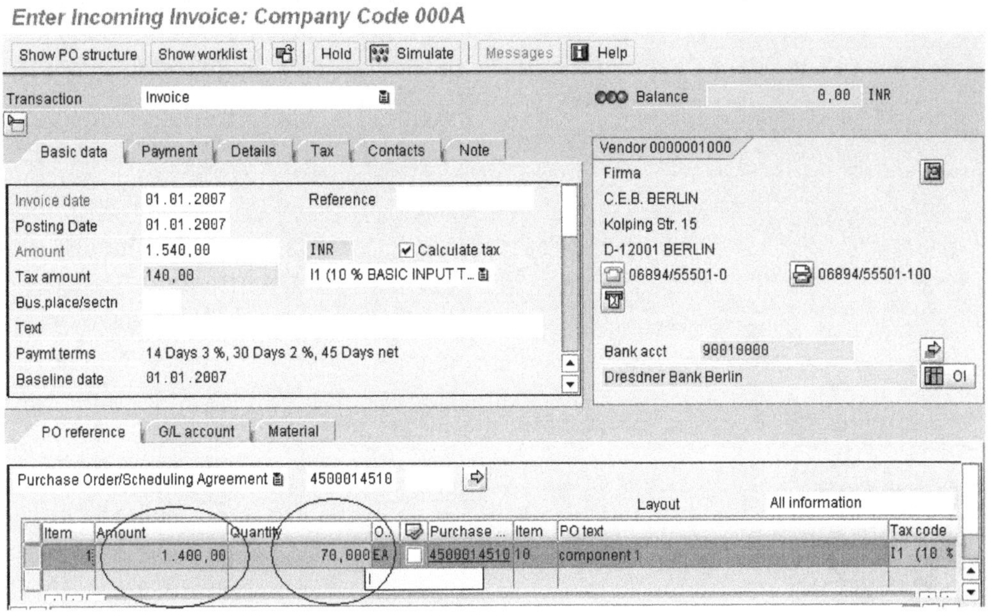

Now you will be able to see one line item. Here you can see total received quantity 70. You can receive invoice as total quantity received. Enter tax code in the appropriate field. Put a check in the calculate tax field check box. On the right side in the balance field you can see total amount to be paid. Enter same amount in the Amount field on the left side. It should be a total of tax amount and total due amount for material received. Simulate the document. If everything is ok then save the invoice receipt document. There will be no problem in this process.

On simulation you will see following screen.

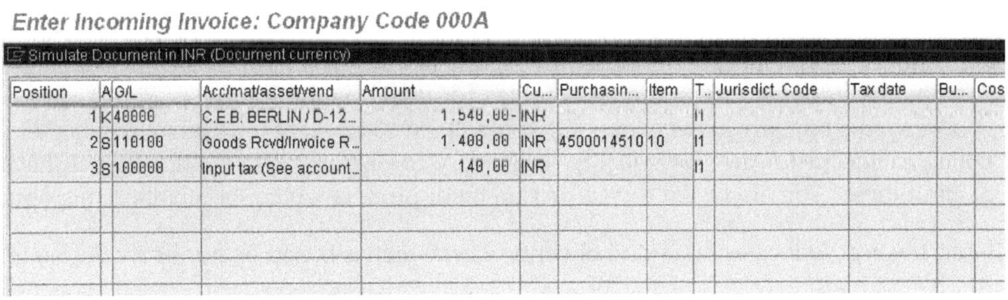

Position	A	G/L	Acc/mat/asset/vend	Amount	Cu...	Purchasin...	Item	T..	Jurisdict. Code	Tax date	Bu...	Cos
1	K	40000	C.E.B. BERLIN / D-12...	1.540,00-	INR			I1				
2	S	110100	Goods Rcvd/Invoice R...	1.400,00	INR	4500014510	10	I1				
3	S	100000	Input tax (See account...	140,00	INR			I1				

Now think about a scenario. Suppose in one delivery of material you found some problem in the material. You are not satisfied with the received material's quality and you are not willing to pay for that. It may be that you have returned goods to the vendor or not but you are not ready to accept invoice. Now think on the last procurement. Do you have any option of rejecting one invoice for the delivery which is in dispute? The answer will come out as no.

So to face such problem and be prepared for such disputes you will have to make some settings as we will do in the system. This will be discussed in the chapter GR Based Invoice Verification.

Chapter

27

GR BASED INVOICE VERIFICATION

Introduction:-

We have already discussed in the last chapter on PO Based Invoice Verification. PO Based Invoice Verification is a kind of verification which is not based on goods receipt quantity. It is based on purchase order and invoice is received for total quantity received. You do not have any option of rejecting any invoice amount. You will have to accept total quantity whether you are willing to accept for any low quality or delivery in dispute or not. But you will have to accept all of these. You also have seen a procurement process which has clarified this option.

GR Based Invoice Verification is a kind of verification which is based on goods receipt quantity.

Thinking on the last scenario as discussed in the last chapter think about a scenario. Suppose in one delivery of material you found some problem in the material. You are not satisfied with the received material's quality and you are not willing to pay for that. It may be that you have returned goods to the vendor or not but you are not ready to accept invoice. Now think on the last procurement. Do you have any option of rejecting one invoice for the delivery which is in dispute? The answer will come out as no.

So to face such problem and be prepared for such disputes you will have to make some settings as we will do in the system. This whole process will be discussed in the current chapter.

Prerequisites:-

Create Material Master:-

Create material master record as usual.

Vendor Master:-

Create Vendor mater as it is created normally. On the purchase data screen pay attention that the 'GR based inv. Verif.' field is not checked if you are creating new vendor master record. If you are changing any existing vendor master record then put a check in the field check box. This is shown in the picture below. You can see that field in the picture as checked. Save the vendor master record.

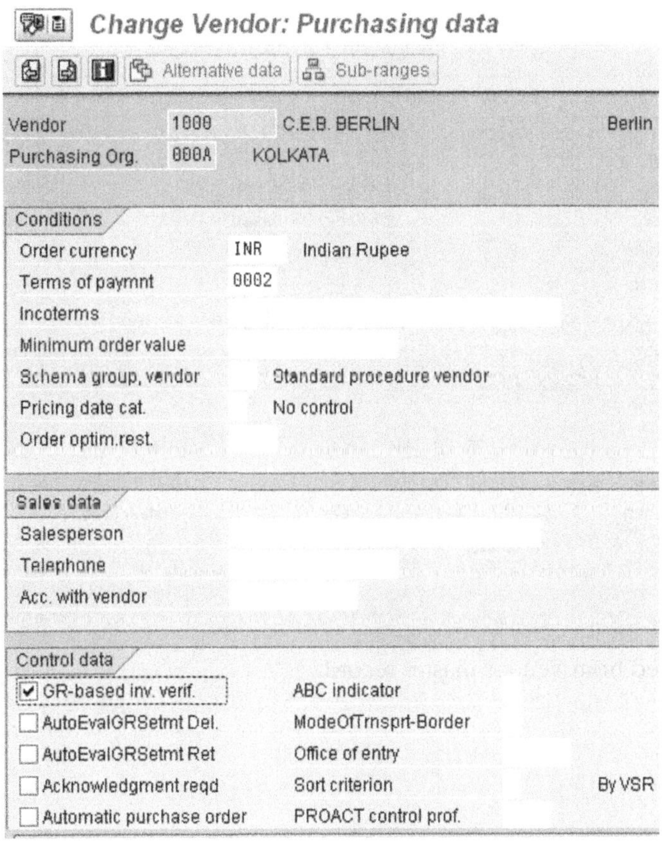

Source List:-

Create Source list as normally it is created.

Purchase Info Record:-

Create purchasing info record as it is created normally but pay attention on the purchasing organization data screen. The field GR Based IV field should be checked. As this information is adopted from the vendor master record so it will show checked as it is checked in the picture below. Save the purchasing info record.

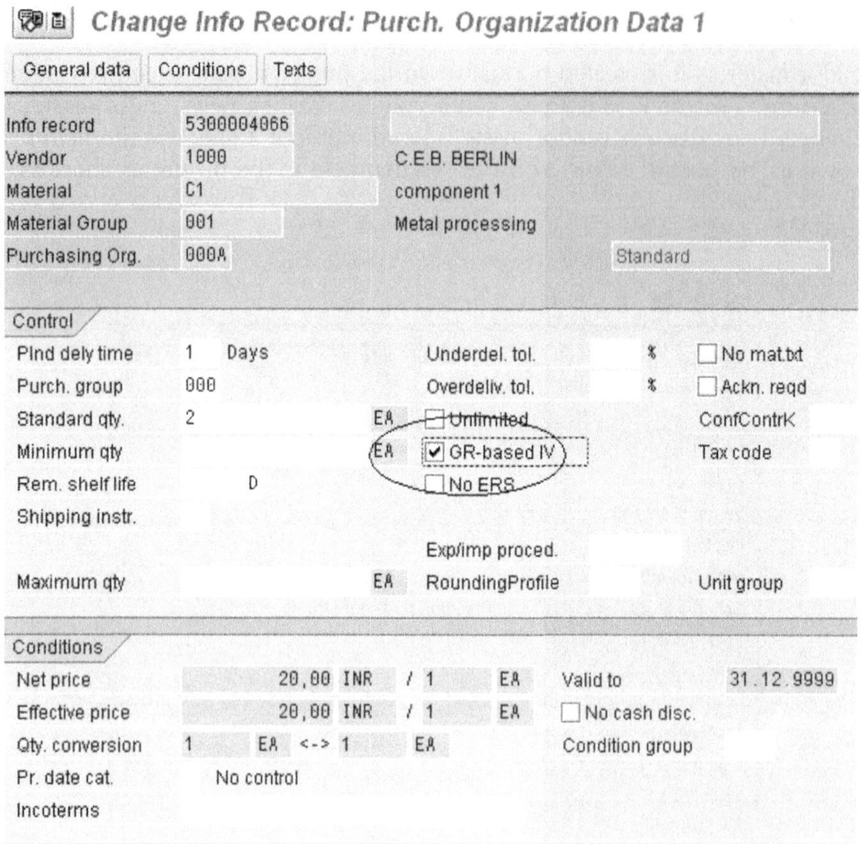

This data is adopted from Vendor master record.

Purchase order:-

Create purchase order as usual. Again here you have to pay attention on the Invoice tab page as there you will see information on GR Based IV. It is shown in the picture below and check. This field check box should be checked.

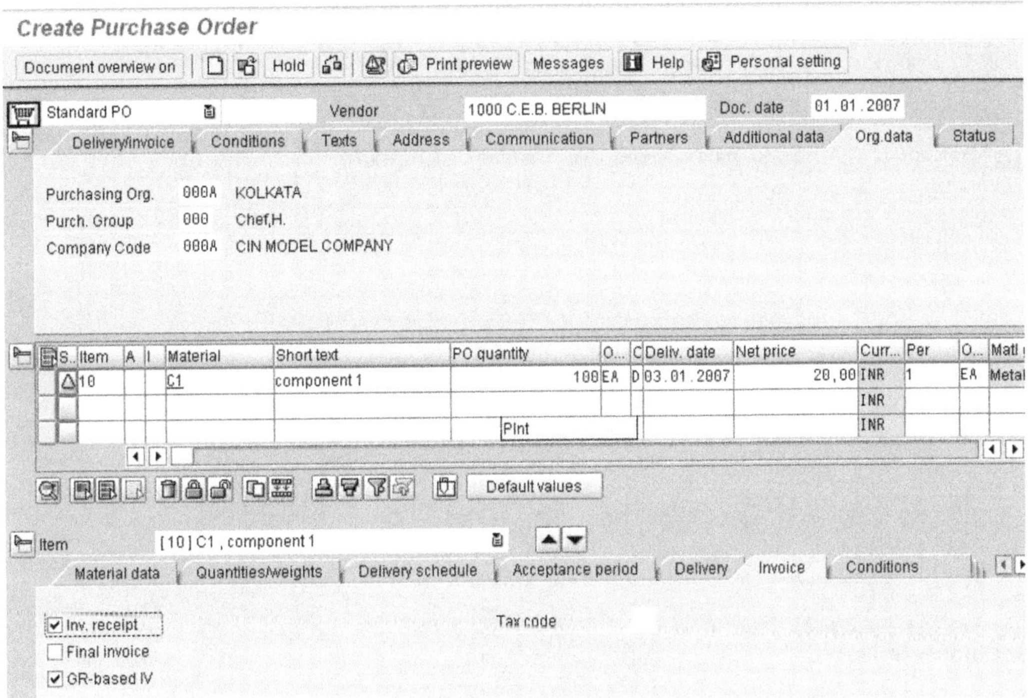

In the quantity field input quantity as 100. Save the purchase order after checking it.

Goods Receipt:-

1ST Goods receipt: Now go to MIGO screen. Perform goods receipt process as usual. On the quantity screen check total quantity to be received as with reference to purchase order. There you will find quantity as 100 as total quantity. In this field check and change the quantity and input there as 10 as quantity. Check the document and save it. Check the material document and FI document. Check quantity received in the transaction MMBE in stock overview.

2nd Goods receipt: Repeat same transaction twice with receiving quantity 20 and 40. This time also goods receive should be with reference to purchase order. When entering goods receipt 2nd time check total quantity left to be received. It should show as 90 pieces. Change the quantity as 20, check it and save it

3rd Goods receipt: Repeat again goods receipt with reference to purchase order third time. This time quantity should show as 70. Change the quantity as 40. Check quantity and save it.

Purchase Order History:-

Go to transaction code ME21N. Go to other purchase order. Enter the purchase order number that you are procuring. Go to Purchase order history tab page. Here you will be able to see the processing that has happened with this purchase order. Multiple goods receipt with reference to this purchase order is tracked in and recorded here. You can see in the picture below.

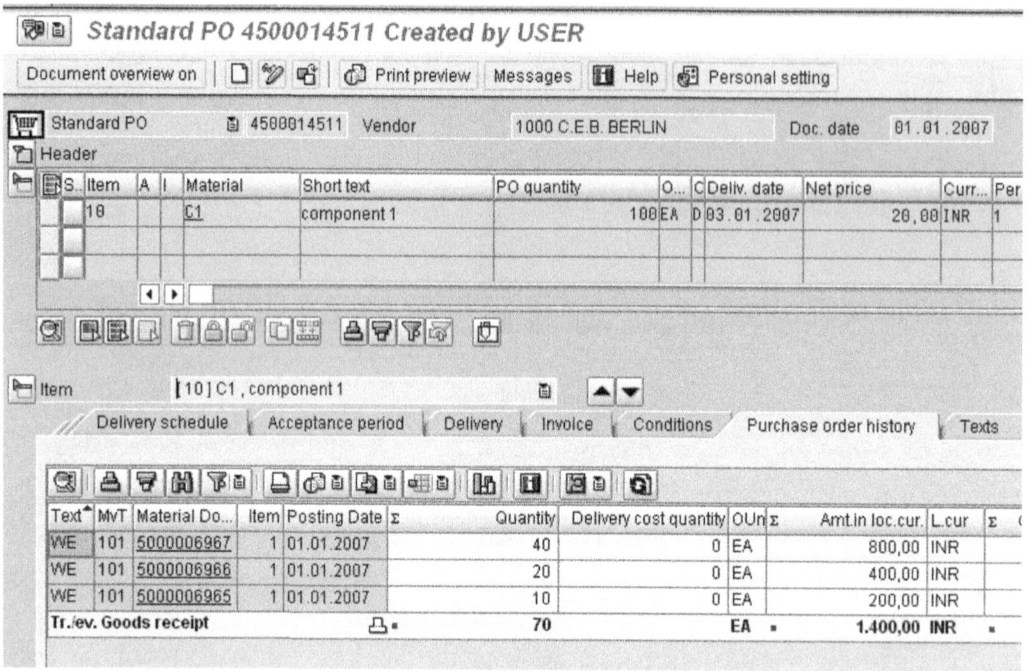

Incoming Invoice Verification:-

Enter invoice in the transaction code MIRO in the command line. There take purchase order as reference document. Enter document number and adopt that.

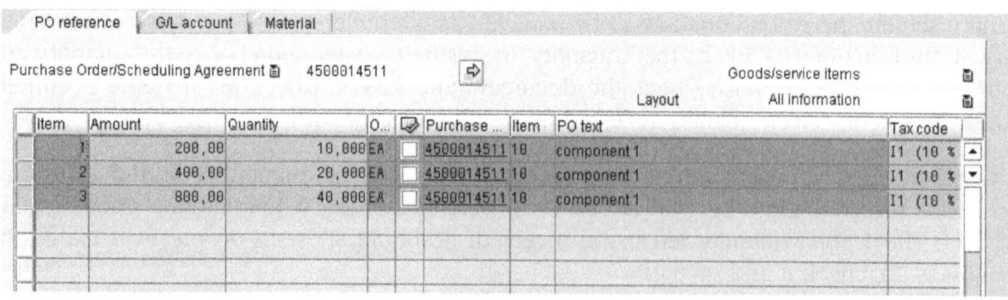

Now you will be able to see 3 line items for each goods receipt and not in one line item. You can see total received quantity 70. You can receive invoice as total quantity received. Enter tax code in the appropriate field. Put a check in the calculate tax field check box. On the right side in the balance field you can see total amount to be paid. Enter same amount in the Amount field on the left side. It should be a total of tax amount and total due amount for material received. Simulate the document. If everything is ok then save the invoice receipt document. There will be no problem in this process.

Now simply compare two processes, one is PO Based invoice verification and 2nd is this GR Based invoice verification process. You have seen in the PO based invoice verification one line item while invoice entry, but in GR based one line item for each Goods receipt. Now in this GR based invoice verification process you have freedom to accept that you want to accept and to reject the invoice which you do not want to accept.

After simulation you can see following screen.

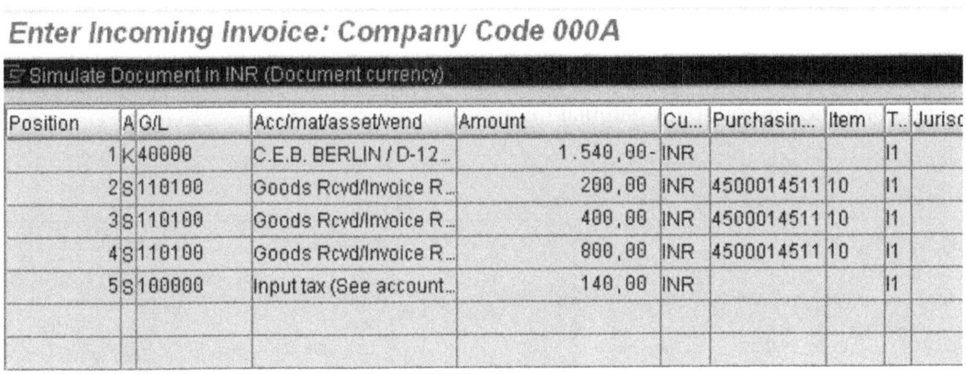

Here you also have an option of not accepting one delivery due to any reason. You can do simply this by deselecting the rejected line item, and by confirming with a stroke of enter.

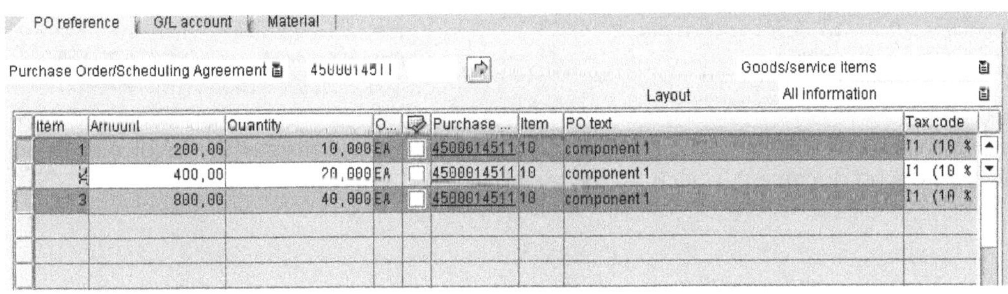

You can see total amount in the balance field changes to the total line item selected.

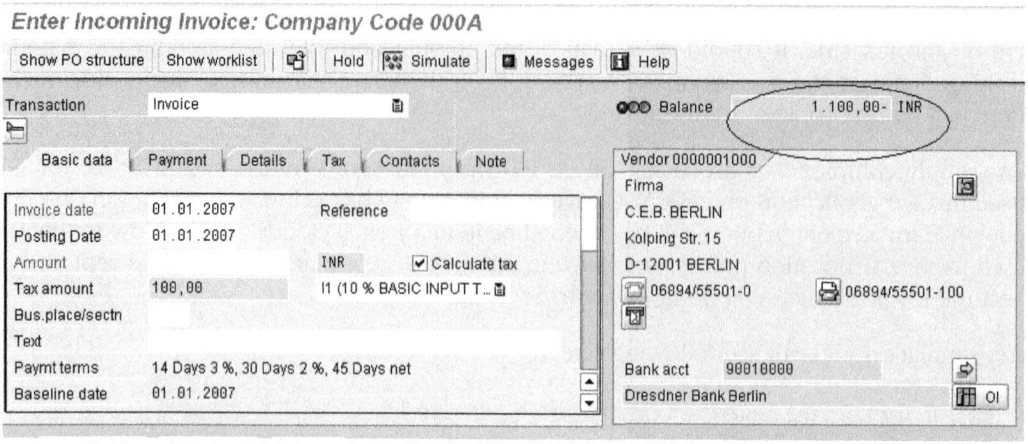

Enter the confirmed amount and simulate it and post it.

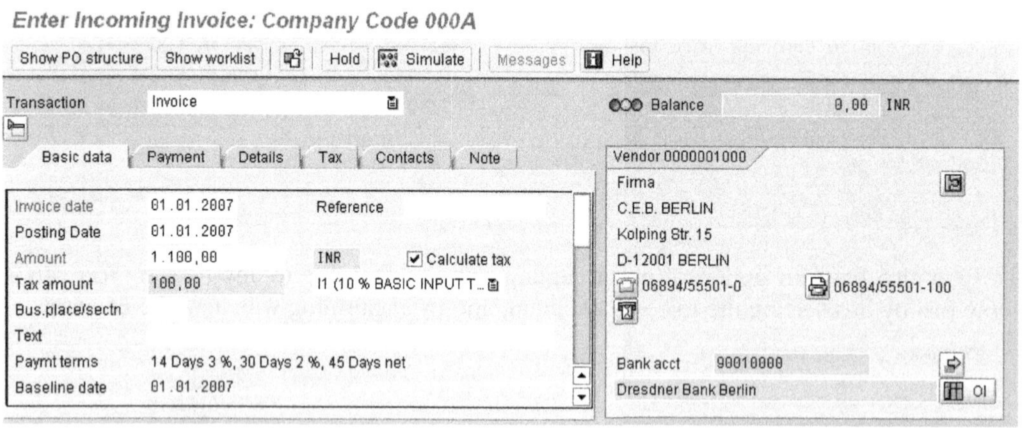

If every thing is ok then post the document. After posting again display the invoice document. Go to follow on document. Check FI documents.

Chapter

28

PHYSICAL INVENTORY

Introduction:-

Physical inventory is a component which enables you to handle physical inventory counting of you company's warehouse stocks for balance sheet purposes. In the standard system, a physical inventory can be carried out for the following stock types:

- **For a company's own stock**
  - Unrestricted-use stock in the warehouse
  - Quality inspection stock
  - Blocked stock
- **For Special stock**

(such as consignment stock at customer, external consignment stock from vendor, or returnable packaging)

  - Unrestricted-use stock in the warehouse

- o Quality inspection stock
- o Blocked stock

These physical counting must be taken separately in different physical inventory documents for different stock levels.

- o **Storage location level**
  - o **Batch level** (If batch management is active for the material)
- o **And Special stock level.**
  - o **Batch level** (If batch management is active for the material)

Physical inventory takes place at storage location level. A separate physical inventory document is created for every storage location and for special stock level.

In the stock counting following stocks types are not taken into account.

- o Blocked stock returns
- o Stock in transfer

If you need to count these also then first you have to transfer post these stocks to other stocks.

Physical Inventory Procedures

There are following physical inventory procedures:

- o Periodic inventory
- o Continuous inventory
- o Cycle counting
- o Inventory sampling
- o Periodic Inventory

Periodic inventory

In this procedure following are the key features.

- o Material movement remains blocked (From the start of the counting to the end of counting)
- o Every material is counted physically
- o Counting is done on balance sheet key date

Continuous Inventory

Following are the key features in this procedure.

- o Stocks are counted continuously during the entire fiscal year.

- o Every material is physically counted at least once during the year.

Cycle Counting

Following are the key features in this procedure.

- o Counted at regular intervals within a fiscal year
- o These intervals (or cycles) depend on the cycle counting indicator set for the materials.
- o The Cycle Counting Method of Physical Inventory allows fast-moving items to be counted more frequently than slow-moving items.

Inventory Sampling

In MM Inventory sampling randomly selected stocks of the company are physically counted on the balance sheet key date. If the variances between the result of the count and the book inventory balance are small enough, it is presumed that the book inventory balances for the other stocks are correct.

Updating the Logistics Information System (LIS)

When inventory differences are updated in the logistics information system, they are displayed both on a quantity and on a value basis.

Constraints

There are some constraints for difference posting.

- o Posting period is set automatically
- o Posting period has to be same for during entire counting process.
- o The inventory difference must be posted in the same posting period or to the previous period if allowed.

Chapter

29

INVENTORY COUNTING

Introduction:-

By this time in you must have created some material or at least one material that you would have procured from vendor through any procurement process and would have kept that in different stock types. Also you might have put the stock in different storage locations. Now in this chapter we simply take a look how this entire physical inventory counting process takes place. Where you need to start with the process? Where to end?

Whatever be the physical inventory method, but the process of physical inventory can be divided into three phases:

Preparation

In this phase you

- Create a physical inventory document.
- Blocking Materials for posting resulting from any goods movement.
- Print and distribute the physical inventory document.

Counting

In this step you

- Get the physical inventory document
- Start Counting stocks
- Enter the result of the count on the physical inventory document printout

Analysis

In this step you

- Enter the result of the count into the system
- Initiate a recount, if necessary
- Posting inventory differences if any into the system
- With the posting of inventory count system unblocks posting blocks which was set at the beginning of creation of physical inventory document.

Menu path

To perform a physical inventory count in your system or your company following is the menu path that you can see in the picture. SAP Easy Access > Logistics > Materials Management > Physical Inventory > Physical Inventory Doc > Create > ENTER.

Transaction code:-

Transaction code for this is MI01. On entering this you will see following screen as in the picture below.

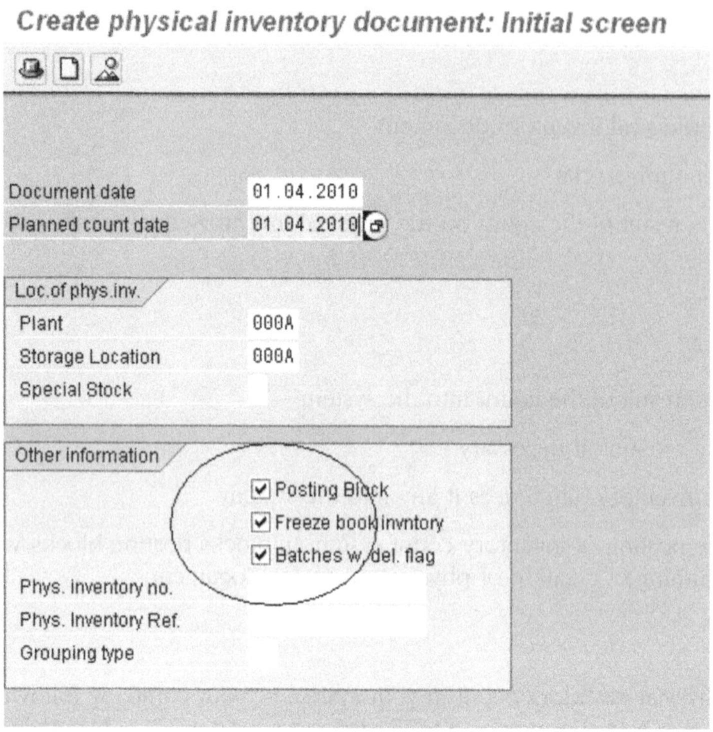

In the picture above you can see following information on the initial screen.

Document date:-

This is the current date of your system that you are working on. Set it to current or the date of counting.

Planned count date:-

This is the date on which the counting will take place.

Plant:-

This is the plant for which inventory counting will take place. This is the first level for counting.

Storage location:-

This is the specific storage location for which inventory counting will be done. This is the 2nd level of counting.

Special Stock:-

This is the 3rd level of counting. In the picture above you can see multiple special stock type that your company is dealing in. You can select any of these if you have any special stock available in your system and you want to count that only separately.

Posting Block:-

This check box should be checked. Reason is that if you do not check this check box then material movement postings will keep on taking place and you might not get correct physical count of the material.

The blocking indicator can be set in one of two ways:

- Directly upon entry of the physical inventory document (if the count is to take place immediately)
- Shortly before the count (if the count is to take place later). You can set the indicator by choosing Physical inventory document > Change in the header data of the physical inventory document or via batch input.

Freeze book inventory:-

This check box is to be selected if you want to freeze the inventory stock status of that plant and storage location for which counting is to be done. If this field is selected and posting block is not set even then counting will be done effectively without stopping the goods movement. Because system will take a snap shot of the stock status and later on after physical count you can post the difference with regards to freezing time point stock book inventory status.

Error: Freezing of book inv. Balance in storage location is not allowed.

To allow freeze book inventory you have to set it in the customization at the plant level in the transaction code OMBP. This is shown in the picture below.

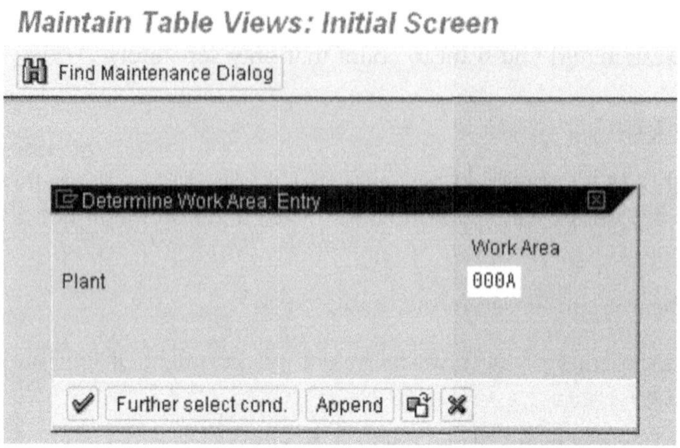

Here you have to enter your plant in which you want to freeze book inventory.

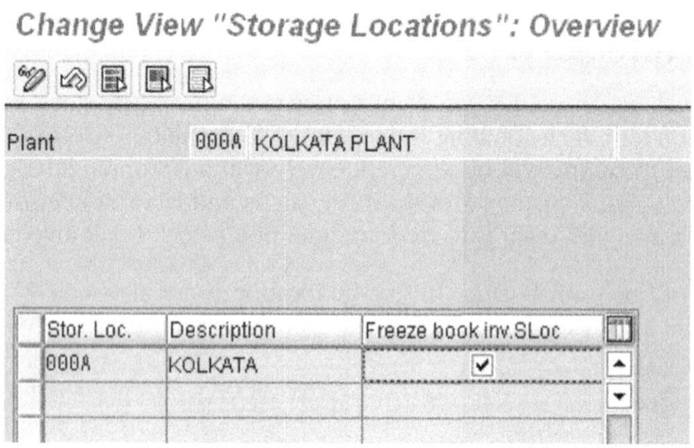

Another error Entering material and quantity:-

In the next screen you have to enter the material that is to be counted along with specific batch number if batch number is activated in the system for that material.

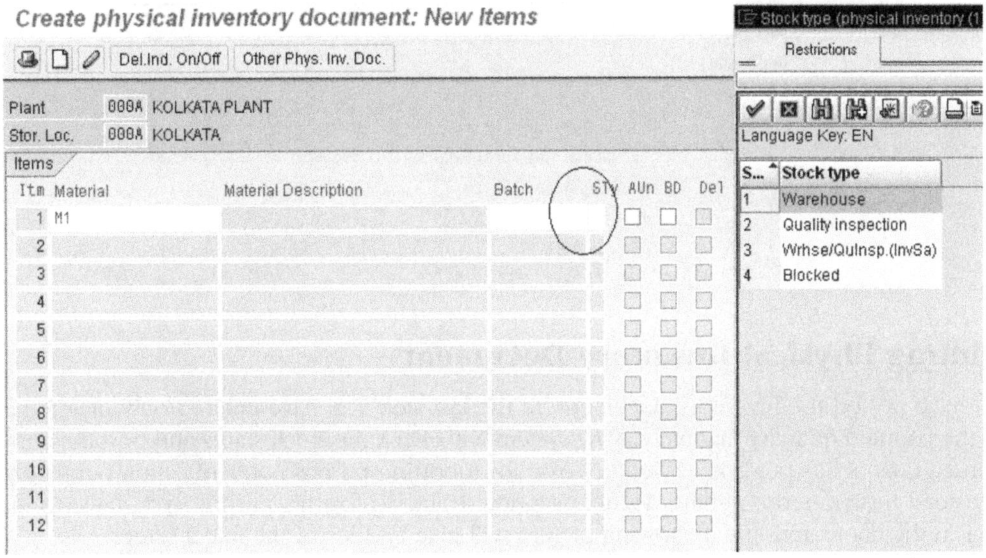

As in the picture above you can see the material entered for counting and special stock types that you can select. After entering material, batches and special stock indicator simply post or from here through Environment you can navigate to different functions relating to stock and material.

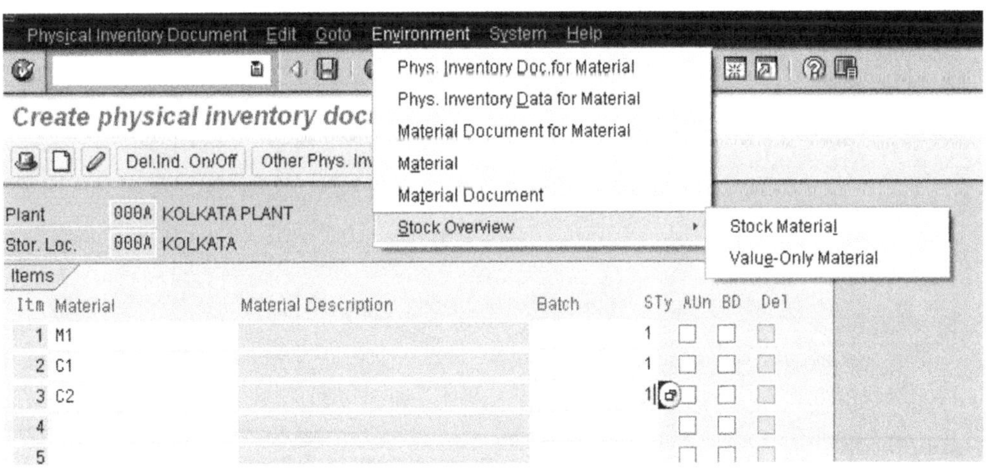

Here if you click on overview then system will show the list of materials for counting.

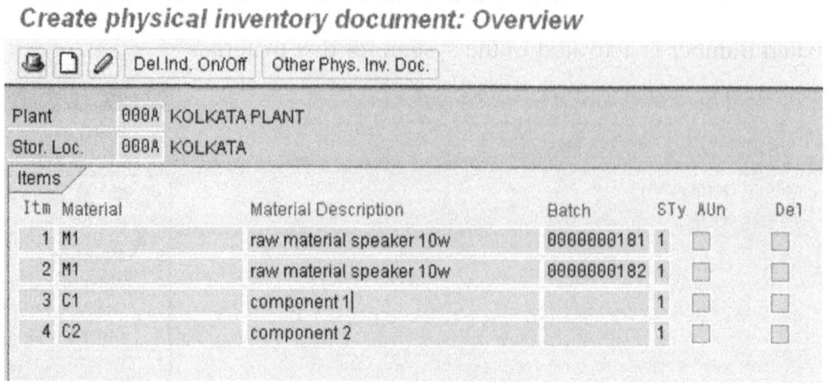

Printing Physical Inventory Document

You have posted the inventory document. In the last step you have entered only material and not the counted quantity manually. Now system will check the stock status and post the current counted quantity as per book inventory. You for reporting purpose or verification purpose you may need this posted counting document printed out. So for this purpose you have to enter MI21 in the command line. Following picture will give an idea of the initial screen.

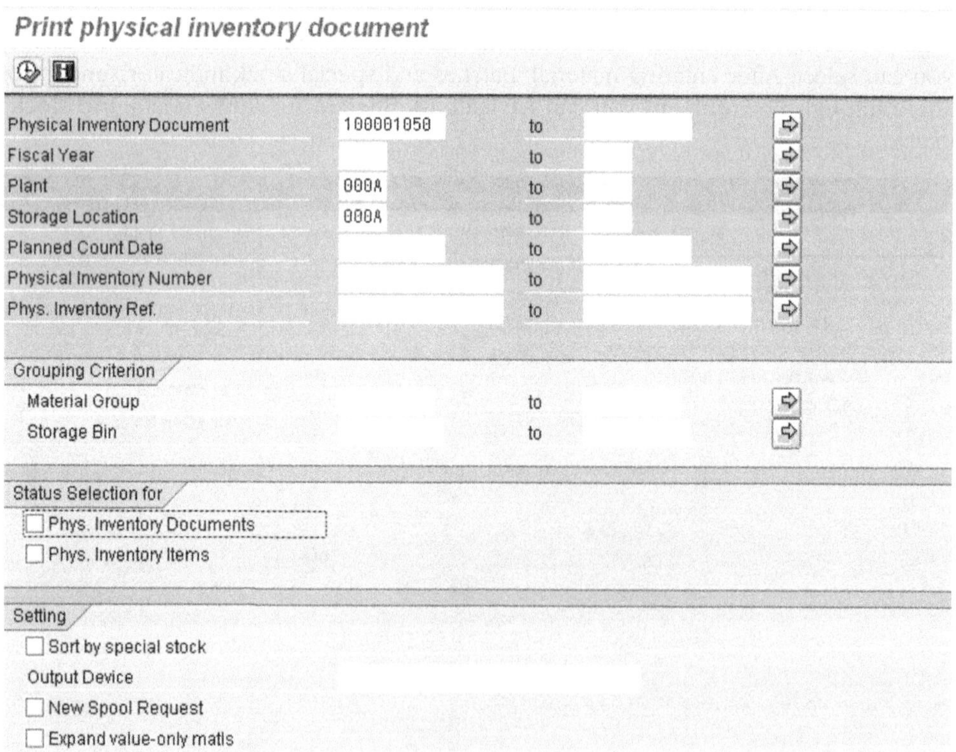

Here you need to enter following information on the initial screen.

- Physical inventory document one or a range of the document number
- Fiscal year in which posting is to be take place
- Plant in which stock counting will be done
- Storage location is the level for stock counting
- LP01- Enter this as output device for printout or physical printer name.

Execute the process.

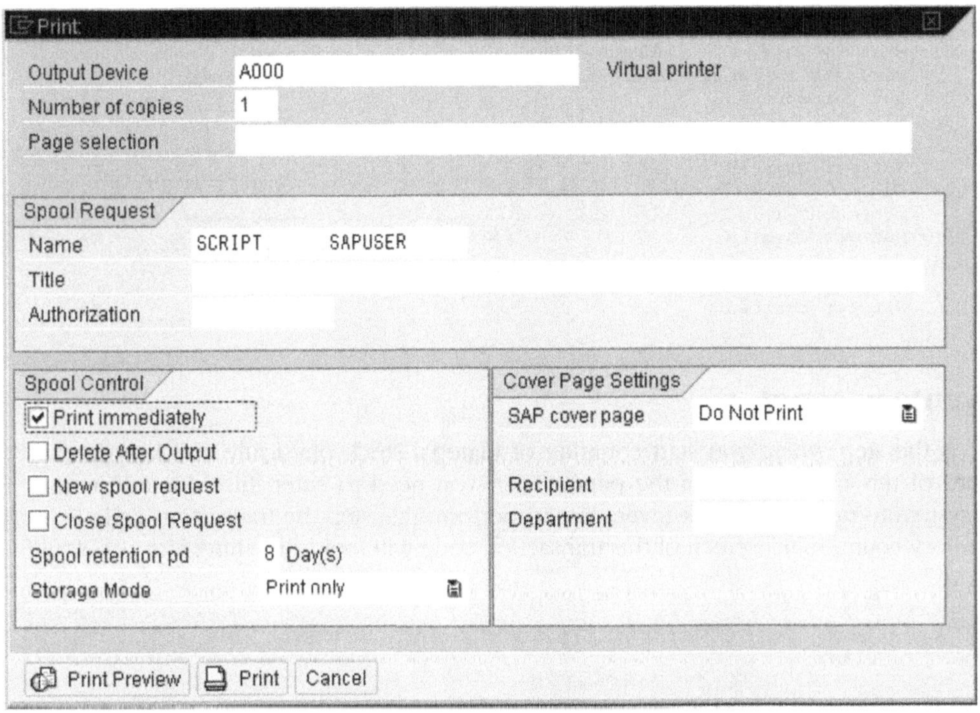

System will prompt you for printer name confirmation and other printer settings. On this screen select Print preview. On pressing print preview the printable document will be displayed. Get it printed and distribute it to the related people for counting.

Print Preview of A000 Page 00001 of 00001

```
Plant                 : 000A
Description           : KOLKATA PLANT
Phys. inv. doc.       : 100001050
Created by            : SAPUSER
Planned count date    : 01.01.2007
Phys. inv. reference:
Phys. inv. no.        :
--------------------------------------------------------------------------
Itm  Material             Batch                          SLoc Stor. bin
     Mat. short text                                     Stock type
     Status of item                                      Counted qty.    Un
-----------------------
001  M1                   0000000181                     000A
     raw material speaker 10w                            Warehouse
     Not yet counted                                     _______________ EA
002  M1                   0000000182                     000A
     raw material speaker 10w                            Warehouse
     Not yet counted                                     _______________ EA
003  C1                                                  000A
     component 1                                         Warehouse
     Not yet counted                                     _______________ EA
004  C2                                                  000A
     component 2                                         Warehouse
     Not yet counted                                     _______________ EA
```

Inventory count

This is the step where you start counting of material stock physically and keep on tracking record of this one by one on the paper. Then you need to enter this counted quantity into the system to match the book inventory. To perform this step the transaction code is MI04 as inventory count. Initial screen of this transaction code will look something like as below in the picture.

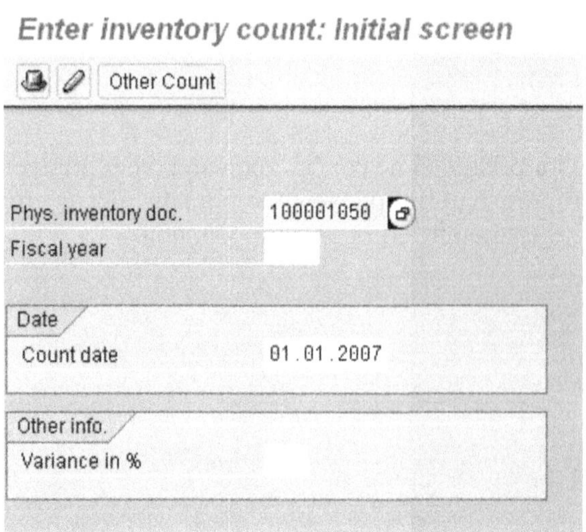

Physical inventory doc:-

On the initial screen you have to enter physical inventory document number as it will be matched document wise.

Fiscal year:-

In this field you need to enter the same fiscal year in which the document of physical inventory document was posted.

Count date:-

This is the field where you need to enter counting date on which counted quantity will be entered into the system.

Press ENTER.

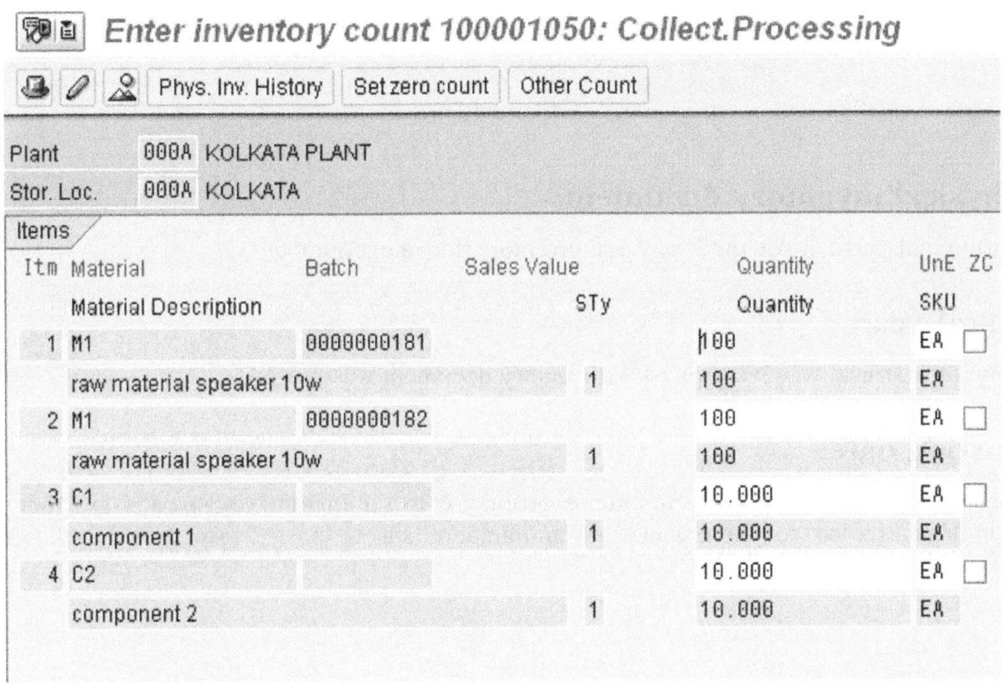

As in the picture above you need to enter counted quantity in the quantity field. As we have entered for material's counted quantity as you have counted.

Post the document.

Posting the Differences:-

While counting you came to know the difference in the book inventory and the physically counted quantity. You have to post the difference in T-code – MI07

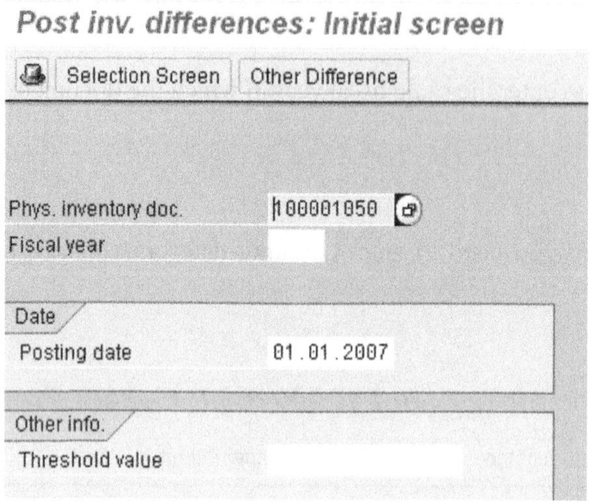

Physical inventory document:-

On the initial screen you enter physical inventory document number.

Fiscal year;-

This is the year in which the physical inventory document was posted.

Posting date:-

This is the date on which the difference quantity is to be adjusted and posted to either as a profit or as a loss for the organization and amount is to be posted respectively to the G/L accounts.

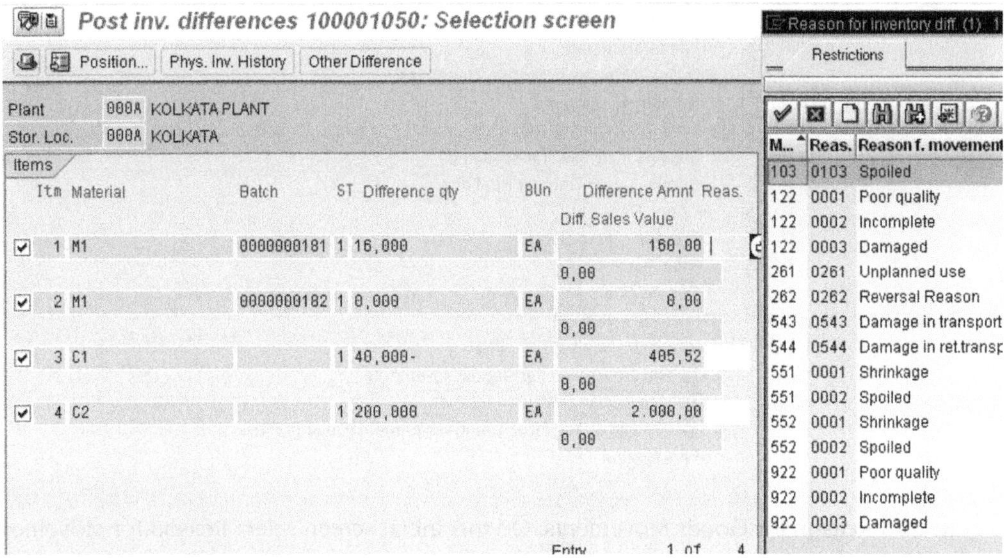

On the next screen you need to enter the reason for the difference of ### pieces. You know that counted quantity came as ### pieces and had been entered as that in the system. But in the MMBE transaction code for stock overview it is showing as ### quantity as total stock for that storage location as in the screen below.

Quantities may be remaining in quality inspection. But system will take only unrestricted quantity as not special stock type was selected while inventory document creation.

Loss:-

In the above scenario as there is a loss then for that you will have to entered difference quantity as loss to the organization and respective amount will be posted via movement type 702 with the reason entered or declared.

Profit:-

Now in the same scenario if the counted quantity would have been found as ###, then there would have been a gain of ### pieces on the book inventory. So the excess quantity of ### pieces and respective amount would need to be posted as a profit for the organization with the movement type 701 with appropriate reason. If appropriate reason is not configured in your system for the movement type then you have to customize that in the system. Following picture will guide you on that.

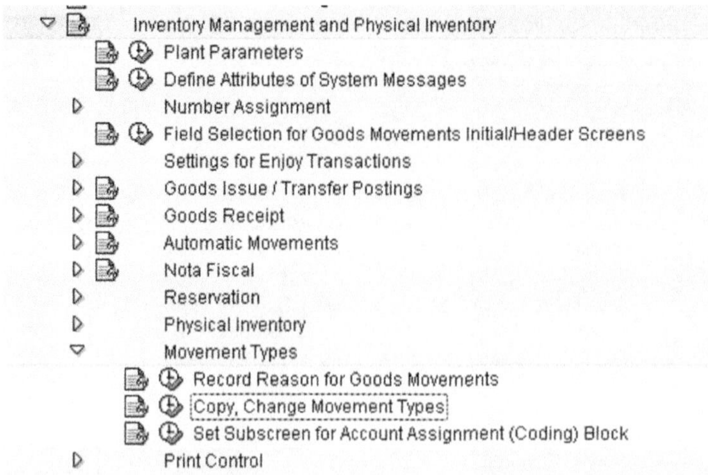

Select Record Reason for Goods Movements. On this initial screen select Reason for Movement.

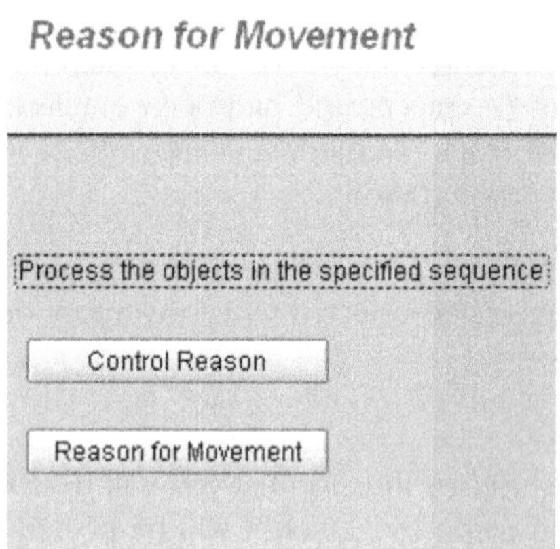

Here go to new entries.

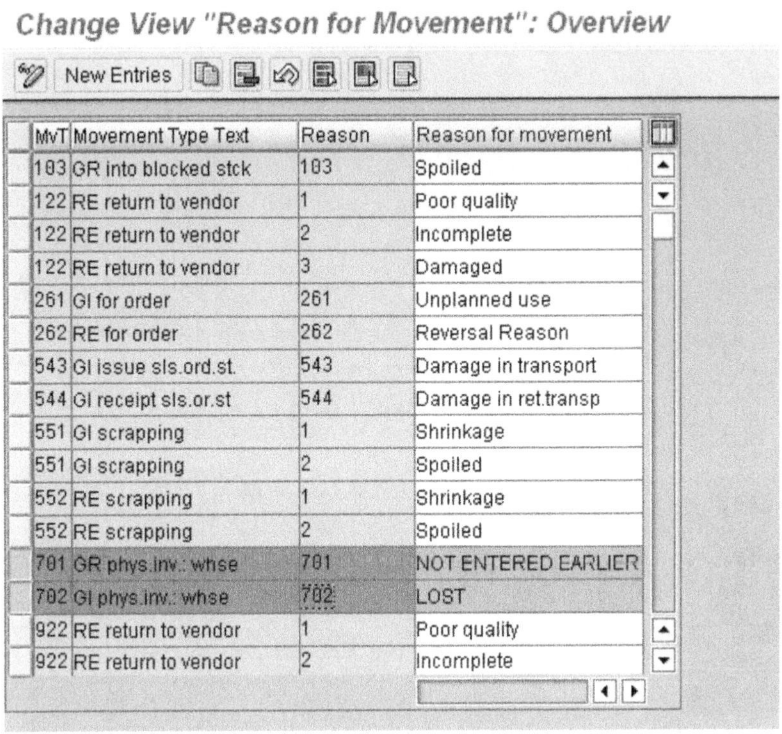

Change View "Reason for Movement": Overview

New Entries

MvT	Movement Type Text	Reason	Reason for movement
103	GR into blocked stck	103	Spoiled
122	RE return to vendor	1	Poor quality
122	RE return to vendor	2	Incomplete
122	RE return to vendor	3	Damaged
261	GI for order	261	Unplanned use
262	RE for order	262	Reversal Reason
543	GI issue sls.ord.st.	543	Damage in transport
544	GI receipt sls.or.st	544	Damage in ret.transp
551	GI scrapping	1	Shrinkage
551	GI scrapping	2	Spoiled
552	RE scrapping	1	Shrinkage
552	RE scrapping	2	Spoiled
701	GR phys.inv.: whse	701	NOT ENTERED EARLIER
702	GI phys.inv.: whse	702	LOST
922	RE return to vendor	1	Poor quality
922	RE return to vendor	2	Incomplete

Select movement type 701 for any gain amount posting and goods receipt will be posted and 702 for any loss amount posting.

ENTER and save the settings. Later on when you will be entering the difference in the system these reasons will be optioned and you will be able to select that.

Again go back to the screen for difference posting MI07.

Enter proper reason.

Save post the document.

Go back to MMBE transaction code to see the stock overview status.

Here you can see that total book inventory is reduced by the difference quantity and it has been set as much as counted quantity of material as was entered in MI04.

So following the above process now you know how the inventory counting takes place and how it is performed in different steps.

Chapter 30

SERVICE MASTER RECORD

Introduction:-

If you wish record a data base or master record for frequently procured services. Now we will create a sample service master record. The menu path for this is as shown in the picture below.

Requirement of service master:-

A service master record provides following valuable information to the process.

- Service number
- Service category
- Descriptive texts (short and long text)
- Base unit of measure
- Material group
- Valuation class

Prerequisites:-

Relevant settings are already maintained for maintenance of service master records in Customizing for *External Services* under *Service Master Record*.

Service master record:-

This is a Single Screen Function. In the left side you can see list o short texts for different service numbers which are already existing in the system. This screen is always in display mode. From this screen you can:-

Display:-

This single screen function is always in display mode.

Create

You can see create option up there. From here you can create a new service master record as per your specification as this process is shown below with the pictures.

Change:-

You can change the master record at any point of time by clicking display change option.

Copy:-

This function is used by clicking the already existing service master number which is applicable, to create a new service number. You have to click the service number and then select copy as option.

Find:-

Through this option you can search for a service master record.

Delete:-

Service master record can be deleted only if conditions are not maintained for the records.

The next screen will look something like as below.

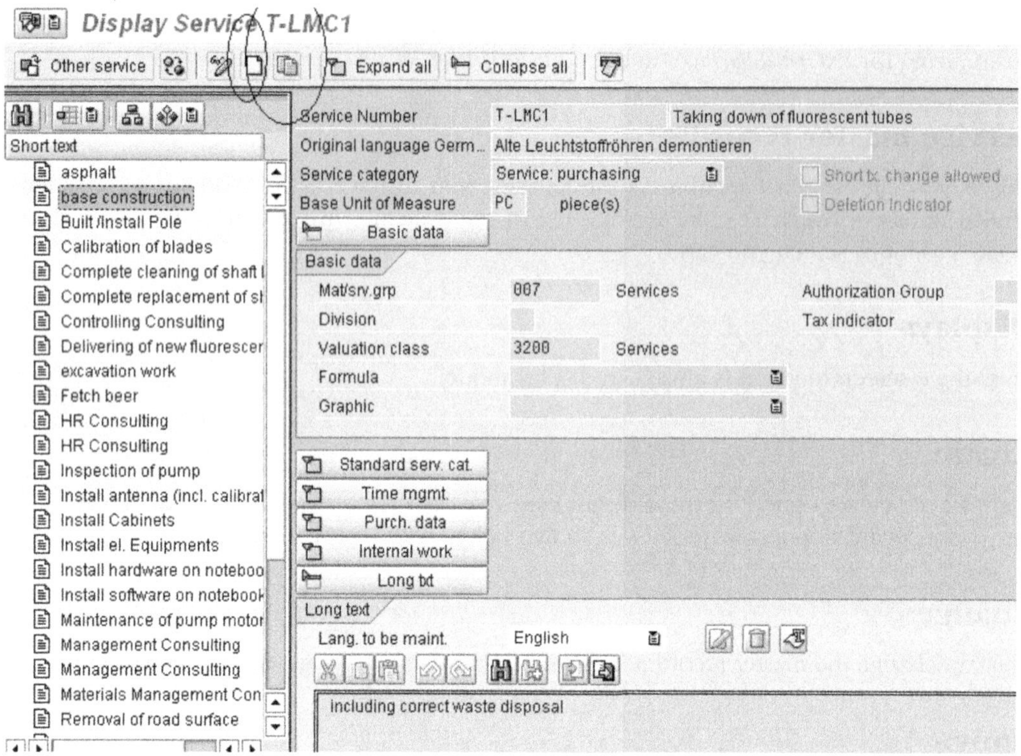

Activity number:-

In this screen you will have to first input the activity number for the service. Just like material master record this number is the name for the service.

Number Range:-

It depends on the process that your firm follows. If external number assignment has been defined, then enter the number of your master record.

You can check and define if required the number range in Customizing for *Service Master ® Define Number Ranges*

Service Category:-

This field is just like material type in material master record. This selection will determine the type of service with number range allowed. It also defines that the service number may be allotted externally or not.

Base Unit of Measure:-

This field captures that this service will be calculated and counted in days or hours or any other Unit of measure. Based on this later all the performance monitoring and payment will be recorded.

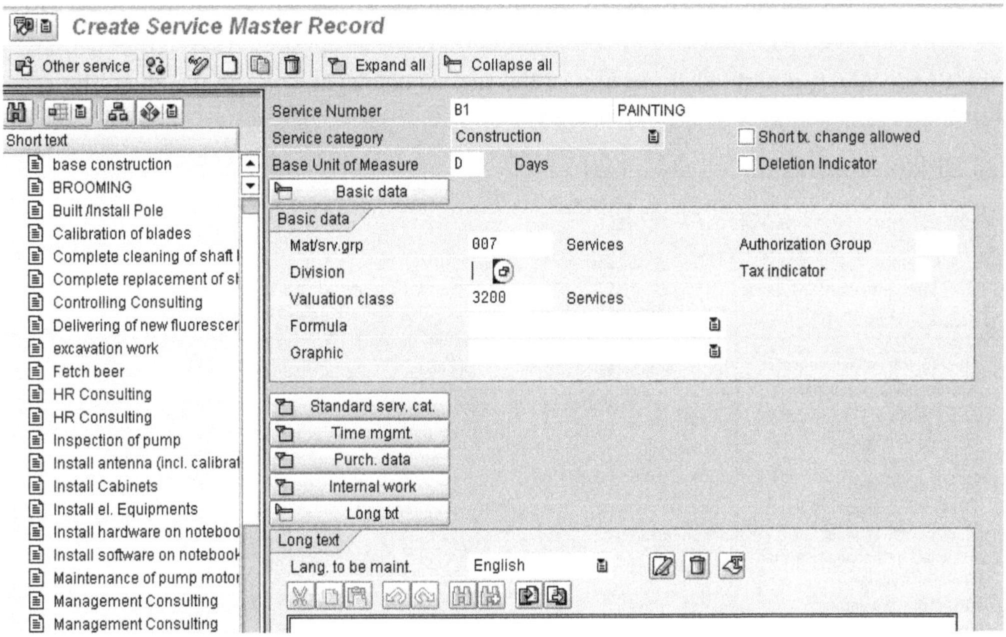

Mat/srv. Grp:-

This is a field for input of material or service group. Just as in material master material group is assigned, in the same way here also a service has to be assigned with the service group 007.

Valuation Class:-

As in the material master we assign valuation class in the Accounting 1 tab page, here also we have to assign a valuation class which will be used for automatic account assignment for value update in the respective general ledger accounts. These settings are done in automatic account assignment process customization.

Tax indicator:-

You can also assign tax indicator as applicable in the field Tax indicator.

Long text to be maintained:-

Here you can maintain any text for this service as description.

So these were basic information which is required to input to create a service master record for a service. Apart from these there are some other fields also which may or may not be required for basic process but only for specific reason and on requirement.

Save the master data.

*** Copy option of creating the service master

In the t code AC01, double click on any of the text as displaying on the left side. The screen will become on display mode of that service.

Then click on copy icon.

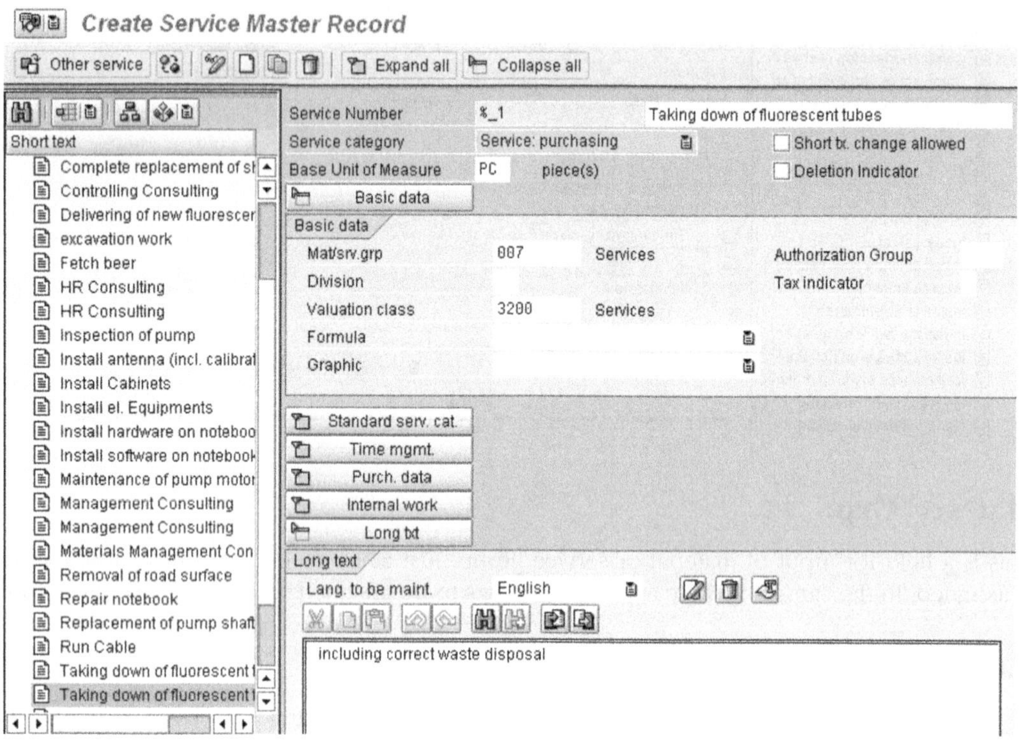

Enter text in the service number and description. Also change the base unit of measure. You can see this in the picture below.

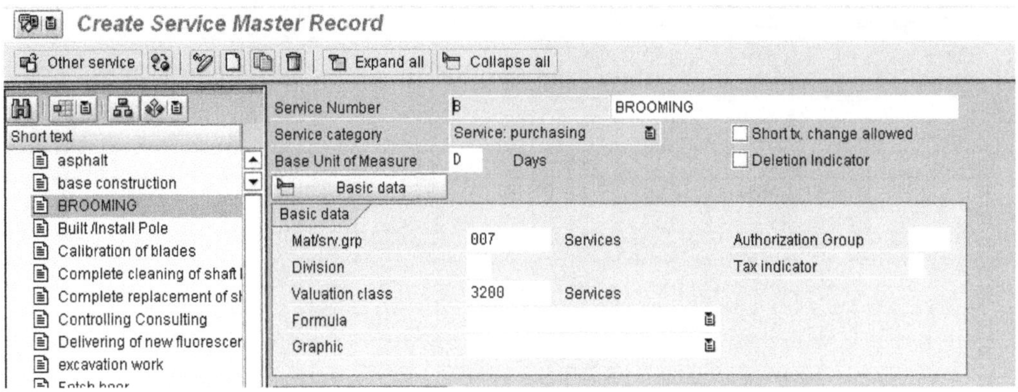

After changing these details save the master record.

*** Service condition record

You can also maintain service condition record for the service. The t code for this is ML33.

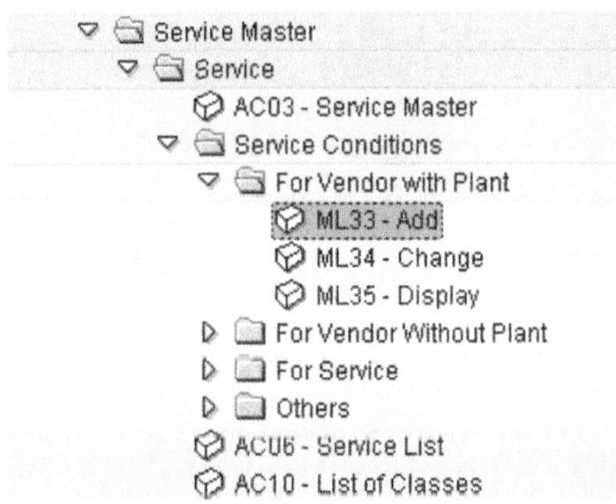

In the initial screen you can enter all the details like service code, amount per unit of service, base unit of measure for that service, validity date range etc.

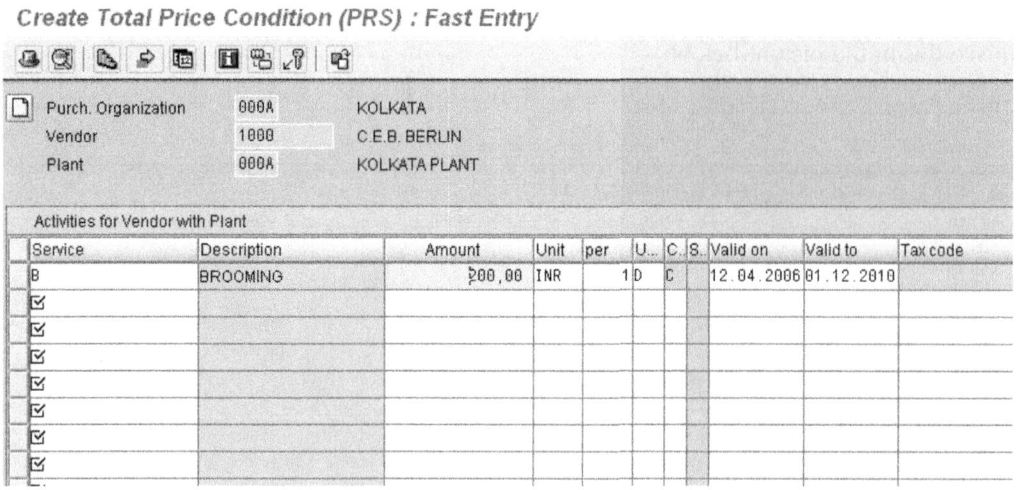

After entering all these details save the master record.

Chapter

31

SERVICE PURCHASE REQUISITON

Introduction:-

Create purchase requisition for service as you create standard purchase requisition. You can follow the process as mentioned below.

Menu path:-

You can see menu path in the picture below. SAP Easy Access > Logistics > Materials Management > Purchasing > Purchase Requisition > Create

Transaction code:-

Enter ME51N in the command line for purchase requisition initial screen.

Item category:-

On the initial screen in the item category field first of all enter item category D for service.

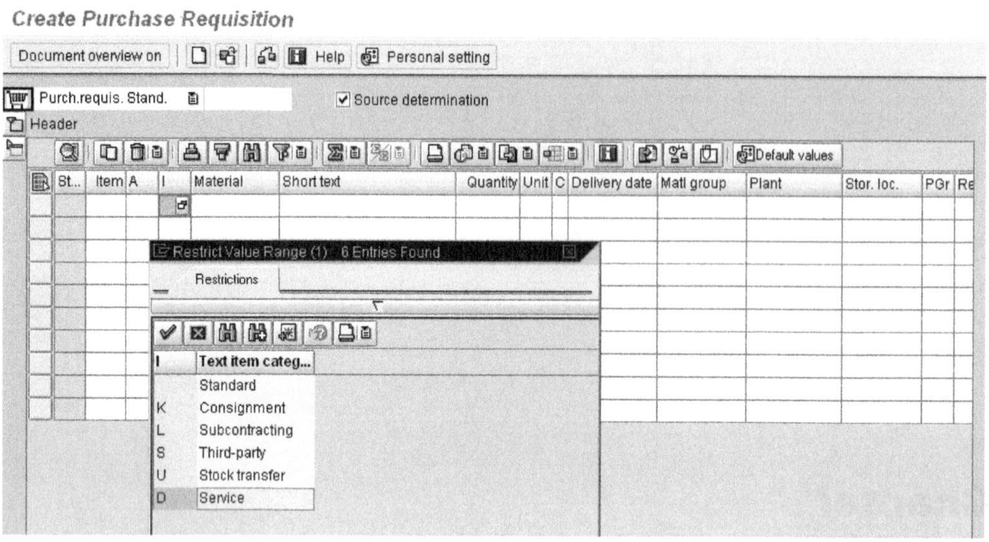

Press ENTER.

Account assignment category:-

In the account assignment category field enter U for unknown account assignment category. Unknown is selected here because at the time of purchase requisition creation the center or reason for which cost will occur is not known.

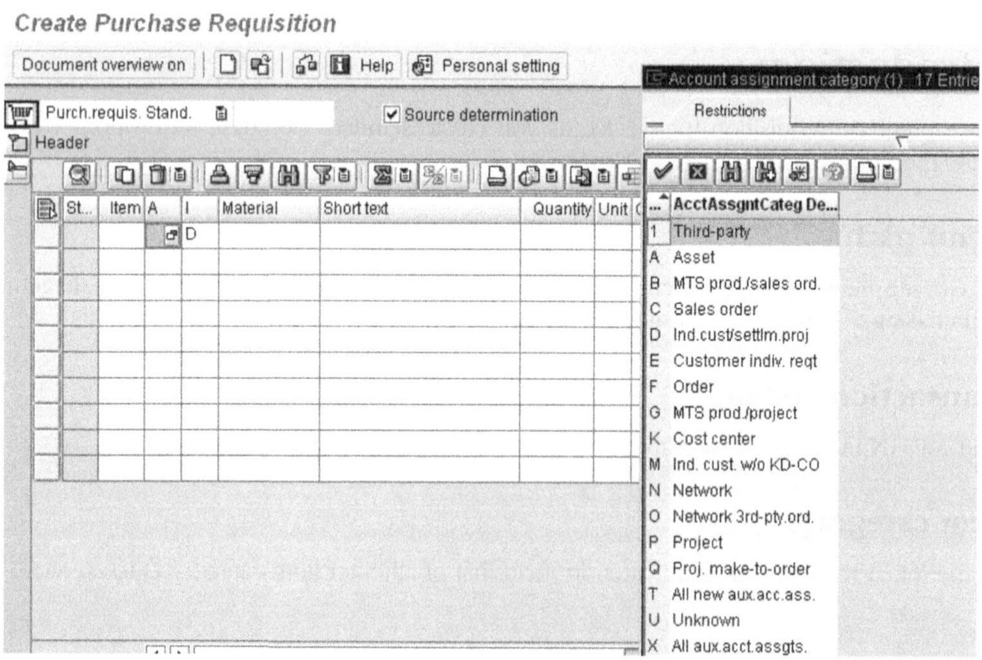

Plant:-

On entering information system will ask for plant. Enter plant 1000.

Purchase group:-

Enter responsible purchase group such as 000 in the purchase group field.

On the item details screen go to service tab page. Here you enter service number that you have created in the create service master data. Such as B that is created in the last step in this book.

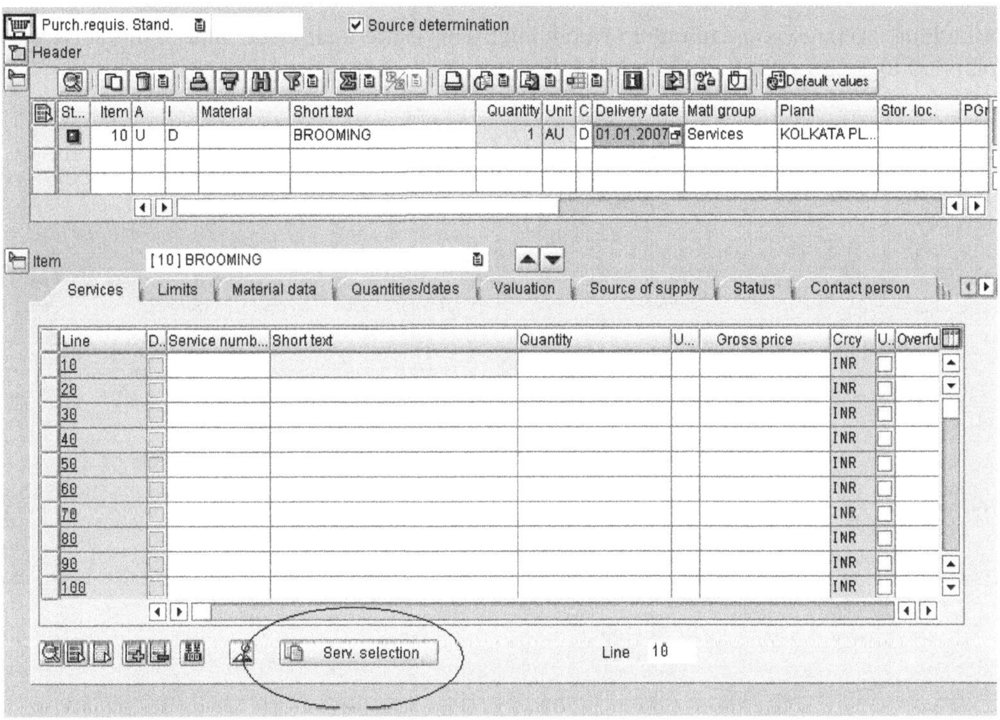

Service selection:-

You can also click on serv selection for selection of service id or service number code. Other wise you can also manually enter service number as B or any of your service.

Quantity:-

You have to enter the number in unit of measure that is required to be performed as for example 100 days in the picture above.

Gross Price:-

You need not enter any value here as you can see that this field is populated automatically. This value is taken from the condition record that you had created earlier.

Conditions:-

Select the line of the service number and go to conditions. This operation is shown in the picture above.

In the screen above you can see that you can add additional Cnty that is condition type as per your specific requirement.

On Limit tab page

Overall limit:-

On the limit tab page you can enter Overall limit. This is the total value limit of this service that is planned to be procured. Enter here 5000.

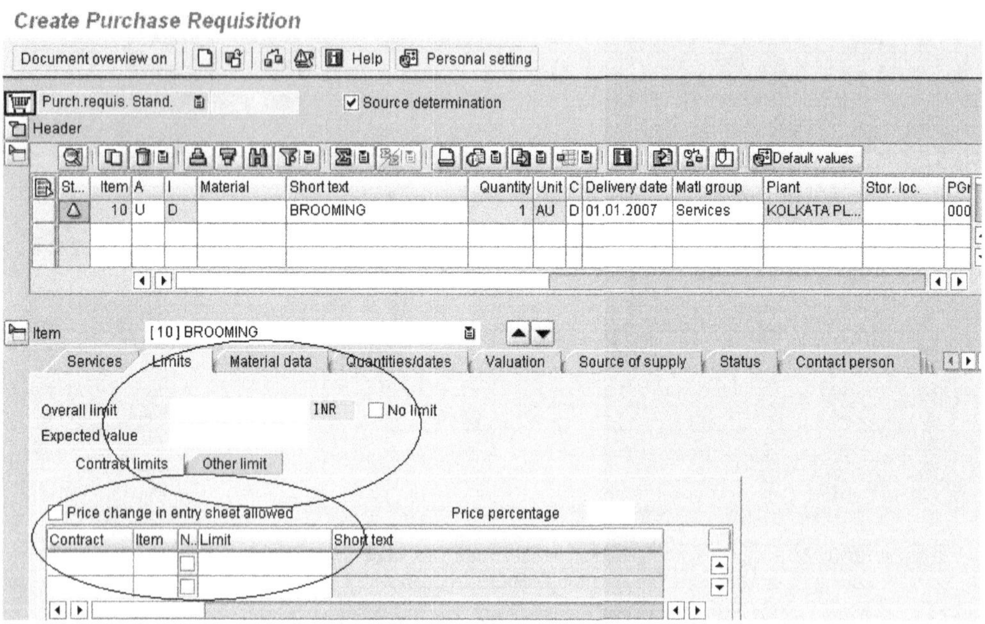

Expected value:-

This is the expected value that is required to be procured but not more that overall limit value. Enter here 5000.

Contract:-

On the limit tab page you can enter contract document number if this service is to be procured against any specific contract document.

Short text:-

Go back to the main screen and enter a short text on the item line for the service.

Check the document and Save it.

Chapter

32

SERVICE PURCHASE ORDER

Introduction:-

Service purchase requisition is created in the last chapter. Now you have to create a purchase order with reference to the purchase requisition. For this go to ME21N screen. On the item line move right words and put cursor in the purchase requisition field. Press F4. From here select purchase requisition number from the purchase requisition list as you can see in the picture below.

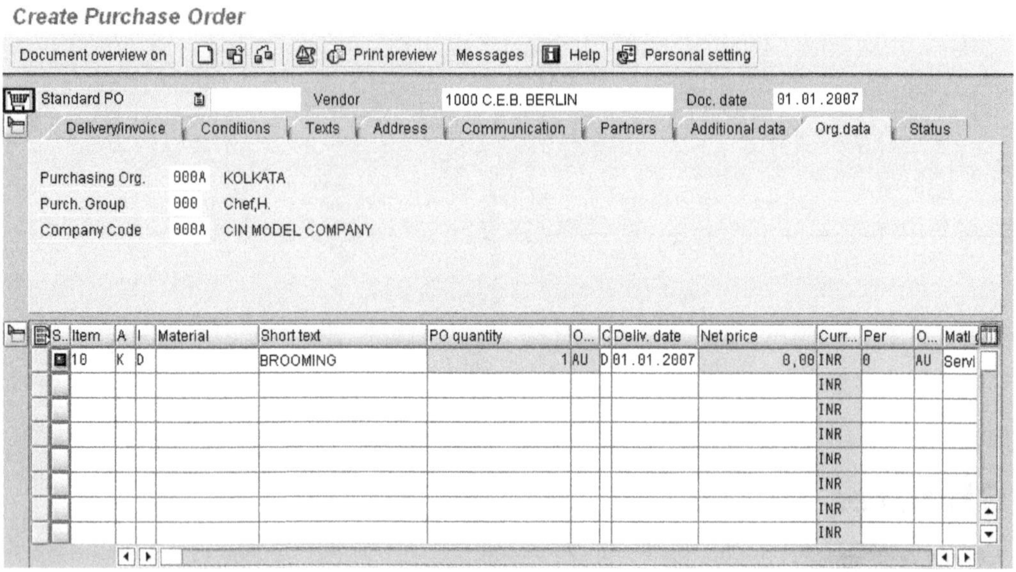

After entering these details like-

Purchase organization

Company code

Vendor

Enter

Purchase group

Item category D

Account assignment category K

Short Text

PO Quantity

Enter

Then click on Service selection as in the picture below on the line item details.

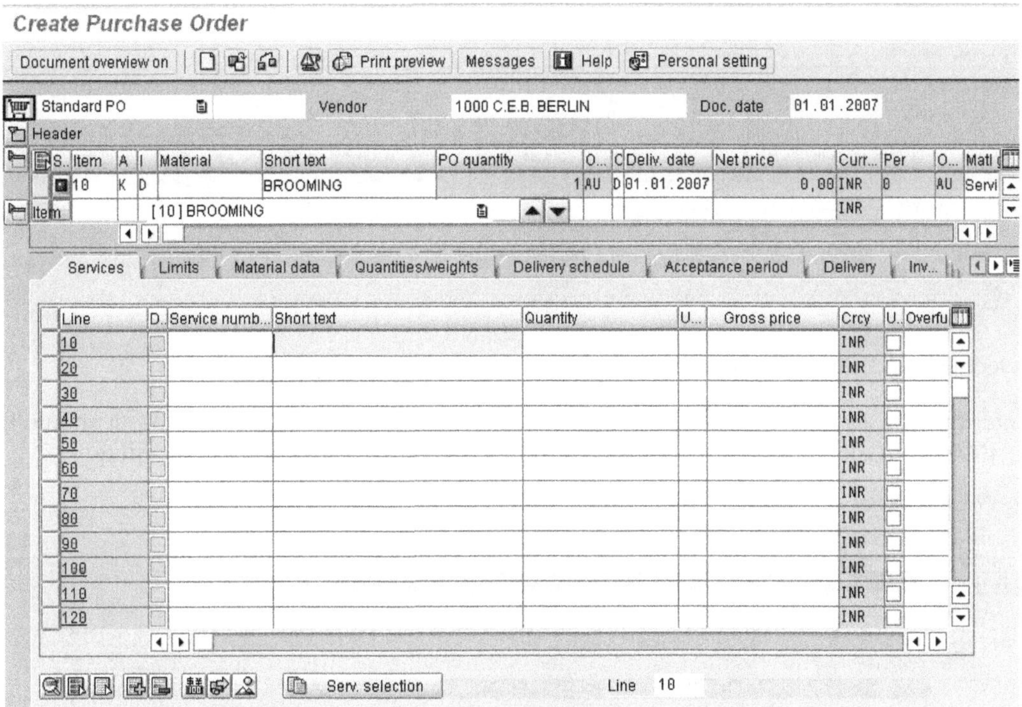

Enter.

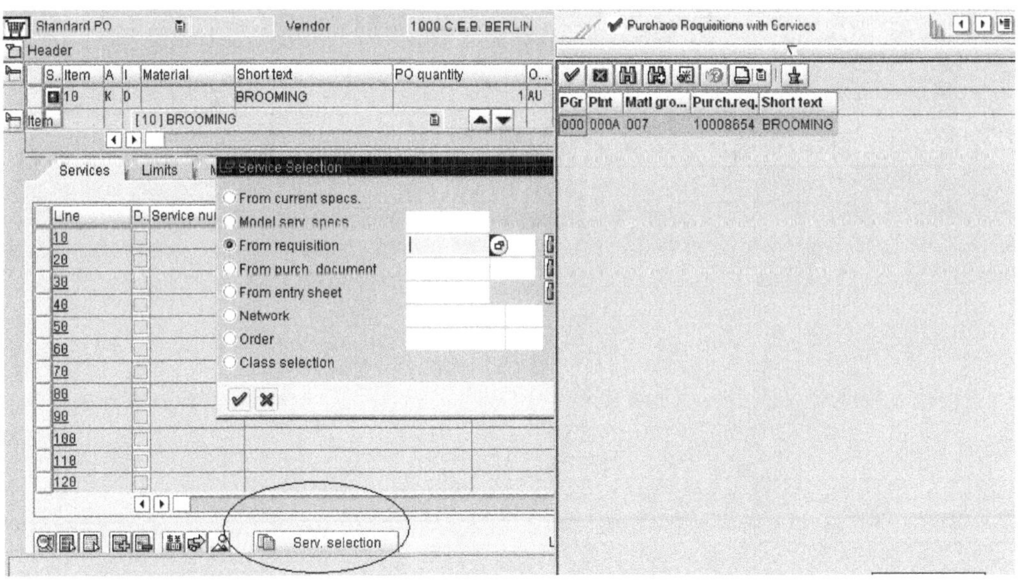

Select purchase requisition number.

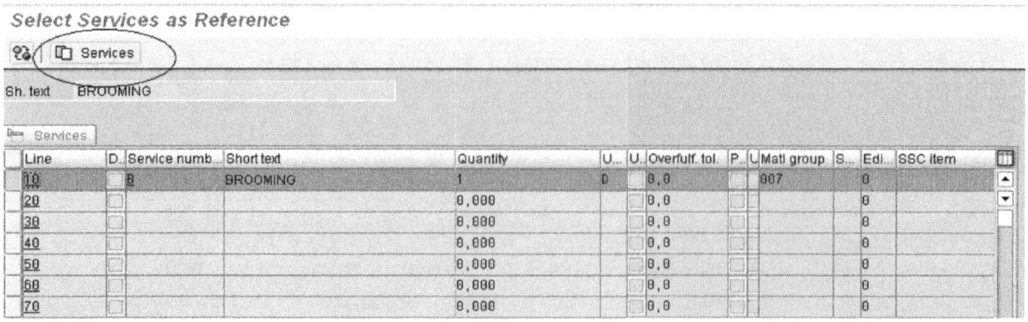

Select line and cline on Services.

Enter the G/L account meant for the cost center and the cost center. In your case it should be as 400000 as G/L account and 1000 as cost center, to complete the process smoothly.

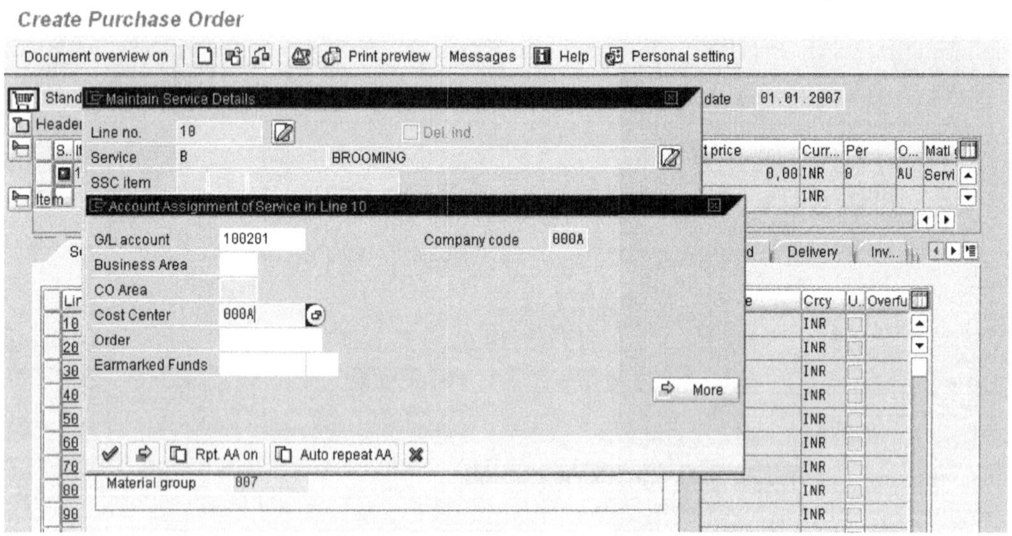

Enter.

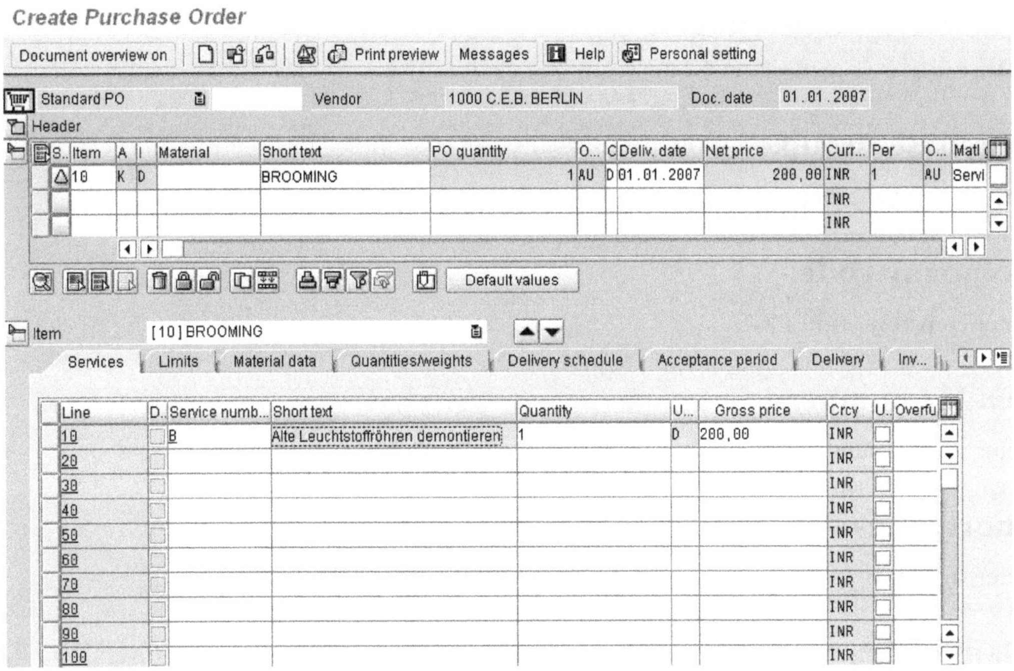

You will be able to see the details with the price which was maintained in the service condition record.

You can also check the condition tab page.

You can see all the details are copied.

At this point check the document in both the process as mentioned above and save the purchase order.

Service selection:-

Except then the above procedure you can also select the purchase requisition number through an another process. You can follow this process as mentioned below.

Item category:-

Enter item category D.

Account assignment category:-

Enter account assignment category U/K

Purchase organization:-

Enter purchase organization 1000.

Purchase group:-

Enter purchase group 000.

Company code:-

Enter company code 1000.

Vendor number:-

Enter vendor number that will supply the material.

Short text:-

Enter short text.

Plant code:-

Enter plant code as 1000.

Press enter.

Service selection:-

Go to service selection on the service tab page. This is shown as below in the picture.

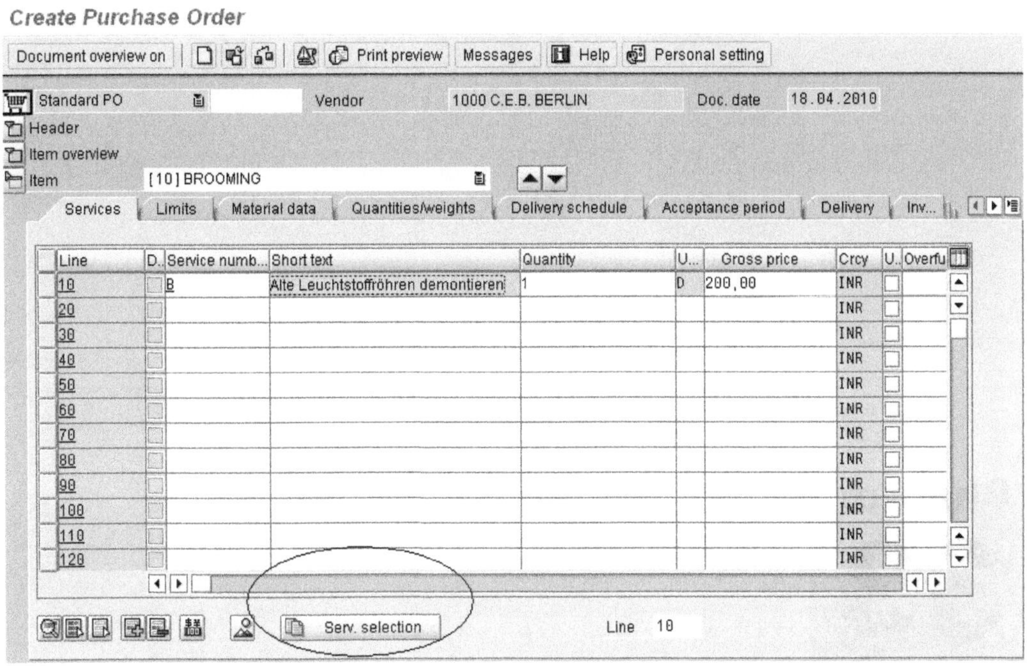

If you are creating service PO manually then you can select the service from this service selection icon. Otherwise you can copy the required doc from purchase requisition.

Follow the options to search the required purchase requisition. This process is shown below in the picture.

Select the purchase requisition number.

Press ENTER.

You can see following screen. On this screen select the line of the service and go to services as to adopt services . You can also press F9 to function this.

Purchase requisition with quantity will be adopted.

Here you can change the quantity as per your requirement.

Set limit in this process as limit is not adopted from the purchase requisition.

At this point check the document in both the process as mentioned above and save the purchase order.

Chapter

33

SERVICE ENTRY SHEET

Introduction

This is the step where you accept the performed service. In the process earlier you sent the purchase requisition to the vendor. He performed the service as per your need and submitted the report of work performed. Now you will check the performed functions and record it in to the SAP system. This document accepting and posting process is called as service entry and material document is called as service entry sheet.

Menu path:-

To do this you can follow menu path as shown in the picture below.

Transaction code:-

You can also enter ML81N in the command line.

Initial screen:-

The initial screen will appear. The initial screen will always appear in display mode.

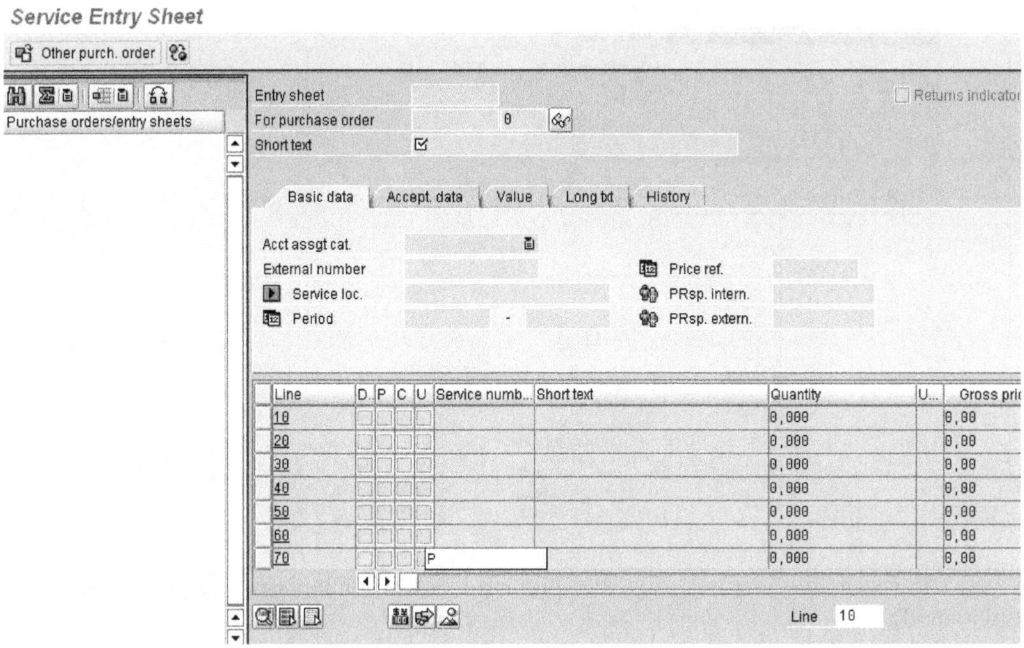

Othcr documcnt:-

On this screen select other purchase order as it is shown in the picture above or press Shift+F5.

Reference purchase order:-

Below in the picture you can see how the required purchase order is searched.

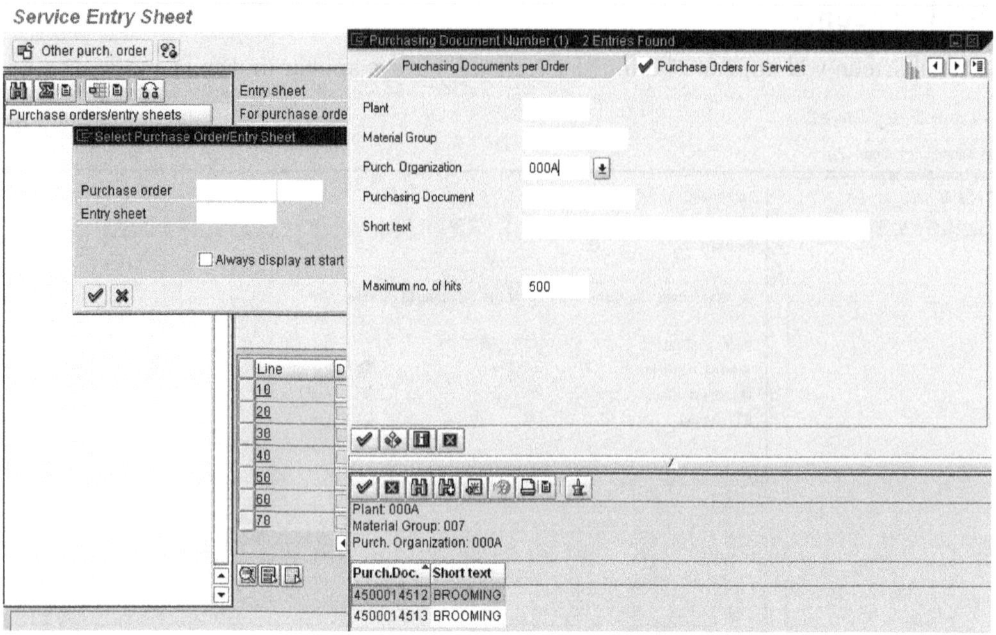

As you can see in the picture below the purchase order number is accepted and visible in display mode.

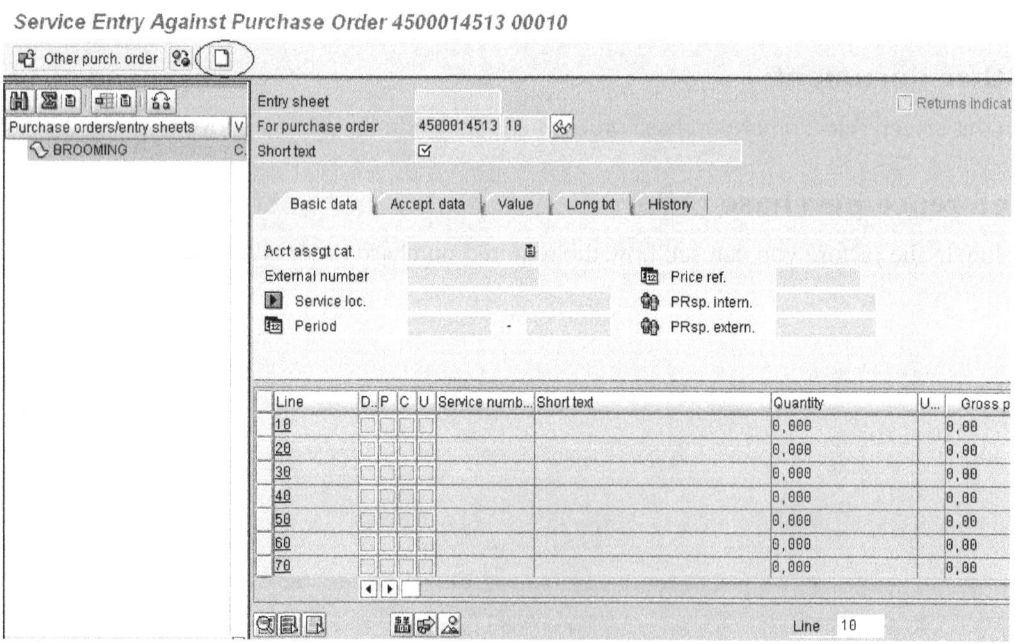

Account assignment category:-

Here you need to select create entry sheet as it is shown in the picture above. You can also press Shift+F1.

Then following screen will appear.

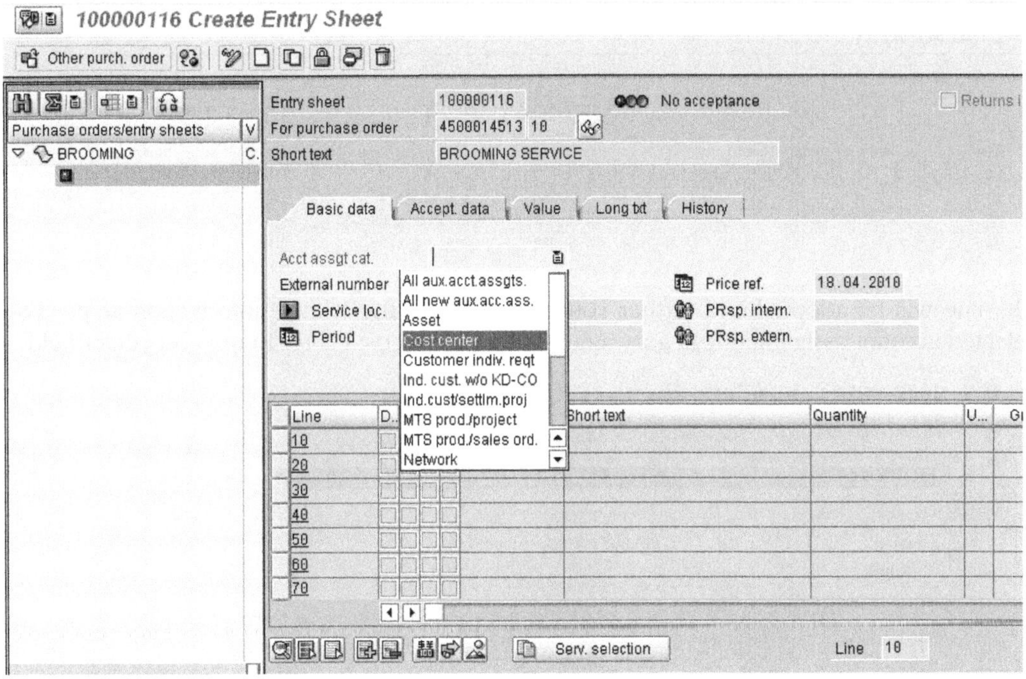

On this screen select account assignment category. You need to select this as because you had selected unknown account assignment category type in the purchase requisition and then in the purchase order. Select here cost center. Press enter.

Following screen will be visible.

Short text:-

On this screen enter short text in the field.

Service selection:-

Then go to service selection at the bottom of the entry sheet screen.

On pressing service selection following screen will appear.

Here you can adopt full quantity but selecting the check box. Or alternatively you can press enter. This will bring you in the screen as it is shown below.

Here you can select the line as it is performed.

Adopt service:-

Go to services as to adopt services or press F9.

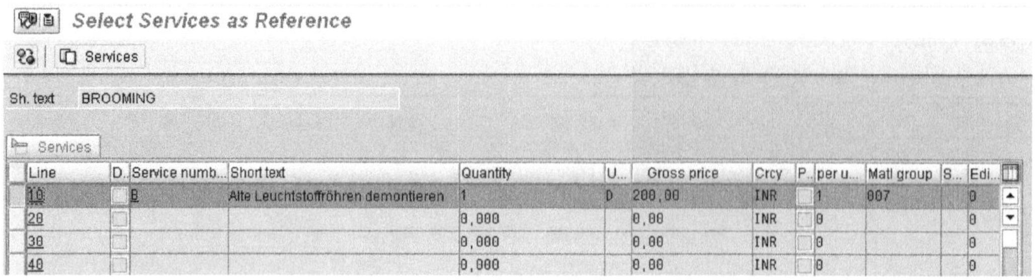

The line will be adopted and further you need to enter the relative information as per your selected account assignment category. Enter 1000 for the cost center in the cost center field.

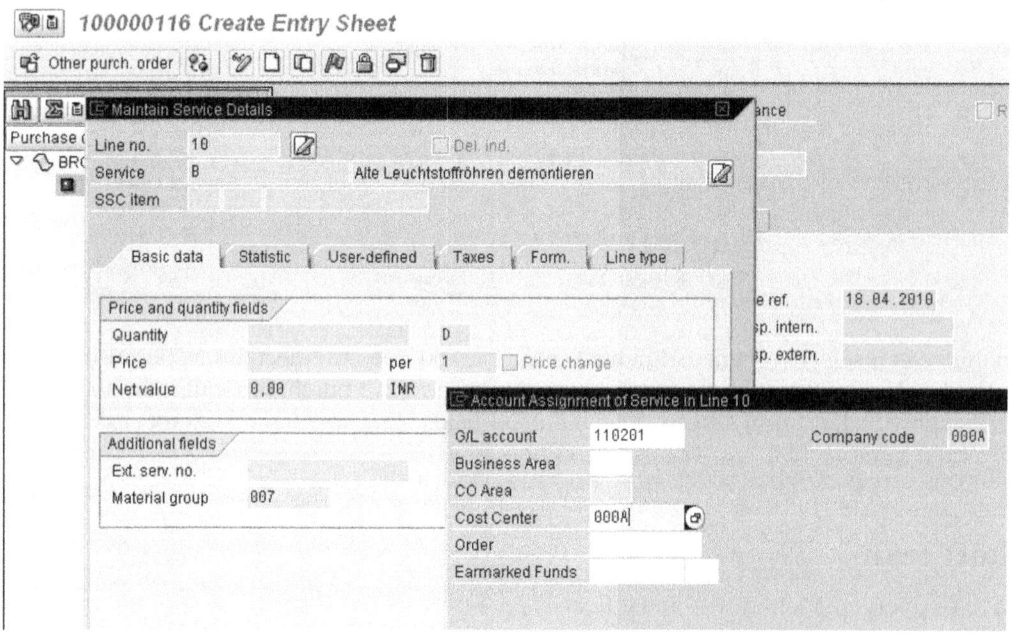

Other information will be copied automatically.

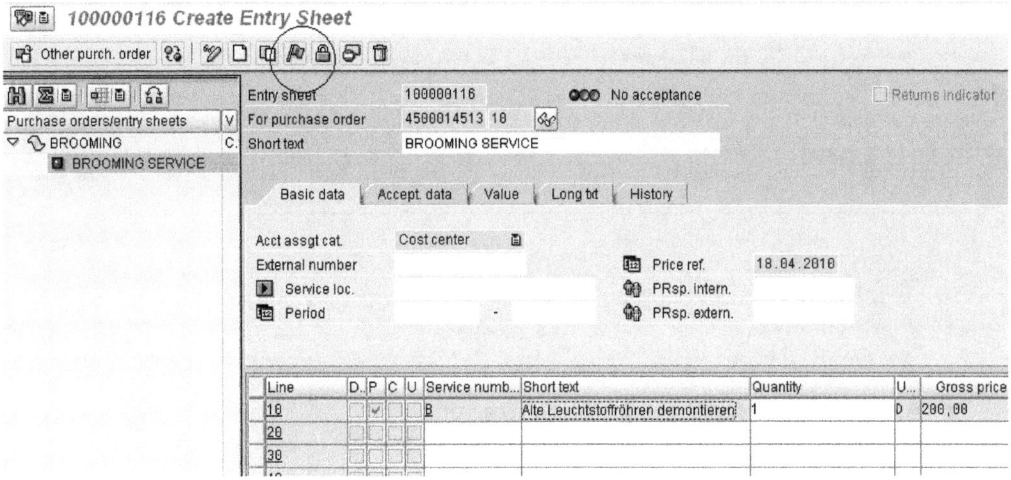

You can even change the quantities as per work done or performed.

Accept:-

After inputting this information press the green flag icon on the top of the screen to accept the entry sheet. Or press Ctrl+F1.

Save the document.

Purchase order history:-

You can go to purchase order display screen and there input the purchase order number.

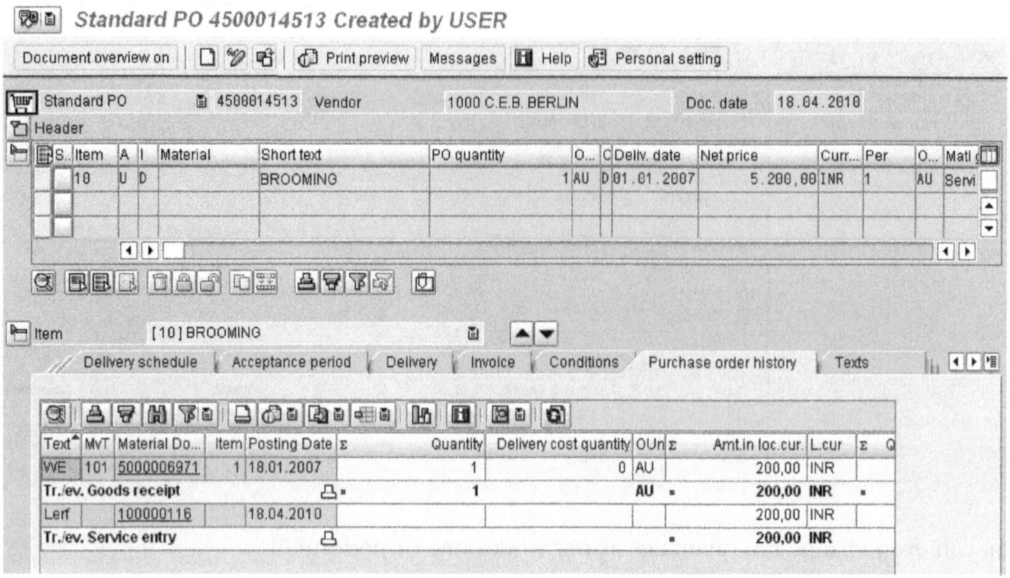

Then on the purchase order history tab page you can see the history of the service performed and accepted.

Or on the service entry sheet screen you can go to other purchase order, select relative purchase order number and adopt. Then go to environment and go to purchase order history.

Document type for service entry sheet:-

Here Lerf document type is for service entry sheet document. If you press this document number then it will take you to the service entry sheet screen.

WE document type is for goods receipt material document. Pressing this document number will take you go display material document screen.

Chapter

34

INVOICE ENTRY FOR SERVICE PROCUREMENT

Introduction:-

In the last chapter we have received and accepted the service performed by the vendor. We have also seen the material and financial documents created by those transactions. Now in the next step we need to make incoming invoice entry for the performed service. The process same as the standard invoice entry procedure. You can follow below mentioned process.

Transaction code:-

Enter MIRO transaction code in the command line or follow menu path as below.

Menu path:-

You can also follow the menu path as mentioned below. SAP Easy Access > Logistics > Materials Management > Logistics Invoice Verification > Document Entry > Enter Invoice

Initial screen:-

You will be on the initial screen of invoice entry. You can see that in the picture below.

Document Date:-

On the initial screen enter document date.

Posting Date:-

On the same screen enter posting date.

Reference Document:-

Go to PO reference as you can see in the picture below.

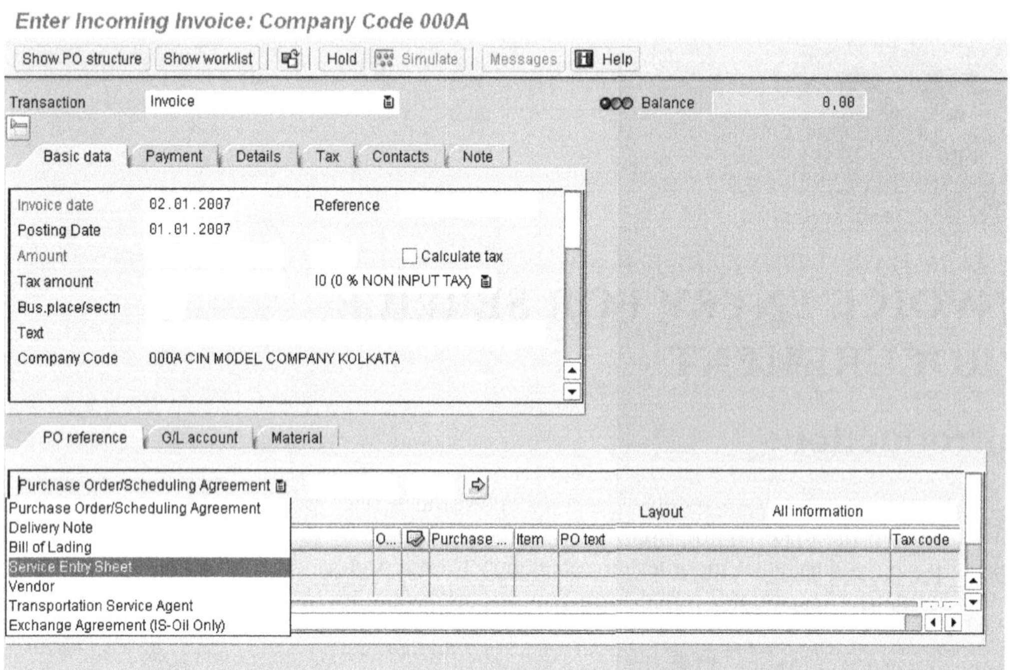

From this drop down you can select either purchase order or service entry sheet as reference document. We will perform now with reference to service entry sheet. Select the service entry sheet option.

Press F4 to find the entry sheet.

Select proper entry sheet.

Press ENTER.

Adopted information:-

The information will be adopted on the invoice entry screen.

Payment tab page:-

On the payment tab page at the header you can enter payment related information like base line date, payment terms and other information.

Base line date:-

This is the date from which due date and discount date is calculated. Here enter a date.

Tax code:-

There are two options of tax code. One is at the header level and another is at the line item level. In the tax code field Select proper tax code in the tax code field both on the header and line item.

Check in the calculate tax box:-

Select a check in the calculate tax check box.

Balance:-

You can see total amount as 2436 appearing on the right side in the balance field.

Amount:-

Enter same amount in the amount field.

Press ENTER.

Simulate:-

This option is selected to see whether the document information which is entered is correct or not. Simulate the entry as it is sown in the picture blow by pressing simulate document Ctrl+Shift+F7.

From here you can hold, park, save as complete form or even simply can post the document as there is not error found while simulation in the document.

Post the document.

Payment blocked:-

There may be a message as invoice posted but payment blocked. This happens due to same variance in any of the pre customized reason. To resolve such problem you have to first know the reason and correct that and release the document for payment. Otherwise the vendor will not be able to get any payment.

Materials Management Transaction Codes

Go to SE16 t-code.

Enter Table name as TSTCT

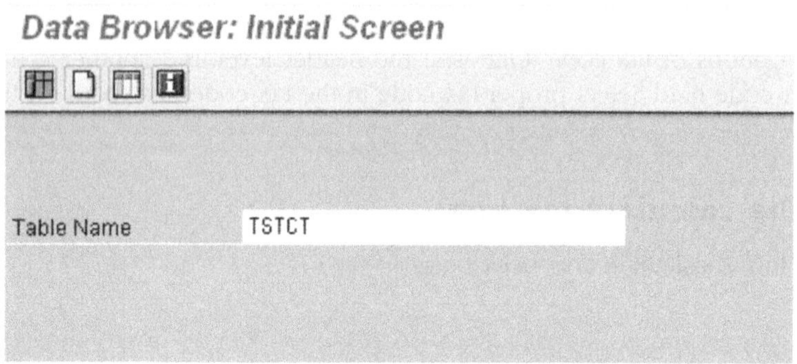

Press Enter

Execute.

In the TCODE field enter first letter of the T-CODE series. This is shown in the picture below.

Execute.

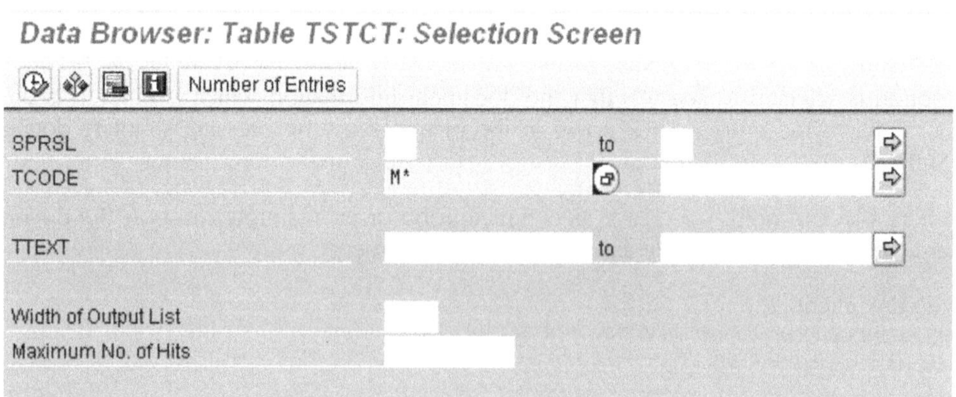

A whole list of TCODE is displayed.

Appendix A

Standard Organization for a company code in MM module

Client	800 – Assumed Production client(server)											
Controlling area	1000											
Chart of accounts	1000											
Company code	1000			1100			1200			2000		
Purchase organization	1000			1100			1200			2000		
Plant	1000	1001	1001	1100	1101	1102	1200	1201	1202	2000	2001	2002
Storage location	0001	0001	0001	0001	0001	0001	0001	0001	0001	0001	0001	0001
	0002	0002	0002	0002	0002	0002	0002	0002	0002	0002	0002	0002
Purchasing Group	001 , 002, 003, 004,.............											

Some Important and Transaction Codes (T-Code List)

ME01	Maintain Source List
ME03	Display Source List
ME04	Changes to Source List
ME05	Generate Source List
ME06	Analyze Source List
ME07	Reorganize Source List
ME08	Send Source List
ME11	Create Purchasing Info Record
ME12	Change Purchasing Info Record
ME13	Display Purchasing Info Record
ME14	Changes to Purchasing Info Record
ME15	Flag Purch. Info Rec. for Deletion
ME16	Purchasing Info Recs. for Deletion
ME1E	Quotation Price History
ME1L	Info Records Per Vendor
ME1M	Info Records per Material
ME1P	Purchase Order Price History
ME21N	Create Purchase Order
ME22N	Change Purchase Order
ME23N	Display Purchase Order
ME28	Release Purchase Order
ME29N	Release purchase order
ME2A	Monitor Confirmations
ME2B	POs by Requirement Tracking Number
ME2C	Purchase Orders by Material Group
ME2J	Purchase Orders for Project
ME2K	Purch. Orders by Account Assignment
ME2L	Purchase Orders by Vendor
ME2M	Purchase Orders by Material
ME2N	Purchase Orders by PO Number
ME2O	SC Stock Monitoring (Vendor)
ME2S	Services per Purchase Order
ME2V	Goods Receipt Forecast
ME2W	Purchase Orders for Supplying Plant

ME31K	Create Contract
ME31L	Create Scheduling Agreement
ME32K	Change Contract
ME32L	Change Scheduling Agreement
ME33K	Display Contract
ME33L	Display Scheduling Agreement
ME34K	Maintain Contract Supplement
ME34L	Maintain Sched. Agreement Supplement
ME35	Release Outline Agreement
ME35K	Release Contract
ME35L	Release Scheduling Agreement
ME37	Create Transport Scheduling Agmt.
ME38	Maintain Sched. Agreement Schedule
ME39	Display Sched. Agmt. Schedule (TEST)
ME3A	Transm. Release Documentation Record
ME3B	Outl. Agreements per Requirement No.
ME3C	Outline Agreements by Material Group
ME3J	Outline Agreements per Project
ME3K	Outl. Agreements by Acct. Assignment
ME3L	Outline Agreements per Vendor
ME3M	Outline Agreements by Material
ME3N	Outline Agreements by Agreement No.
ME3P	Recalculate Contract Price
ME3R	Recalculate Sched. Agreement Price
ME3S	Service List for Contract
ME41	Create Request For Quotation
ME42	Change Request For Quotation
ME43	Display Request For Quotation
ME44	Maintain RFQ Supplement
ME45	Release RFQ
ME47	Create Quotation
ME48	Display Quotation
ME49	Price Comparison List
ME4B	RFQs by Requirement Tracking Number
ME4C	RFQs by Material Group

ME4L	RFQs by Vendor
ME4M	RFQs by Material
ME4N	RFQs by RFQ Number
ME4S	RFQs by Collective Number
ME51N	Create Purchase Requisition
ME52N	Change Purchase Requisition
ME53N	Display Purchase Requisition
ME54N	Release Purchase Requisition
ME55	Collective Release of Purchase Reqs.
ME56	Assign Source to Purch. Requisition
ME57	Assign and Process Requisitions
ME58	Ordering: Assigned Requisitions
ME59	Automatic Generation of POs
ME59N	Automatic generation of POs
ME5A	Purchase Requisitions: List Display
ME5F	Release Reminder: Purch. Requisition
ME5J	Purchase Requisitions for Project
ME5K	Requisitions by Account Assignment
ME5R	Archived Purchase Requisitions
ME5W	Resubmission of Purch. Requisitions
ME80	Purchasing Reporting
ME80A	Purchasing Reporting: RFQs
ME80AN	General Analyses (A)
ME80F	Purchasing Reporting: POs
ME80FN	General Analyses (F)
ME80R	Purchasing Reporting: Outline Agmts.
ME80RN	General Analyses (L,K)
ME81	Analysis of Order Values
ME81N	Analysis of Order Values
ME82	Archived Purchasing Documents
ME84	Generation of Sched. Agmt. Releases
ME84A	Individual Display of SA Release
ME85	Renumber Schedule Lines
ME86	Aggregate Schedule Lines
MM01	Create Material &

MM02	Change Material &
MM03	Display Material &
MM04	Display Material Change Documents
MM06	Flag Material for Deletion
MM11	Schedule Creation of Material &
MM12	Schedule Changing of Material &
MM13	Activate Planned Changes
MM14	Display Planned Changes
MM15	Display Changes (Migration)
MM16	Schedule Material for Deletion
MM17	Mass Maintenance: Indus. Matl Master
MM50	List Extendable Materials
MM60	Materials List
MMAM	Change Material Type
MMBE	Stock Overview
MMPV	Close Periods
MMRV	Allow Posting to Previous Period
MB1A	Goods Withdrawal
MB1B	Transfer Posting
MB1C	Other Goods Receipts
MB21	Create Reservation
MB22	Change Reservation
MB23	Display Reservation
MB24	Reservation List
MB25	Reservation List
MB1A	Goods Withdrawal
MB1B	Transfer Posting
MB1C	Other Goods Receipts
MB21	Create Reservation
MB22	Change Reservation
MB23	Display Reservation
MB24	Reservation List
MB25	Reservation List
MB59	Material Doc. List
MB5A	Evaluate Batch Where-Used Archive

MB5B	Stocks for Posting Date
MB5C	Pick-Up List
MB5S	Display List of GR/IR Balances
MB5T	Stock in transit CC
MB5TD	Stock in Transit on Key Date
MB5W	List of Stock Values
MBLB	Stocks at Subcontractor
MBSM	Display Cancelled Material Docs.
MI01	Create Physical Inventory Document
MI02	Change Physical Inventory Document
MI03	Display Physical Inventory Document
MI04	Enter Inventory Count with Document
MI05	Change Inventory Count
MI06	Display Inventory Count
MI07	Process List of Differences
MI08	Create List of Differences with Doc.
MI09	Enter Inventory Count w/o Document
MI10	Create List of Differences w/o Doc.
MI11	Recount Physical Inventory Document
MI12	Display changes
MI20	Print List of Differences
MI21	Print physical inventory document
MI22	Display Phys. Inv. Docs. f. Material
MI23	Disp. Phys. Inv. Data for Material
MI24	Physical Inventory List
MIGO	Goods Movement
MIR4	Call MIRO - Change Status
MIR5	Display List of Invoice Documents
MIR6	Invoice Overview
MIR7	Park Invoice
MIRA	Fast Invoice Entry
MIRO	Enter Incoming Invoice
ML01	Create Standard Service Catalog
ML02	Maintain Standard Service Catalog
ML03	Display Standard Service Catalog

ML81N Service Entry Sheet

ML84 List of Service Entry Sheets

MR21 Price Change

MR22 Material Debit/Credit

MR8M Cancel Invoice Document

MRBR Release Blocked Invoices

MRKO Settle Consignment/Pipeline Liabs

MRRL Evaluated Receipt Settlement

MSRV3 PO List by service codes

XK01 Vendor create

XK02 Vendor change

XK03 Vendor Display

MKVZ Vendor list by purchasing organization

If you yourself want to know a particular t-code list then you can follow following process

Enter transaction code - SE16N in the command line.

In the field for table enter TSTC as table name and press enter.

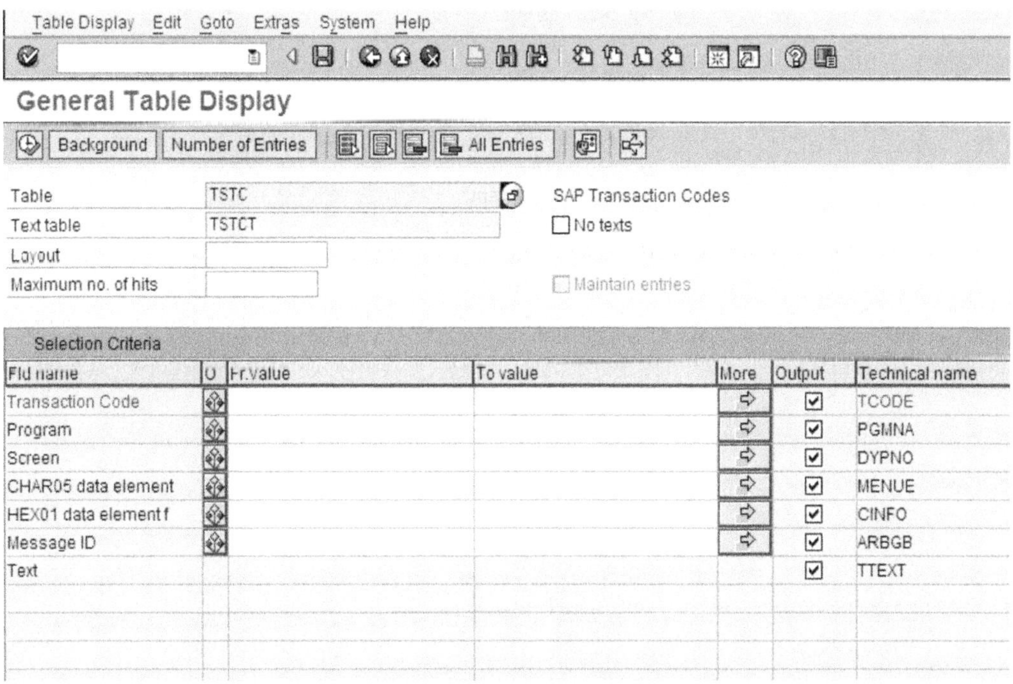

Enter M* or any other letter with ending with '*' in the field for Transaction code and execute. It will display all the transaction codes starting from M. Generally in the domain of Materials management maximum of the transaction codes start from M letter. In ECC6 there are more than 106,200 T-codes some of which may or may not be interlinked.

How to display technical name of a particular transaction code in menu path

While surfing around menu path you can also make t-codes visible by following a simple process.

Step 1 Login into the SAP SYSTEM.

Step 2 Click on Extras menu

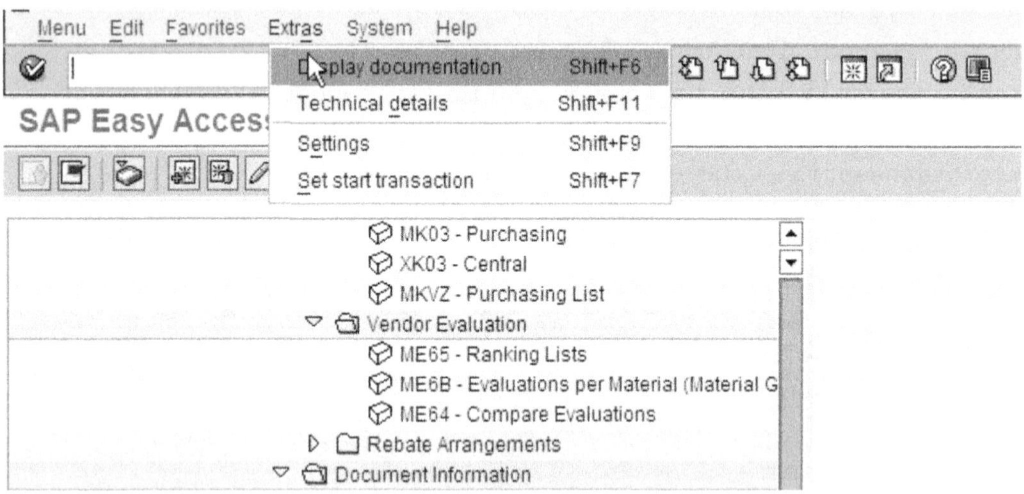

Step 3 Click on Settings in the drop down

Step 4 Put a check in the check box in front of Display technical names

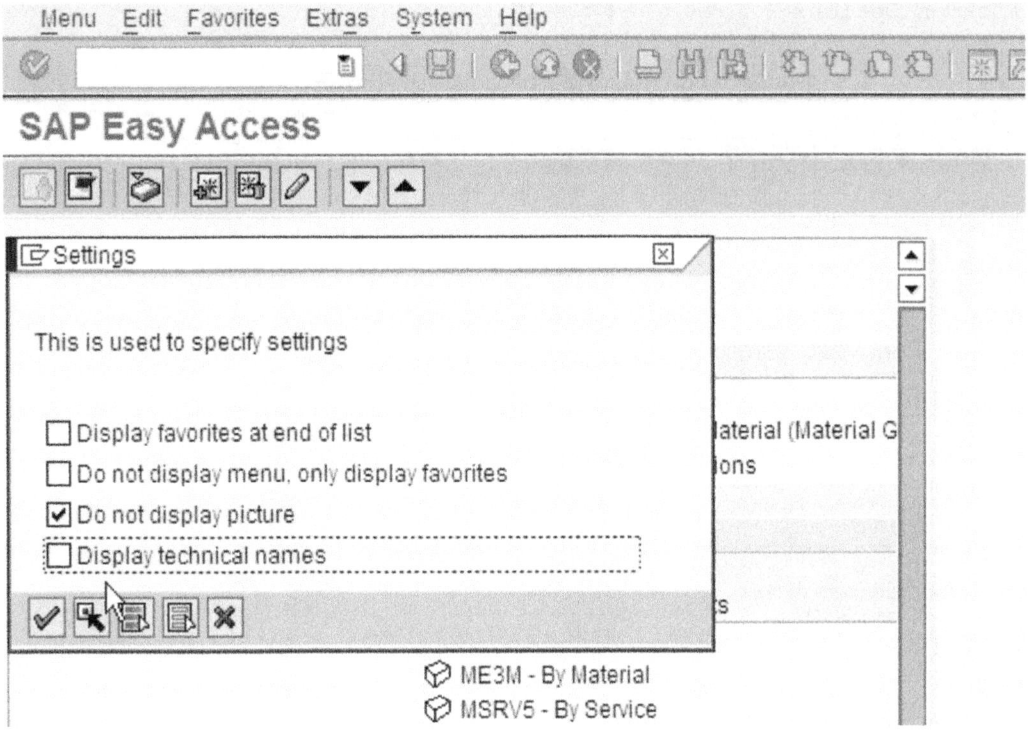

Step 5 Again surf menu path. It will display technical names too.

How to make document types in the drop down list or reference list while creating a document or making an entry

Step 1

Step 2 Click on Customize local layout

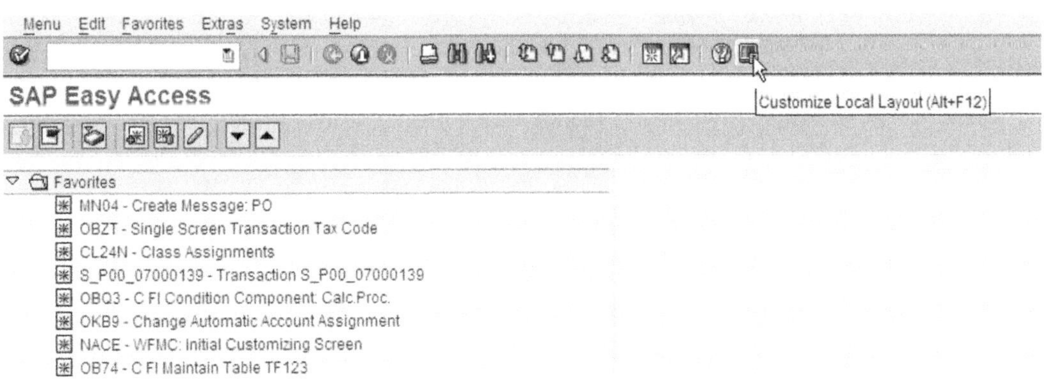

Click on Options

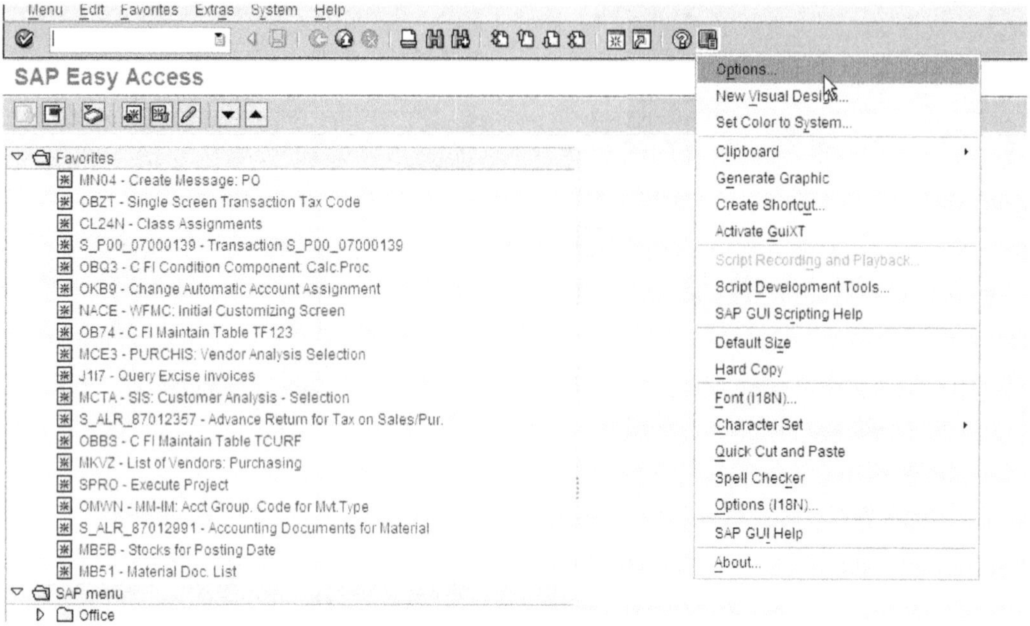

Click on expert and put check in the box meant for show key in all dropdown lists and a check in sort items by key.

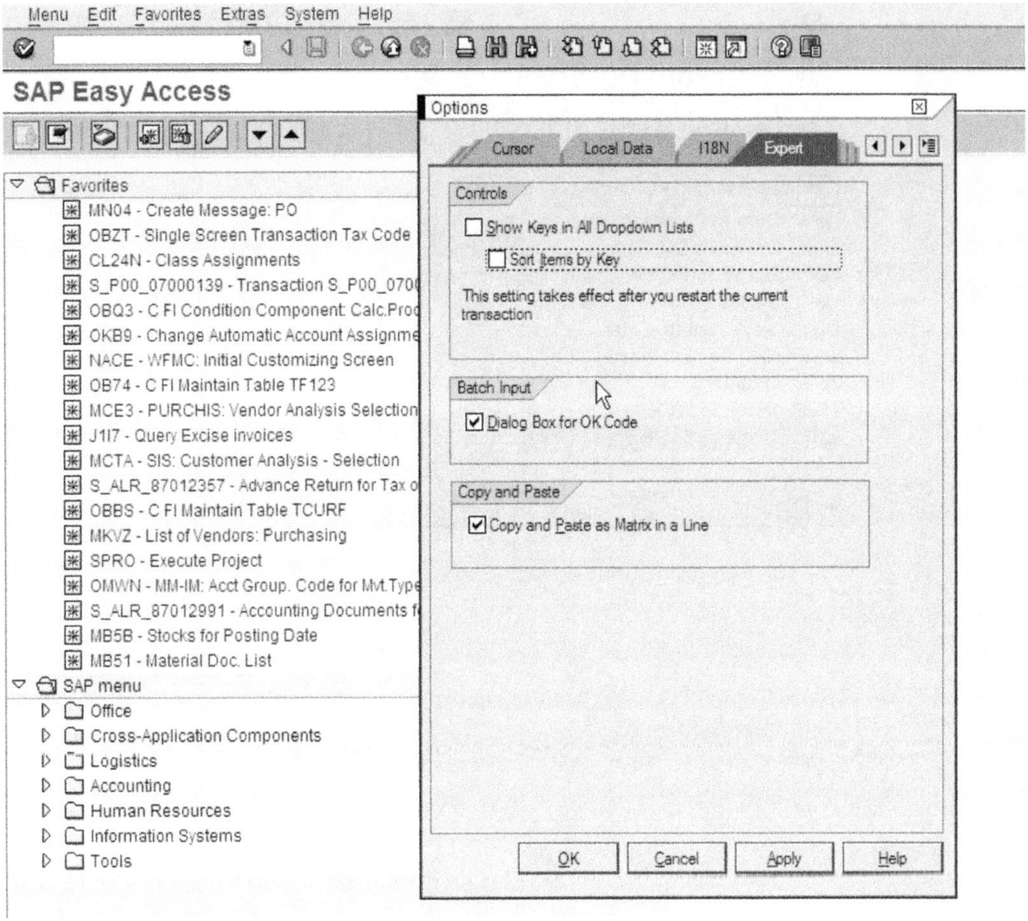

It will display while making with short codes.

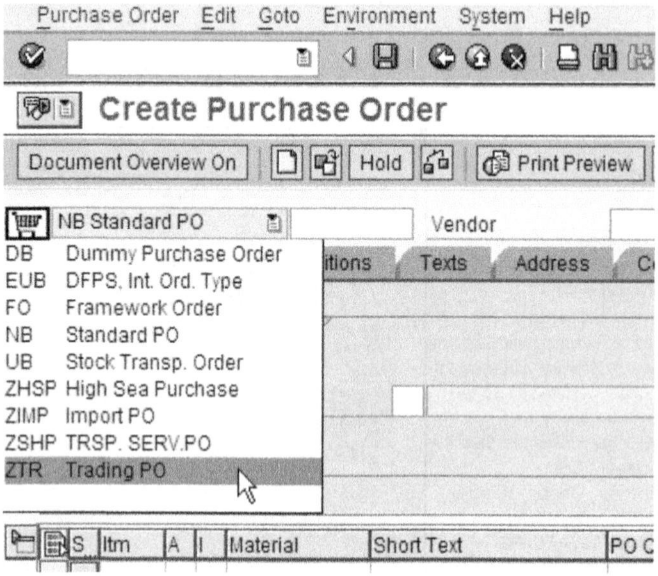

CPSIA information can be obtained at www.ICGtesting.com
Printed in the USA
BVOW10s1455051013

332641BV00006B/104/P

9 781619 030466